RITY

A S... P REFERENCE GUIDE

WEB SECURITY

A STEP-BY-STEP REFERENCE GUIDE

Lincoln D. Stein

ADDISON-WESLEY

An imprint of Addison Wesley Longman, Inc.

Reading, Massachusetts • Harlow, England • Menlo Park, California
Berkeley, California • Don Mills, Ontario • Sydney
Bonn • Amsterdam • Tokyo • Mexico City

The publisher offers discounts on this book when ordered in quantity for special sales. For more information, please contact:

Corporate, Government, and Special Sales Group
Addison Wesley Longman, Inc.
One Jacob Way
Reading, Massachusetts 01867
800-238-9682

Library of Congress Cataloging-in-Publication Data

Stein, Lincoln D., 1960–
Web security : a step-by-step reference guide / Lincoln D. Stein.
p. cm.
Includes bibliographical references and index.
ISBN 0-201-63489-9 (alk. paper)
1. Computer networks—Security measures. 2. World Wide Web (Information retrieval system)—Security measures. 3. Web sites—Security measures. I. Title.
TK5105.59.S74 1997 97-44554
005.8--dc21 CIP

ISBN 0-201-63489-9

Text printed on recycled and acid-free paper.

2 3 4 5 6 7 8 9 10 - DS - 02 01 00 99 98
Second printing, March 1998

Contents

Preface

This is the "how not to shoot yourself in the foot" book about Web security. Enough theory to be interesting, but not so much that it gets dry and academic. Enough war stories to be fun, but not so many that they overwhelm the rest. No political agenda. No favoritism. You'll find here nothing but practical, commonsense advice for sidestepping the hoard of little gotchas that currently plague the Web, plus you'll find a framework for deciding for yourself how to handle all the gotchas that are yet to be.

Who is this book for? The first third of the book deals with problems that are relevant to anyone who uses the Web: privacy threats, the potential of the Web to spread viruses and other malicious software, the practice and pitfalls of electronic commerce. The remainder gives advice directed to Webmasters, system administrators, system security officers, and others who worry that their organizations' Web sites might be broken into or that their local area network can be compromised by nasty stuff brought in by their employees' Web surfing. If you already run a Web site, you'll want to read this book through. If you're a casual Web surfer, read the first part now and save the rest for later. If current trends continue, everyone will have a Web site and will have to worry about keeping it safe.

Web Security: A Step-by-Step Reference Guide began life about two years ago as the World Wide Web Security FAQ. I was concerned that new Web sites were going up at an amazing rate, with little appreciation for the security implications. I was dismayed that much of the advice being dispensed was incomplete or simply misinformed. So I put together 30 or so frequently asked questions (with answers) to advise Webmasters on how to keep their sites safe from attack by unwanted intruders, and I posted it on my Web site. Over a period of months, the FAQ grew considerably as readers mailed in requests for more information, suggestions, and in some cases contributed their own questions and answers. To the original sections on server-side security, I added sections dealing with client-side (browser) security, privacy issues, sections on cryptography and digital money, and an ever-growing list of security holes in specific pieces of software. In 1996, the first of an epidemic of Web site break-ins shook the Web; in its aftermath, the number of "hits" on the FAQ grew tremendously. The FAQ is now mirrored on five continents and has been translated into Russian, Italian, and Chinese.

When my editor initially suggested I turn the FAQ into a book, I was skeptical. First of all, the information was already on line. Second, the Web is changing so rapidly that any book on security issues is out of date by the time it hits the shelves. Finally, the whole FAQ was less than 50 typeset pages and I was dubious that it could be bulked up into a full-length book. To the first two objections, my editor responded that printed books and the Web are complementary. Printed books provide depth and comprehensiveness. The Web provides vast breadth and information that is always (we hope) up to date. As for my last objection, well, would you believe that the working title for this tome was "The Pocket Guide to Web Security."

Acknowledgments

I am grateful to everyone who helped during the conception, research, writing, and production of this book. Bob Bagwill, Jim Carroll, Tom Christiansen, Ian Redfern, Laura Pearlman, Bob Denny, and countless others contributed substantially to the WWW Security FAQ. Their insight and understanding has enriched the FAQ and this book, as well. Many thanks to Lewis Geer at Microsoft Corporation, who helped me sort out the ins and outs of Internet Explorer and active content, and to Brian Kendig at Netscape Corporation, who performed a similar role with Java and JavaScript. My warmest thanks also to my technical reviewers Mike Stok, Tom Markham, and Fred Douglis, each of whom came through with many helpful corrections and suggestions, in record time.

At the MIT Genome Center, many thanks to Lois Bennett and Susan Alderman, two tirelessly cheerful system administrators who never seemed to mind my turning the Web site and LAN into a laboratory bench for every new scheme I wanted to try out. I gravely promise to them that I will never again rip out all the server software and replace it with "new and improved" code at the start of a four-day weekend.

At Addison Wesley Longman, I am indebted to Carol Long, my first editor and the one who convinced me to launch this project, to Karen Gettman, who took over the project when Carol's career took her elsewhere, and to Mary Harrington, who kept everything from unraveling during the transition. Thanks also to Marilyn Rash, who coordinated the production effort.

Last, many thanks to Jean Siao, who blinked not an eye as her Macintosh was slowly swallowed by tangled mats of network cabling and spare parts. Yes, you can play SimCity now without fear of electrocution.

Nanjing
August 1997

Chapter 1

What Is Web Security?

Web security is different things to different people. For some, it's the ability to browse the Web in peace, knowing that no one is looking over their shoulders. For others, it's the ability to conduct financial and commercial transactions safely. For the operators of Web sites, it's confidence that their sites will not be vandalized by pranksters or used as a gateway to break into their local area network.

One of the problems with talking about Web security is that the topic has been distorted by software vendors and the press. Makers of Web browsers would have you believe that Web security is all about using cryptography to protect credit card numbers. Firewall vendors offer their systems as the only path to safety. Sun Microsystems views Web security as a matter of converting everything to Java as quickly as possible, a position hotly disputed by Microsoft. Meanwhile, sensational press reports muddy the debate with headlines that scream about "poison cookies" and "hostile applets."

In actuality, Web security is both more simple and more complex than the vendors would have you believe. More simple because it is easy to break the Web down into its components and see where the problems lie. More complex because there are no simple solutions, no magic formulas for making the Web "safe."

The Three Parts of Web Security

When you get right down to it, a Web connection is a very simple thing (see Figure 1.1). There are only three parts.

1. The Web browser
2. The Web server
3. The connection between the two

FIGURE 1.1 Web connections have three parts: the browser, the server, and the connection between the two.

The user, via her browser, connects to a remote Web server and requests a document. The server returns the document, and the browser displays it. What could go wrong?

Look at the transaction in a little more detail, however, and you'll see that the integrity of the system rests on a whole set of assumptions.

From the User's Point of View

- The remote server is owned and operated by the organization that it seems to be owned by.
- The documents that the server returns are free from dangerous viruses and malicious intent.
- The remote server will not record or distribute information that the user considers private, such as her Web browsing habits.

From the Webmaster's Point of View

- The user will not attempt to break into the Web server computer system or alter the contents of the Web site.
- The user will not try to gain access to documents that she is not privy to.
- The user will not try to crash the server, making it unavailable for others to use.
- If the user has identified herself, she is who she claims to be.

From Both Parties' Views

- The network connection is free from third-party eavesdroppers listening in on the communications line.
- The information sent between browser and server is delivered intact, free from tampering by third parties.

The whole purpose of Web security is to ensure that these assumptions remain valid. Because Web connections have three parts, Web security has three parts.

1. **Client-side security** These are security measures that protect the user's privacy and the integrity of her computer. Technological solutions include safeguards to protect users against computer viruses and other malicious software, as well as measures that limit the amount of personal information that browsers can transmit without the user's consent. Also in this category are steps that organizations can take to prevent employees' Web browsing activities from compromising the secrecy of the company's confidential information or the integrity of its local area network.
2. **Server-side security** These are measures that protect the Web server and the machine it runs on from break-ins, site vandalism, and denial-of-service attacks (attacks that make the Web site unavailable for normal use). Technological solutions run the gamut from firewall systems to operating system security measures.
3. **Document confidentiality** These are measures that protect private information from being disclosed to third parties. One risk to document confidentiality is eavesdroppers who intercept documents as they cross the network. Another risk is fraudulent identities—for instance, a user who misrepresents herself to a Web server as someone authorized to download a document, or a Web server that tricks a user into sending it confidential information by pretending to be a trusted site. The main technological fix in this category is cryptography, although simpler measures, such as the use of passwords to identify users, also play an important role.

None of these three aspects of Web security is independent of the other two. The strongest cryptography in the world will not keep a Web page secret if the computer that it is stored on is broken into. An impregnable Web server still won't protect an organization from public humiliation if a prankster can manage to hijack its *name* long enough to convince the world that the site was really vandalized.

Risks

What can go wrong? The risks depend on whether you're the person surfing the Web or the person administering the Web site. Sometimes, the interests align. Because eavesdropping hurts everyone, document encryption is in the interests of both parties. Sometimes, however, the interests of the Web site and the user are at odds. For example, when a Web site operator rewrites a CGI script as a Java applet, the risks from buggy software have been moved squarely off the Web site and onto the end user.

Indeed, client-side security and server-side security often overlap in complicated ways. Large organizations are just as concerned that confidential information will leak out through their employees' Web surfing sessions as they are that their Web servers will be broken into.

Risks That Affect Both Client and Server

Anything that affects the security of the network connection between Web site and end user is of equal concern to both parties. While this also includes things such as interruption of network services, in practice, the two main risks are network eavesdropping and Internet fraud.

Eavesdropping

In the days when Web browsers were passive vehicles that could do little more than fetch URLs and render HTML on-screen, eavesdropping was the major security concern. To someone using the Internet, a network connection between computer A and computer B seems as direct and simple as a piece of wire connecting the two machines. In fact, it's anything but. Unless the two computers are on the same local network, the data from each machine touches down at several locations before it reaches its final destination (Figure 1.2). A message from the browser may first travel by telephone line to a router at the user's Internet service provider (ISP). From there, it's shunted via a leased line to the ISP's regional service provider (RSP). It's now transferred across a high-speed trunk line to an RSP in some other part of the world. From there, the message travels to the Web site's ISP, to the Web site's local area network, and finally to the Web server machine itself.

At any point in this long and convoluted path, the message may be intercepted by unscrupulous individuals. Small software programs called "packet sniffers" can be set up to listen to network traffic, looking for interesting patterns in the data (passwords or credit card numbers, for example) and reporting back the information. To intercept the conversation between a Web browser and server, a packet sniffer can be installed at any point along the path between the two.

In order to set up such a packet sniffer, an unscrupulous individual must first break into one of the computers along the path: a machine at one of the ISPs, either of the RSPs, a computer connected to the local area network of the organization that runs the Web site, or even on the Web server itself. Because small ISPs are generally more vulnerable than the large regional providers, they are the obvious targets for such an attack. The local area network of the organization that runs the Web site is also a tempting target.

Once a packet sniffer is installed, someone can listen in to the entire conversation between browser and server. Among the things that can be intercepted are the URL that the browser requests, the document that the server returns, passwords given by the user to access restricted areas of the site, and the contents of any fill-out forms that the user submits. A malicious and technically savvy individual can go even further and alter the contents of the data en route. To give a dramatic example, a cyber-thief could conceivably alter the contents of a message you send to your bank, modifying an elec-

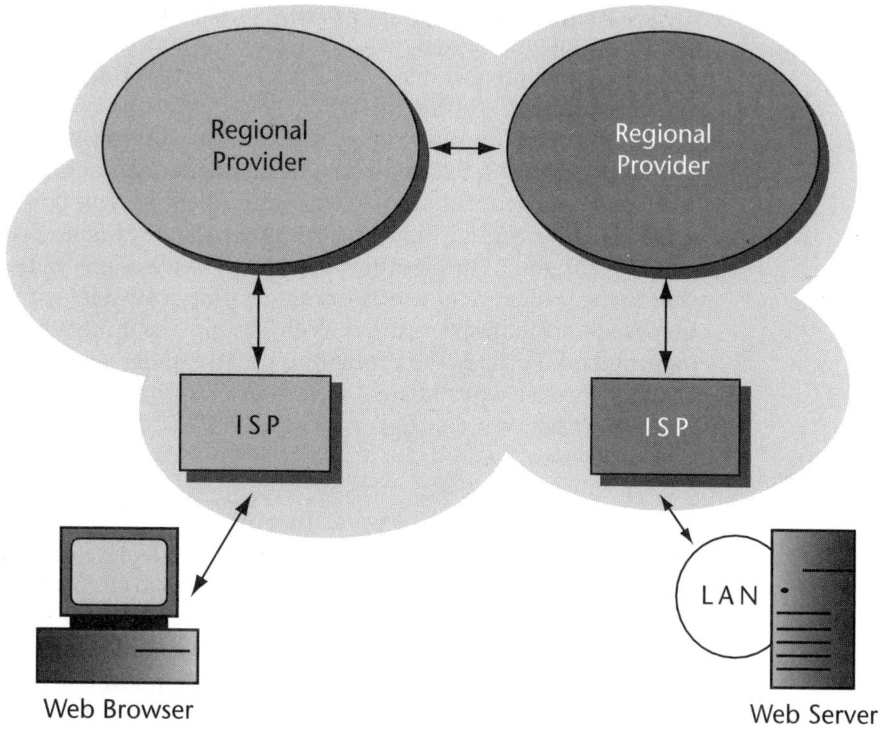

FIGURE 1.2 Data passes through many intermediaries on its way from the browser to the server.

tronic funds transfer so that the money is transferred into the thief's account rather than your own.

Packet-sniffer "kits" are readily available on the Internet and are among the first programs to be installed when a system is broken into. It is not uncommon for a server administrator to stumble across a sniffer that has been quietly running on a system for days or weeks; until the sniffer was discovered the administrator had no idea that the system had ever been broken into. In corporate environments, packet sniffers are something that nosy insiders can install on their desktop computers to listen in to the traffic on the local area network. Your coworker may be surreptitiously watching your Web-surfing sessions!

The new generation of cable modems also increases the risk of packet sniffing. In a typical cable modem system, everyone in the neighborhood served by a single cable distribution area shares packets. Because a cable distribution area may span many city blocks, you have to worry about all your neighbors listening in, party-line style.

Cryptography is the main defense against eavesdropping. By encrypting all communications between Web browser and server, the information can be kept safe from prying eyes. This is the first and still most widely held interpretation of Web security.

Despite the obvious risks from packet sniffers, the problem remains largely theoretical. Surprisingly, there has not yet been a single publicized case in which a confidential Web communication was compromised by network eavesdropping (as of June 1997). Although some software vendors might want you to think otherwise, the absence of any major incidents is *not* due to the widespread use of cryptographic software. Although encrypting browsers are common, most Web surfing is done with the encryption switched off. Perhaps the problem is greatly underreported, or perhaps there are much easier ways to steal information.

Fraud

Related to the problem of eavesdropping is the problem of Internet fraud. When a user connects to a Web page that looks like the L.L. Bean site and places an order, how does she know that it's really L.L. Bean and not a rogue Web server that has copied the legitimate site's pages and set up a lookalike site? When a bank implements a Web-based teller system, how does it determine that the user who transfers $10,000 from one account to another is authorized to do so? On the Internet, there's no face-to-face contact between people, no picture ID cards, no driver's licenses or personal references. To conduct business on the Internet, there must be a way to reliably authenticate individuals and organizations.

Conveniently, the same techniques that are used to encrypt communications can also be used to create unforgeable "digital signatures" for the purpose of authentication. The system works by assigning "certificates" to various Internet participants. Certificates are electronic vouchers issued by companies whose job it is to guarantee the identity of individuals and organizations. Web sites authenticate themselves with site certificates, and individual users authenticate themselves with personal certificates. Specific types of certificates also vouchsafe the identities of software publishers, credit card companies, and banks.

Although encryption and authentication usually go hand in hand, you can authenticate without encrypting and encrypt without authenticating. The latter combination allows you to have a secure, yet anonymous, Internet conversation.

Risks to the End User

Some Web security risks only affect the end user. Ironically, these risks have grown as Web browsers have become more powerful.

Active Content

In the days of 1,200-baud modems, security gurus preached "software celibacy": Don't run software downloaded from unknown bulletin board systems and Internet sites because you might catch a virus. Many people took this advice to heart. Others averted problems by thoroughly scanning all downloaded files with virus checkers before running them.

The Web has made software celibacy much harder. The problem is that the distinction between active software and passive documents has blurred. Things that we used to assume are safe, such as word processor files, can now launch virus attacks on our systems. Making matters more difficult, Web pages contain "active content." Browsers can download and run software without advance notice. All you have to do is view a page.

Active content embraces a motley collection of technologies that make Web pages more interesting and interactive. Java applets and ActiveX controls are the best known of the active-content technologies, but browser plug-ins, helper applications, JavaScript, and VBScript are also members of the family. Well-written active content enhances Web pages with animations, interactive games, and serious applications, such as database browsers and groupware products. Buggy active content, on the other hand, may contain security holes that compromise the user's privacy or the integrity of the data stored on her computer. More worrisome, active content written for malicious purposes may attempt to damage a user's system or seek to gain unauthorized access to a local area network.

Like network eavesdropping, active content remains more a potential problem than a real one. A variety of "malicious applets" have been demonstrated, but few serious attacks have been reported so far. The main problem has been "annoying applets," pages that contain active content tailored to make the browser crash or freeze.

Privacy Infringement

The other major risk to the end user is the loss of privacy. Although Web surfing feels like an anonymous activity, it is hardly that way. Big brother is watching. Every time a user fetches a page from a remote Web site, she leaves a calling card. It may be no more than the Internet address of her computer, or it may be more personal information. What are the remote sites doing with this information? There's no way to know for sure.

Web sites can get information about a user in a variety of ways. The most basic is the server log, which records the time and date of the connection, the address of the user's machine, the identity of the document that the user requested, and the URL of the previous document the user was viewing. More information is available to ISPs whose proxy servers keep track of every Web site visited by the ISP's customers.

Another way that Web sites can collect information about users is through Internet "cookies," small identifiers that Web sites use to tag browsers. Cookies allow servers to remember a particular browser when it returns to the site after a period of time. They were designed to enhance Web surfing by allowing users to customize pages, browse databases, navigate complex maps, and perform other tasks that require continuity across browsing sessions. But as we'll see, cookies have been abused by advertising agencies to tag people, allowing them to collect detailed information about users' Web-browsing habits.

The greatest threat to personal privacy is not information that is stolen in sneaky ways, but information that users voluntarily give away—in user surveys, news postings, e-mail messages, and on-line orders. Once this information leaves the user's hands, there's no control over how it's used, and Web sites routinely trade it, aggregate it, and correlate it with information gathered by other Web sites. The same worldwide integration that has made the Web such a compelling medium gives it the potential to become a vast network of spy cameras.

The handling of personal information is a hotly debated topic. The need to maximize user's privacy is at odds at a fundamental level with businesses' need to minimize fraud. The first goal seeks to maximize users' anonimity. The second goal requires users to be strongly and unequivocally identified. Somehow, a compromise must be struck.

Risks to the Web Site

Some risks primarily affect the Web server's side of the connection. These include Webjackings, break-ins, and denial-of-service attacks.

Webjacking

Perhaps the event that strikes the most fear into Webmasters' hearts is the possibility that their organizations' sites will be broken into and modified by vandals. Often, the contents of the site are replaced with crude parodies or by political messages. The results can be merely embarassing for an organization, or they may have more lasting effects. For example, an organization that has built up a reputation for security, such as a branch of the government or a finanical institution, may suffer persistent damage to its reputation after a Webjacking event. In contrast to some of the risks discussed earlier, Webjackings are far from rare. Hundreds of sites have been attacked and vandalized, including such technically sophisticated organizations as the U.S. Central Intelligence Agency, the U.S. Air Force, and NASA.

Vandals can Webjack a site by exploiting holes left open by a poorly configured operating system, a misconfigured Web server, or buggy software. Web servers, whose rapidly expanding feature sets tend to outrun vendors' quality control systems, have a poor track record in the security arena. Many older Web servers contain bugs that open up large security holes, and the list includes several well-known commercial servers that were called "secure" because of their ability to encrypt communications. There is no doubt that unknown security holes exist in the current generation of servers.

Another fertile source of security problems is CGI scripts and server modules. These small pieces of computer code extend the ability of the server to create dynamic Web pages, interface to search engines and databases, and respond to input from the user. CGI scripts are easy to write, easy to install, and easy to use. Popular sites make heavy use of them, and some have hundreds of custom scripts installed. But CGI scripting's main blessing is also its biggest curse. Scripts are so easy to write that many of them are created by programmers with no prior experience in network programming and little appreciation of security issues. The list of security holes in popular CGI scripts is long and growing.

A Web server is no stronger than its weakest link. The operating system must be secure, the file system must be secure, the Web server software must be secure, and each of the server's CGI scripts and modules must be secure. A failure in any of these components makes all the other security measures meaningless.

Server and LAN Break-ins

Although some vandals break into a Web server just for the purpose of parodying its content, others may have a more serious agenda: to use the server as a staging base for further attacks on the organization's databases, file servers, and other mission-critical systems. Too often, the Web server provides a portal of entry for intruders, a wide open door set in the walls of a forbidding castle.

You can defend against this type of break-in by making the Web server as secure as possible. But the fundamental problem with Web sites is that they're complex, ever-changing systems that are under constant pressure to grow. Even the best Webmaster will eventually make a mistake that will open up a security hole.

When used properly, firewall systems protect mission-critical systems against threats that enter via the Web server. They can also effectively tighten defenses against attacks on the Web server itself. Used improperly, a firewall will make a Web site unusable. Worse, a misconfigured Web server can punch a hole in a firewall, rendering it useless.

Denial-of-Service Attacks

Even if a vandal can't break into a Web site, he can make it look bad by making it crash, hang, or process requests so slowly that it is unusable. For a site that depends on 24-hour availability, this can be disastrous.

Denial-of-service attacks can be aimed at the operating system, Web server software, CGI scripts, and Web site services. Although there is no magic formula for avoiding denial-of-service attacks, you can lessen their impact by placing limits on the resources used by the Web server and other programs, as well as closing known vulnerabilities in the operating system and other software.

The Layout of This Book

This book is divided into three sections corresponding to the three parts of Web security. The first section, Document Confidentiality, starts with a general introduction to cryptography. It then moves on to discuss the specifics of the two cryptographic protocols that are most relevant for the Web: the SSL protocol, used for general-purpose document encryption; and SET, used to secure credit card transactions.

The second section, Client-Side Security, looks at Web security issues from the end user's point of view and provides practical recipes for avoiding the biggest pitfalls. Its three chapters describe how to use Web browsers to prevent electronic eavesdropping and fraud, how to avoid being bitten by active content, and how to avoid privacy infringements.

The last section, Server-Side Security, is the longest. It deals with Web security from the Web site administrator's point of view. Webmasters will find practical advice on everything from configuring the operating system securely to controlling access to the site to safe CGI scripting. Firewalls, remote authoring tools, and access control based on client-side certificates all receive special attention.

Commercial Products

A large number of commercial software and hardware products are mentioned in this book. An even larger number aren't. Although I would have liked to have personally examined each and every security-related product, time (and my editor) wouldn't permit. When confronted with too many products and too little space, I chose first those that I am experienced with, and second those that, whether for merit or for historical reasons, are market leaders and most likely to be encountered by readers. Please don't construe the inclusion of one product over another as an endorsement.

For Web browsers, I use Netscape Navigator and Microsoft Internet Explorer as my exemplars throughout this book. For Web servers, I chose Microsoft Internet Information Server as representative of the Windows NT world, and Apache (and its encrypting cousin, Stronghold) as a model UNIX server. Much of the advice on safely configuring these two servers applies as well to other popular products. In cases in which there are unique and pressing security issues that affect other popular servers, I have pointed them out.

Checklists

Staring with Chapter 3, chapters end with a checklist of dos and don'ts, intended as a quick review of the chapter's main points. You can use them as the starting point for a poor man's security audit, but don't place blind faith in them. Security is more than checking off items in a checklist. The important thing is to understand the basic concepts so that you can formulate and implement your own checklist.

Online and Offline Resources

Web security is a huge subject, and there's no way that one book can hope to cover it all. Further, because technology is changing at a remarkable rate, parts of this book will be out of date by the time it hits the shelves. Rather than reach for an unrealistic comprehensiveness, each chapter is designed to touch on the essentials of the subject. Further information resources, in the form of online URLs and offline books, can be found at the end of each chapter.

To save you the trouble of retyping long URLs, links to all the online resources mentioned in this book are mirrored at its companion Web site, located at

http://www.awl.com/cseng/titles/0-201-63489-9/

Errata and updates will be posted to this site periodically.

Much of this book is derived from the *World Wide Web Security FAQ*, an online document that I wrote and maintain. The FAQ is updated frequently, every two weeks or so, and is a good place to watch for breaking Web security issues. It is mirrored at various locations around the world, but the master document can always be found at:

http://www.w3.org/Security/faq

Online Resources

The WWW Consortium security pages

A good survey of security-standards-making activity by the W3C and others.

http://www.w3.org/Security/

The NCSA Web security pages

A very readable tutorial on web security for the Webmaster.

http://hoohoo.ncsa.uiuc.edu/security/

The Digicrime Web site

Many pointers to computer security information, plus examples of hostile applets and other exploits.

http://www.digicrime.com/

Netscape's security pages

A good overview of technological fixes, lightly slanted to one company's producers.

http://home.netscape.com/info/security-doc.html

Yahoo security pages

Links to public and commercial Web sites dealing with Web security

http://www.yahoo.com/companies.and.Internet/Internet/World.Wide.Web/security/

Printed Resources for Web Security Information

There are two good books devoted specifically to security on the World Wide Web:

Garfinkel, Simson, with Gene Spafford, *Web Security and Commerce* (O'Reilly & Associates, 1997).

A thoughtful book that considers the social, legal, and economic sides of Web security, as well as the practical side.

Rubin, Aviel, Geer, Daniel, and Ranum, Marcus, *Web Security Sourcebook* (John Wiley and Sons, 1997).

A more academically oriented book that looks at Web security protocols in depth.

The following are several general computer security books:

Amoroso, Edward, *Fundamentals of Computer Security Technology* (Prentice-Hall, 1994).

A complete introduction to computer security.

Garfinkel, Simson, and Spafford, Gene, *Practical UNIX & Internet Security* (O'Reilly & Associates, 1996).

Although targeted at UNIX systems, this book provides an excellent overview of Internet security.

Pfleeger, Charles, *Security in Computing* (Prentice-Hall, 1996).

Another good general security reference guide.

PART I

Document Confidentiality

Can your coworker monitor your Web-surfing habits? Can unscrupulous individuals intercept the passwords used to access confidential documents on a Web site? Is that a trusted Web site at the other end of the connection or a rogue site impersonating it?

This section takes a close look at cryptography, the key technology for protecting against these and other threats.

Chapter 2

Basic Cryptography

When people think about Web security, cryptography is often the first thing that pops into their minds, thanks to browser developers' success in raising consumer consciousness about the risks of transmitting credit card numbers across the World Wide Web. Despite the hype, cryptography does play a crucial role on the Web. It enables confidential information to be transmitted from location to location across insecure networks without risk of interception or tampering, and it allows the two communicating parties to verify each others' identities without meeting in person.

This chapter introduces the principles of cryptography and shows how those principles are applied to real-life problems on the Web. It shows you what you can expect from the Web cryptographic protocols and, more important, what their limitations are.

How Cryptography Works

The word *cryptography* comes from the Greek for "secret writing." Cryptography has been used by militaries since the days of the Hellenic wars, and has grown steadily in sophistication in parallel with mathematics and information technology.

All cryptographic systems, no matter how complex, have the following four basic parts (Figure 2.1).

1. **Plaintext** This is the message before anything has been done to it. It is either human-readable or in a format that anyone with the proper software can use.

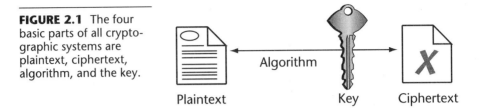

FIGURE 2.1 The four basic parts of all cryptographic systems are plaintext, ciphertext, algorithm, and the key.

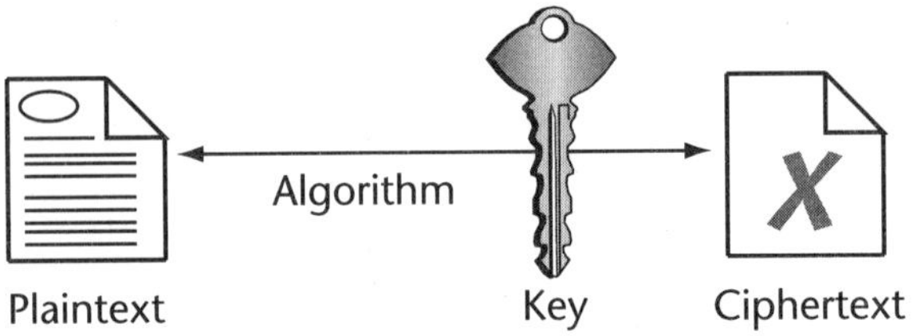

2. **Ciphertext** This is the plaintext message after it has been modified in some way to obscure it, rendering it unreadable. The process of converting plaintext into ciphertext is "encryption," while the opposite operation is known as "decryption."
3. **Cryptographic algorithm** This is the mathematical operation used to convert plaintext into ciphertext, and vice versa.
4. **Key** This is a secret key used to encrypt and/or decrypt the message. Each key transforms the same plaintext into a different ciphertext. If the cryptographic system works properly, only people who know the correct key can decrypt a piece of ciphertext.

The beauty of cryptography is that the ciphertext can be transmitted across unsecure, public communications channels. Even if the ciphertext is intercepted, it is useless to anyone who does not possess the decryption key. Before the advent of digital computers, plaintext, ciphertext, and key were usually in the form of human-readable text. Now the three are, typically, streams of arbitrary binary information. Video, sound, and software can all be encrypted as easily as plaintext.

An important feature of good cryptographic systems is that the security of the system depends completely on the secrecy of the decryption key. It is *not* necessary to keep the workings of the cryptographic algorithm secret. This allows the same algorithm to be reused by many people and avoids any need to protect crytographic software from curious eyes.

Ciphertext can be "cracked" and read by unauthorized users in several ways. One way is through cryptanalysis. Trained cryptographers analyze the ciphertext for residual patterns left over from the original plaintext. Any such patterns can be used to reconstruct either the original message or the key used to encrypt it. A mark of a good cryptographic algorithm is that it contains no patterns: The ciphertext is indistinguishable from random noise. All algorithms commonly used on the Web have this property and are thought to be resistant to cryptanalysis for this reason.

Another way to crack ciphertext is to guess the decryption key. Try each possible key in turn until you find one that returns a readable message—the so-called brute-force attack. This may sound impractical, but remember that a high-speed computer may be able to try millions of guesses in a second. Even if the individual computers aren't remarkably fast, they can be networked to work on the problem in parallel, guessing passwords at a remarkable rate. This is the reason that the length of the key is so important. A key that is 16 bits long has $2^{16} = 65{,}536$ different possibilities and will fall to brute-force attack immediately. A key that is 40 bits long has more than 10^{12} (one thousand billion) possibilities. Although this seems like a lot, 40-bit keys are still considered too weak to entrust with valuable information. The keys used to encrypt sensitive information are typically 128 bits or higher (10^{38} possibilities, more than the number of water molecules in all the oceans of the planet). (See Key Length and U.S. Encryption Policy later in this chapter for a discussion of the length of keys used in Web software bound for the U.S. domestic and export markets.)

The easiest way to crack an encrypted message is to find a way to work around the system. You could break into the machine where the plaintext is stored and steal the file, bribe someone into revealing the decryption key to you, surreptitiously replace the software used to encrypt messages with a doctored copy, or discover flaws in the way the encryption software works.

Symmetric Cryptography

For much of the history of cryptography, encryption algorithms were symmetrical, meaning that the same secret key was used to both encrypt and decrypt a message (Figure 2.2). For the system to work, the sender and recipient have to agree on a secret key in advance by some secure means. For example, you could have a courier hand-deliver a locked briefcase containing the secret key on a floppy, read the key over a secured telephone line, or agree in advance to pick a key based on the first letters of the words appearing in the headline of today's *New York Times*.

Common symmetrical algorithms you are likely to encounter include the following five.

1. **DES** DES is the Data Encryption Standard sanctioned for the encryption of unclassified information by the U.S. National Institute of Standards and Technology (NIST). It has been widely used since its introduction in the '70s. DES's 56-bit key length was secure during its first two decades, but 56 bits is now too small to protect DES-encrypted messages from a determined attack. (See the DES Cracked box for a discussion.) Because DES encrypts data in discrete blocks of 64 bits, it is often used in combination with a mode called CBC (cipherblock chaining). In this system, the encryption of each block depends on the contents of the previous one, preventing an interloper from tampering with the message by rearranging the encrypted blocks.

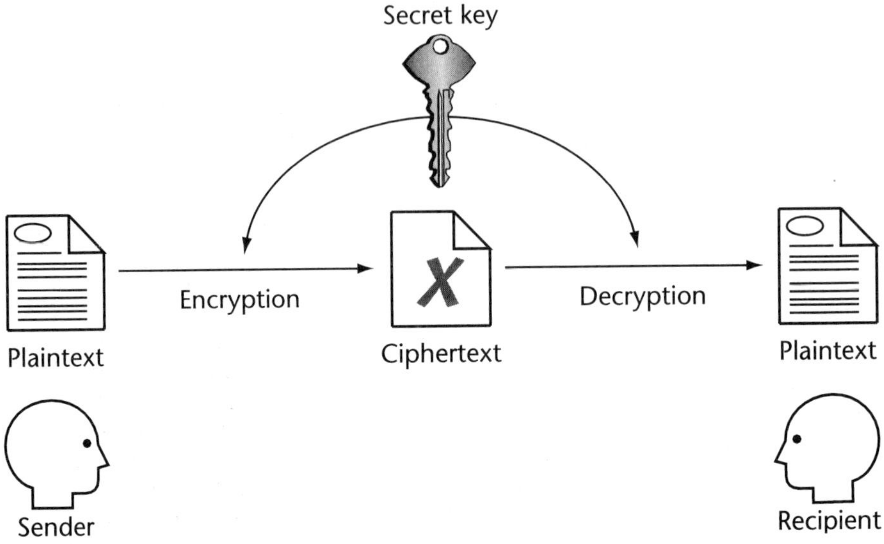

FIGURE 2.2 In symmetric cryptography, the same key is used for encrypting and decrypting the message.

2. **Triple DES, DESX, GDES, RDES** These are variants of DES that decrease the risk from brute-force guessing by using longer keys. In the widely used triple-DES, the message is first encrypted with one secret key, next decrypted with a second secret key, and finally encrypted again with the first secret key. This gives an effective key length of roughly 168 bits.
3. **RC2, RC4, RC5** These are proprietary algorithms invented by RSA Data Security, Inc. They use keys of variable lengths ranging as high as 2,048 bits. RC2 and RC4 are of particular interest to Web users, as crippled versions that use 40-bit keys have been licensed for export beyond U.S. borders. As a result, these are the algorithms most frequently used by encrypting Web browsers and servers.
4. **IDEA** The International Data Encryption Algorithm, first proposed by Xuejia Lai and James Massey, is a patented algorithm held by Ascom-Tech AG. It is popular in Europe, but less so in the United States. With a 128-bit secret key, it is considered to be significantly more secure than unmodified DES. IDEA is one of the algorithms at the heart of the popular e-mail encryption software, Pretty Good Privacy (PGP); the other is RSA, discussed on page 21.
5. **Blowfish** This is an unpatented symmetric algorithm invented by Bruce Schneier that is gradually making its way into many commercial and freeware encryption products. It uses a variable-length secret key up to 448 bits long.

DES Cracked

At a conference held in January 1997, the RSA Data Security Corporation issued a challenge to the world. It encrypted a short English phrase with the DES algorithm and posted it to its Web site, offering $10,000 to the first person to crack the message.

Five months later the prize was claimed by the concerted effort of a team of volunteers called the DESCHALL group.

DESCHALL cracked the message using a brute-force attack. It tried each of the possible DES keys in turn until one worked. In order to make the attack feasible, DESCHALL turned the effort into an Internet-wide lottery. The list of possible keys was divided up into many small segments. Each segment was given to a volunteer, along with a key-testing program to be run on the volunteer's desktop computer. The person who got the lucky number would receive a 40-percent share in the RSA prize money. DESCHALL started with a few hundred volunteers, but as word of the contest spread, the number of participants swelled to thousands. As predicted, someone eventually hit the jackpot. The lucky winner was Michael Salders of Houston, Texas, whose 90-MHz desktop Pentium cracked the challenge phrase, "Strong cryptography makes the world a safer place."

Although it made headlines, the result was hardly surprising to cryptographers, who had been warning for years that DES was no longer a match for modern computers. Keys that are 56 bits long are just not long enough to withstand a concerted brute-force attack by conventional computers, let alone an attack by one or more high-speed machines.

Web users need not be alarmed by this development. The SSL protocol used to encrypt Web communications is not much threatened by DES's weakness. Although DES is one of the encryption options that SSL recognizes, it uses the stronger RC2, RC4, and triple-DES algorithms when it can. At other times, SSL uses a much weaker 40-bit algorithm when the software has been deliberately crippled for export. However, if you use DES to encrypt personal or organizational files for long-term storage, you should be concerned by this development because these documents are now vulnerable. Upgrade to a system that uses a longer key length as soon as feasible.

Unfortunately, symmetric algorithms present problems for use on the Internet where parties often need to communicate without having previously met. Communications are likely to be spontaneous, and there is rarely an opportunity to exchange secret keys in advance. Another troublesome requirement for Internet cryptography is the need for multiway communications. Typically, many people need to communicate with a single server. Even if it were possible to securely distribute a Web server's secret key to the thousands of users who might like to communicate with it, it would be impossible to keep the key secret for long. Once a symmetric key is divulged, it and every message that it has been used to encrypt become forfeit. A new key has to be chosen and distributed.

Public Key Cryptography

During the 1970s, a new type of cryptographic algorithm known as "public key cryptography" was invented (also known as "asymmetric cryptography," although no one uses that term). In public key systems, keys come in pairs: one used for encryption and the other for decryption. Surprisingly, an encrypted message cannot be decrypted even if you know the key that was used to encrypt it. Only the matching decryption key can be used to retrieve the original message.

Everyone who participates in a public key cryptography system owns a unique pair of keys. One of the keys, called the "public" key, is made publicly available. Far from being a secret, the public key is widely distributed to anyone who wants it. The other key, called the "private" key, is a closely guarded secret. To send a secure message to someone, you look up her public key and use it to encrypt the message (Figure 2.3). The message can now be sent over an insecure channel without fear of interception. So long as the matching private key remains in the possession of its intended recipient, there is only one person in the world who can decrypt and read that message.

This behavior is perfect for the Internet. You can send an encrypted message to anyone without making arrangements in advance. Multiple people can send messages to the same party without the need to share any secrets.

In contrast to the many algorithms available for symmetric cryptography, there are only two practical public key algorithms (see next page). Of these, only one is widely implemented.

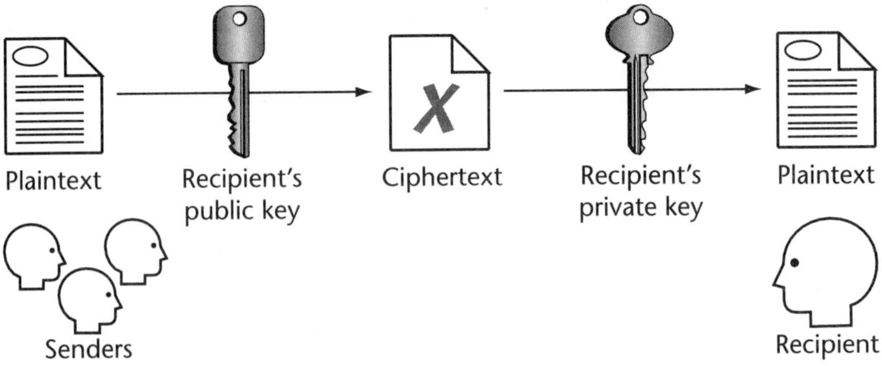

FIGURE 2.3 In public key cryptography, multiple people encrypt messages using the recipient's well-known public key. The recipient decrypts it with her private key.

1. **RSA** Named for its inventors, Ronald Rivest, Adi Shamir, and Leonard Adelman, RSA is patented by RSA Data Security, Inc. It forms the basis for essentially all the Web and secure e-mail software you are likely to encounter. RSA uses variable key lengths, typically ranging from 512 to greater than 1,024 bits.
2. **ElGamal** This algorithm, named for its inventor, Taher ElGamal, uses variable key lengths between 512 and 1,024. Unlike RSA, it is unpatented, but its use has been limited because of a patent infringement dispute with the inventors of the Diffie-Hellman algorithm (described on page 28). However, the Diffie-Hellman patent expired in April 1997, and cryptographic systems based on ElGamal should be appearing shortly.

The mathematics of public key algorithms are beyond the scope of this book. Suffice to say that they rely for their security on computationally difficult problems, such as the difficulty of finding the prime factors of very large numbers. Barring fundamental breakthroughs in mathematics (which isn't such a far-fetched idea), solving these problems is very labor intensive, and the amount of labor required increases dramatically as the keys get longer. The longer the length of the key pair, the more computer time it takes to guess the private key. The keys typically used for Internet applications would take millions of years to crack using current technologies.

The main limitation of public key cryptography is speed. The fastest implementation of the RSA algorithm is still a thousand times slower than a typical symmetric algorithm, making it impractical for encrypting long messages. In real-world applications, public key and symmetric cryptography are usually combined in a way that takes advantage of their best features. (See Digital Envelopes later in this chapter.)

Digital Signatures

Public key cryptography provides one other great benefit. It allows one to create unforgeable digital signatures. Digital signatures are a clever reversal of the public key encyption/decryption scheme (Figure 2.4). Messages encrypted using an individual's *private* key can only be deciphered with her *public* key. This provides a simple recipe for creating an unforgeable statement of identity.

1. Create a short statement of identity—for instance, "I am Mary Anne."
2. Encode it with your private key, creating an encrypted signature.
3. Attach the encrypted signature to the message and encrypt the whole thing with the public key of the intended recipient.
4. Send the message.

The message's recipient decrypts the message with her private key and detaches the encrypted signature. She now decrypts the signature with the

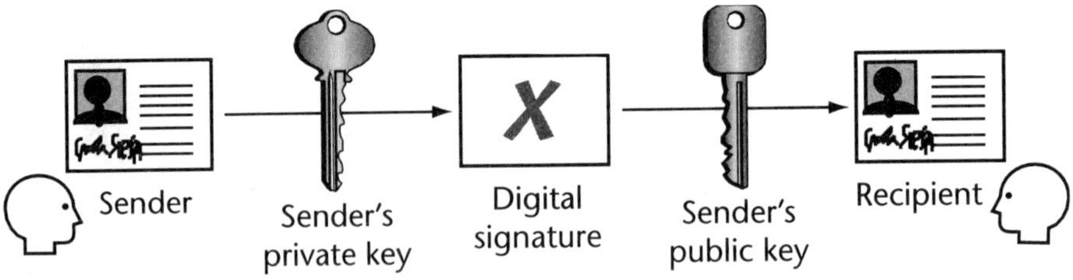

FIGURE 2.4 By using her private key to encrypt a short message, the sender can generate a digital signature.

sender's well-known public key. If it decrypts correctly, the recipient knows that only someone with access to the sender's private key could have signed the message.

In real life, digital signature protocols are more complicated than this. This is because the scheme I've just described does nothing to prevent malicious individuals from cutting and pasting the sender's encrypted signature from an old message onto a new, fraudulent one. There are several ways around this, however. In one variant, most often used when two parties are initiating a prolonged conversation, one party generates a random "challenge" phrase and sends it to the other. The other signs the challenge with her private key and returns it. If the challenge decrypts correctly with the other's public key, her identity is confirmed. Another scheme uses message digest functions, described in the next section.

Any public key algorithm can be used to create digital signatures. However, an algorithm that was specifically designed for this purpose is the Digital Signature Algorithm (DSA), issued in 1994 by the U.S. National Institute of Standards and Technology (NIST) for use in its proposed Digital Signature Standard (DSS). This algorithm, developed in conjunction with the National Security Agency (NSA), is a variant of ElGamal and uses a variable key length between 512 and 1,024 bits. Although the NIST has encouraged both the public and private sectors to use DSS for the protection of unclassified information, its adoption has been spotty because of political fighting and lingering suspicions over the involvement of the NSA in its development.

Message Digest Functions and Message Integrity

Both symmetric and public key cryptography provide some built-in integrity checking. If a message is modified in transit, because of either a communications error or someone's deliberate intervention, the message won't decrypt correctly. However, this is not a good integrity check because messages are typically encrypted in small blocks of text. It's possible for a portion of an encrypted message to be deleted or a section duplicated without causing any obvious problems.

"Message digest functions," also known as "one-way hashes," provide reliable integrity checking. In some ways, a digest function is similar to an encryption algorithm. It takes a plaintext message and transforms it into something that looks random. Unlike an encryption algorithm, however, the transformation is one way. Message digest functions generate short, fixed-length values, known as "hashes." The hash is much shorter than the original—information is lost during digestion. There's no way to decrypt a hash, nor any known way to create two different messages that generate the same hash.

A message digest acts as a digital fingerprint for the original message. If the message changes even slightly, its digest will change dramatically. In combination with encryption and digital signatures, message digests allow you to send tamper-proof messages across the Internet. Here's one popular recipe, which, as it happens, is the basis for the Digital Signature Standard:

1. Run a message through the digest function, obtaining its hash.
2. Sign the hash with your private key.
3. Send the signed hash and the original message to the recipient.

The recipient now decrypts the hash using the sender's public key and compares this with the result of running the message through the digest function anew. If they match, the recipient has verified both the sender's identity and the integrity of the message.

There are other ways to use message digests for message integrity checking and/or authentication. Many methods require both sender and recipient to share a secret key that they've exchanged at some prior time. For example, the SSL protocol (described in the next chapter) uses message authenticity check (MAC) values calculated in the following manner:

```
MAC = digest(secret + digest(secret + message))
```

In this equation, the plus sign (+) means concatenatation, so the MAC is the digest of the secret key concatenated with the digest of the key and the message. The two rounds of digestion foil any attempt by an evil-doer to intercept the message and append false information to the end.

There are a variety of message digest functions. The ones you are most likely to encounter are

1. **MD4** A fast one-way hash function designed by Ronald Rivest of MIT. It produces 128-bit hashes. After publication, it was found to have some minor weaknesses and was replaced by MD5.
2. **MD5** Rivest introduced this as a replacement for MD4. It is the most widely used message digest function. Like MD4, it produces a 128-bit hash.

3. **SHA** SHA is the Secure Hash Algorithm, designed by the NIST (with help from the NSA) for use in the Digital Signature Standard. It produces a 160-bit hash.

Digital Envelopes

Although public key encryption systems seem ideal for the Internet, they have one serious drawback. They are orders of magnitude slower than symmetric systems, making them unsuitable for transferring large documents. The solution to this is to combine the two systems (Figure 2.5). Here's the basic recipe.

1. Generate a secret key at random. This secret key is often called the *session key* because it is discarded after the communications session is done.
2. Encrypt the message using the session key and the *symmetric* algorithm of your choice.
3. Encrypt the session key with the recipient's public key. This becomes the "digital envelope."
4. Send the encrypted message and the digital envelope to the recipient.

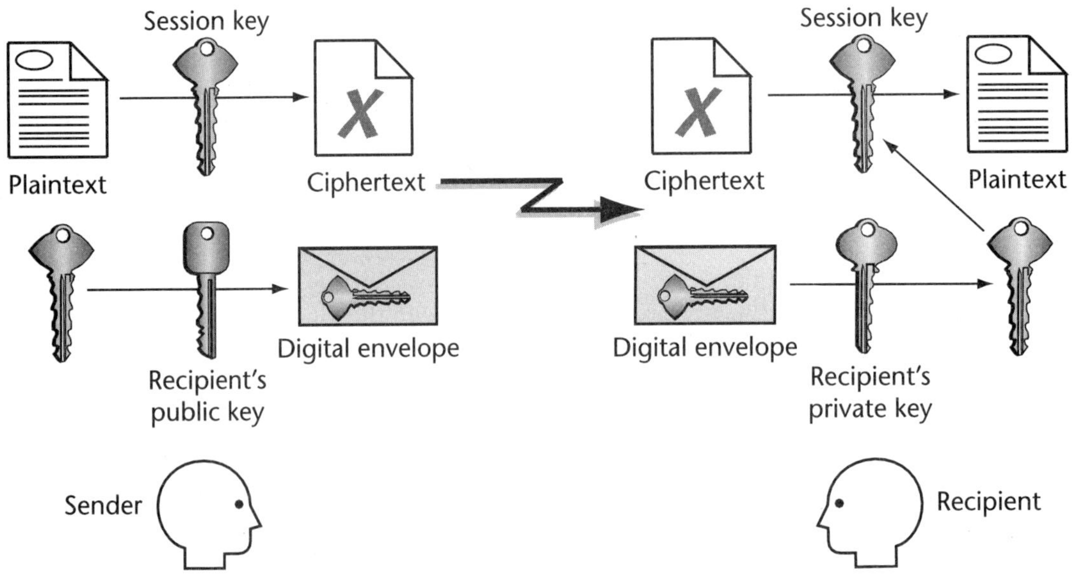

FIGURE 2.5 To make a digital envelope, the sender generates a random session key, encrypts the message with it, then encrypts the session key with the recipient's public key.

When the recipient receives the envelope, she uses her private key to decrypt it, recovering the session key. She now uses the session key to decrypt the message. The message is secure because it is encrypted using a symmetric session key that only the sender and recipient know. The session key is secure because it is encrypted in such a way that only its intended recipient can decrypt it.

The digital envelope system can be used to establish secure two-way communications. One party chooses the session key, encrypts it, and sends it as described previously. The two parties now use this shared secret key to encrypt their entire conversation. When the conversation is over, the session key is discarded.

Certifying Authorities and the Public Key Infrastructure

Some readers may have noticed that there's a gaping hole in what I've described so far. Public key cryptography works well only so long as you know the intended recipient's public key in advance. This is a tricky thing to arrange. In a world of hundreds of thousands of Web servers and millions of people, you certainly don't want to keep everyone's public key in a database on your hard disk. Nor can you ask the recipient for her (or its) public key before sending a secure message, because there's no assurance that the person on the other end of the connection is who or what you think it is.

One solution to this problem would be to rely on a large networked database to keep track of everyone's public key and distribute them on demand. When you wanted to send someone a message, you'd connect to the database securely (everyone must know the database server's public key in advance) and send it a query for the user or organization you're looking for.

Although the network database sounds like it might work, it has some practical problems such as: Who's going to maintain the thing? How well will it perform when there are a hundred million public keys on file?

Certifying Authorities

A more practical solution is to rely on trusted third parties, called "certifying authorities" (CAs), for public key validation. A certifying authority is a commercial enterprise that vouches for the identities of individuals and organizations. Instead of keeping everyone's public keys on your hard disk, you keep the public keys of a few well-known and trusted CAs. Before sending a message to someone, you ask that they present you with a "digital certificate" that has been signed by one of these CAs. From the certificate, you can verify the recipient's identity and recover his or her public key.

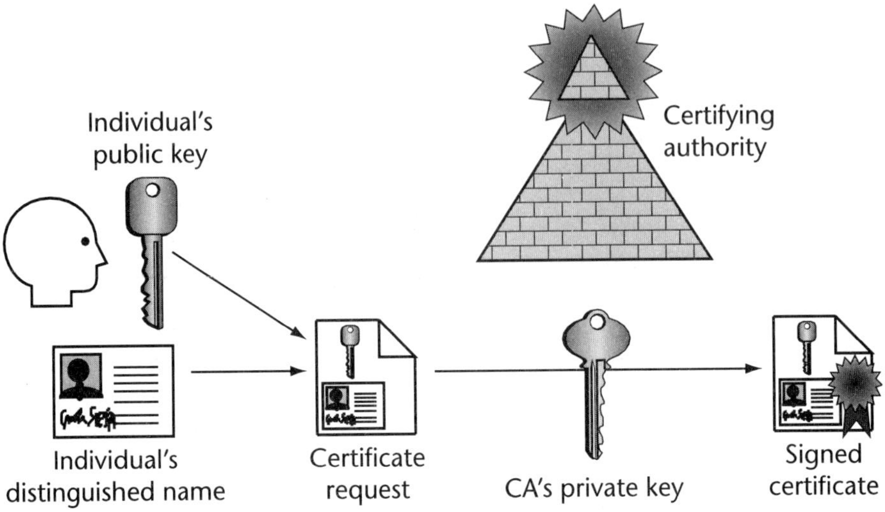

FIGURE 2.6 Certifying authorities grant digital certificates by signing the individual's public key with the authority's own private key.

Digital certificates are untamperable and unforgeable. The system works like this (Figure 2.6):

1. Generate a public/private key pair.
2. Keep the private key, and send the public key to a CA, along with identifying information, in the form of a "certificate request."
3. Pay the CA's fee.
4. The CA will now verify that you are who you claim to be. The verification may be thorough or cursory, depending on the CA's policies and the size of the fee.
5. If everything checks out, the CA will create a certificate that contains your public key, along with identifying information. If this is a certificate for use in a Web browser, it may contain your name and e-mail address. A certificate intended for use by a Web server will contain the Web site's home URL.
6. The CA generates a message digest from the certificate and signs the hash with its private key, creating a signed certificate. It now returns the signed certificate to you.

Before you send someone a secure message, you ask the person to present a signed certificate. You decrypt the signed hash with the CA's known public key to verify that the public key, name, and other identifying information have not been altered since the certificate was signed. You can now use the public key to send a message with confidence that it is the correct one.

CAs and signed certificates are central components of the developing public key distribution system known as the "public key infrastructure." A variety of certificates are used for different purposes. Certificates used to authenticate Web servers are "site certificates"; those that authenticate individual users are "personal certificates"; those used by software companies to sign executables (see Chapter 5) are known as "software publisher certificates." There are, of course, certificates that hold the CA's own public keys, which are known as "certifying authority certificates." Although they are used for different purposes, all certificates share a common format, known as X.509v3 (version 3 of the X.509 format).

To prevent fraud, reputable CAs validate the identity of any person or organization requesting a certificate. As proof of identity, the applicant may have to produce articles of incorporation, pass checks with credit bureaus, exchange notarized letters, or sign affidavits. The level of proof required depends on the individual policies of each CA. When you visit a particular CA's Web site, you will find a long and legalistic certification practice statement (CPS), which details the CA's validation policies and its limits of liability.

Root CAs and Certificate Chains

Web browsers and other encrypting software are delivered with the signed certificates of a dozen or so well-known certifying authorities preinstalled. These are known as "root CAs," and they bear certificates that are self-signed. You trust that the public keys contained within these certificates are correct because you trust the software vendor and believe that the software has not been tampered with.

In addition to signing end user's certificates, a root CA can sign another CA's public key, granting it signing authority. This starts a "certificate chain." The secondary CA can now sign end-user certificates or sign the certificates of CAs further down the chain. When an end user presents a certificate signed by one of these nonroot CAs, it presents the certificates of all CAs on the signing chain. If you trust the root CA, you can use its public key to validate the certificate of the second CA on the chain. You can now use the second CA's public key to validate the third CA's certificate, and so on down the line until you recover the end user's public key. This is called a "hierarchy of trust."

Currently, certificate chains are most often found in intranet environments, where they are used to authenticate Web browsers on the basis of client certificates. However, they also appear in the SET protocol and other digital payment schemes. More information can be found in the next chapter and in Chapter 12.

Certificate Expiration and Revocation Lists

Public keys don't last forever. There are a number of events that can invalidate a public/private key pair, including the loss or corruption of a private key, its theft, a change in the identifying information contained within the certificate, and the compromise of the CA's private key itself. When any of these things happens, the affected certificate should be revoked so that it cannot be used.

An essential part of the public key infrastructure is the idea of a "certificate revocation list" (CRL), a database of some sort that holds the IDs of all certificates that have become invalid. In theory, everyone wishing to send a message should check the intended recipient's public key against the CRL before sending the message.

In practice, this doesn't generally happen on the Internet because of the impracticality of maintaining a master CRL database. With the exception of software publishers' certificates and some intranets, no one maintains a network-accessible CRL. Instead, all certificates have an expiration date, typically a year from the time they were issued. If someone presents a certificate that has expired, the software that checks it for validity will catch the problem and complain.

There are obvious problems with waiting as long as a year for a compromised certificate to expire. Until its certificate expires, a fraudulent person or Web site may continue to use a revoked certificate without anyone being the wiser.

Diffie-Hellman: Encryption Without Authentication

Public key cryptography usually goes hand-in-hand with authentication. Because at least one party must produce a signed certificate that identifies her, truly anonymous communications are not possible. However, it is possible for two parties to set up an encrypted communications session without using signed certificates at all. Diffie-Hellman key exchange allows two parties to negotiate a session key without ever sending the key itself across the network. This elegant algorithm works by having the two parties pick a partial key independently. Each one sends the other just enough information about its partial key so that the other can independently calculate a common key value, but not enough information so that the would-be eavesdropper can reconstruct the key by listening in on the conversation. The key is now used in a symmetric encryption algorithm to encrypt the contents of the communications session. When the session is done, the key is discarded.

Diffie-Hellman was covered by a U.S. patent that expired in April 1997. Not now widely used, it is likely to be found in an increasing number of cryptographic products over the next few years. Unlike encryption protocols based on certificates, Diffie-Hellman can provide secure communications while preserving the anonymity of both parties.

Diffie-Hellman has an important drawback, however. Because it provides no authentication, it is susceptible to a man-in-the-middle attack, a type of attack that is easier to explain than to accomplish. Users A and B want to communicate with each other, but C imposes himself in the network between the two without arousing any suspicions. User A unwittingly negotiates a secret key with C, thinking that C is B. B negotiates a secret key with C, thinking that C is A. A and B now send each other messages, with C relaying the information back and forth. A and B think they're communicating securely, but in reality C is able to read and modify every message they send.

Securing Private Keys

The security of public key cryptography depends on the security of the private keys. If a private key is compromised, all messages that are encrypted with its corresponding public key can be read. Worse, the private key can be used by an impostor to forge the digital signature of its owner.

To prevent this eventuality, private keys are usually stored on the user's hard disk in encrypted form. When the software is first launched, it prompts the user for a pass phrase to unlock the key. The key is then read into memory and used when needed.

There are problems with this approach, the most significant of which is the risk that the user's computer will be compromised by a virus or other malicious software that seeks to intercept the private key. One way to avoid this problem is to seal the private key in a ROM chip contained within a "smart card" that is physically carried around by the user. The private key never leaves the card. Instead, the card is inserted into an interface port (often a PCMCIA slot) on the user's machine. When data needs to be decrypted or signed, the system transfers the data to the card, where a built-in CPU does the calculations; the results are then returned to the computer.

There are a large number of smart card systems. For its part, the U.S. government is currently promoting an NSA-designed smart card called Fortezza. The Fortezza card uses a classified (that is, secret) encryption algorithm known as Skipjack, which uses a controversial key escrow system to allow U.S. law enforcement agencies to decrypt messages sent by suspected criminals. Partly because of the controversial nature of key escrow, companies have been slow to adopt the Fortezza system. See the Key Escrow and Key Recovery box for more details.

Key Length and Security

The longer the encryption key, the more secure the message. But how long is long enough, and how secure is secure enough?

Provided that the encryption algorithm is a good one, that it is implemented correctly, and that there are no cracks in key management that allow the secret key to be divulged, the only way to crack an encrypted message is to try all possible values of the key until one works. This brute-force approach will take time and money, but determined opponents can find a variety of ways to speed up the process.

Dedicated Hardware

It's possible to design a specialized machine that does nothing but try cryptographic keys. In the most famous instance of this, Michael Wiener published in 1995 the design of a DES-cracking machine, complete with specialized chips and integrated circuits. The machine was predicted to be able to crack a 56-bit DES key in an average time of 3.5 hours. The total cost: $1 million. This is within easy reach of most governments, large companies, and criminal organizations. However, it may be possible to do better than this. Rumor has it that the NSA has hardware devices that can crack 56-bit keys in a matter of minutes.

Networked Hardware

Brute-force guessing is easy to parallelize. If you distribute the workload across 1,000 computers, it will take 1/1,000th the time to crack a key. In 1997, a group of cryptographic enthusiasts demonstrated that they could crack a 56-bit DES key in a matter of months by dividing the work among a number of conventional home and office computers. Although the key-guessing activity was done openly in this case, it isn't hard to imagine it being done without the participants' knowledge—for example, as a hidden side effect of playing a popular network game.

As the key size increases, so does the cost and time of a brute-force attack. Every bit doubles the number of possible keys. A 57-bit key will take twice as long to crack as a 56-bit key. A reasonable approach is to choose a length whose cost to crack exceeds the value of the encrypted message by some comfortable margin. No one will spend $100,000 to crack a message whose value is only $1,000.

The calculation of comfortable key length must also take Moore's Law into account. This empirical law observes that computers double in speed every 18 months, meaning that the cost of cracking a message decreases by a factor of 10 every five years or so. In assessing key length security, you need to weigh the value of the message against the cost of cracking it and the expected longevity of the message. The $1,000 message that isn't worth cracking today will reach the break-even point in the course of a decade.

You also need to balance key length against performance. The longer the key, the more time-consuming the encryption and decryption process. To get a sense of the security of various key lengths, see Table 2.1. It estimates the time and cost, in the year 1997, for cracking various symmetric algorithms using specialized hardware. The first column estimates how long it will take to crack a key if your opponent is willing to make an initial investment of thousands of dollars. The second column estimates the time it will take if the opponent can spend millions.

TABLE 2.1 Estimated Time to Crack Symmetric Algorithms with Various Key Lengths

	Cost ($)	
Key length	**$ thousands**	**$ millions**
40 bits	Seconds	<1 Second
56 bits	Days	Hours
64 bits	Months	Days
80 bits	Eons	Millennia
128 bits	>Age of the universe	>Age of the universe

For technical reasons, the keys used by public key algorithms need to be larger than symmetric keys in order to provide the same level of resistence to brute-force attacks. A 384-bit public key pair provides approximately the same level of security as a 40-bit symmetric key. Unlike symmetric keys, which are typically used to encrypt a single communications session and then discarded, public key pairs have to remain secure for a long time. A single key pair may be used to encrypt millions of session keys during its lifetime. For this reason, even 512-bit keys are considered to be low security. Most vendors of cryptographic software recommend keys of 1,024 bits or higher.

Key Length and U.S. Encryption Policy

The federal government strictly restricts the export of encryption technology beyond U.S. or Canadian borders. Strong encryption is classified as a munition, along with Sidewinder missiles and nuclear arms. Encryption software must be granted a license by the Department of Commerce (DOC) in order to be exported legally. Violation of the export restrictions is punishable by fines and prison terms, and even the re-export of software acquired overseas is considered to be a violation.

Certain types of encryption software can win exemption from the export restrictions. If the encryption system is sufficiently weak, the DOC will grant it a license. The RC2 and RC4 symmetric algorithms have both received such licenses. Under the terms of the agreement, however, the algorithms are crippled to use keys of 40 bits or less. Similarly, a version of the RSA public key algorithm limited to 512 bits is exportable.

Cryptographic software that cannot be used to encrypt arbitrary messages can also be licensed for export. This includes software that generates digital signatures but doesn't encrypt messages, as well as software that uses message digests to guarantee the integrity of messages. Also specifically exempted are programs that are specialized for financial transactions. For example, the Quicken personal finance management package has won an exemption for export even though it uses strong encryption to communicate with participating banks.

The justification for the U.S.-export restrictions is that the availability of strong encryption will allow international terrorists and other criminals to shield their electronic communications, financial records, and other evidence from law enforcement officials. Although the effect of the law in slowing

Key Escrow and Key Recovery

U.S. software developers have long resented the export restrictions on cryptography. This resentment has grown steadily as developers have watched European and Japanese companies release cryptographic products that are unfettered by U.S. law. In response to this concern, the Clinton administration proposed a "key escrow" plan in 1996. Under this plan, software developers could export software that used long keys but only if they deposited the private keys of each user of the program with a government-managed escrow agency. If the law enforcement agencies needed to, they could obtain the appropriate court orders and recover the escrowed keys.

The original plan was wildly unpopular for practical and political reasons. No individual or corporation was eager to give the federal government the ability to read all its encrypted messages. And no vendor was up to the monumental task of registering all its customers with a new federal agency.

In response, the Clinton administration floated a modified plan later that same year. This proposal uses a modified type of escrow called "key recovery." In key recovery, each encrypted message is accompanied by two digital envelopes. The first digital envelope contains the session key encrypted with the recipient's public key, as usual. The second digital envelope contains the same session key encrypted with the public key owned by a federal key recovery agency. If need be, the key recovery agency can use this second digital envelope to decrypt and read the message. As with the original proposal, a court order would be required before the key recovery agency would decrypt a message.

To make the deal attractive to software developers, the Clinton administration initially promised to allow software developers to begin exporting software using 56-bit DES encryption if they would commit to developing a 64-bit key recovery system. However, in early 1997, the administration backpedaled on this promise, linking stronger encryption to implementation of a working recovery system.

Key recovery differs from the original plan in that session keys are escrowed, not a user's private key. This means that inadvertent disclosure of the private key by the escrow agency does not compromise all the user's messages. There's an important trade-off, however. If the key recovery agency's own private key happens to be leaked, then everyone's messages, past and present, are forfeit.

In March 1997, Netscape Corporation issued a press release announcing that it would incorporate the Clinton key recovery scheme into its future software, a move that took many industry observers by surprise. What happens next is anyone's guess.

international terrorism is unknown, the chilling effect on U.S. software development is undeniable. Strong cryptographic software has been slow to come to market because of software companies' reluctance to maintain different products for domestic and export use.

This policy explains the perplexing fact that U.S.-made Web browsers, e-mail packages, and other Internet software often come in two versions. The domestic product, available only as a shrink-wrapped product on the shelves of American software outlets, incorporates strong cryptography with long, secure keys. The export product, available on shelves overseas, is limited to keys that are crackable in seconds with specialized hardware or in days using networks of conventional machines.

Because of the difficulty in controlling distribution over the Internet, U.S. software distributed on FTP and Web sites is almost always limited to the export versions. Consequently, the vast majority of Web browsers in use around the world are crippled. Web servers sold overseas are likewise crippled. It is important to realize that strong encryption is only possible if both the Web browser and server support it. If either piece of software is crippled, the entire session will be.

As this book went to press, there were signs that the government had begun to relax its export restrictions. In June 1997, the U.S. government granted both Netscape and Microsoft a limited exemption from the export restrictions. Versions of these companies' browser and server products are allowed to use strong 128-bit keys, but only when customers are using the Web to communicate with their banks. Special bankers' certificates are used to enforce these rules.

Online Resources

The Cryptography Source Pages

http://www.cs.hut.fi/crypto/

Ray Kopsa's Shortcut to Cryptography

A huge list of cryptography-related links.

http://www.subject.com/crypto/crypto.html

RSA Data Security

http://www.rsa.com/

Netscape's Cryptography Pages

http://www.netscape.com/newsref/ref/rsa.html

Microsoft's Cryptography Pages

http://www.microsoft.com/workshop/prog/security/pkcb/cryptl.htm

A long list of cryptography-enhanced software products

http://www.semper.org/sirene/people/gerrit/secprod.html

Information on DES cracking

http://www.frii.com/~rcv/deschall.htm

Information on other brute-force key cracking attempts

http://www.cl.cam.ac.uk/brute/

Printed Resources

Schneier, Bruce, *Practical Cryptography,* 2nd Edition (John Wiley & Sons, 1995).

Everything you need to know about cryptography in one highly readable source.

Smith, Richard E., *Internet Cryptography* (Addison-Wesley, 1997).

Cryptography as it is used on the Internet.

Chapter 3

SSL, SET, and Digital Payment Systems

The previous chapter described how cryptography works in principle. In practice, cryptographic principles must be incorporated into working communications protocols and software. There are a variety of cryptographic protocols on the Internet, each specialized for a different task (see Table 3.1). Some were designed to secure specific modes of communication, such as e-mail and remote login. Others are generalists, providing cryptographic services to multiple modes of communication.

On the Web, SSL (Secure Sockets Layer) is the dominant protocol for encrypting general communications between browser and server, while SET

TABLE 3.1 Internet Cryptographic Protocols

Protocol	Purpose
CyberCash	Electronic funds transactions
DNSSEC	Domain name system
IPSec	Packet-level encryption
PCT	TCP/IP-level encryption
PGP	E-mail
S/MIME	E-mail
S-HTTP	Web browsing
Secure RPC	Remote procedure calls
SET	Electronic funds transactions
SSL	TCP/IP-level encryption
SSH	Remote login
TLS	TCP/IP-level encryption

(Secure Electronic Transactions) is a specialized protocol for safeguarding credit-card-based transactions. This chapter takes an in-depth look at these two protocols, then turns to the current menagerie of competing digital payment systems.

Secure Sockets Layer

Secure Sockets Layer (or SSL) is a flexible, general-purpose encryption system. You've probably used it, even if you weren't aware of it, since it is built into both the Netscape and Microsoft browsers. This section looks at SSL in depth.

SSL History

SSL was introduced in 1994 with the first version of the Netscape Navigator browser. The ability of Navigator to encrypt communications was a major selling point for Netscape, a feature emphasized by frequent warnings displayed by the browser when cryptography was not in use.

In the same year, a competing cryptographic protocol known as S-HTTP was introduced by a coalition of business groups known as CommerceNet. Although the cryptographic principles used by S-HTTP and SSL were the same (digital envelopes, signed certificates, message digests), there were two important differences between S-HTTP and SSL.

1. S-HTTP was designed to work with the Web protocols only. SSL is a lower-level protocol that can be used to encrypt many types of network connections.
2. SSL was incorporated into a free browser that became wildly popular. S-HTTP was initially available in a modified version of NCSA Mosaic that users had to purchase.

SSL rapidly became the predominant secure protocol on the Web, and S-HTTP sank into oblivion (although it is still supported by some browsers and servers).

There have actually been three versions of SSL. SSL 1, used internally in Netscape, contained some serious flaws and was never released. SSL 2.0 was incorporated into Netscape Navigator versions 1.0 through 2.X. V2.0 had some weaknesses related to man-in-the-middle attacks. In addition, there was an embarrassing episode in which two college students cracked the implementation of SSL v2.0 in minutes by exploiting a bug in Netscape's random number generator (see the box SSL Cracked).

SSL Cracked

In 1995, there were several well-publicized incidents in which SSL was "cracked." In the first episode, Damien Doligez, a French self-described cipherpunk, used a network of computers at his university to mount a brute-force attack on a secret message encrypted by the crippled export version of SSL. After about a week of computation, the key was discovered and the message revealed. Although this event made headlines at the time, it was not unexpected, as 40-bit keys are not secure. In fact, this feat, when repeated in January 1997, took just 3.5 hours.

In September of that year, Ian Goldberg and David Wagner, students at Berkeley at the time, discovered a much more significant flaw. The UNIX version of Netscape Navigator 1.2, they discovered, generated its session keys in a predictable way, using a combination of the process ID, the parent process ID, and the current time as the seed for its random-number generator. Because these values are all constrained to a relatively small range, it was easy to set up a program that guessed session keys from the possibilities. Their program proved effective against even strong 128-bit keys. It could crack any SSL message in a matter of minutes (the students boasted that it took so long only because they hadn't optimized their program).

The following month, the same pair of students discovered yet another attack on Netscape Navigator. Using packet sniffer technology, they were able to intercept and modify the Navigator binary as it passed through their network's file sharing system. This modification patched the random number generator so that it always generated the same, predictable session key, rendering SSL useless.

Netscape repaired the random-number generator bug in browser versions 1.3 and higher. The file sharing attack, however, is not so easy to fix because it is a vulnerability in the file sharing protocol itself, not in the Netscape browser. The moral of the story is that even though your cryptography is the best money can buy, all bets are off if there is a flaw anywhere else in the system.

In an attempt to leverage public uncertainty about SSL's security, Microsoft introduced the competing PCT protocol in its first release of Internet Explorer, in 1996. Netscape responded by introducing SSL v3.0, a version that addresses the problems in 2.0 and adds many new features, most notably support for Diffie-Hellman anonymous key exchange and the Fortezza smart card.

At this point, Microsoft backed down and agreed to support SSL in all versions of its Internet software (although its software still supports PCT for backward compatibility). SSL v3.0 is implemented in Netscape Navigator 3.0 and higher and by Internet Explorer 3.0 and higher. Other browsers should support it as well by the time you read this.

SSL has recently become the focus of Internet standards activity by the Internet Engineering Task Force (IETF). TLS, the proposed Transport Layer Security protocol, is a derivative of SSL v3.0 that uses a different message digest function and a slightly different set of encryption algorithms. Because of the IETF's historical suspicion of protocols that originate with the NSA, it is uncertain whether TLS will support Fortezza. See the listing of URLs at the end of this chapter for links to TLS.

SSL Characteristics

The SSL protocol operates at the TCP/IP transport layer, one level below such application-specific protocols as NTTP (news), HTTP (Web), and SMTP (e-mail) (Figure 3.1). This is in contrast to the Web-specific S-HTTP protocol. This feature gives SSL flexibility and protocol independence. Any program that uses TCP can be modified to use secure SSL connections by making a few source code changes. In addition to SSL-capable Web browsers and servers, there are SSL-ized TELNET programs, news readers, and e-mail transport programs.

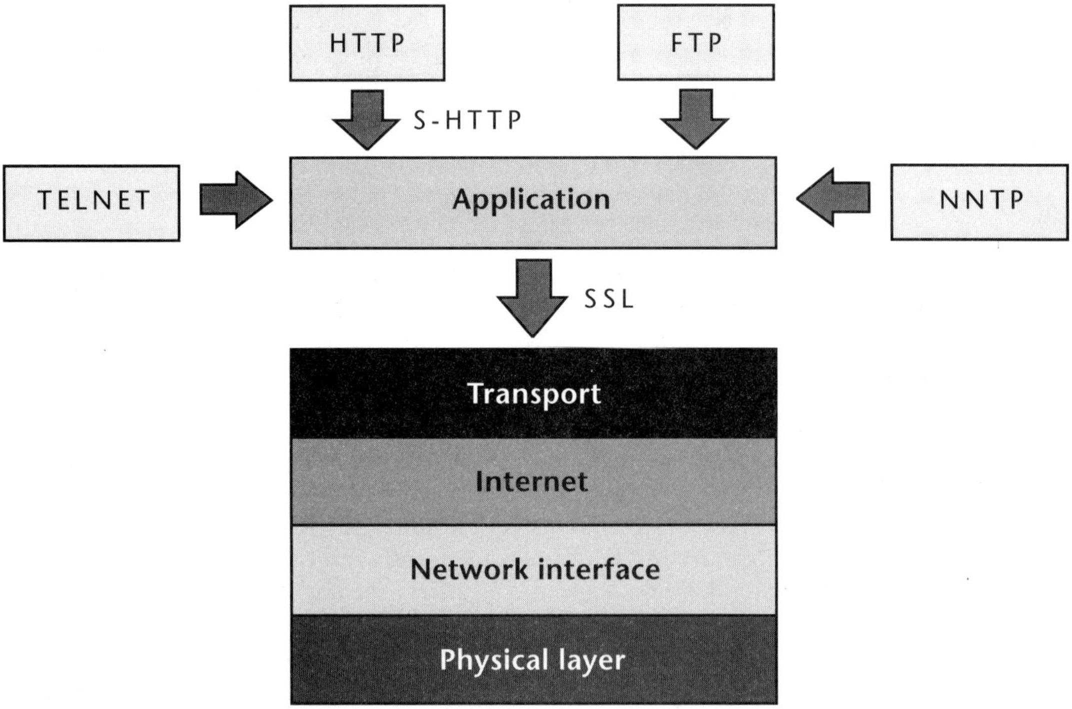

FIGURE 3.1 The SSL protocol operates at the TCP/IP transport layer, in contrast to S-HTTP, which operates at a higher level.

The main trade-off of putting SSL at the transport layer is that it is not specifically tuned for the HTTP protocol and, therefore, may not be as efficient for Web browsing as it might have been. A minor limitation is that an SSL connection must use a dedicated TCP/IP socket. When a Web server is running in SSL mode, it uses a distinct network port (usually port 443) for its encrypted communications.

Another important feature of SSL is flexibility with regard to the choice of symmetric encryption algorithm, message digest function, and authentication method. For symmetric encryption, SSL can use any of DES (in CBC, cipher block chaining, mode), triple-DES, RC2, or RC4. For message digests, SSL can use either the MD5 or SHA hashing algorithms. For authentication, SSL can use RSA public keys and certificates or operate in an anonymous mode in which the Diffie-Hellman key exchange algorithm is used. A variety of key lengths are available for the encryption algorithms, including the crippled lengths used by U.S. export versions of SSL software. The combination of symmetric encryption algorithm, message digest method, and authentication is known as a "cipher suite." Table 3.2 lists the cipher suites currently supported by SSL. Note that some are supported by SSL 3.0 only.

When an SSL client first makes contact with a server, the two negotiate a common cipher suite. In general, the two try to pick the strongest encryption methods that they both have in common. If a crippled export Web browser that only supports 40-bit session keys contacts a Web server that does not have this limitation, the server will negotiate down to 40 bits. Similarly, the server will derive a valid 512-bit RSA public key from its full-length 1,024-bit key when communicating with a crippled client. Some Web servers allow

TABLE 3.2 SSL Cipher Suites

Suite	Strength	SSL Versions	Description
DES-CBC3-MD5	Very High	v2.0, v3.0	Triple-DES in CBC mode, MD5 hash, 168-bit session key
DES-CBC3-SHA	Very High	v2.0, v3.0	Triple-DES in CBC mode, SHA hash, 168-bit session key
RC4-MD5	High	v2.0, v3.0	RC4, MD5 hash, 128-bit key
RC4-SHA	High	v3.0	RC4, SHA hash, 128-bit key
RC2-CBC-MD5	High	v2.0, v3.0	RC2 in CBC mode, MD5 hash, 128-bit key
DES-CBC-MD5	Medium	v2.0, v3.0	DES in CBC mode, MD5 hash, 56-bit key
DES-CBC-SHA	Medium	v2.0, v3.0	DES in CBC mode, SHA hash, 56-bit key
EXP-DES-CBC-SHA	Low	v3.0	DES in CBC mode, SHA hash, 40-bit key
EXP-RC4-MD5	Low	v2.0, v3.0	Export grade RC4, MD5 hash, 40-bit key
EXP-RC2-CBC-MD5	Low	v2.0, v3.0	Export grade RC2 in CBC mode, MD5 hash, 40-bit key
NULL-MD5	N/A	v2.0, v3.0	No encryption, MD5 hash, authentication only
NULL-SHA	N/A	v3.0	No encryption, SHA hash, authentication only

the administrator to fine-tune the negotiation process. For example, a Webmaster can choose to allow access to a particular directory only for those clients that support strong cryptography.

SSL provides built-in data compression, which is important because once a message is encrypted it is no longer compressible. (Compression works by finding common patterns in data streams and removing the redundancy. Encryption works by removing all patterns from the data, rendering it uncompressible.)

When an SSL connection is in place, all browser-to-server and server-to-browser communications are encrypted, including

- The URL of the requested document
- The contents of the requested document
- The contents of any submitted fill-out forms
- Cookies sent from browser to server
- Cookies sent from server to browser
- The contents of the HTTP header

The only thing that can't be disguised by an SSL session is the fact that a particular browser is talking to a particular server. To get around this, one can use SSL in conjunction with an anonymizing proxy (see Chapter 6).

The SSL Transaction

An overview of the SSL protocol is shown in Figure 3.2. For the full technical details, consult the SSL specification given in the URLs at the end of this chapter. The goal of the protocol is to authenticate the server and, optionally, the client, and to end up with a secret symmetric key that both client and server can use for sending encrypted messages.

Briefly, the steps of the process are

1. **The client (that is, browser) opens a connection to the server port and sends a "ClientHello" message.** "ClientHello" lists the capabilities of the client, including the version of SSL it uses, the cipher suites it supports, and the data compression methods it supports.
2. **The server responds with a "ServerHello" message.** The server returns a message that contains the cipher suite and data compression method it has chosen, along with a session ID that identifies the connection. Note that the server is responsible for choosing the cipher suite and compression methods. If there is no match between the suites supported by the client and server, then the server sends a "handshake failure" message and hangs up.
3. **The server sends its certificate.** If the server is using certificate-based authentication (which is currently almost always the case), the server

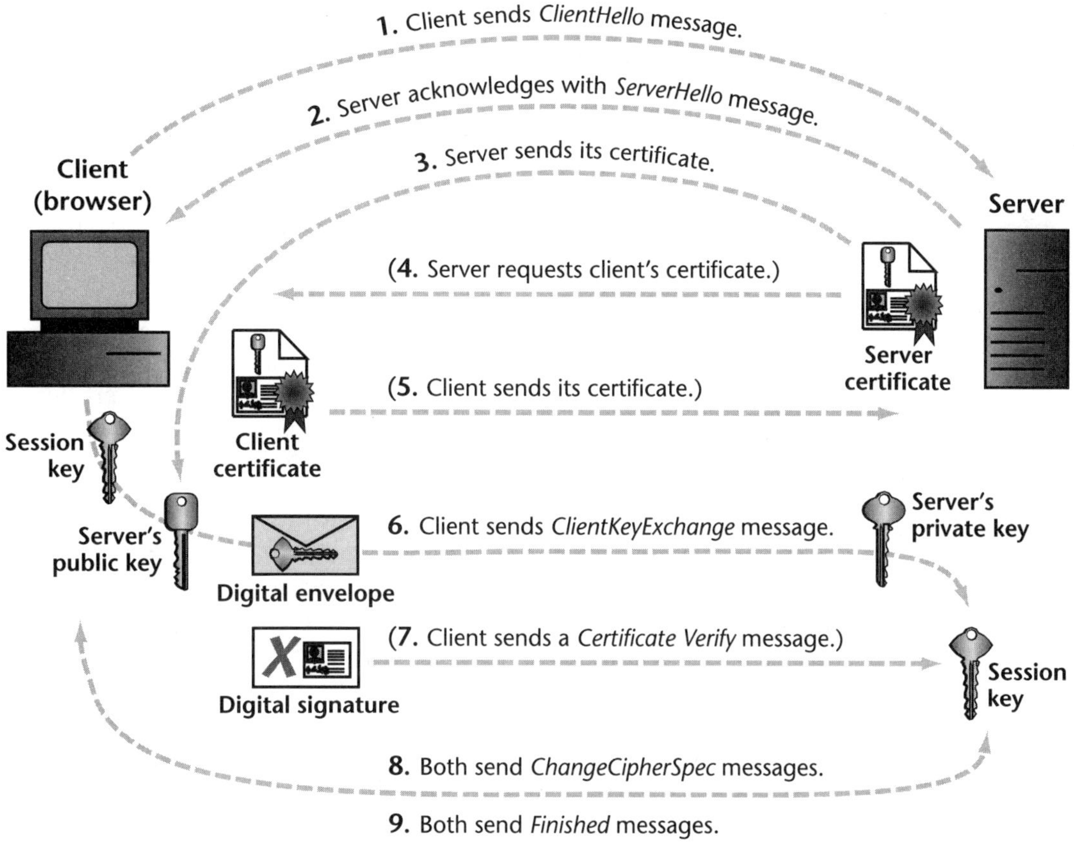

FIGURE 3.2 The SSL handshake consists of nine steps that authenticate the two parties and create a shared session key.

sends its signed X.509v3 site certificate. If the certificate is signed by a non-root certifying authority, the server also sends the chain of signed certificates that lead up to the primary CA.

4. **The server sends a client certificate request (optional).** If client certificates are used for client authentication (currently rare but likely to be seen more often in the future), the server next sends the client a certificate request message.

5. **The client sends its certificate (optional).** If the server has requested it, the client returns its signed X.509v3 client certificate. If the client has no certificate, it sends a "no certificate" alert. The server may choose to abort at this point with a handshake failure, or continue onward.

6. **The client sends a "ClientKeyExchange" message.** This is where the symmetric session key is selected. The details vary depending on the cipher suite chosen, but in the most typical case, the client generates a premaster secret using a good random-number generator. This secret will be used on both the client and the server sides to generate the true master secret that is used as the session key (because different symmetric ciphers use different-length keys, the session key is not generated directly). The browser encrypts the secret using the server's RSA public key (recovered from the server's certificate) to create a digital envelope. The envelope is now forwarded to the server.
7. **The client sends a "CertificateVerify" message (optional).** If client authentication is in use, the client must authenticate itself to the server by proving that it knows the correct RSA private key. The "Certificate-Verify" message consists of the premaster secret generated in step 6, which has been manipulated in various ways to make it harder to tamper with by someone listening in on the conversation. The secret is signed with the client's RSA private key and forwarded to the server, which proceeds to check it for validity against the client's certificate. Notice that the server doesn't have to prove its identity. Because the client sends the premaster secret to the server using the server's public key, only the legitimate holder of the server's certificate can decrypt and use it.
8. **Both client and server send a "ChangeCipherSpec" message.** This is a simple message that confirms that both client and server are ready to start communicating using the agreed-on symmetric cipher and session key.
9. **Both client and server send "finished" messages.** These messages consist of MD5 and SHA hashes of the entire conversation up to this point and allow both parties to confirm that their messages were received intact and not tampered with en route.

At this point, both client and server switch into encrypted mode, using the session key (generated from the premaster secret) to symmetrically encrypt subsequent transmissions in both directions.

In addition to the nine steps outlined here, there is an additional transaction available to SSL 3.0 servers. Instead of sending its certificate in step 3, the server can send a "ServerKeyExchange" message. This is used to negotiate a session key without the server sending a certificate. This can happen in any one of the following three cases.

1. The server is using the anonymous Diffie-Hellman key exchange protocol.
2. The server is using the Fortezza smart card encryption suite.
3. The server has a signature-only private key (for instance, a DSS key, see Chapter 2).

IPv6 and IPSec

There seem to be a lot of Internet encryption protocols out there. Why so many? Part of the problem is that TCP/IP itself is not secure. Designed as an experiment in internetworking, its creators never dreamed that it would some day run something as vast as the Internet or that people would be entrusting it with confidential data. Nothing in a TCP/IP packet is protected against prying eyes: not its header, which contains the addresses of its source and destination machines, nor the data it carries.

To address the security issues in TCP/IP and to solve other pressing problems, the IETF has been working on version 6 of the venerable TCP/IP protocol, IPv6. Among its other features, IPv6 offers optional encryption and data integrity checking at a deep layer of the internetworking stack, a facility known as IPSec (for IP security) Any two computers can authenticate themselves to each other and encrypt their communications. The protocol allows only the data portion of each packet to be encrypted, or for both the data and header information to be encapsulated within an encrypted data stream (this is a scheme commonly used in virtual private networks). Unlike SSL, IPSec does not require existing software to be modified in order to take advantage of its encryption; it is completely transparent. IPv6 may also be the fastest encrypting protocol available, as it was designed to be supported by the coming generation of IPv6-compatible hardware routers.

However, because of its low-level nature, there are a number of features that IPSec cannot support. The main missing feature is user-level authentication. Although IPv6 can authenticate machines—network interfaces, routers, and bridges—it cannot authenticate individual users and processes. Another drawback of IPv6 is that it uses the 56-bit DES protocol for encryption. As noted in Chapter 2, many people now consider DES to be inadequate for high-security applications. This choice may change before IPv6 is released, however. Finally, IPv6 will not become widespread until the majority of Internet routers are upgraded to support it, a process that will take years.

For these reasons, there will continue to be a role for higher-level protocols, such as SSL and SET, in the IPv6 world.

The most interesting of these scenarios is the use of the Diffie-Hellman key exchange algorithm. In this case, client and server negotiate a shared session key without ever identifying each other. Because there's no certificate exchange, the interaction is completely anonymous. This also means that the transaction is vulnerable to a man-in-the-middle attack.

Although part of the SSL v3.0 protocol, Diffie-Hellman key exchange wasn't supported by any commercial Web browser at the time this was written. This may well have changed by the time you read this. Practical advice on using SSL with popular brands of browsers and servers is given in Chapters 4 and 10, respectively.

SET and Other Digital Payment Systems

We now turn our attention to SET, a cryptographic protocol designed to handle credit card transactions on the Web.

What Is SET?

SET stands for Secure Electronic Transactions and is a cryptographic protocol jointly developed by Visa, Mastercard, Netscape, and Microsoft. Unlike SSL, which is a general-purpose system for encrypting communications, SET is highly specific. It can be used only to secure credit and debit card transactions between customers and merchants.

At a low level, the SET protocol provides the following essential services.

- **Authentication** All the parties in the credit card transaction are authenticated using digital signatures. This includes the customer, the merchant, the bank that issued the customer's credit card, and the bank that handles the merchant's checking account.
- **Confidentiality** The transaction is encrypted so that eavesdroppers cannot listen in.
- **Message integrity** The transaction cannot be tampered with by devious individuals to alter the account number or the amount of the transaction.
- **Linkage** SET allows a message sent to one party to contain an attachment that can be read only by another (the rationale for this is described on page 47). Linkage allows the first party to verify that the attachment is correct, without being able to read the contents of the attachment.

At a high level, the SET protocol supports all the features of the current credit card system, including

- Cardholder registration
- Merchant registration
- Purchase requests
- Payment authorizations
- Payment capture (funds transfer)
- Chargebacks (refunds to consumers for returns and disputed charges)
- Credits
- Credit reversals
- Debit card (check card) transactions

SET can handle real-time transactions, batch transactions, installment payments, and such scenarios as the use of credit cards by hotels to set aside a large chunk of the guest's credit in order to cover room service and telephone charges.

At the time this was written, the final SET specification had just been released (May 1997). Although a large number of software vendors had announced support for the protocol, only the Verifone Corporation released a SET product. The vWallet application for customers and the vPOS extension for the Microsoft Merchant Web server use a preliminary version of the SET specification. Web browsers will eventually provide direct support for SET, by either incorporating the protocol in the browser software itself or by downloading it in the form of an ActiveX control, Java applet, or plug-in.

Despite the current scarcity of software, SET is likely to assume a major role in Web financial transactions sometime in 1998, if only because of its sponsors' clout.

Why Not Just Use SSL?

Before we get into SET specifics, the obvious question is: Why is a special-purpose protocol necessary at all? Why not just use SSL to submit credit card numbers using a fill-out form?

It's certainly possible to use SSL to accept credit card payments. This is, in fact, the way it's most often done on the Internet, and it is the basis for the turnkey "commerce systems" sold by Netscape, Microsoft, Open Market, and others. However, there are a number of drawbacks to using straight SSL for this purpose.

For one thing, although SSL solves the problem of transmitting the credit card number safely from the customer to the merchant, it doesn't help with the rest of the transaction: checking the number for validity, checking that the customer is authorized to use this credit card number, authorizing the transaction with the consumer's bank, and actually processing the transaction. In a simple system, a CGI script can check the credit card number for typographical errors using its built-in checksum (see the Checking Credit Card Numbers for Validity box) and write the number to a file or database for manual verification later. However, for many applications online credit card authorization is a necessity. High-end commerce systems validate orders as they come in by contacting a server run by a credit card authorization service via SSL or a proprietary protocol. Such systems may also manage refunds, chargebacks, back orders, transaction logging, shopping cards, online catalogs, and inventory control. A fully functional credit card processing system is either a lot of custom programming or an expensive packaged solution.

Another problem with SSL-based schemes is server-side security. Because the credit card number is transmitted to the merchant's Web server, there's a fair chance that the merchant will choose to save it to a file or database. If someone succeeds in breaking into the merchant's server, the entire database of credit card numbers may be compromised. This is, in fact,what happened in 1994 when someone broke into the Netcom Internet service provider. In

Checking Credit Card Checksums

Multidigit credit card numbers are not quite the random numbers they appear to be. The first four digits indicate the bank that issued the card. The last digit is a checksum that can be used to check the number for entry errors. At a minimum, software that accepts credit card numbers should verify the checksum for correctness. This is no substitute for verifying the credit card number with an online authorization service, but it's a start.

The checksum algorithm is

1. Multiply each digit in the card by its "weight." Weights alternate 1,2,1,2. For cards with an even number of digits, the series of weights begins with 2; otherwise it begins with 1.
2. If the weighted digit is greater than 9, subtract 9.
3. Sum the weighted digits and calculate their base-10 modulus.
4. The result should be zero.

Here's a short Perl script to validate a credit card number. It will return "1" for a valid number, or "0" otherwise.

```
sub check_cc {
    my $num = shift;
    my $sum = 0;
    my @digits = $num=~/(\d)/g;;
    my @weights = (1,2) x (@digits/2 + 1);
    shift @weights unless @digits % 2;
    foreach (@digits) {
        my $weighted = $_ * shift @weights;
        $weighted -= 9 if $weighted > 9;
        $sum += $weighted;
    }
    return ($sum % 10) == 0;
}
```

addition, some people worry that merchants will use their credit card numbers to compile mailing lists and marketing information.

Another problem with using SSL for credit card transactions is the vulnerability of poorly written systems to misuse as credit card number guessing systems. The unscrupulous remote user first generates a series of trial credit card numbers. All of them satisfy the basic checksum validation, but he doesn't yet know which of them correspond to real accounts. He then feeds the numbers to a script that makes a series of bogus purchases on some innocent Web merchant's server. If the credit card number is invalid, the server returns an error and the script discards the number. If the credit card number is authentic, the server accepts it. The script then cancels the purchase and records the number. In short order, such a system can discover hundreds of valid credit card numbers. SET avoids these problems by providing an integrated system that handles the entire transaction, including card authorization and finalization of the sale. To prevent theft of the credit card number, the protocol never gives the merchant direct access to the customer's number; instead he is notified whether the purchase was approved.

Finally, there is the issue of U.S. export restrictions. Systems that use strong cryptography are banned from export, including those that use SSL. However, because the law exempts systems that can be used for financial transactions only, software vendors can ship full-strength SET systems overseas, something that is currently not possible with general-purpose SSL products.

SET in a Nutshell

The SET protocol is an intricate dance between four parties: the cardholder, the merchant, the bank that issues the credit card, and the merchant's bank (also known as the "acquiring" bank). Like other encrypting protocols, SET uses public/private key pairs and signed certificates to establish each player's identity and to allow them to send private messages to one another.

During a sales transaction, the SET protocol works like this (Figure 3.3).

1. **The customer initiates a purchase.** The customer browses the merchant's Web site, decides she wants to buy something, and fills out an order form containing the description of the merchandise and shipping information. This is all done before the SET protocol starts by using CGI scripts or other server-side software. The SET protocol begins when the user presses a "pay" button.

   The server now sends the customer's computer a message that launches SET software on her personal computer (the exact implementation details are up to the browser vendors; it will probably be done by sending the browser a document with a special MIME type, an ActiveX control, or a Java applet).

2. **The client's software sends the order and payment information.** The customer's SET software creates two messages. The first message contains order information consisting of the total purchase price and the order number. The second message is payment information that consists of the customer's credit card number and bank information.

   The order information is encrypted using a random symmetric session key and packaged into a digital envelope using the merchant's public key. The payment information is likewise encrypted, but this time using the merchant's *bank's* public key. This prevents the merchant from peeking at the credit card number or the bank from peeking at the order information.

   The software now computes a hash of the order and payment information jointly and signs it with the customer's private key. This creates a

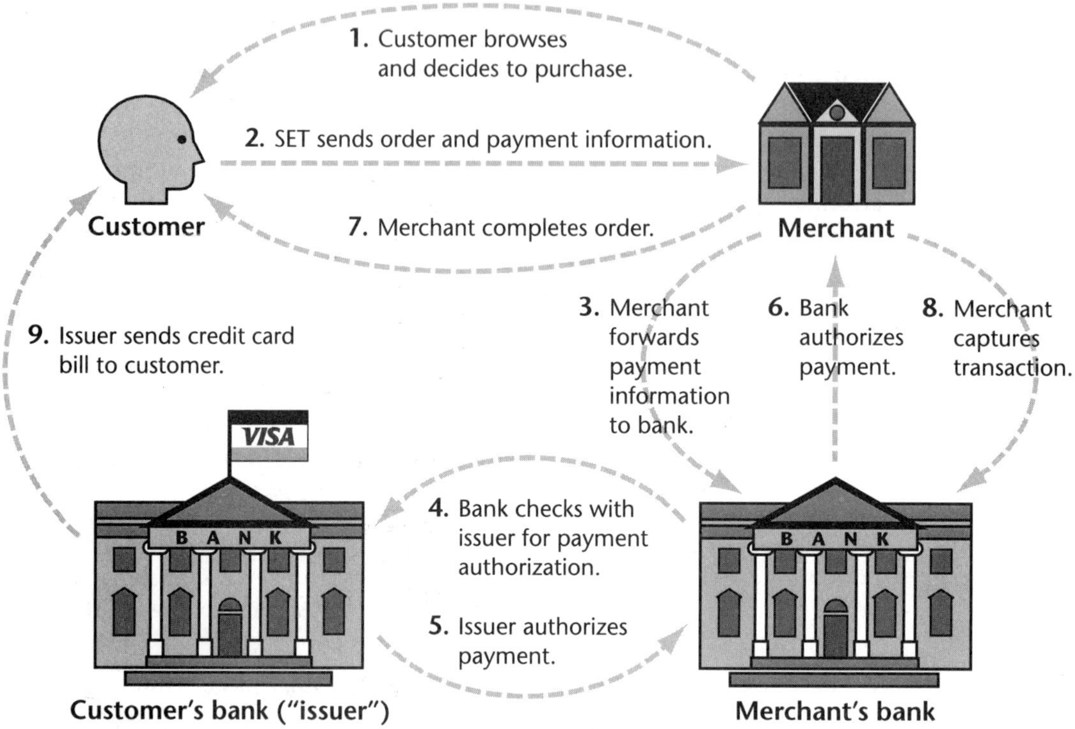

FIGURE 3.3 The SET protocol coordinates the activities of the customer, merchant, merchant's bank, and card issuer.

"dual signature" that allows both merchant and merchant's bank to validate the integrity of both messages without being able to read the part addressed to the other party.

3. **The merchant passes payment information to the bank.** SET software on the merchant's Web server generates an authorization request, forwarding the customer's payment information to a SET server maintained by the merchant's bank (or more likely, a "payment gateway" working on behalf of the bank). The merchant signs a hash of the authorization request with its private key in order to prove its identity to the bank. This request is encrypted with a new random session key and incorporated into a digital envelope using the bank's public key.
4. **The bank checks the validity of the card.** The bank decrypts the merchant's authorization request and verifies the merchant's identity. It then decrypts the customer's payment information and verifies the customer's identity. Now the merchant's bank needs to check with the customer's bank for authorization. It generates its own authorizaton request, signs it, and forwards it to the card issuer.

5. **The card issuer authorizes and signs the charge slip.** The customer's bank confirms the merchant's bank identity, decrypts the information, and checks the customer's account. If the account is in good standing, the card issuer approves the authorization request by signing it and returning it to the merchant's bank.
6. **The merchant's bank authorizes the transaction.** The merchant's bank now authorizes the transaction and signs it, sending the OK back to the merchant's Web server.
7. **The merchant's Web server completes the transaction.** The merchant's Web server acknowledges that the card was approved by showing the customer a confirmation page and then enters the order into the merchant's order processing system. In due course, the merchant ships the goods or provides the service.
8. **The merchant "captures" the transaction.** In the final phase of a typical SET interaction, the merchant sends a "capture" message to its bank. This confirms the purchase and causes the customer's credit card account to be charged. The merchant's checking account will be credited.
9. **The card issuer sends a credit card bill to the customer.** The SET charge appears on the customer's monthly statement, along with other charges.

There are authentication steps in every phase of the SET protocol. This is vital to prevent an unknown third party from inserting herself into the transaction. To accomplish this, SET uses a variation on the hierarchy of trust (Figure 3.4). A trusted certifying authority will issue X.509v3 certificates to both the credit card issuer and the merchant's bank. Before either a merchant or a cardholder can use the SET system, they must register themselves. When a consumer electronically registers a credit card with the SET system, the SET software generates a public/private key pair. The public key is signed by the issuing bank and returned to the user as a signed X.509v3 certificate. Likewise, the merchant's bank gives the merchant a certificate when it opens an account for accepting credit card payments.

Unlike the SSL protocol, in which the same public/private key pair is used for both encryption and digital signatures, SET uses two key pairs for certain parts of the protocol. The merchant, the merchant's bank, and the bank that issues the customer's credit card all have two key pairs, one used for encryption and the other used for digital signatures. Hence, each of these parties actually owns two certificates. As an interim measure until card issuers are set up as certifying authorities, SET has the capability of running in a mode in which cardholders have no certificates and are unauthenticated. This is no worse than using SSL to send credit card numbers directly to the merchant.

Technically, the SET protocol uses the Secure Hash Algorithm (SHA), which produces a 160-bit hash. Its public/private key pairs use the RSA encryption algorithm and are 1,024 bits long. Although SET can use a variety

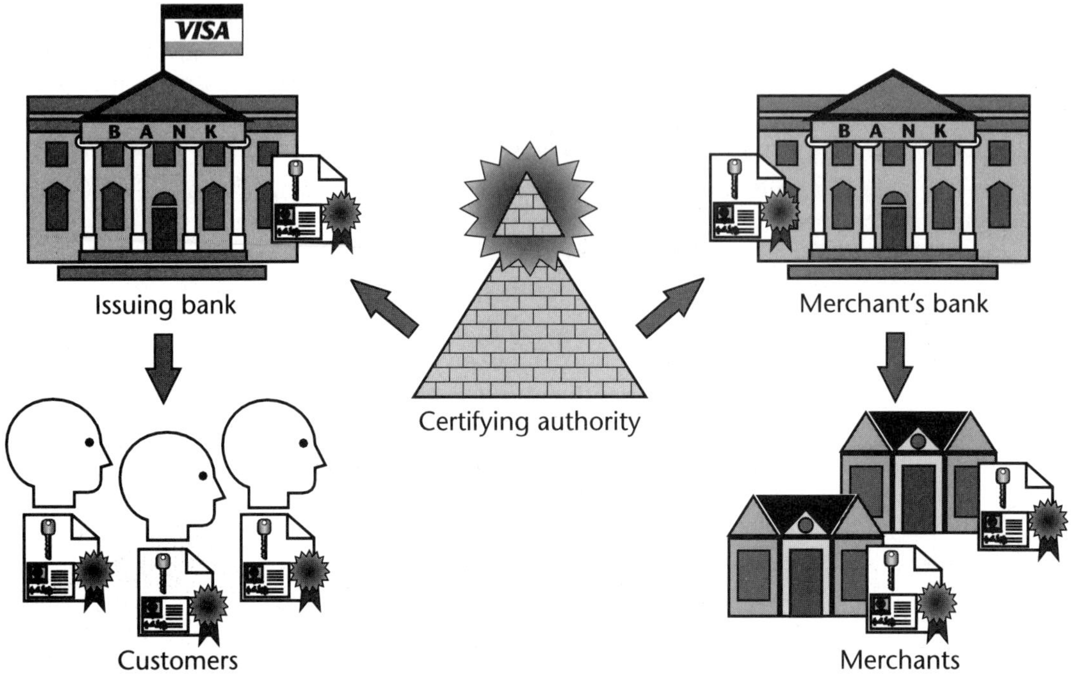

FIGURE 3.4 SET uses a hierarchy of trust. All parties hold certificates signed directly or indirectly by a certifying authority.

of algorithms for symmetric encryption, its default is DES, which uses a 56-bit key. Because DES is susceptible to brute-force guessing, this choice suggests that SET's designers consider the cost of cracking a DES message larger than the value of a single credit card transaction.

The SET User Interface

Although SET-enabled software is hard to come by, the Microsoft Wallet application illustrates what it will probably look like to consumers. Microsoft Wallet is built into Internet Explorer 4.0, and is available as an add-on for IE 3.0 and Netscape browsers. Although Wallet currently uses SSL to transmit credit card information from the user's computer to the Web server, it does contain hooks for SET and other payment protocols. Future versions of the software will support SET directly.

Microsoft Wallet's user interface presents two panes of information, one for the user's billing information and the other for payment information (Figure 3.5). Billing information contains the user's name and address and is transmitted directly to Wallet-savvy servers, saving the user the annoyance of retyping the same information for each purchase. The payment information is a list of credit and check cards the user owns. The address and the payment information are encrypted on the user's disk and must be unlocked with a password before Wallet can be used. When the user goes to buy something from a server that supports Wallet, the software prompts the user to select the credit card she wishes to charge. To complete the transaction, the user presses a "pay" button, transmitting the information to the merchant's server.

On the server side, Microsoft provides a free Webmaster's kit for Wallet development. The kit is compatible with Internet Information Server and other servers that support server-side includes. In its current form, Wallet is a convenient way to transfer the user's address and payment information to the server. Although it can be controlled using no more than HTML and a few lines of JavaScript code (provided as examples in the kit), Wallet is only useful when integrated with custom CGI scripts that interface to the merchant's order processing system. Nor does Wallet provide live authorization of credit card purchases, although this will certainly be added when

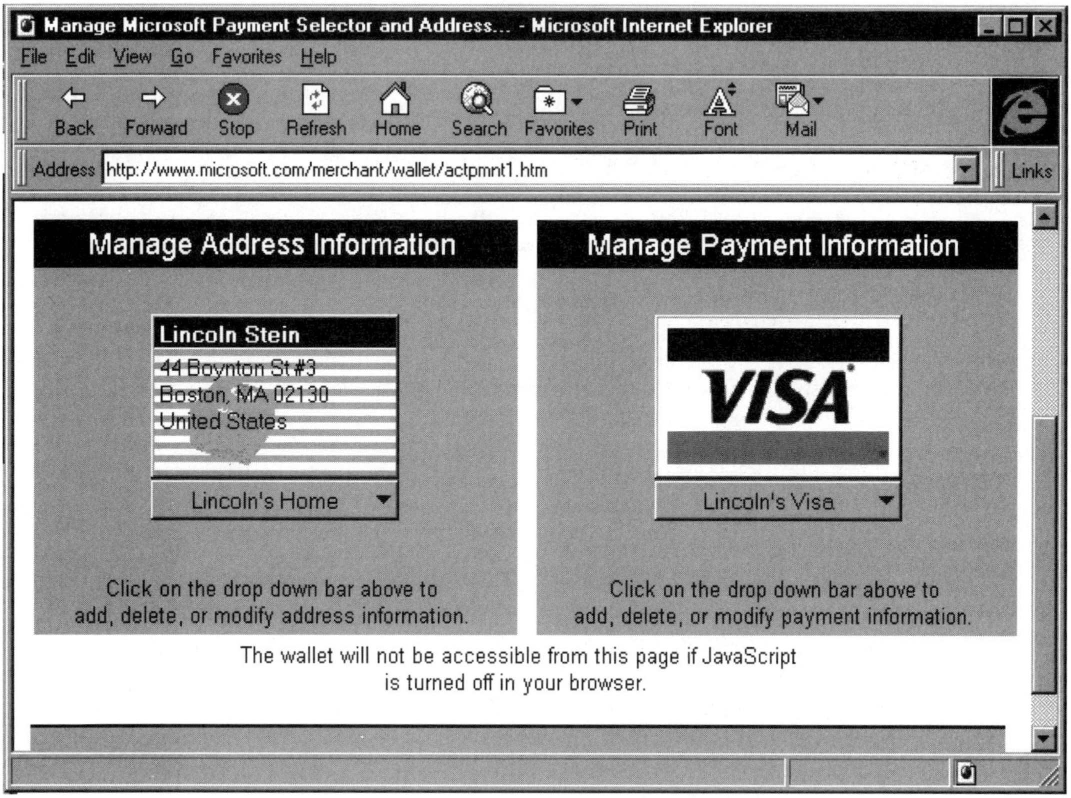

FIGURE 3.5 Microsoft Wallet has two panes of information: one for address information, the other for payment options.

the SET-compatible version is released. Of course, the Microsoft Merchant Server (whose name has recently changed to Microsoft Commerce Server) is preconfigured for Wallet support, and supports live authorization, order entry, credit processing, and all the other frills.

Who Pays for the Credit Card System?

The credit card system is a complicated machine, with banks, authentication terminals, and leased telephone lines spanning the globe. The system will only become more complicated as Internet payments through SET come online. Who pays for it all?

The answer, of course, is: You do. Consumers subsidize the system through annual fees and interest payments made to card-issuing banks. Merchants pay for the system with per-transaction fees charged by their banks. They also pay the bank a percentage on each purchase. This fee is called, oddly enough, the "discount."

The credit card system is set up to minimize the cost of fraud. Cardholders can dispute charges by claiming billing errors, unsatisfactory merchandise, or unauthorized use of their card numbers. The cardholder's bank will now initiate an investigation. If the merchant is found to be at fault, the investigation may ultimately result in a chargeback, in which funds are debited from the merchant's account and credited to the cardholder. This is one of the transactions that SET is designed to handle.

Things get more interesting if the cardholder refuses to pay a charge by alleging that it was used fraudulently. By federal law, cardholders cannot be held responsible for more than $50 of unauthorized credit card charges. In practice, this fee is usually waived by the issuing bank (*Caveat:* The limit does not apply to check cards; see Chapter 4). Who gets stuck paying the price of a fraudulent transaction depends on the agreements between the merchant and the two banks. In the case of face-to-face transactions, such as at a walk-in store, the merchant generally can't be held liable as long as it can prove that it followed the standard procedures for verifying the credit card (checking the signature, authorizing the payment, and so forth). Unless the card-issuing bank can prove that the charge was really authorized, it ends up paying the merchant's bill.

Things are different when a mail-order or telephone-order transaction is involved. In the case of this type of high-risk transaction, it is the merchant who ends up with the liability for unauthorized card use. The only exception is when merchants use an address verification service to confirm the cardholder's billing address and send the merchandise to that address using a shipping service that will certify that the goods were delivered and signed for. Although credit card authorization systems provide billing address confirmation for free, shipping certifications can be pricy—and are irrelevant for software and information delivered directly over the Internet.

Because banks now lump Internet commerce among high-risk mail-order purchases, merchants pay for disavowed online purchases, at least for the time being.

Other Digital Payment Systems

SET's main strength is also its biggest limitation: It is strongly tied to the credit card system. Because merchants pay a fee for each credit card transaction, it only makes sense to use SET for transactions of $10 or more. Items with smaller price tags, such as pay-per-view Web pages and online games, don't work economically unless the merchant and the customer work out a long-term subscription relationship in advance, effectively precluding impulse buying and pay-per-play sites. Debit cards suffer from a similar problem. Micropayment schemes, such as CyberCoin and Millicent, seek to overcome this limitation by allowing for transactions with very low overhead.

Another problem with the credit card model is that it isn't anonymous. By design, the customer identifies herself with every purchase and her identity is recorded by the merchant and both banks. Although this system offers many advantages, such as credit on demand and the ability of cardholders to dispute charges, it provides little in the way of privacy. Digital cash schemes, such as DigiCash, attempt to provide the equivalent of electronic cash on the Internet—reliable yet completely anonymous.

Most E-money schemes require cryptography to ensure the sanctity of the transaction. This raises the bar for online merchants who must install and manage complex software packages in order to accept digital payments. Offline schemes, such as First Virtual, work around these problems by sending the confidential part of the transaction separately by a secure channel, such as voice telephone.

First Virtual

The First Virtual scheme is one of the earliest entries into the Internet commerce marketplace. It is designed for low- to medium-priced software sales, fee-for-service information purchases, and other types of intangible merchandise that can be delivered over the Internet. It is not designed for the purchase of tangible items, such as computer hardware, dishwashers, and dream trips to Hawaii. First Virtual's main feature is that it does not rely on any encryption technology to protect the confidentiality of the user's payment information. Instead, all confidential information is transmitted in advance by voice telephone.

Before making purchases with the First Virtual system, the consumer signs up for a First Virtual account by filling out an online application form at First Virtual's Web site. The consumer then completes the process by telephone. During the sign-up procedure, she provides her credit card number and contact information and receives a First Virtual personal identification number (PIN) in return. There is a $2 sign-up fee, after which the customer pays no additional fees to First Virtual.

When a user wants to purchase some software, download a restricted Web page, or play an online game, she types her First Virtual PIN into a text field in a fill-in form. A CGI script on the merchant's server does a quick validation of the PIN, then makes the software or Web page available for download. First Virtual will later contact the consumer by e-mail, describe the charge, and give her the chance to approve or disapprove the purchase before her credit card is billed. Ordinarily the customer will mail the message back with the word "approved" in the message body. However, if the customer feels the product wasn't worth its purchase price, she is free to disapprove it. The charge is waived and the merchant doesn't get paid for the purchase. Because the merchandise is intangible, this doesn't cause significant financial loss for the merchant. To prevent users from abusing this privilege, those that cancel an unusually large number of purchases will eventually lose their First Virtual privileges. If a user's PIN is used fraudulently, she can alert First Virtual of the fact. It will be canceled and a new PIN issued. Again, because the merchandise is intangible, fraud doesn't threaten anyone with a large financial loss.

Merchants wishing to accept First Virtual payments open an account with First Virtual for a one-time processing fee, currently $10. First Virtual provides the merchant with a simple CGI script to validate users' PIN numbers and to notify First Virtual when a purchase has been made. In addition to the one-time fee, First Virtual charges the merchant a fixed transaction fee, currently $0.29 per transaction, plus 3 percent of the purchase price.

The First Virtual system provides a simple but limited way to accept financial transactions on the Web. Because of its limitations and its awkward payment model, it has gained little consumer acceptance.

CyberCash

CyberCash, a product of the CyberCash Corporation, is a SET-like system suitable for credit and debit card transactions. Like SET, it uses specialized software on the merchant's and customer's sides of the connections to provide for secure payments across the Internet. In contrast to SET, the system is mature, and working software is readily available for both the server and client sides of the connection.

For a consumer to make CyberCash payments, she must first download a free piece of software called the CyberCash Wallet from CyberCash's Web site and initialize it with payment information and personal identifying information. Payment options currently include credit card numbers and bank account numbers, which are then safely stored in encrypted form on the user's personal computer. There is no charge for the installation or use of this software.

When a user orders an item from a CyberCash-accepting merchant and presses the "pay" button, Wallet pops up and requests the user to select a payment system in much the way Microsoft's similarly-named product does. The user may choose to charge the purchase against a credit card, in which case the charge will appear on her next credit card statment, or against her checking account, in which case the sum will be debited immediately via a wire transfer. Software installed on the merchant's side of the connection validates and records the transaction by connecting to a server maintained by CyberCash, a process that takes 10 to 15 seconds. Wallet maintains a record of each transaction, allowing the user to rapidly review her purchases and check them against her credit card and/or bank statements. This is a nice feature that Microsoft Wallet does not have.

Like SET, CyberCash uses strong cryptography to prevent transaction information from being intercepted by unauthorized third parties. Furthermore, because actual credit card account numbers are never recorded on the merchant's server, there is no chance that credit card numbers can be stolen by individuals who have broken into the merchant's computer system.

To accept CyberCash payments, a merchant must open an account with an acquiring bank that supports the system. The accounts are similar to mail-order and telephone-order credit card accounts and have a similar fee structure. The merchant must also install CyberCash Electronic Cash Register software on the Web server. The software generates a transaction log that can be fed into the merchant's order entry and shipping systems; it also handles chargebacks, refunds, and the like. The Cash Register is downloadable free of charge and available for many platforms, including Windows NT and UNIX. Electronic commerce Web server packages from both Microsoft and Netscape come with hooks for the CyberCash system that allow for tightly integrated operation.

CyberCash shares SET's high per-transaction overhead and is impractical for small purchases. However, a CyberCash micropayment service called CyberCoin allows the customer to pay a lump sum into the CyberCash system in advance and then make small purchases against it. This allows credit card fees to be amortized into a single lump sum, making pay-per-play and small impulse buys economically feasible. Individual purchases can be as small as $0.25. Although there is no upper limit on the size of the transaction, customers are not allowed to pay more than $80 into their CyberCash accounts per month. The client and server software used for CyberCash and CyberCoin are the same, but the agreement between the merchant's bank and CyberCash is not. Some banks support one system but not the other.

The CyberCash Corporation has announced that future versions of its software will support SET.

DigiCash

DigiCash, a product of the Netherlands-based DigiCash Company, is a digital cash system that works something like phone cards and subway tokens. Under this system, users mint money by creating "CyberBucks," electronic vouchers that, like dollar bills, carry unique serial numbers and a denomination. Before a

CyberBuck can be used, however, it must be digitally signed by a bank that supports the DigiCash system. The fee the bank charges to sign a CyberBuck is the denomination of the bill: a $10 CyberBuck costs the user $10 to sign. Once signed, a CyberBuck can be used just like real cash. When a customer wishes to purchase some merchandise from an online store, she electronically transfers some number of CyberBucks to the merchant's server, receiving smaller denomination bills as change. The merchant now owns the money and can use it in other electronic transactions or trade it in at a participating bank for real money.

Because CyberBucks are digitally signed using public key cryptography, they cannot be counterfeited. The recipient of DigiCash can check the signature against the public key of the bank, verifying that it is a valid bill. DigiCash transactions are fully anonymous and untraceable, more so than real cash. When real cash is involved, banks can record the serial numbers of bills and identify whom a particular piece of currency was issued to. DigiCash uses a blinding system that prevents banks from associating a particular CyberBuck with the individual who presented it for signing.

A complication with the DigiCash system is that a user can copy a CyberBuck and attempt to spend it twice. To get around this, the system uses centralized servers that allow someone who has received DigiCash in payment to verify that the money has been used only once. This can be done immediately on-line or delayed until a more convenient time. Because of the way the DigiCash protocol works, the person who spends the same piece of currency twice automatically discloses her identity, allowing the bank to trace the fraud to its source. Under other circumstances, this feature works in the user's favor. If a particular payment is in dispute (for example, a provider of online services claims the user missed a payment), the user can disclose just enough information to prove that the CyberBuck the merchant recently deposited did indeed come from her.

Another feature that sets DigiCash apart from the other payment schemes is that it can be used to transmit money safely between peers. Ordinary people can barter and trade CyberBucks across the Internet without going through banks or other financial institutions.

DigiCash has its risks too. If a customer makes a DigiCash purchase and the merchant absconds before providing the goods, the customer can't stop payment (although she can provide sufficient information to trace the bill when it is deposited). If the user's hard disk crashes with $1,000 in DigiCash on it, the money's gone. Fortunately, CyberBucks can be backed up, just like any other electronic document.

DigiCash requires special software to be installed on both the consumer's and the merchant's computers. It is currently available for Windows NT, Windows 95, and some UNIX systems. Although the system has been available for more than a year, its adoption by banks, merchants, and consumers has been slow, although acceptance seems to be better in Europe than in the United States. This may be due more to users' unfamiliarity with the system than to any inherent limitations.

Millicent

The Millicent protocol, introduced by Digital Equipment Corporation in late 1996, is designed as a low-overhead system to handle small electronic purchases between a tenth of a cent and $5. Its innovation is the use of "brokers" and "scrips." A scrip is similar to the gift certificates we encounter in the real world. Like a gift certificate, a scrip has a small face value and can be redeemed only at a particular merchant's store. If the value of the scrip is larger than the item's purchase price, the merchant returns the difference to the customer in the form of a new scrip.

Where do scrips come from in the first place? Again, like gift certificates, they are minted and issued by the merchants themselves. They are numbered serially and digitally signed so that the merchant can rapidly verify that a scrip is valid and has not been spent more than once. However, unlike gift certificates, which are ordinarily purchased directly by consumers, Millicent scrips are purchased in bulk by brokers at wholesale prices. The brokers then resell the scrips to individual customers at a markup. The inventors of the system envision that large organizations like banks and credit card companies will want to get into the Millicent broker business.

Because the scrips are produced and signed by the merchant, there is no need for a centralized server to validate scrips and check that they are being used only once. The merchant does all the checking itself. This eliminates one of the major bottlenecks in the SET, CyberCash, and DigiCash systems and helps keep costs down. Because Millicent is intended to handle small sums of money only, it doesn't need to use very strong cryptography or to rely on a public key infrastructure for authentication. If the user loses a scrip, she's only out a dollar or so—no worse than losing a coin in a vending machine. If a merchant tries to cheat the user, she can complain to the broker. As a result, the system has a very low transaction overhead.

At the time this was written, the Millicent system was in trial phase. See the Millicent home page for up-to-date information.

Checklist

SSL

1. What level (export-grade or U.S. domestic-grade) of encryption does your browser or server use?

   ❍ Export-grade SSL (40-bit keys)

   ☑ Domestic-grade SSL (128- to 168-bit keys)

Forty-bit keys are too weak to withstand a brute-force attack by a determined foe. Forty-bit encryption may be sufficient for personal information and perhaps even to transmit credit card numbers, but not for transactions that involve large sums of money or valuable information, such as trade secrets and business plans. Remember that to use strong encryption, both the server *and* browser must use domestic-grade encryption. Browsers downloaded from FTP and Web sites are almost always crippled for export.

2. Are you using a recent version of Netscape Navigator?

❍ No

☑ Yes

Prior to version 2.0, Netscape Navigator's implementation of SSL was seriously flawed. If you are an end user, upgrade to a more recent version. If you administer a Web site, and you rely on SSL to keep certain confidential documents secret, make sure that no one who routinely accesses your site is using an old browser. All versions of Internet Explorer that support SSL are thought to be free of this problem.

Digital Payment Systems

This checklist will help you compare the features of various digital payment systems.

1. Does the system transmit payment information in the clear?

☑ No

❍ Yes

Although there are few, if any, examples of credit card information being intercepted in transit, this is a major source of concern for users. A digital payment system should protect this information, either by sending it by some out-of-band route (for instance, voice telephone) or by encrypting it.

2. Does the system store payment information in unencrypted form on the server?

☑ No

❍ Yes

A bigger source of concern is the risk that someone will break into the merchant's computer or database system and steal credit card information. Systems that store customer payment information in unencrypted form are to be avoided, including those that store the information transiently in temporary files.

3. Does the system store payment information in unencrypted form on the customer's computer?

   ☑ No
   ❍ Yes

   For the same reasons that payment information shouldn't be stored in the clear on the server, it shouldn't be stored on the user's personal computer without a pass phrase to encrypt and decrypt it.

4. Does the system log transactions?

   ❍ No
   ☑ Yes

   Logging is essential to catch problems. Digital payment systems should log all transactions—including the aborted ones—in a reliable manner. Both the server side and the client side software should keep logs.

5. Does the system prevent double-charging?

   ❍ No
   ☑ Yes

   With Web-based forms, it's easy for a user to get confused and submit the same order twice. The payment software should check for this event and prevent it.

6. Does the system permit chargeback credits?

   ❍ No
   ☑ Yes

   In credit card-based payment systems, you occasionally need to process a customer credit or make a refund. The digital payment system should provide an interface to accomplish this.

7. Can the system be used as a credit card validator?

   ☑ No
   ❍ Yes

   Some payment systems can be used by unscrupulous individuals as an oracle to validate credit card number guesses. Make sure that yours isn't one of these.

Online Resources

SSL Protocol

http://home.netscape.com/newsref/std/SSL.html
http://home.netscape.com/newsref/ref/internet-security.html

TLS Protocol

http://www.consensus.com/ietf-tls/

IPv6 Specification

http://www.globecom.net/(nocl,sv)/ietf/rfc/rfc1883.shtml

IPv6's Security Contrasted with SSL's

http://www.seas.gwu.edu/student/reto/ipv6/index.htm

SET and Other Digital Money Systems

SET specification

http://www.visa.com/cgi-bin/vee/sf/standard.html

A discussion of SET in relationship to banking regulations

http://www.citynet.net/personal/till/set1.htm

Microsoft Wallet

http://www.microsoft.com/commerce/wallet/

Netscape Commerce Server

http://www.netscape.com/

Microsoft Merchant

http://www.microsoft.com/merchant/

First Virtual

http://www.fv.com/

CyberCash

http://www.cybercash.com

DigiCash

http://www.digicash.nl/

Millicent

http://www.millicant.digital.com/

PART II

Client-Side Security

Will some evil hackers' group grab your credit card numbers? Will a rogue Web site infect your hard disk with a plague of viruses? Can cookies steal your soul?

The next three chapters break through the hype and scare stories and take a level look at Web security from the end user's point of view.

Chapter 4

Using SSL

Network eavesdropping is a major potential problem on the Internet. Packet sniffers installed on the path anywhere between Web browser and server can monitor the entire conversation, including the information submitted in fill-out forms and stored in cookies. The SSL protocol, described in the previous chapter, dramatically reduces the risk by emptying the browser-server data stream. In the process, it also solves another Internet problem, reliably identifying the party at the other end of the network link.

The previous chapters showed how SSL works internally. This chapter gives a more practical guide for making the best use of SSL-enabled browsers. Practical information for administering SSL Web servers is postponed until Chapter 11.

SSL at Work

It is easy to use SSL. In fact, the process of setting up a secure connection happens so fast and easily that many people use it regularly without knowing it.

Establishing an SSL Connection

Microsoft Internet Explorer, Netscape Navigator, Spry Mosaic, and other commercial browsers offer support for the SSL protocol. To see SSL in action, point one of these browsers at the URL *https://www.fedex.com/track_it_adv.html,* which happens to be a fill-out form on the Federal Express company's secure Web server. Notice that the URL begins with *https* (for "HTTP-secure") rather than *http*. Figure 4.1 shows how this appears in Netscape

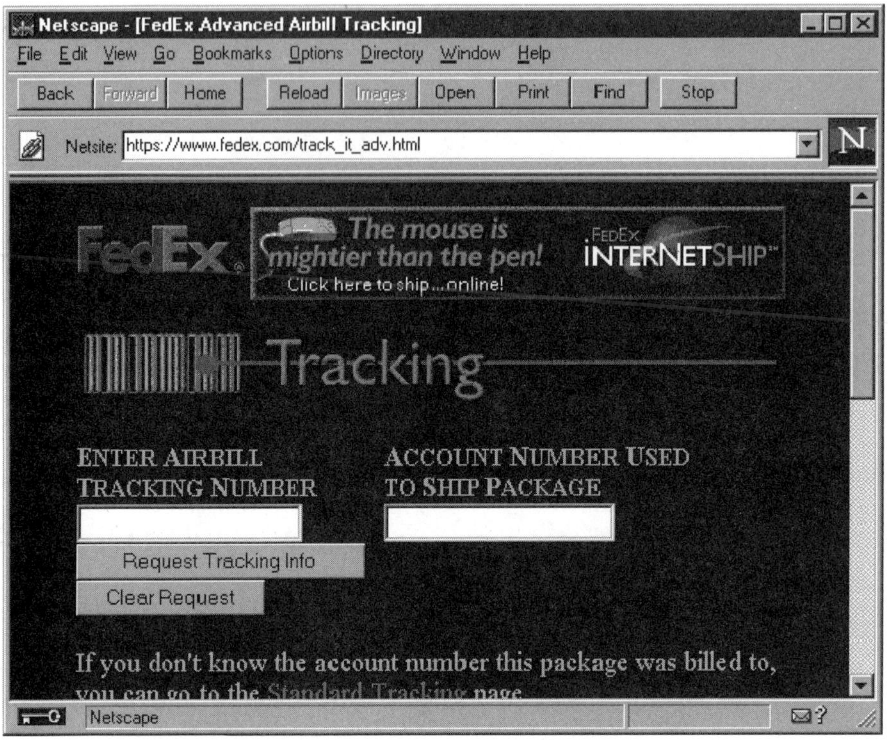

FIGURE 4.1 The FedEx site uses SSL to keep delivery information confidential.

Navigator 3.01. It looks just like an ordinary Web page, with a few subtle differences. First, there is a thin blue line between the Web site address and the page contents (because of the black-and-white illustration, you'll have to try it yourself or take my word for it). Second, the key icon at the bottom left of the browser, which is usually displayed as a broken key on a pink background, is now a solid key on a blue background. If you look *really* carefully at the key icon, you'll notice that the key has two teeth. This means that the browser is using crippled export-grade encryption. Instead of a key, Navigator 4.0 (aka Netscape Communicator) uses a padlock icon to indicate an encrypted document.

To get more information about the encrypted session, you can either click on the key icon or choose *View->Document Info* from the browser menu bar (or choose *Security* from the toolbar in Navigator 4.0). This will display a multi-pane window that contains information about the current document. If you scroll down to the bottom of the lower panel, you will see information about the document's encryption method (Figure 4.2). In the paragraph labeled *Security,* we learn that the page was transmitted in encrypted form using "a medium-grade encryption key suited for U.S. export." Below this,

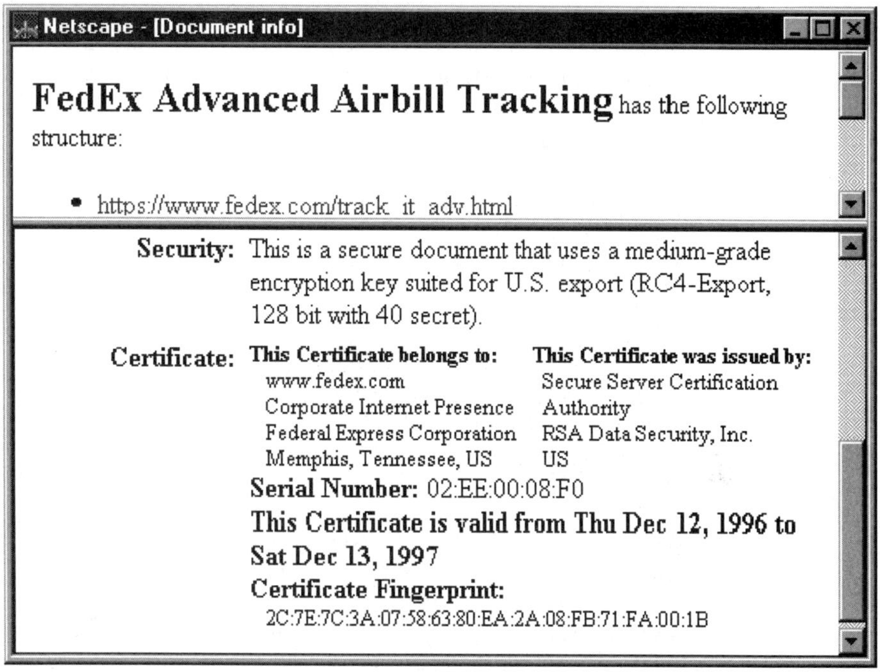

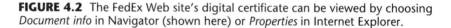

FIGURE 4.2 The FedEx Web site's digital certificate can be viewed by choosing *Document info* in Navigator (shown here) or *Properties* in Internet Explorer.

in the section labeled *Certificate,* is the signed certificate that the FedEx site used to authenticate itself. The column to the left gives the Federal Express Web site's address and its postal address. To the right of this is information about the certifying authority that signed the certificate, in this case RSA Data Security, Inc., the company that owns the better-known VeriSign Corporation. Other information provided in this window includes the certificate's expiration date, a serial number, and a "certificate fingerprint" (actually an MD5 hash) that can be read over the phone to Fed Ex's Webmaster if there's ever any doubt as to the validity of a certificate.

When Internet Explorer establishes an SSL connection, the user interface clues it gives are more subtle. The only difference from a normal Web page is that a small padlock icon appears in the lower right-hand corner. You can view the session's encryption and certificate information by choosing *File->Properties* and then selecting the *Security* tab. All the information provided by the Netscape browser can be found here, but formatted differently. In contrast to Netscape's description of export-grade cryptography as "medium-grade," Microsoft uses the more accurate term "low strength."

Because SSL connections are noticeably slower than unencrypted connections, most sites use ordinary HTTP for their public pages. When you enter a restricted part of a site or need to submit confidential information, the link that takes you there is an *https* URL. You may not even realize that SSL is in use unless you look for the clues. As long as the solid key or padlock icons are displayed, you can be confident that your communications are being encrypted. The URL you requested is protected, as are the contents of the document. Any information that you submit in a fill-out form or that is transmitted to and fro in cookies (Chapter 6) are also encrypted.

Things to Watch For

Although using SSL is straightforward, there are a few complications. This section discusses the most frequent gotchas and gives some advice on what to do when you encounter them.

Site Name Mismatches

When a Web browser connects to an SSL server, it does some basic validation of the site's certificate. Among the things that it checks is whether the name listed on the certificate matches the site's URL. If the two do not exactly match, the browser presents a warning. You can observe this behavior by fetching *https://www0.fedex.com/track_it_adv.html*, where *www0* is the internal name of one of the servers that FedEx uses to handle its Web transactions.

After displaying the warning, the browser will allow you to continue the transaction or cancel. It is up to you to determine which is the correct course to take. In the case of *www0.fedex.com* and *www.fedex.com*, you might elect to continue to fetch the page. If the name on the certificate were *www.bobs-spa.com*, you might well suspect that you are dealing with an impostor and elect to cancel the transaction. To be completely safe, you should always double-check the remote site's certificate manually before submitting any truly confidential information.

Mixed Pages

It is possible for HTML pages to contain a mixture of encrypted and unencrypted information. The main page may have been fetched using SSL, but its inline images may have come from a different server that does not use encryption. In this case, the document information window will show the security information for each element separately. Ordinarily, such a situation should not be cause for concern. If you wish, some browsers allow you to be warned when viewing a page with mixed content.

A cause for greater concern is when a page is retrieved via SSL but the fill-out form contained within it submits its contents to the remote site using unencrypted HTTP. This is a rare event that usually points to an innocent mistake made by the Web site author or operator, but it has the unwanted efect of lulling you into thinking that the contents of the form are secure, when in fact they are not. You can detect this type of error by having the browser warn before submitting fill-out forms in unencrypted form. Unfortunately, this setting generates so much unwanted noise that most users turn it off.

Export and Domestic-Grade Cryptography

As explained in the last chapter, browsers destined for export beyond the United States and Canada are crippled to use insecure 40-bit session keys. These keys are sufficient to deter casual nosiness but not enough to protect valuable secrets. If you have downloaded your browser from an FTP or Web site, you are probably using a crippled version.

U.S. and Canadian users are urged to purchase shrink-wrapped copies of browser software in order to have access to strong encryption. For other users, a workaround can be found in the form of Safe Passage, a joint product of C2Net Inc. and Thawte Communications Ltd. Safe Passage is a small Web proxy that runs on your desktop machine. To use it, you configure your export-crippled browser to send all its URL requests to the Safe Passage proxy. Safe Passage, in turn, forwards your request to the remote server, using strong encryption. Because Safe Passage was developed outside U.S. borders, it is free of export restrictions. At the time this was written, the software was available for Windows 95 and NT systems.

Certificate Revocation and Expiration

Under a number of circumstances, a site's certificate may be revoked. Sometimes, there is an innocent explanation for this, as when a new certificate replaces one that contained a typographical error. In other cases, a certificate is revoked because the site's private key was compromised, allowing the certificate to be used fraudulently. In all such cases, the serial number of the revoked certificate is stored in a certificate revocation list maintained by the certifying authority.

Unfortunately, for reasons explained in the previous chapter, Web browsers do not currently check CAs' revocation lists. The only time you know that a site certificate has been revoked is when it eventually expires. If a remote server offers your browser a certificate that is past its expiration date, the browser will present a warning and offer you the chance to cancel the connection. Either the certificate has been revoked or a lazy Webmaster has neglected to renew the site's certificate in time. If confidential information is involved, it is prudent to cancel.

CA and Site Certificates

Each Web browser that's shipped comes with the public keys of several certifying authorities preinstalled. The public keys are installed in the form of "self-signed" certificates, which are digital certificates that the CA itself has

A Packet Sniffer at Work

During the preparation of this book, I looked around for a packet sniffer program capable of intercepting Web access passwords. I was unable to find one at the usual hackers' sites, although I did find plenty for intercepting TELNET passwords. So I decided to roll my own. It was remarkably easy.

I took advantage of the *tcpdump* network administrator's diagnostic tool that comes with many standard UNIX distributions, including the version of Linux installed on my laptop. This does all the hard work of putting the network interface card into "promiscuous" mode, intercepting network packets and filtering the ones destined for HTTP ports. Around this program, I placed a small Perl wrapper script to reassemble packets, scan them for their source and destination addresses, and pull out Web access passwords. The whole program was a mere 22 lines.

A few weeks later I demonstrated the program during a tutorial on Web security at the Sixth International WWW conference, in Santa Clara. I plugged my laptop into the network outlet conveniently located near the speaker's podium and started up the program. Within seconds, the program was capturing all the activity on the network of Web kiosks down the hall in the main reception area. As we watched, we saw each URL requested by unsuspecting surfers, as well as the user names and passwords they provided to gain access to "protected" areas. Here's a brief excerpt to give you an idea of what we saw (the names and passwords have been changed to avoid embarassment):

```
207.218.76.108->vrml.organic.com    GET /VRML2.0/FINAL/Overview.html
207.218.76.106->gfx.hotmail.com     GET /spacer.gif
207.218.76.106->www.hotmail.com     POST /cgi-bin/start/paulxhogan/207.82.250.70_d5
207.218.76.70->ice.wco.com          GET /cgi-bin/www6/ice/main.pl
207.218.76.70->ice.wco.com          Authorization: Basic isaacxc:wabbit
207.218.76.42->tmstv.com            GET /cgi-bin/tvcgi.sjm/gridref+s0+g040712000?51,11
207.218.76.67->ice.wco.com          POST /cgi-bin/www6/ice/main.pl
207.218.76.67->ice.wco.com          Authorization: Basic fredrg:Frederic
207.218.76.40->ice.wco.com          GET /cgi-bin/www6/ice/main.pl?x-a=v&x-id=2386
207.218.76.40->ice.wco.com          Authorization: Basic marym:zebra97
207.218.76.48->pasture.purdue.edu   GET /~agenhtml/agenmc/usage/usage.graph.small.gif
```

Notice that even though the sniffer was plugged into the network at the WWW6 convention center, the information it gathered affected remote Web sites, as well as nearby ones.

If you are using a UNIX system, you can fetch the sniffer and tcpdump from the URLs given at the end of the chapter. With these tools, network administrators can learn what kind of information their sites may be exposing. Please don't use them for unethical purposes.

signed ("I am XYZ corporation. Trust me."). Netscape Navigator recognizes about 15 such certifying authorities (Table 4.1). Internet Explorer recognizes a smaller subset of these. You can view the certificates recognized by your browser by selecting *Options->Security Preferences->Site Certificates* in Netscape Navigator 3.X (Figure 4.3) or by selecting *View->Options->Security ->Sites* in Internet Explorer. In Netscape Navigator 4.0, the information can be found by clicking on *Security* in the toolbar and then selecting *Certificates ->Signers*. Both the Netscape and Microsoft browsers allow you to view the contents of the certificates. If you wish, you can delete a certificate entirely, something you might want to do if, at some point, you've accepted the certificate of a nonstandard authority (see below).

For unknown reasons, beta versions of Netscape Navigator 4.0 come with the certificate of a CA called *Netscape Test CA* preinstalled. This CA is used to sign the limited-time test certificate that accompanies trial versions of Netscape Web servers. Because Netscape doesn't verify the identities of Web sites that request this test certificate, an endorsement by this CA is meaningless. If you find the Netscape test CA among the certificates recognized by your browser, remove it.

Both Netscape and Microsoft browsers give you the option of deactivating a certificate without deleting it entirely. With Internet Explorer, you can deactivate a CA's certificate by unchecking the checkbox displayed to the left

TABLE 4.1 Certifying Authorities Recognized by Netscape Navigator 4.0

AT&T Certificate Services	Netscape Test CA*
AT&T Directory Services	RSA Commercial CA
ATT CA	RSA Secure Server CA
ATT Research CA	Thawte Personal Basic CA
BBN Certificate Services CA Root	Thawte Personal Freemail CA
Canada Post Corporation CA	Thawte Personal Premium CA
CertiSign BR	Thawte Premium Server CA
CommerceNet CA	Thawte Server CA
GTE CyberTrust Root CA	United States Postal Service CA
GTE CyberTrust Secure Server CA	Uptime Group Plc. Class 1 CA
GTIS/PWGSC, Canada Government Secure CA	Uptime Group Plc. Class 2 CA
GTIS/PWGSC, Canada Government Web CA	Uptime Group Plc. Class 3 CA
IBM World Registry CA	Uptime Group Plc. Class 4 CA
Integrion CA	VeriSign Class 1 Primary CA
KEYWITNESS, Canada CA	VeriSign Class 2 Primary CA
MCI Mall CA	VeriSign Class 3 Primary CA
	VeriSign Class 4 Primary CA

**Netscape Test CA should be deleted.*

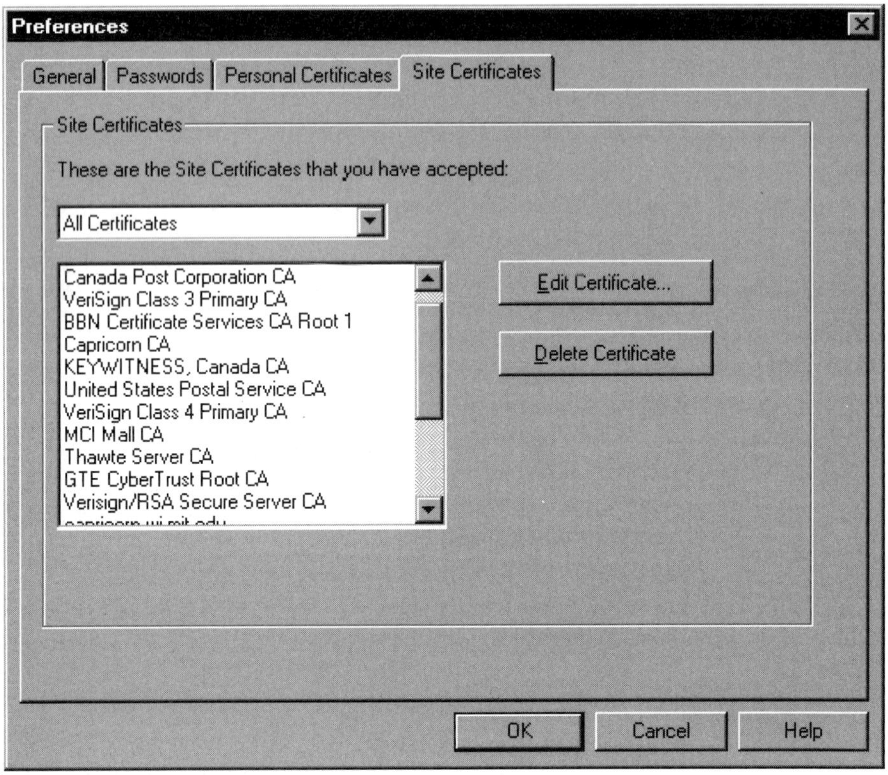

FIGURE 4.3 This is the list of recognized certifying authorities as it appears in Netscape Navigator 3.X.

of its name. With Netscape Navigator, you do this by selecting on the certificate and pressing a button labeled "Edit Certificate." This brings up a window that displays certificate properties and options. To deactivate a certificate without deleting it, select the radio button labeled "Do not allow connections to sites certified by this authority." If a site tries to send your browser a certificate signed by a deactivated CA, the browser will refuse the connection. You can, of course, reactivate a certificate at any time.

The Netscape browsers also offer an intermediate between accepting a certificate signed by a particular CA unconditionally or rejecting it completely. After bringing up the certificate's properties window, select the checkbox labeled "warn before sending data to sites certified by this authority." The browser will now display an alert before establishing an SSL connection to a site certified by this authority, giving you the option to continue the connection or cancel.

What happens if a Web server presents your browser with a certificate signed by some CA that is not on the list? In this circumstance, the Netscape and Microsoft servers have different behaviors. Netscape puts up a warning that asks if you wish to accept this site's certificate. If you accept, Netscape gives you the option of accepting the certificate for this session only or for future sessions, as well. Netscape will then install the site's certificate among the list of CA certificates. You can view the site certificate, deactivate it, or delete it in the same manner as you can for those belonging to certifying authorities.

In contrast, if a Web server tries to present a certificate signed by an unknown certifying authority to Internet Explorer, the browser will reject the certificate, display a warning, and tell you that it cannot complete the connection.

Both Internet Explorer and Netscape Navigator also allow you to install additional CA certificates, allowing the browser to recognize sites that have been certified by them. Certificates can be distributed on floppy disk or via the Internet. They're merely a file with a special MIME type (see Chapter 11 for details). To load such a certificate, click on a link that points to it. The browser will display a dialog warning that you are attempting to install a CA certificate and asking if you want to proceed (Figure 4.4). If you accept, the certificate will be installed among the other CA certificates and the browser will now recognize the authority of that CA to sign Web server certificates.

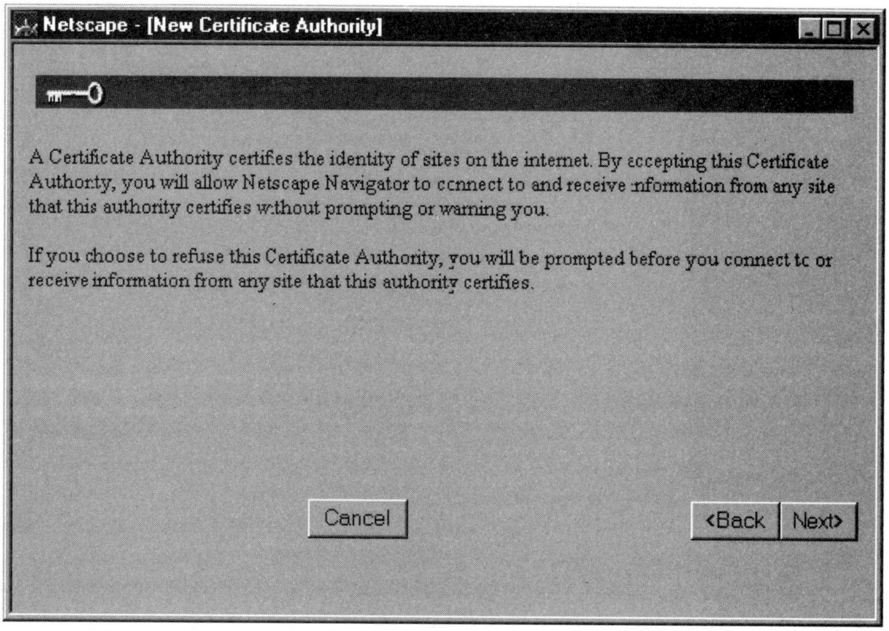

FIGURE 4.4 When a site asks a browser to recognize a new certifying authority, it displays a warning message.

There's a crucial difference between a site certificate and a CA certificate. If you acccept an individual site's certificate, you are telling the browser that you are willing to exchange SSL-encrypted messages with that one site. If

Sending Credit Card Numbers Across the Web

A frequently asked Web security question is: Can I send my credit card number over the Web? The answer is: Go ahead.

The whole issue of Internet-based credit card theft is a straw man. It was set up in part by the Netscape Corporation in order to provide a compelling reason to convince users to shift from the freeware Mosaic browser to its line of encrypting products. In actuality, consumers in the United States and Canada are protected against credit card theft by a $50 cap on liability. In practice, the fee is routinely waived by financial institutions. Other countries follow similar practices. At most, the user whose credit card number has been stolen suffers some inconvenience until a replacement card is issued. (See the bottom of this section for important caveats about check cards.)

In restaurants, we give our credit cards to some unknown college student who takes it into a back room for a few minutes and does who knows what with it. We routinely read our credit card numbers over the phone to salespeople we are never likely to meet. Weighed against the cavalier way we treat our credit card numbers every day in the real world, the risks of Web-based interception are small.

Credit card companies feel differently about this matter, however, as they bear the costs of fraud. Interestingly, these companies aren't so worried about the risks of a credit card number being sniffed in transit as they are about the vulnerability of Web sites to break-ins. In the single largest case of Internet credit card fraud to date, intruders broke into a large Internet server provider's computer system. There they discovered and made off with an unencrypted file containing the credit card numbers of each of the ISP's several thousand customers. In the aftermath of the theft, each of the customer's credit cards had to be canceled and reissued. To prevent this from happening, SET, the encrypting protocol preferred by the credit card companies, manages credit card purchases without ever giving the merchant access to the customer's card number.

An important caveat to what I've just said applies to check cards, also known as debit cards, which many banks have begun issuing to customers. Although these cards look and act like credit cards in many ways, they are covered by different banking regulations. As a result, the $50 liability limit applies only to check cards if the loss is noticed and reported within two business days. After that, the liability limit rises quickly to $500 and can become unlimited if the theft is not reported within 60 days of a bank statement. You might want to think twice before sending your check card number over the Web, or even before using your check card for more conventional transactions!

you accept and install a CA certificate, however, you are telling the browser that you trust every site whose certificate has been signed by that CA. Do not install a CA certificate unless you are sure you know what you're doing. If the certificate installation dialog box ever appears unexpectedly, you should cancel the request.

In Netscape Navigator 4.0, the interface for managing site certificates and other aspects of encryption has been redesigned. You can find the options under *Communicator->Security Info.*

Personal Certificates

In addition to the site certificates that you can use to verify the identity of remote Web servers, there are personal certificates that you can use to prove your identity to the server. Both Netscape and Microsoft aggressively promote personal certificates. Some browser versions have even incorporated the process of applying for a "digital ID" into the standard installation script. Personal certificates are completely analogous to site certificates. They contain your name, your e-mail address, and the public-key-half of a public/private key pair, all signed by a certifying authority. Some personal certificates contain other information as well, such as gender, birth date, mailing address, and social security number.

Personal certificates can be used to gain access to members-only Web sites, to log in to corporate intranets, or, potentially, to conduct legally binding business transactions. They can be issued by a public certifying authority, such as VeriSign, or by a private concern, such as your employer.

VeriSign Personal Certificates

VeriSign is the first public certifying authority to offer personal certificates. For a small fee, you can obtain your very own digital ID. VeriSign currently offers two types of personal certificate: a Class 1 certificate suitable for casual use; and a Class 2 certificate that provides some guarantee that you are who you claim to be.

To obtain a Class 1 certificate, you need only complete a form on VeriSign's Web site. The application is processed automatically without any attempt by VeriSign to validate the information you provide. When the signed certificate is ready, you will receive an e-mail message giving a URL and access code for retrieving it.

To obtain a Class 2 certificate, you must provide a mailing address, a driver's license, and a social security number. The certificate will be issued after VeriSign validates the information with a credit bureau. To prevent fraudulent applications, the information necessary to retrieve your certificate is sent to you by surface mail, not electronically.

There is an annual fee of $9.95 for Class 1 certificates, although at press time, VeriSign was offering Class 1 certificates on a free six-month trial basis. Class 2 certificates cost $19.95 per annum.

What can you do with a VeriSign ID? At the moment, not very much. A few Web sites collect personal certificates in order to customize the site according to the user's preferences. When the user returns to the site, the server recognizes her certificate and restores her preferences. In the future, some Internet sites may use certificates to create members-only areas, for electronic billing, or as legal proof of age for access to adult material. Much of this seems a long way off.

VeriSign personal certificates do offer one tangible incentive, however. They allow you to send and receive encrypted e-mail using the new S/MIME (Secure Multipurpose Internet Mail Extensions) system, a feature supported by e-mailers from Netscape, Microsoft, Frontier Technologies, and others. VeriSign's Web site allows you to search for the personal certificate of any registered user. If the search is successful, you can install her certificate on your browser and use it to send her secure e-mail. This feature, announced for Internet Explorer 4.0 and Netscape Communicator, was not yet fully functional in the beta versions that were available for testing when this chapter was written.

Although S/MIME may become popular in the future, today a better solution for securing e-mail is PGP (Pretty Good Privacy). This system has the advantage of being free, widely used, and free of reliance on a third party for certification. More information on PGP can be found in the references at the end of this chapter.

How reliable are VeriSign personal certificates? Class 1 certificates provide no proof of identity. At most, they verify your e-mail address because the information needed to retrieve the certificate is returned by e-mail. There's nothing to stop a malicious individual from applying for a certificate in your name and substituting his or her e-mail address for yours. Class 2 certificates, while providing better assurance of identity, are not foolproof. Anyone with access to your credit bureau report (or the contents of your wallet) will have the information necessary to apply for a certificate in your name. However, because the information necessary to install the newly granted certificate is returned by surface mail, that person would also have to have access to your letterbox. Whether this is a significant risk depends on where you live and whether your letterbox has a lock.

VeriSign has announced, but not yet made available, a Class 3 personal certificate intended for high-security applications. The application for this certificate would involve a notarized letter and legal proof of identity using a birth certificate or passport.

What warranties are associated with certificates? In June 1997, VeriSign announced a warranty program called NetSure, which provides some protection against damages resulting from the loss or misuse of a certificate. There are caps of $1,000 and $25,000 on damages resulting from fraudulent use of Class 1 and Class 2 certificates, respectively. Among the circumstances covered by this plan are

- Loss or compromise of the user's private key
- Issuance of a certificate to an incorrect or unauthorized person
- Impersonation resulting from falsified information
- Revocation of the certificate by VeriSign without due cause
- Unreasonable delay in processing a revocation or renewal request

There is no warranty associated with Class 1 trial certificates. There are also many legal caveats contained within the warranty's fine print. In particular, the warranty requires you to exercise "reasonable care" to protect your private key from disclosure. It isn't clear what precautions are necessary to satisfy this requirement.

What are the disadvantages to using a personal certificate? By definition, if you use a personal certificate, you give up anonymity. A Web site that uses SSL can require your browser to present its certificate in order to establish a secure connection. The information on the certificate is now available to the operators of the site. For Class 1 certificates, this information will include your name and, optionally, your e-mail address, nationality, age, and gender (none of this is verified, so it may not be correct). For Class 2 certificates, the information consists of your correct name and e-mail address (required) and, optionally, your mailing address. There is no limit to what the remote site will do with this information, and some people worry that it will be used to generate marketing information or mailing lists.

Despite the uncertain usefulness of the personal certificates issued by VeriSign for general Internet use, digital certificates do have a great deal of importance in other applications. In SET financial transactions (see Chapter 3), certificates are used to identify customers, financial institutions, and merchants. In corporate intranets, the corporation may set up its own internal certifying authority and issue certificates to all its employees. These certificates are then used to control access to confidential documents on the Web server (see Chapter 11).

Obtaining a VeriSign Personal Certificate

To give personal certificates a try, you may apply for a VeriSign Class 1 or Class 2 certificate using the steps that start on page 77. Certificates are currently supported only for recent versions of Internet Explorer, Netscape Navigator/Communicator, and Frontier Technologies' e-mail products. If you use Microsoft Internet Explorer, ActiveX must be activated before you apply for a personal certificate (see the next chapter).

Managing Passwords Safely

Passwords have a way of cropping up wherever you look. If you use a LAN at your workplace, you probably have a password for logging in. Web servers use passwords to control access to confidential documents. Web browsers use passwords for encrypting sensitive information, such as the private keys used for digital signatures. Often, the entire security edifice stands or falls on how well passwords are chosen and maintained. Here's some general advice on passwords that is valid for many different circumstances.

Don't share your passwords or write them down. Pick a password that is easy to remember but hard to guess. Bad passwords include:

- Any English word or name
- Any foreign word or name
- Your telephone number, credit card number, social security number, office number, or street number (all can be obtained in a variety of ways)
- a predictable sequence of digits, such as *12345*
- a predictable sequence of letters, such as *abcde* or *qwerty* (the letters on the second row of the keyboard)
- A common phrase, such as *a stitch in time*
- Anything shorter than six letters

Good passwords should be six letters or longer and consist of a combination of upper and lower case letters, numbers, and punctuation marks. The current trend in security circles is to recommend the following method for choosing passwords.

1. Pick an easy to remember but idiosyncratic phrase, such as *My origami got 2 wet 2day!* Mispellings and numeric substitutions are encouraged.
2. Create the password by taking the first letter of each word: *Mog2w2*. For variety, take the last letter of each word: *yit2t!*

As subscription-only Web sites proliferate, you may find that you have to juggle many passwords and PINS—one for the LAN at work, one for your credit card, one for your bank account, one for your cellular phone, and one for each Web site you have an account with. Try to control the temptation to use the same password for all your accounts. Some types of account are less secure than others. Unless you are careful to use SSL to connect to sites that require a user name and password to log in, that password may be intercepted by network eavesdroppers. Even if you do use SSL to encrypt the password, there's still a possibility that the Web site is not maintained as securely as you might wish. Unscrupulous individuals who break into the site may steal your password directly from the Web server. I use different passwords for each of the accounts that I care about (my bank account and my LAN account at work) and another password for all the Web subscriptions that I wouldn't be too upset to have someone break into.

You should make it a practice to change your passwords frequently. Change them once every two months at the minimum. The more often you change them, the less likely it is that someone will figure one out and start using it.

1. Connect to VeriSign's Digital ID Center at *http://digitalid.verisign.com/.*
2. Find and select the *Enroll* icon.
3. Find and select the icon corresponding to your browser or e-mailer.
4. You will be presented with a page that gives you a choice between a free six-month trial certificate, a full-service Class 1 certificate, or a full-service Class 2 certificate. Choose the one you prefer.
5. You will now see a fill-out form similar to the one shown in Figure 4.5. For Class 1 certificates, your name and e-mail address are required. No verification of your name is done, so you can use a nickname or alias. However, the e-mail address must be correct in order to receive the certificate. For Class 2 certificates, there are several more required fields, including your postal address.

   At the bottom of the Class 1 form are optional attributes that can be included in the certificate. They include your nationality, your birthdate, and your gender. Because this information is sent to remote sites when your browser presents its certificate, it can be used for customizing content—or for generating mailing lists. If you wish, you can choose to suppress the inclusion of your e-mail address in the certificate, something you might want to do if you are concerned about junk e-mail (aka "spam"). However, the e-mail address is required in order to send and receive secure e-mail using S/MIME.
6. Below this form, you will find another set of fields concerned with verification information. For Class 1 certificates, this area contains a single field in which you can enter a challenge phrase. This challenge phrase will be required if you ever need to revoke your certificate. For Class 2 certificates, there are other fields in addition to the challenge phrase. You are requested to provide your birth date, driver's license number, social security number, phone number, spouse's and employer's name, and other information that is used to verify your identity through a credit bureau. This information is used for verification only, and is *not* incorporated into the final certificate.
7. Below this is payment information, with fields for your credit card number, expiration date, and billing address. Fill this in if you are requesting a full, nontrial certificate.
8. Last, you are required to read VeriSign's certification practice statement, which you can read online or download as a Microsoft Word file (one megabyte) or Adobe Acrobat file (600K). By requesting the certificate, you agree to the terms of the agreement. This long, densely legal document sets out your rights and obligations as a VeriSign certificate holder. Among other obligations, you agree to keep your certificate's private key safe from disclosure.
9. If you agree to the terms, press the "Accept" button.

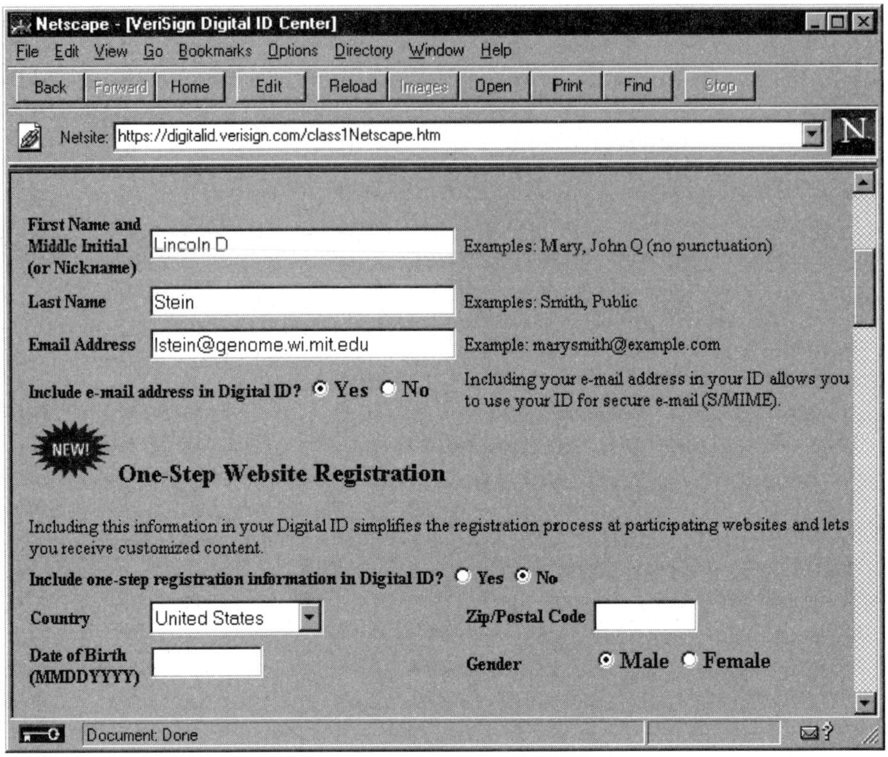

FIGURE 4.5 Applying for a VeriSign personal certificate involves filling out a form with your name and e-mail address.

10. VeriSign will now send your browser an HTML page containing certain tags that cause it to generate a public/private key pair and the certificate request (see Chapter 11). While this is going on, both the Netscape and Microsoft browsers display dialog boxes explaining what they're doing and warning you to keep the private key secret. Netscape's dialog is shown in Figure 4.6. Internet Explorer's dialog is less laden with jargon, but it says much the same.

    After reading the dialog, press "OK."

11. If you are using Netscape, the browser will now ask you to provide a password. This password is used to encrypt the private key before storing it to a file on your computer's hard disk. Because it is encrypted, the private key cannot be stolen by someone with access to your machine. You will need this password in order to unlock the private key and use the certificate, so don't forget it. The password should be different from the challenge phrase entered in step 6 because, unlike the challenge phrase, which is shared with VeriSign, the password is your personal secret. Internet

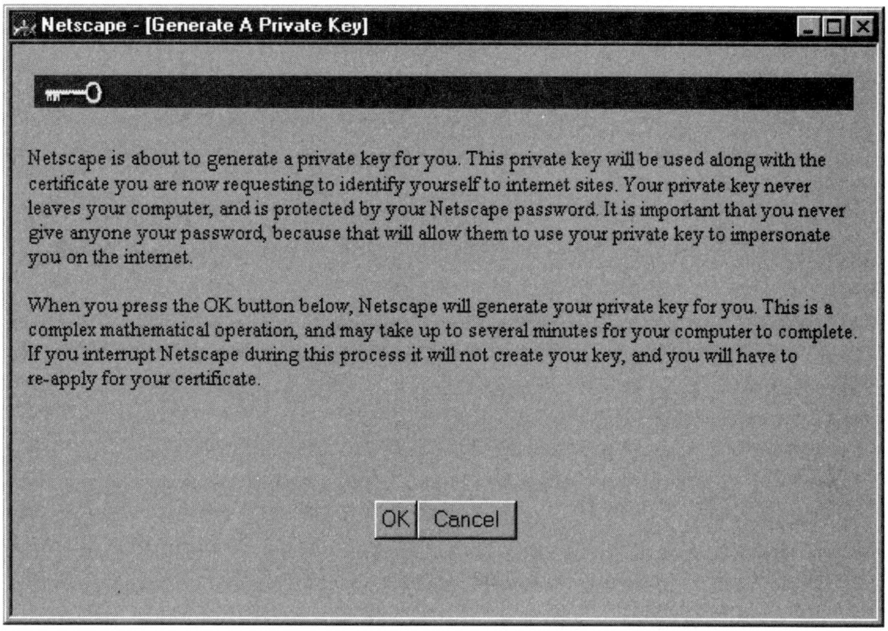

FIGURE 4.6 When Netscape generates a public/private key pair, it displays this message.

Explorer skips this step, as it stores the private key encrypted with your system login password.

12. At this point, if you are using Internet Explorer, the browser prompts you to choose a nickname for the certificate. This name has no particular significance except as a simple way to keep track of multiple certificates. Netscape browsers skip this step but give you a chance to change the name of the certificate when you install it (see below).
13. If all goes well, VeriSign will display a confirmation page. Now you wait. When the signed certificate is ready, VeriSign will send you information for downloading the certificate. This information consists of a URL and a PIN. For Class 1 certificates, the information is sent via e-mail message within minutes of completing the application. For Class 2 certificates, the information will arrive in a postal letter delivered after VeriSign completes its credit bureau check (days to weeks).
14. After receiving the URL and PIN, you will retrieve and install the signed certificate. Using the *same computer and browser* that you used to request the certificate, connect to the URL provided in the message. Type in the PIN and press "Submit."

15. VeriSign will send you the signed certificate in a format recognized by the browser. The browser will now launch a wizard that leads you through the process of installing the certificate. You can review the certificate and, in Netscape browsers, give it a name. The name has no particular significance other than to give you a simple way to keep track of multiple certificates. When you reach the last page of the wizard, press "Finish" to install the certificate.
16. The browser will display a final dialog box confirming that the certificate has been installed.

You can review your personal certificate(s) at any time by selecting *Options->Security Preferences->Personal Certificates* (Netscape), or *View->Options->Security->Personal Certificates* (Internet Explorer). As with CA certificates, you can view them, activate and deactivate them, and remove them entirely.

Once a personal certificate is installed on your browser, a remote server may request it whenever the browser initiates an SSL connection. If you have only one certificate installed, the browser will quietly return it without bothering you. If you have more than one certificate installed, which can happen if you have both a public certificate from VeriSign and a private one from your employer, there is the issue of which certificate the browser will present when asked.

In Netscape, the personal certificate preferences page allows you to choose whether the browser will always use a particular certificate, try to guess automatically, or to ask you to choose the certificate to present each time one is required. I recommend that you choose the last option, at least at the beginning. This way, you will be alerted whenever a site requests a certificate. Internet Explorer always chooses the certificate to use automatically.

Maintaining a Personal Certificate

VeriSign's Digital ID Center has a number of options in addition to the enrollment one. The options are available in a navigation bar at the top of *http://digitalid.verisign.com/*. You can

1. **Revoke your certificate.** You will want to do this if you think your private key has been compromised. The revocation process requires your certificate's serial number and the challenge phrase from step 6. You can find the serial number by viewing the certificate in your browser or by searching for your e-mail address in VeriSign's certificate database (see below). A small annoyance is that the serial number displayed by Netscape is a 32-digit hexadecimal number with colons inserted between each pair of digits. You must remove the colons before entering the serial number in VeriSign's pages.

2. **Renew an expiring certificate.** Serial number and challenge phrase are again required.
3. **Request a replacement certificate.** You will want to do this after revoking a certificate. It is essentially a repeat of the original application procedure.
4. **Find someone's certificate in VeriSign's database.** You can search by name, e-mail address,or certificate serial number. When you find the person you want, you can install their certificate on your browser for the purpose of sending secure e-mail via S/MIME.

One of the hassles of personal certificates is that they are difficult to transport from one machine to another. In some cases, you can move a certificate from one machine to another by copying the files that contain the certificate and its private key. For Netscape Navigator, certificates and public/private key pairs are kept in a series of configuration files with names like *cert5.db*, *cert7.db*, and *key.db*. On Windows 95 systems, these files can be found in *C:\Program Files\Netscape\Navigator*. The files live in different locations on Windows NT, UNIX, and Macintosh systems and are not guaranteed to be in the same places in different browser versions. You'll need to do some detective work. Once you identify the key files, copy them to the corresponding directory on the target machine. While you're at it, copy the files to a floppy and store it in a safe place. This will enable you to restore your digital ID in case of a disk crash.

There appears to be no way to copy or back up a personal certificate from Microsoft Internet Explorer (through version 4.0 beta 1). The certificate and key information are kept in the system registry, and no documentation describes how to safely move this information to a new machine. However, you can and should back up the certificate by the simple expedient of backing up the entire machine. Hopefully, future versions of browser software will provide some mechanism for copying the certificate and its private key to a floppy for transport and backup purposes.

When upgrading browser software, use the upgrade option in the vendor's installation program. If you delete the old version before installing the new one, your certificate may be lost. If you have a backup, you may be able to restore it. Otherwise, you'll have to revoke the old one and request a replacement. I know of no way to move a personal certificate from a Netscape browser to a Microsoft browser or vice versa.

Browser SSL Settings

You've already seen how to view the encryption status of a page and to review personal and site certificates. Here are other relevant settings as they appear in Netscape Navigator 3.02 and Microsoft Internet Explorer 4.0.

Because new features are being added to browsers at a breathless pace, the details may be slightly different by the time you read this.

Microsoft Internet Explorer

To adjust Internet Explorer's SSL-related settings, choose the *View->Options...* menu command to bring up the Options window (Figure 4.7). Select the tab labeled *Advanced* to view 30 or so checkboxes that turn various options on

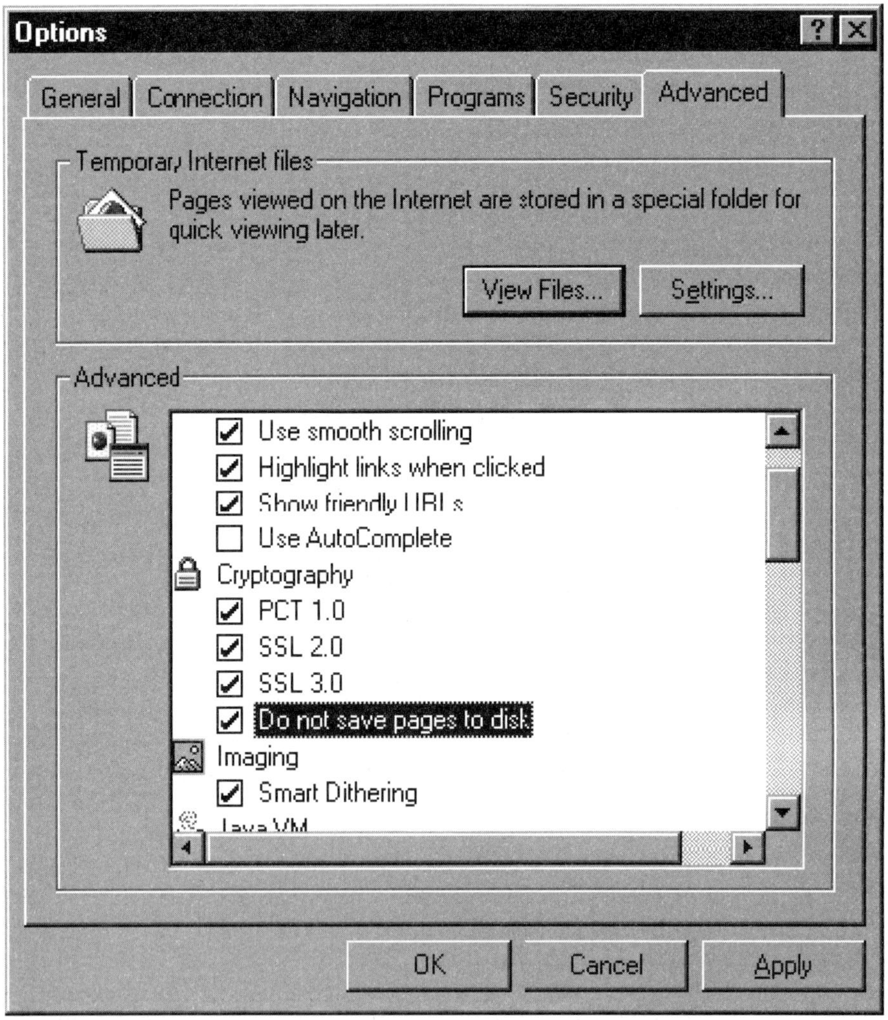

FIGURE 4.7 Internet Explorer's SSL settings can be found under *View->Options-> Advanced.*

and off. Oddly, most SSL-specific settings are not located on the Security page, which is concerned with active content and other issues.

Among options dealing with scrolling rate and the way images are dithered are the following SSL-related settings.

Under the heading *Cryptography,* there are

☐ PCT 1.0
☐ SSL 2.0
☐ SSL 3.0
☐ Do not save pages to disk

These four checkboxes control which cryptographic protocols to use. PCT is the cryptographic protocol that Microsoft briefly pushed as an alternative to SSL and later withdrew. It is still offered for backward compatibility with certain corporate intranets. The SSL 2.0 and SSL 3.0 checkboxes, if selected, will enable these two versions of SSL. Unless you are running in a corporate environment that dictates that only one protocol should be used, all three of these protocols can safely be selected.

The final checkbox controls whether Web documents retrieved via SSL or PCT should be cached to disk among the other documents. Selecting this checkbox will speed the perceived performance of SSL-using sites. However, it also opens the possibility that a confidential document might be compromised if someone gains physical or networked access to your machine. If in doubt, leave the option disabled.

Under the heading *Warnings,* there are

☐ Warn about invalid site certificates
☐ Warn if changing between secure and unsecure mode
☐ Warn before sending over an open connection
  ○ Only when I'm sending more than one line
  ○ Always
  ○ Never

The first checkbox, if selected, will present a warning if a Web site presents a server certificate that has expired, doesn't match its domain name, or has been signed by an unrecognized certifying authority. This option should always be turned on.

The second checkbox controls whether the browser will display an alert when you move between an SSL connection and a non-SSL connection. Because IE ordinarily indicates the presence of an SSL connection with the most subtle of clues, you may wish to activate this option. Unfortunately, the warnings get annoying rapidly.

The last option is a set of three radio buttons that control how Internet Explorer treats an attempt to use an unencrypted connection to send information submitted via a fill-out form. Because the SSL protocol was developed in part to avoid the possibility of personal information being intercepted from forms, it makes sense to warn if it's not in use. The problem is that if the browser warns every time a fill-out form is submitted insecurely, it will generate annoyance messages for such banal submissions as keyword searches and guestbooks. The first alternative attempts to minimize the noise problem by warning only if the submitted form contains more than one line of text, the assumption being that longer fill-out forms are more likely to contain personal information than ones containing a single line. The second alternative warns every time a fill-out form is submitted, regardless of its length. The last alternative turns off the warnings completely.

Netscape Navigator

Most of the relevant settings are found under *Options->Security Preferences* (Figure 4.8). In addition to the personal certificate and sitecertificates sections that you have seen before, this window contains two other tabbed pages labeled General and Passwords.

In the General section, there are four checkboxes to control the warning boxes that appear whenever the status of an SSL connection changes. Unfortunately, the warnings are annoying and tend to increase the noise level in the user interface. Whether they actually help avoid security problems is unclear.

Show an Alert Before:

- **Entering a secure document space (server)**
  A warning box will appear when you jump from a conventional Web page to one that uses the SSL protocol. Because SSL connections are still relatively rare on the Internet, turning this warning on will not usually increase the noise level. However, it adds little additional information to the "solid key" icon and the solid blue bar that appear when SSL is active.
- **Leaving a secure document space (server)**
  A warning box will appear whenever you leave a Web page protected by SSL to retrieve an unencrypted page. Turning this option on will add little to the noise level and may help avoid situations in which you mistakenly believe you are still working in an encrypted environment.
- **Viewing a document with a secure/insecure mix**
  Netscape will warn if you view a page that contains some elements that are encrypted and others that are not, such as inline images or applets. These situations are rare, so turning it on will not add to the noise level. However, it is hard to know what to do when the warning does appear. Is this type of page a security risk?
- **Submitting a form insecurely**
  Netscape will warn before submitting a fill-out form without using SSL. This is the most useful of the warnings because it alerts you whenever

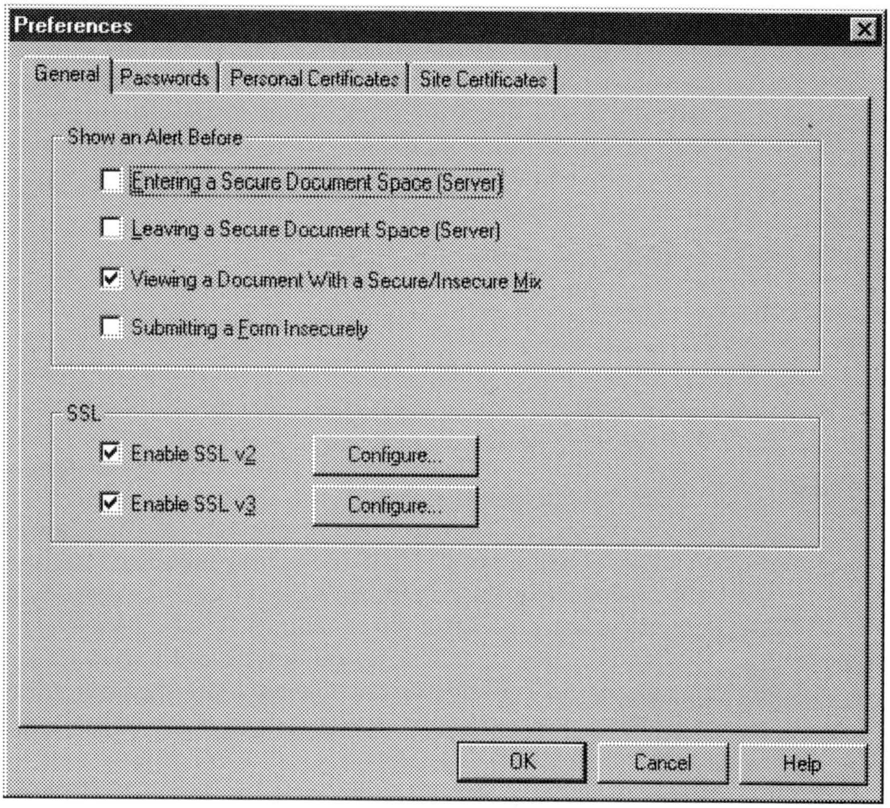

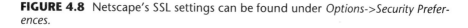

FIGURE 4.8 Netscape's SSL settings can be found under *Options->Security Preferences.*

you send potentially confidential information across the network in unencrypted form. Unfortunately, it greatly increases the noise level. In addition to appearing before you submit your credit card number, the warning window appears for such humdrum things as keyword searches, user feedback forms, and guestbooks. Most users turn the warning off.

At the bottom of the General window are settings that control the SSL protocol itself. Two checkboxes enable SSL 2.0 and 3.0. To communicate with the largest number of servers, you will wish for both SSL versions to be enabled. Adjacent to the checkboxes are buttons labeled "Configure," which allow you to fine-tune the SSL protocols. Pressing either button raises a window that allows you to view and selectively enable and disable the cipher suites used by SSL. Unless you know what you are doing, you should leave the settings at their defaults. See Chapter 2 for a description of cipher suites.

The Passwords page of the Security Options window controls the password used to encrypt the private keys of personal certificates. If you have a personal certificate and your computer is not physically and electronically secure, it is wise to use such a password. Otherwise, an individual could steal your private key and impersonate you. This page allows you to change your encryption password and adjusts how frequently Netscape will ask for the password. Options include

1. Once, when the browser is first launched
2. Every time a personal certificate is needed
3. After some user-adjustable period of inactivity

If you are in the habit of leaving your computer running unattended with a browser window open, the second and third options are prudent. The password-changing options allow you to remove the password entirely if you wish. In this circumstance, the private key will no longer be encrypted.

One more Netscape option that is relevant to SSL is found in *Options ->Network Settings* under the *Caching* tab. A checkbox labeled "Allow Persistent Caching of Pages Retrieved through SSL" controls whether Web documents retrieved via SSL are cached locally on disk. By default, this setting is turned off. Turning it on allows Web pages viewed with SSL to be saved to the document cache, along with ordinary pages, opening up the possibility that confidential documents could be compromised if an individual gains physical or network access to your machine.

In Navigator version 4.0, all SSL settings have been reorganized into a new window. Press the "Security" button in the toolbar to display and edit the settings. Except for this reshuffling, the various SSL options are unchanged in 4.0. The one exception to this is the ability to control whether encrypted pages are cached to disk, which seems to have vanished in 4.0. Presumably, encrypted pages are never stored to disk in this version of Navigator.

Checklist

1. Do you use a Web browser that supports the SSL protocol when viewing or submitting confidential information?

   ❍ No

   ❍ No, but my browser is protected by the company's firewall

   ❍ No, but I only browse my company's intranet server, although sometimes I do so from home

   ☑ Yes

   ❍ No, but I only browse my company's intranet server from within the local area network

If there is any stretch of untrusted network between your browser and the Web server, there is a possibility that the information passing either way could be sniffed. This is true whenever the connection passes across the Internet, even if one end or the other is protected by a firewall system. If both ends of the connection are within the local area connection, it can't be sniffed by an outsider; however, there is still no protection against a nosy coworker or an intruder with physical access to the local network. If SSL is in use, the connection is secure against eavesdropping even if it passes across the Internet.

2. Do you view or submit extremely confidential information using a browser with crippled export-grade cryptography?

   ☑ No

   ❍ Yes

   Web browsers designed for export are crippled so that they can use encryption keys no longer than 40 bits. If the information being transmitted has only modest value, such as a credit card number, no one will invest the effort to crack it. However, if the information is valuable, 40-bit encryption will not discourage a determined eavesdropper. Users in the United States and Canada should obtain the shrink-wrapped versions of the software. Overseas users should consider using an encrypting proxy, such as Safe Passage.

3. Do you password-protect your personal certificate(s)?

   ❍ No

   ☑ Yes

   Although not widely used at the time this chapter was written, personal certificates (digital ID's) will become an important way to verify identities on the Internet. To avoid having your identity "stolen" by someone with physical or network access to your personal computer, you should encrypt it with a hard-to-guess password.

4. Have you ever accepted a CA certificate offered by an unknown Web site?

   ☑ No

   ❍ Yes

   Although this is unusual, a Web site may attempt to offer you a new certifying authority certificate. If you accept it, the browser will extend trust to all sites signed by that authority. Unless you know for a fact that you trust the new CA (for example, it's an authority run by your own company to control access to its intranet servers) you should refuse this type of offer. Table 4.1 lists CAs that Netscape Navigator is preconfigured to recognize. You may wish to check the CA certificates installed in your browser against this list and delete any that you don't recognize.

5. Have you backed up your personal certificate(s), if you have any?

   ❍ No

   ✓ Yes

   If you use a personal certificate for identification or to send and receive secure e-mail, you should back it up to prevent loss in case of a disk crash or inadvertent deletion. With the Netscape browsers, you can simply copy the certificate database files. With Internet Explorer, the certificate is stored in the system registry and the most direct way to back it up is to back up the entire disk (a good idea in any case).

Online Resources

VeriSign

http://www.verisign.com/

Safe Passage

http://www.c2.net/ (United States and Canada)
http://www.stronghold.ukweb.com/ (Overseas)

PGP

http://www.pgp.com/

RSA Data Security's listing of S/MIME e-mail software

http://www.rsa.com/rsa/S-MIME/

Simple Perl-based packet sniffer

http://www.genome.wi.mit.edu/~lstein/talks/WWW6/sniffer/

Tcpdump and libpcap (required for sniffer)

ftp://ftp.ee.lbl.gov/tcpdump.tar.Z
ftp://ftp.ee.lbl.gov/libpcap.tar.Z

Printed Resources

Garfinkel, Simson, *Pretty Good Privacy* (O'Reilly & Associates, 1995).

A reference guide for the popular PGP program for securing e-mail. In addition to explaining how to use the software, this book is a good general introduction to encryption systems and a good source for information on the politics of strong cryptography.

Chapter 5

Active Content

Web browsers have the capacity to download and execute software automatically without warning. All one needs do is look at a page. In many cases, you may not even know that something special has happened; the software just adds a subtle touch here and there to enhance the behavior and appearance of the page. This capacity is broadly known as "active content."

Because of active content, life for users and network administrators has become more interesting. Users who would ordinarily be reluctant to download software from an FTP site think nothing of surfing to sites they've never heard of. Unbeknownst to them, the site may choose to run untrusted software on their machines via active content. If the software is buggy, it may crash the browser. If the software is written with malicious intent, it may try to damage the user's system or violate her privacy. From the network administrator's point of view, active content is of concern because it can be used to circumvent a firewall system or to seed viruses throughout the computers on the LAN.

This chapter talks about active content: the traditional kind, as well as the newer, exotic varieties. We'll take a realistic look at the risks and talk about what you can do to avoid them.

Bad by Design or Bad by Accident?

It is helpful to distinguish between programs that were designed for the purpose of inflicting harm and those that are well intentioned but contain bugs that can be exploited by others for nefarious ends. Is the bad behavior a "bug" or a "feature"?

Purposefully bad programs get most of the attention. Examples include the external viewer program used for the Moldovan telephone scam (see The Moldovan Connection box) and the Chaos Computer Club's malicious ActiveX control (see ActiveX on pages 100–104). Because purposefully bad programs are often written and distributed by rogue programmers, you can avoid many of them by accepting only software from trusted software developers. For now, we'll leave aside the slippery question of how to determine which software developers to trust.

Despite the press attention devoted to deliberately malicious software, that may not account for the greatest risk to Web surfers. Any piece of software can contain a bug, even one from a well-respected developer. The larger and more featureful a program is, the more likely it is to be buggy, and every bug is a potential security hole. This means that the most capable programs, those that are most likely to be widely installed, are the ones most likely to pose risks. There are already several examples of this phenomenon, including problems with older versions of the Macromedia ShockWave plug-in for Netscape Navigator and the Microsoft PowerPoint viewer for Internet Explorer (both discussed in the next section). If one of the vulnerable versions of these programs is installed on a user's system, the operator of a rogue Web site could exploit it to steal information or to inflict damage on the system.

It is not even unheard of for a reputable software vendor to distribute shrink-wrapped software contaminated with a virus that crept in at some point during the development cycle.

Unfortunately, the distinction between software that is bad by intention and bad by accident is not always as clear as we'd like to think. Is the security hole in a trusted vendor's software an honest mistake or a back door deliberately placed there in case certain contingencies arise? Imagine the following (completely hypothetical) scenario: The MegaComm Corporation designs and distributes an ActiveX control that interfaces to its popular paging systems. The control becomes popular and is widely used in corporate environments. One day someone exploits a back door in the software to steal trade secrets from Intelligenix, MegaComm's arch-rival. Bug or feature?

Traditional Threats

Malicious software has been with us since the early days of electronic bulletin boards. A typical scenario goes like this: A new game sounds enticing, so you download it to your machine and install it. When you run the game, it displays a welcome screen that says "Initializing high scores." A few seconds later, your computer crashes. When you try to boot it up again you discover that the game wasn't initializing the high scores. It was reinitializing

The Moldovan Connection

The biggest Web scam to date came to light in early 1997, when it was discovered that thousands of Internet users had been swindled into making expensive long distance telephone calls to Moldova. The scam worked like this:

1. Internet users in search of pornography stumbled across one of two promising Web sites called sexygirls.com and erotic2000.com.
2. In order to view the pornography, the Web site instructed users to download a special external viewer application, a Windows 95 program called david7.exe.
3. When users downloaded and ran the viewer, the program disconnected the users' computer's modems from their own ISP's, turned off the speakers, and reconnected them to the Internet via an ISP located in Moldova.
4. Users were then taken to an adult site where they could view the pornography—while paying for an expensive long distance telephone call.
5. Even after users left the site, they continued to be connected long distance to the Moldovan ISP at a rate of $2 per minute.

The scam made money for the Moldovan ISP because the number was equivalent to a U.S. pay-per-minute 900 number. The rest of the long distance fees were split between the user's long distance carrier and the Moldovan phone company.

Several thousand people in the United States and Canada fell victim to this scam before it was shut down, with phone bills ranging from $4 to $4,400. This scam is similar in many ways to more-traditional schemes that entice unwary users to dial long distance 900 or 809 numbers. The main novelty is its sophisticated use of the Internet.

your hard disk. This type of program is called a Trojan horse. It is only one of a whole bestiary of malicious programs.

Trojan horses The most basic of mischief-makers, the Trojan horse fools you into running it by pretending to be something it's not. Trojans are often used as vehicles to introduce viruses, worms, and other beasts into a user's computer.

Viruses Viruses are small bits of computer code that have the ability to replicate themselves and insert themselves into an executable program, a file, a floppy disk, or a portion of the hard disk. Once infected with a virus, a program itself becomes infectious. The virus can spread to other files or to other computers on the network via file sharing.

Macro viruses Macro viruses are viruses written in the macro language of a word processor, spreadsheet, or other application and make their home in whatever type of document the application produces. This makes them infectious across any operating system that the application runs on.

Rabbits These are programs that, when launched, make many copies of themselves. They can copy themselves in memory, filling up RAM and perhaps crashing the computer, or they can fill up hard disk space. Unlike viruses, rabbits do not attach themselves to existing files. However, they may attempt to camouflage themselves by assuming an innocent name or by turning on a hidden file-listing attribute.

Worms These are similar to rabbits, but they are capable of spreading from one machine to another across the network by exploiting loopholes in Internet protocols.

Viruses must be fun to write because there are many thousands of distinct species and new ones are appearing constantly. Most of the new species are existing viruses that have been captured, improved, and rereleased by programmers who are anxious to make their mark on the world.

Helper Applications and Plug-Ins

Helper applications and plug-ins are launched by browsers to display documents with specialized MIME types that the browser cannot display directly, such as streaming audio files, animations, database applications, and VRML files. Helper applications, also known as "external viewers," are full-fledged applications that can be run independently of the browser. They create their own windows, process their own menu commands, and interact directly with the mouse and keyboard. Any program can be a helper application, including programs like the Windows Notepad that weren't specifically designed for the purpose.

Plug-ins, in contrast, are small code libraries that can execute only in the context of a browser session. The browser does much of the dirty work for the plug-in, which is typically responsible only for drawing its processed data into the browser window. Plug-ins are generally written by third-party vendors to give the browser access to a vendor-specific document type. For example, the Macromedia Company distributes a plug-in called Shockwave that gives Netscape browsers the ability to display Macromedia Director animations.

You install plug-ins by downloading the code and running its Install program. During installation, the plug-in library is copied into a designated directory and the browser is alerted to its existence. Plug-ins are a Netscape invention. Although Internet Explorer can run Netscape plug-ins, they are deprecated in favor of ActiveX controls, a topic we'll visit later.

To see what helper applications are installed in your system, choose *Options->General->Helpers* in Netscape Navigator, or choose *View->Options ->Programs->File Types...* in Microsoft Internet Explorer. You will be present-

Cross-Platform Viruses: The New Plague?

In the natural world, biological variability prevents every new germ from becoming a plague that will wipe out a species. No two individuals are entirely alike. Some are susceptible to a disease; others are resistant. The disease spreads through the population, attacking the susceptible ones. The resistant ones, however, live on to perpetuate the species.

In the software world, the differences among operating systems are roughly equivalent to biological variability. The virus that is lethal to Windows machines can't harm a hair on a Macintosh's chin. This heterogeneity has helped to prevent the unrestricted spread of viruses across the Internet.

This is changing. As today's personal computers transform themselves into "network computers," there is an imperative to have machines of all makes and models run the same programs without modification. The most likely source of this great cross-platform equalizer is Sun Microsystem's Java. The major software vendors are now moving to incorporate Java interpreters into the next generation of operating systems, enabling Java programs to run on any machine connected to the Internet.

If Java programs can run on all computers, so can Java viruses. Java viruses don't exist yet, but it's only a matter of time before they make their appearance. A Java virus will be able to spread from machine to machine across the Internet unimpeded by small details like operating system and hardware type. This is similar, but even more threatening, to the cross-platform Microsoft Word macro viruses, which spread easily from Windows machines to Macintoshes concealed in Word document files.

Get out your virus checkers, here they come!

ed with a long table of MIME types and the helper applications used to view them. You can add new MIME types or change the applications associated with them. You can also get information about plug-ins by choosing *Help ->About Plugins* from Netscape Navigator's menu bar.

Despite their differences, both helper applications and plug-ins are similar from a security standpoint. They are pieces of native computer code that have complete access to your computer's disk and other resources. A buggy viewer or plug-in can crash your computer. A viewer or plug-in written with malicious intent can ruin your day.

Fortunately, both helper applications and plug-ins require manual intervention to install. If you attempt to view a document type that has no viewer or plug-in configured, the browser will complain. You will need to track down the appropriate viewer or plug-in and go through several steps to download and install it. The process makes it abundantly clear that viewers and plug-ins are foreign pieces of software. Cautious users will think twice before installing a plug-in found on some random Internet site, and the annoyance of installing a new plug-in discourages other users from doing it frequently.

A viewer or plug-in written with the best of intentions is not guaranteed to be safe. Plug-ins, in particular, have a well-deserved reputation for bugs that cause browser crashes and hangs. Most of these problems are small annoyances, but some can be more sinister. Both viewers and plug-ins may contain viruses just like any other software. A viewer may be inadvertently infected while it's still with the developers, or a virus-infected viewer may be deliberately uploaded to the Internet by an unscrupulous individual.

Another thing to watch out for is external viewers that contain command interpreters. Even if the viewer itself is bug-free, the risk is that some malicious individual will create a set of commands that, when interpreted by the viewer, cause it to behave badly. When does an application contain a command interpreter? Sometimes it's pretty obvious. The DOS *command.com* program, used to process *.BAT* files, is definitely a command interpreter. Do not configure a browser to use *command.com* as the helper application for a DOS batch file. A one-line file could easily erase your hard disk. For similar reasons, avoid using the Perl interpreter as a viewer for Perl scripts, or the BASIC interpreter as a BASIC source code viewer. On UNIX systems, eschew the various command shells, such as *sh*, *csh*, and *ksh*.

In other cases, identifying programs that contain command interpreters can be more difficult. As a general rule, anything that contains a macro processor is probably dangerous. Both Microsoft Word and Excel contain macro processors that run automatically when the program is asked to open certain documents. These macro facilities can be abused by technically knowledgeable pranksters. UNIX users should avoid using the Emacs text editor as an external viewer.

Any program that can launch external applications is also at risk. For example, Microsoft PowerPoint has a feature that allows it to run applications from within presentations. By enticing Internet users to view a presentation that invokes Windows commands, an unscrupulous Web author can inflict damage on any user who has innocently configured her browser to use PowerPoint as a viewer. Instead, if available, use the stripped-down document viewers that Microsoft and other vendors provide for those who haven't purchased the full product. In these versions, the command interpreters are often disabled. Check the viewer's documentation to be sure.

Even if you use a stripped-down viewer application, you may not be entirely safe. Prior to a fix released on March 19, 1997, the Shockwave plug-in for Netscape Navigator, which allows browsers to display Macromedia Director movies, could be tricked into uploading local files from the user's hard disk onto a remote server, leafing through the user's e-mail, or accessing an internal Web site protected by the corporate firewall system. The immediate cause of these security holes was Shockwave's ability to read and write files on the user's hard disk, coupled with an obscure bug in the interaction between Shockwave and Navigator. The fundamental cause, however is the essential way that Shockwave works: It receives a stream of commands from a remote site and acts on them. In other words, it contains a command interpreter.

The best advice that I can offer is to keep the number of installed viewers and plug-ins to the bare minimum. Use plug-ins from software developers you trust. Even then, be sure to check the vendor's support pages on a regular basis, before you're taken by surprise by a known security hole.

Java

The much-hyped Java is a programming language invented by Sun Microsystems for use in embedded systems and later adapted for use on the Web. Its main claim to fame is its interpreted nature. A single Java program can run on any computer that has a Java interpreter installed, which is in contrast to compiled languages like C, which must be recompiled for each combination of computer hardware and operating system. Both Internet Explorer and the Netscape browsers come with a Java interpreter built in, and many operating system vendors are now moving to make Java interpreters a standard part of their systems.

Strictly speaking, Java is partially compiled. Java source code, contained in files with a *.java* suffix, is compiled into a compact byte code contained within *.class* files. These files can then be packaged and stored in a compressed form in *.jar* (Java archive) files. It is the intermediate byte code rather than the original source code that is recognized and executed by the Java interpreter.

Developers like Java because of its cross-platform nature. A single Java program will run without modification a large number of operating systems, including Windows, Macintosh, and a variety of UNIX systems. They also like it because it dispenses with many of the technical hassles that make programming difficult and programs unreliable. Java manages memory dynamically, allocating and deallocating blocks of memory as needed. This prevents the single major class of programming error. Java gives programmers no access to physical memory or to memory pointers, avoiding many traps for the unwary. And because Java is a strongly typed language, it catches errors that result from typographical errors and general sloppiness.

Java is a "safe" programming language because it prevents many errors that can lead to crashes or inadvertent security holes. But safe languages are not necessarily secure ones. To the credit of Java's developers, they also thought carefully about Java's security before releasing the language to the world. Java programs run in two modes: an "application" mode similar to the way that full-blown stand-alone applications run, and an "applet" mode, in which Java objects are downloaded from a Web site and execute in the context of a Web browser. To incorporate an applet into an HTML page, Web authors add an <APPLET> tag to their pages. A typical <APPLET> tag looks something like this

```
<APPLET CODE="example_applet"
          CODEBASE="http://www.capricorn.org/java/"
          WIDTH=500 HEIGHT=100>
<PARAM NAME="image" VALUE="example.gif">
<PARAM NAME="color" VALUE="blue">
</APPLET>
```

The <APPLET> tag contains attributes that tell the browser the applet's name ("example_applet" in this case), where to find it (at the URL *http://www.capricorn.org/java/* in the file *example_applet.class*), and what its size requirements are. Notice that, like inline images, the applet's code doesn't have to reside on the same server as the HTML page that refers to it. A series of <PARAM> tags pass runtime information to the applet, allowing its behavior to be customized. The running applet can also be controlled on the fly by using JavaScript (see below).

When the browser sees an <APPLET> tag, it fetches the *.class* or *.jar* file from the location indicated, starts the Java interpreter, and executes the applet. The applet is then free to load other class files that it needs to run, each of which must reside on the same server that the applet was downloaded from. The applet typically appears as an interactive inline image in the browser window. It can perform animations, play sounds, and respond to mouse clicks and keyboard input. It can also create its own windows and menu bars. In current browser implementations, applet windows are clearly marked as belonging to the applet rather than to the operating system—they display a prominent label that says either "Untrusted Java window" or "Unsigned applet window," depending on the interpreter.

The security implications of Java applications and Java applets are quite different. When running in application mode, Java programs have all the rights and privileges of any other program on the system. They can read and write files, send data to the printer, open up network connections, and so on. In contrast, when Java programs run as applets, they are limited to something Sun calls the "sandbox." In Java's original incarnation, sandbox restrictions were strict.

1. Applets cannot read from or write to the local disk.
2. Applets cannot access physical hardware such as memory, disk drives, or the drivers that control keyboard, printer, and screen.
3. Applets cannot access system environment information, including information that would help them determine what operating system they're on.
4. Applets cannot invoke system commands or run external programs.

5. Applets cannot open network connections to any machine except the one they were originally downloaded from (the so-called phone-home restriction).

Together, these sandbox restrictions lock Java applets into an opaque bubble. Having no access to any of the resources on the local machine, they are incapable of peeking at any private data, let alone modifying it. The phone-home restriction allows them to open a network connection to databases and to other types of servers on the machine that they were downloaded from, but they are not allowed to make network connections to any machine on your local area network or on the Internet at large.

This security model is enforced in two ways. First, a Java class called the "security manager" oversees all security-sensitive system calls. If a piece of Java code attempts to make a call that violates the applet security policy, the security manager raises an exception that causes the applet to abort. (You may occasionally see buggy applets crash with a security exception—this doesn't necessarily mean that they were written with evil intentions.)

Second, the Java interpreter incorporates a package called the "bytecode verifier," which is responsible for examining Java programs as they are downloaded from the remote site. The verifier confirms that the program was generated by a Java compiler and follows the rules and restrictions of the Java language. This is to prevent a programmer with an intimate knowledge of Java internals from hand-crafting an applet that bypasses the security manager.

Hostile Applets

In principle, Java applets are secure. In practice, Java's good name has been marred by a series of well-publicized implementation bugs that allowed its security restrictions to be bypassed. Many of these bugs were discovered by Edward Felten's computer security research group at Princeton University.

1. **Failure of the phone-home restriction.** The earliest bug to attract attention was a failure in Java's restrictions on network connections. In March 1996, Steve Gibbons and Edward Felten independently discovered that by temporarily subverting the domain-name system (something a technically sophisticated hacker can do), a malicious individual could circumvent the network connection restriction and send out a hostile applet that could contact any machine on the Internet, including one on the user's side of the corporate firewall. This bug was identified in Netscape Navigator 2.0 and reportedly fixed in 2.01 and later versions.
2. **Ability to execute arbitrary machine instructions.** Java applets are not supposed to be able to execute unchecked machine code, but a bug in the way the Java interpreter loads machine-specific code libraries allowed

remote users to circumvent this restriction. The attacker first tricks the browser into downloading a code library (disguising it as a "broken" inline image, for example). This places the library in the browser cache. The attacker than sends the unsuspecting user an applet that loads this code. Because the library code is not restricted by the security manager, the applet has broken out of the sandbox and can do whatever it wishes. This bug, discovered in March 1996 by Edward Felten, was present in versions 2.0 and 2.01 of Netscape Navigator and fixed in versions 2.02 and later.

3. **Ability to bypass the Java security manager with hand-crafted bytecode.** In March 1997, an internal security audit at Sun revealed a bug in the Java bytecode verifier. By carefully hand-crafting Java bytecode, a programmer with extensive knowledge of Java internals could bypass the Java security manager completely and execute forbidden commands. The bug is present in Microsoft Internet Explorer 3.01 and in Netscape Navigator 3.01. It is fixed in later versions.

Just as this book went to press, it was discovered that yet another bug in the Java implementation of the phone-home restriction allowed Java applets to make network connections to machines located behind corporate firewall systems. This hole, affecting Netscape Navigator 3.02 and 4.01, had not been fixed at press time. It is not known whether any versions of Internet Explorer are also affected by this bug.

It is important to realize that *none* of these bugs has been known to be used for actual attacks on users. They are all theoretical exploits, most of which have been closed in recent iterations of Java interpreters. Although it is possible that security holes remain in some Java implementations, the security model itself seems sound.

Annoying Applets

While there are no true hostile applets out there, there are plenty of annoying ones. If you wander around the Internet, you might even encounter some. Java applets can launch a variety of irritating denial-of-service attacks against your Web browser and even against your desktop machine.

1. An applet can enter an infinite loop, chewing up CPU cycles and slowing your machine down to a crawl.
2. An applet can allocate a large memory structure or make multiple copies of itself in memory. Like the CPU-hogging attack, this can dramatically slow the response of the system.
3. An applet can open up a window larger than the desktop, preventing you from getting at windows underneath. Or an applet can open new windows more rapidly than you can close them.

4. Applets can perform windowing operations that will crash the browser. This usually happens accidentally as the result of interactions between bugs in the applet and bugs in the Java window toolkit, but it can be made to happen deliberately. (A scrolling text applet on VeriSign's home page makes my browser crash repeatedly. Are they trying to send me a message?)

Browsers currently provide no way to interrupt a running applet. Closing the page may not shut it down, and the denial-of-service attack may make the browser unresponsive to menu commands. You may be forced to quit the browser using a magic key combination (for instance, Option-Command-Escape on the Macintosh), or you might even have to reboot the computer.

In addition to these problems, two applets that are executing at the same time on one browser are not protected from one another. One can detect the other's existence and send it messages. This raises the amusing (but entirely theoretical) possibility that one vendor's applet could deliberately interfere with a competitor's applet in order to make it appear to be behaving erratically.

Inadequate Applets

A more fundamental problem with Java applets is imposed by the sandbox model itself. Because applets are sealed off from the local machine, there are many potentially useful functions that they cannot accomplish, including printing, saving user preferences to disk, converting file formats, and sending a file's contents across the network. In preventing applets from doing anything bad, the sandbox prevents them from doing many good things as well. Although this may work well in a future world of diskless network computers, it's not practical in the current personal computer environment. As a result, Java applets remain, by and large, amusing animations and useless demos.

To address this problem, vendors are modifying the Java security model. Future Java applets will be able to step outside the sandbox in a controlled manner. You will be able to grant the applets of your choice the ability to read and write files in selected directories, access the printer, and make certain network connections.

A key feature of the new Java security model is code signing, similar to the Authenticode system used by ActiveX (see below). Applets that need additional privileges can be cryptographically signed by software publishers in much the way that server certificates are signed by CAs. The fact that the applet is signed makes the publisher accountable for its actions. You may then use certificates as the basis for deciding which applets should have extended access to your system. For example, you might grant additional privileges to all applets signed by software publishers, or you might choose to give capabilities only to those that are signed by a small number of publishers you trust.

At the time this was written, the three major players in the field, Sun, Microsoft and Netscape, all seemed to be creating slightly different dialects of this new Java security model. Sun's proposal, called Java Protected Domains, features a system in which signed applets are by default granted read/write access to a particular directory set aside for them on the file system. On a case-by-case basis, determined by their certificates and the domain names of their home machines, applets can also be given additional access to network resources. Netscape's system, in contrast, has applets making requests for additional privileges at run time and an enhanced security manager granting or denying their requests on a case-by-case basis; additional privileges can include read/write access to files, devices and network resources. Finally, Microsoft's approach, expected to be incorporated into Internet Explorer 4.0, has each applet declare what access privileges it needs within the certificate itself; by examining the certificate the browser can decide whether to run the applet.

Until the new Java security model is available, your options are limited. You can choose to allow the browser to run Java applets... or not. Ask yourself if you really need Java applets for your work or to enjoy the Web to its fullest. If the answer is no, then the most conservative course is to disable the Java interpreter.

ActiveX

Microsoft's ActiveX is a different story from Java. Unlike Java, which is a new programming language designed from the bottom up to be suitable for Web applications, ActiveX is a repackaging of existing technologies. ActiveX is, in fact, a stripped-down version of Microsoft's OLE (object linking and embedding) architecture, a highly successful system that allows multiple Windows programs to interact, exchange data, and share each others' windows.

Like Java applets, ActiveX programs are typically displayed within the browser window as live inline images. These small programs, known as "controls," can do all the things that Java applets can do, including creating animations, acting as viewers for multimedia MIME types, interacting with mouse and keyboard, and creating windows. The notation for incorporating an ActiveX control into an HTML page is also similar to that for creating an applet. A tag for adding a control to a page looks something like this.

```
<OBJECT
    ID="example_control"
    CLASSID="clsid:7223B620-9FF9-11AF-00AA00C06662"
    CODEBASE="http://www.capricorn.org/controls/"
```

```
    WIDTH=70 HEIGHT=40>
<PARAM NAME="image" VALUE="example.gif">
<PARAM NAME="color" VALUE="blue">
<PARAM NAME="_version  VALUE="3">
</OBJECT>
```

The <OBJECT> tag identifies the control by its name (for example, example_control), the URL of the directory containing the control, and a CLASSID attribute that contains a unique hexadecimal serial number for the control. The serial number allows the control to be downloaded automatically from one of several ActiveX control repositories located at Microsoft and elsewhere. Like applets and inline images, a control developed and maintained at one Web site can be incorporated into an HTML page on a site somewhere else. And also like applets, the ActiveX control is passed as runtime information in a series of <PARAM> tags. This allows the page author to customize its behavior. Controls can also be scripted from within the page using Microsoft's JavaScript or VBScript (see pages 106–109).

The most important difference between Java applets and ActiveX controls is that controls are compiled into native machine code. Controls are written in any of several conventional programming languages (often Visual C or Visual Basic) and compiled into a format that allows them to be loaded and unloaded from memory easily. When a browser sees an <OBJECT> tag embedded in an HTML page, it downloads the ActiveX control and then makes a call to the operating system that loads the control into memory and executes it. This means that a control must be recompiled for every combination of operating system and hardware platform.

From the point of view of software developers and users, ActiveX has three important advantages over Java.

1. Developers can use the compilers and computer languages that they are familiar with.
2. Developers can draw on their existing repository of application programs, OLE components, and libraries, allowing them to bring controls to market faster.
3. Controls can do anything. They can save to disk, print, report statistics about hard disk usage, test the network, check for viruses, and so forth.

From the point of view of security, ActiveX controls are scary for one reason: Controls can do anything. They can trash files, commandeer the printer, reformat the hard disk, probe the firewall, install viruses, and so forth.

Because ActiveX controls consist of executable machine code, they are subject to an all-or-none rule. Once an ActiveX control is running on your machine, it has the ability to do anything that any other full-fledged program can do. While this makes ActiveX controls very powerful, it also makes them potentially dangerous. A control written for malicious purposes can compromise your privacy or damage your system in overt or subtle ways. An innocent but buggy control can be subverted by a knowledgeable Web page author into doing something equally compromising.

The Authenticode System

Microsoft was aware of the security risks when it released the ActiveX system. In order to prevent a plague of malicious controls, Microsoft and VeriSign jointly set up a software signing system known as "Authenticode," under which controls are cryptographically signed by their authors before being released. The signature uniquely identifies the software developer and provides a strong guarantee that the software has not been modified since it was signed. When a browser downloads an ActiveX control, it checks its signature for validity. If there is no signature or the signature is from an untrusted software vendor or the control has been modified since it was signed, the browser will catch the problem.

How is your browser to know that a control carrying a particular vendor's signature was, in fact, signed by that vendor and not by some malicious individual signing the control in a reputable vendor's name? The problem is analogous to the problem of trusting remote Web sites, and the solution is the same. A certifying authority, acting as a trusted third party, checks the credentials of software developers who wish to publish ActiveX controls. If the software developer passes muster, the certifying authority grants it a signed "software publisher's certificate." The developer can then use its publisher's certificate to sign controls.

Internet Explorer maintains a list of certifying agencies' certificates, as well as the publishing certificates of individual software vendors that the user has decided to trust. Before executing a signed control, Internet Explorer checks whether the certificate used to sign it belongs to a trusted software vendor. If not, the browser checks whether the certifying authority that signed the vendor's publishing certificate is on the trusted list. If none of these criteria are satisfied, then the browser either puts up a warning dialog and asks you to confirm the execution of the control, or it aborts, depending on its settings.

In principle, any certifying authority can issue software publisher's certificates. In practice, only VeriSign is currently doing so. It is currently issuing two types of publisher's certificate.

1. A "personal" publisher's certificate, whose authentication procedures are similar to VeriSign's personal Class 2 certificates (verification of identity by credit bureau)
2. A "commercial" publisher's certificate, whose authentication procedures require a notarized letter and/or a copy of the vendor's articles of incorporation

To obtain either type of software publisher's certificates, VeriSign and Microsoft require the software vendor to take a pledge. By agreeing to the terms of the pledge, the developer promises to exercise "reasonable care consistent with prevailing industry standards" to keep its code free from viruses, malicious code, and other data that may damage, misappropriate, or otherwise interfere with a third party's operations.

A software vendor who deliberately violates this pledge can have his certificate revoked. (See the Internet Exploder box for an incident in which this actually occurred.) Internet Explorer version 3.01 and higher automatically check a certificate revocation list maintained at VeriSign and refuse to run controls from vendors whose certificates are no longer valid. Like other certificates, publisher's certificates also expire after a period length of time (typically, a year). Internet Explorer complains if asked to run an ActiveX control that has been signed with an outdated certificate.

Is ActiveX Safe?

The Authenticode security model presents some interesting problems. The analogy that Microsoft likes to use when explaining Authenticode is that it provides the same type of quality assurance that consumers get when they buy shrink-wrapped software in a computer store, where the shrink wrapping, embossed hologram, packaging, and printed manual all provide a guarantee that the software contained within the package comes from the developer that claims to have produced it. On the Internet, the software publisher's certificate and the Authenticode signature on the software guarantees the source and integrity of the software.

Is this good enough? The basic premise of the Authenticode system is that the major source of danger on the Internet is software designed with malicious intent by bad people. If we accept this premise for the time being, what assurance does Authenticode give us that this malicious software will not be executed on our systems? Microsoft gives the following answers.

1. **An evil hacker is unlikely to apply for a publisher's certificate.** This may or may not be true. Individual software publishers' certificates are not expensive, and a programmer who writes malicious ActiveX controls by night may very well have a day job in which he uses his certificate to sign legitimate controls.
2. **If a software developer introduces a malicious control, he is breaking the pledge.** This is true. If caught, the developer can have his certificate revoked and might face legal action for the damage his control is responsible for. However, if the malicious control's behavior were triggered only when presented by certain unusual inputs, the developer could plead that the problem was an unintentional bug.

3. **If a malicious control compromises your security, the Authenticode system gives you a way to identify and track down its developer.** Although this may sometimes be true, it's not particularly reassuring ("Here's the serial number of the gun that shot you."). The real problem with this assertion is that it may not hold up when you need it most. Because ActiveX controls have complete access to the system they run on, they have the ability to play many dirty tricks. Among the things they can do is to cover their tracks by erasing the browser's history list, removing all copies of themselves from the cache directory, and leaving a misleading trail pointing at some other culprit. An ActiveX control could quietly patch the Internet Explorer executable, changing its Authenticode routines so that it subsequently allows certain unsigned controls to pass through without warning. Indeed, a control could do its dirty work without arousing any suspicion. While it displays a nice animation, it is scanning the corporate firewall system from the inside for security holes. When the firewall is breached a week later, no one suspects that an ActiveX control was involved.

The Authenticode system contains an implicit assumption that "bad-by-intent" programs are the biggest risk to end-user security. This may not be the case. Historically, the most widespread software security holes have been introduced accidentally by well-intentioned developers. Unscrupulous individuals then discover the holes and go on to exploit them by feeding the software unexpected parameters. Authenticode will not prevent this type of problem. Nor will it prevent the spread of viruses that were inadvertently introduced during the development process. The virus will simply be signed along with the rest of the code.

The main problem with ActiveX is that it uses a binary security model. Either a control is trusted not at all, or it is trusted completely. A better model would allow finer gradations of trust, allowing some controls limited access to certain system resources and allowing others more access or none at all. Unfortunately, because of ActiveX's use of native machine code, this is not feasible without direct operating system support. Possibly, new versions of Microsoft Windows NT will offer the necessary capabilities.

Internet Explorer currently offers several options for controlling ActiveX's behavior. You can choose not to run controls at all, to run signed controls automatically but warn before running any unsigned controls, or to run any control, signed or not. The configuration details are given later in this chapter. Again, your decision vis-à-vis ActiveX should be based on your needs. If you really need to run ActiveX controls, you should enable them. If there is no compelling reason to use this feature, turn it off.

Internet Exploder

Two well-publicized incidents in 1996 and 1997 illustrate ActiveX's mischief-making potential. In the first incident, a software developer named Fred McLain decided to warn the world about ActiveX's security risks. He applied for and obtained a VeriSign personal publisher's certificate and then proceeded to develop an ActiveX control named Internet Exploder. When a browser viewed an HTML page that contained Internet Exploder, the control would perform a clean shutdown of the user's system (on laptops with advanced power management, it also shut off the laptop's power). McLain signed the control with his VeriSign-issued personal publisher's certificate and put it up on the Web among a series of pages that explained what Internet Exploder would do and what it might have done if he had been one of the bad guys.

Internet Exploder generated a significant amount of adverse publicity for ActiveX, and neither Microsoft nor VeriSign were amused. Despite McLain's protestations that he had only written a demonstration program, the two corporations accused McLain of violating the software publisher's pledge by signing a malicious control. McLain's certificate was revoked. This had no immediate practical effect, however, because Internet Explorer 3.0 did not check certificate revocation lists. However, 3.01, issued shortly after the Exploder incident, does implement live revocation list checking. Users who now attempt to view the Internet Exploder page with 3.01 or higher will see a message warning that the control has been signed by an invalid certificate.

In the second incident, members of the Chaos Computer Club (CCC) of Hamburg, Germany, developed an ActiveX control that, when run, searched for a copy of the Quicken financial management program on the user's disk. The control then used OLE interprocess communication calls to make Quicken connect to the user's bank and initiate a wire transfer of a substantial sum to the Chaos Computer Club's account.

Like Internet Exploder, the Chaos control was developed as a demo. Although members of the CCC demonstrated it during a news interview on German television, it has never been released to the Internet. The Chaos control is not particularly sneaky about what it does; the Quicken application and the wire transfer are performed in full view of the user. However, CCC representatives were quick to assure television viewers that they could have disguised their control's actions if they had wanted to.

If you were able to download the Chaos control, your browser would detect that it is unsigned and warn you of that fact—but only if your browser is configured to warn before executing unsigned code. See the section Changing Active Content Settings later in this chapter for details on configuring ActiveX's settings.

JavaScript and VBScript

The Netscape and Microsoft browsers both offer scripting languages in addition to their support for Java and/or ActiveX. Netscape's JavaScript language is available for Navigator and Internet Explorer. VBScript runs on Microsoft browsers only.

Both scripting languages have a similar rationale. While Java and ActiveX offer great power and flexibility, their capabilities can only be exploited by technically skilled programmers. The creation of a Java applet from scratch is beyond the capabilities of many HTML authors. A full-blown applet or control is also overkill for most purposes. If an HTML author needs only to confirm that the value typed into a field of a fill-out corresponds to a correct telephone number, it would be absurd to develop an applet for that purpose.

The scripting languages offer a happy intermediate between HTML authoring and applet/control development. Using nonstandard extensions to the HTML language, page authors can write short programs to check and modify the contents of fill-out forms, open and close browser windows, load new URLs, and generate text dynamically. Another important feature of the scripting languages is that they can be used to send messages to Java applets and ActiveX controls. This allows authors to add third-party applets and controls to their pages, then integrate and customize them to produce useful effects.

JavaScript was developed by the Netscape Corporation and first made its appearance in Netscape Navigator 2.0. Microsoft incorporated a very similar dialect, technically known as JScript, into its browsers beginning with Internet Explorer 3.0. JavaScript's name refers to the similarity of its syntax to Java's. Beneath the surface, however, JavaScript and Java are quite distinct. (JavaScript is actually more similar to HyperScript, the language embedded in Apple Computer's HyperCard product.) Here's a short example of a JavaScript-enhanced HTML page.

```
<HTML> <HEAD>
<TITLE>Welcome to JavaScript</TITLE>
<SCRIPT LANGUAGE=JavaScript>
function greet () {
   alert("Welcome to my page");
}
</SCRIPT>
</HEAD>
<BODY onLoad="greet()">
<H1>Welcome to JavaScript</H1>
</BODY></HTML>
```

The page contains a <SCRIPT> section within its header. This section is where new JavaScript functions are defined, which in this case, consists of a single function named *greet()*. When *greet()* is called, an alert box appears and displays the friendly message "Welcome to my page." The other addition to the page is a new *onLoad* attribute in the <BODY> tag. It specifies that the *greet()* function is to be invoked when the page is first loaded. The effect of this declaration is that the alert box pops up the first time the user views the page. Many of the HTML elements have similar JavaScript extensions, allowing JavaScript functions to be attached to push buttons, form fields, links, images, and so forth. JavaScript provides an interface for controlling Java applets that are loaded and running in the browser. It also allows scripts in one frame or window to control the contents of another. This lets HTML authors create interesting navigation bars and search interfaces.

VBScript, currently available only for Microsoft browsers, made its appearance in Internet Explorer version 3.0. It is a dialect of Visual Basic and draws on the popularity of that language in Microsoft Windows environments. VBScript is conceptually similar to JavaScript. It allows the page author to define functions and then attach them to parts of the HTML page so that they are triggered by certain user actions. It allows the author to control applets and controls elsewhere on the page and to coordinate activities among frames.

JavaScript Security Problems

Since its introduction, JavaScript has received a significant amount of attention from the Internet community. A number of security holes in its design and implementation have been found. Many, but not all, have been patched.

Unlike Java and ActiveX, in which the security model was part of the design process, JavaScript's security model appears to have evolved with time. Early beta releases of JavaScript contained many obvious oversights, such as giving JavaScript authors the ability to retrieve the browser's history list, thereby learning what sites the user has recently visited. As problems were reported, the bugs were patched one by one, usually by disabling certain of the language's features and options. This process continued after JavaScript was released to the public, and still continues today.

The following are some major problems that have plagued JavaScript since its release.

The ability to send e-mail messages in the user's name. Some versions of JavaScript can initiate an e-mail message in the user's name and send it off without her knowledge. This bug was actually exploited by several Web sites to discover visitors' e-mail addresses. The site's home page contained a simple JavaScript function that initiated an e-mail message to the site's Webmaster. When the e-mail arrived, the visitor's e-mail address could be recovered from the mail "From" field. This bug is present in Navigator 2.0, 2.01, and 3.0.

The ability to obtain directory listings of local file systems. Earlier versions of JavaScript were able to obtain directory listings from the user's disks and any network-mounted file systems. After collecting the listing, the script could trick the user into uploading it to a remote server by asking the user to press an innocent-looking button. This bug was present in Navigator versions 2.0 and 2.01.

The ability to upload the contents of a file. JavaScript can also upload the contents of a file without the user's knowledge. In combination with the previous problem, this bug gives unscrupulous page authors the ability to rifle through personal files. This hole was thought to be closed after it was first reported in Navigator 2.01, but it reemerged in June 1997. The problem is present in all versions of Navigator through the 3.01 release, as well as in some of the 4.0 beta releases.

The ability to monitor pages visited by the user. JavaScript pages can quietly open a window with zero width and height, effectively rendering it invisible. A script running in this window can spy on the user's actions, make a record of all the URLs the user visits, then upload the list to a remote machine. This bug originally appeared in Navigator 2.01 and was thought to have been eliminated in later releases. However, the problem reemerged in July 1997. It affects Netscape Navigator 3.0, 3.01, and 4.01. It also affects Internet Explorer 3.0, 3.01, 3.02, and 4.0 beta 1.

The ability to log the images viewed by a user. A JavaScript opened in one frame can spy on the contents of another frame, recording the URLs of all inline images the user views even if the images are from another site (or behind a firewall). The list can then be uploaded to a remote server. This bug was discovered as this book was going to press and had not yet been fixed. All versions of Netscape Navigator through 3.02 and 4.01 are vulnerable to this problem.

Like Java, JavaScript can also be used to launch a variety of annoying denial-of-service attacks. JavaScript programs can start a CPU-intensive task and allocate a large chunk of memory, slowing the system to a crawl. They can make the browser open windows faster than you can close them. Scripts can cause the browser to quit or to crash (although the latter usually happens accidentally).

JavaScript's security history is not reassuring, and there is nothing to suggest that the rate at which bugs are crawling into view has slackened. Fortunately, there may be a glimpse of light at the end of the JavaScript security tunnel. Netscape has announced that future versions of Navigator will support JavaScript code signing using the same technology that allows Java applets to be signed. This facility will enable users to run JavaScripts only if they originate from trusted sources.

Until the new JavaScript signing system is widely installed and proven, it's best to play it safe. Unless there is some page that you absolutely need to see in its full JavaScript-enhanced glory, I recommend turning JavaScript off. See Active Content Settings in Netscape and Microsoft Browsers later in this chapter for instructions on how to do this.

VBScript Security Problems

VBScript, in contrast to JavaScript, has been subject to far less scrutiny by the Internet community. No major security holes had been reported as of spring 1997. Hopefully this means that there isn't anything to worry about, but the possibility exists that the bugs are still waiting to be discovered.

Like JavaScript, VBScript programs can be used to make annoying denial of service attacks. In some cases you may have to reboot the machine in order to regain control.

The Browser as a Security Hole

A web browser doesn't have to run active content in order to compromise user security. It can do it all by itself.

Because browsers are large and complex pieces of software, they are themselves vulnerable to security bugs that can be exploited by knowledgeable remote users. This unpleasant fact was abundantly illustrated in March 1997 by a series of holes found in Microsoft Internet Explorer 3.0.

One problem involved the browser's behavior when opening Windows "shortcut" files. Shortcut files are ordinarily created by individuals to quickly access files and programs on their local machines. Double-clicking on the shortcut launches the original file. This also works in the expected manner when the original file is located on a shared file system.

However, in buggy versions of IE, if a shortcut file was copied onto a Web server and accessed over the Internet, clicking on a hypertext link to the shortcut had a surprising result. Instead of opening a copy of the file on the Web server (or returning an error), the browser tried to open a copy of the file on the user's local machine. If the file were an executable program, such as the Windows registry editor or the DOS command interpreter, this could result in a potentially dangerous program being run on the user's computer, without her knowledge. It was also possible for a malicious individual to wrap several commands into a *.BAT* file, arrange for it to be stored in the unsuspecting user's browser cache and then have this file executed.

Variations of this bug were subsequently found to affect Internet Explorer's e-mail and news readers. All variations of this bug were fixed in IE versions 3.02 and higher.

At about the same time, another set of problems was discovered in the way that Internet Explorer authenticates the user to remote Web servers. Under some circumstances, Internet Explorer for Windows NT and 95 can be fooled into revealing to an untrusted server the user's network login name and password. This information can then be used to break into the user's workplace or to gain access to her personal computer.

The problem involves the challenge/response system that Internet Explorer uses when accessing password-protected documents on Microsoft Internet Information Server systems and Windows NT file servers (see Chapter 9). Here is a somewhat simplified explanation.

When Internet Explorer attempts to fetch a resource from an NT file server or an Internet Information Server Web server, the server sends the client a short, randomly chosen challenge string called a "nonce." The client encrypts the challenge using the user's LAN password and sends the encrypted challenge, the user's name, and other identifying information back to the server. The server looks up the user in its password database, finds the user's password, and uses the password to encrypt the challenge. This is now compared with what the client sent back, and if they match, the server confirms that the user knows the right password.

Now consider what happens when Internet Explorer sees a URL of this form.

file:\\aa.bb.cc.dd\path\to\file

(*aa.bb.cc.dd* is the Internet address of a remote server somewhere.) Because this URL uses the DOS notation for a shared file on a fileserver, Internet Explorer will attempt to access it using the Windows file-sharing protocol. The URL can be hidden inside an inline image so that the browser attempts to load it automatically.

In the first version of this attack, the host at the location indicated by the URL is running a specially modified version of a Windows file server. Instead of sending a random challenge string, it sends the same constant string each time. Internet Explorer trustingly encrypts the challenge with the user's LAN password and sends it back to the server. The server is now free to compare the encrypted password with a dictionary containing tens of thousands of passwords that have previously been used to encrypt the challenge. If it finds a match, it has successfully guessed the password (this is known as a "dictionary attack"). Because many people pick easily guessed passwords, a good dictionary attack can crack an average password about a quarter of the time.

Windows 95 versions of Internet Explorer are prey to a more serious bug. In this case, the browser can be tricked into sending the LAN password in unencrypted form, allowing all users' passwords to be recovered.

There is also a similar trick that does not use the file-sharing protocol at all but takes advantage of a similar vulnerability in Microsoft Internet

Information Server's challenge–response authentication (see Chapter 10). A doctored Web server can fool Internet Explorer into thinking that it is communicating with an IIS system that wants user authentication. The Web server sends Internet Explorer a constant challenge string, which the browser obligingly encrypts with the user's password.

Unfortunately, at the time this was written, these problems had *not* been addressed. Two months after the bug was reported, the vulnerability was still present in Internet Explorer 4.0, Windows NT 4.0 service pack 3, and Windows 95. The problem is that there is no easy solution to this bug; in order to patch it, Microsoft would have to disable one of the core features of the Windows authentication system.

Until a permanent fix is announced, you can work around this vulnerability in the following ways.

1. If you use Windows NT, choose a hard-to-guess password to log into the LAN. This will not prevent a remote server from intercepting your encrypted password but will prevent its operator from recovering it with a dictionary attack. See the Managing Passwords Safely box in the previous chapter for some hints.
2. Use a firewall system that is configured to reject Windows file-sharing requests. This prevents Windows 95 browsers from revealing unencrypted passwords. It does not avoid the IIS challenge–response vulnerability, and therefore allows encrypted passwords to be stolen. However, a firewall does make it more difficult for this information to be exploited by breaking into your account.
3. Don't ever run an NT Web browser under an administrative account. If the administrative password is disclosed, the system is at much greater risk than if an unprivileged user's password is revealed.

Exotic Technologies

As this book was going to press, new technologies, such as server push, XML, dynamic HTML, PointCast, and VRML 2.0 were beginning to roil the waters. Although it is too early to make any judgment on the security of these and other new technologies, there are four simple questions that one can ask when evaluating their security implications.

1. Does the technology involve the interpretation of a command language?
2. Does the technology have the capability to modify files on the user's computer?
3. Does the technology have the ability to transmit information back to the server?

4. Can the technology create a user interface that can mimic a trusted part of the operating system?

If the answer to any of these questions is "yes," be prepared for problems. For example, VRML 2.0 contains hooks that allow bits of Java and JavaScript code to be attached to objects, giving them behaviors. Because this implies that VRML viewers must contain a command interpreter, this is a potential avenue for exploitation.

What You Can Do

What to do about active content risks? On the one hand, active content palpably improves the Web, and is an enabling technology for a new generation of network-based applications. On the other hand, active content is fraught with risks, both confirmed and potential.

This section contains advice for making your system more resistant to active-content attacks.

General Precautions

We look first at general precautions for hardening your system against a variety of attacks from foreign software. Then we consider the options offered by specific web browsers for controlling when and how active content is executed.

User Privileges

If you work in a multiuser operating systems like Windows NT or UNIX, a malicious program launched by your browser will execute with the privileges of your account. Although this affords little protection against compromise of your personal files, it does protect the system itself against damage. Essential system executables, application programs, configuration files, and password files will be protected from modification, and the risk to machines connected to yours via the network will be reduced, as well. Commands that can do extensive damage, such as those to reformat the hard disk, are not usually available to unprivileged users.

On UNIX and NT systems, the following advice is worth taking to heart:

- Never run a Web browser—or any other nonadministrative application—while logged into the system as a privileged user (root on UNIX systems, or, if an administrator, on NT).
- Configure the system so that nonprivileged users do not have write access to system files or application software.

- On Windows NT systems, store the system directory on an NTFS file system rather than on a DOS FAT file system. NTFS provides file access controls that help prevent unauthorized file modifications.

More advice on configuring UNIX and NT systems securely can be found in Chapters 6 through 8.

This advice does not apply to single-user systems like the Macintosh and Windows 95 operating systems. These systems provide very little in the way of operating-system protection against malicious software.

Virus Checkers

If you work on an operating system that is known to be prone to viruses, such as Windows or, to a lesser extent, the Macintosh, you should obtain and use a good virus-checking utility. All virus utilities scan executables, files, and floppy disks for viruses. Scanning can occur on a scheduled basis, such as nightly, or it can be triggered by an action, such as downloading a file. Many checkers are also able to repair infected systems. Because new viruses are being introduced at a rate of hundreds a month, be sure to get the type of checker that can be updated easily by installing a file maintained on the manufacturer's FTP or Web site. Some of the more popular products are listed in Table 5.1.

Verify the Integrity of Downloaded Software

A popular trick is to disguise a piece of malicious software as a trusted software or someone can deliberately infect a popular software package with a virus and place it on an FTP or Web site. For example, in 1995 many users downloaded a file called *PKZIP30B.EXE.* It seemed to be a new version of the popular PKZip file compression utility. In fact, it was a malevolent Trojan horse.

Although it is no guarantee of the software's integrity, it is safer to download a software package from its home site than from a mirror site or FTP

TABLE 5.1 Commercial Virus Checkers

Name	OS	Manufacturer
McAfee VirusScan	Windows 95/NT, Macintosh, Solaris, DOS	McAfee
Dr. Solomon's Anti-Virus	Windows 95/NT, DOS	Dr. Solomon's Software
Norton AntiVirus	Windows 95/NT, DOS	Symantec
IBM AntiVirus	Windows 95/NT, DOS, OS2	IBM
Virex	Macintosh	DataWatch
Symantec AntiVirus	Macintosh	Symantec

repository. The online documentation for many software packages now includes checksum, or fingerprint, information that you can use to verify the package's integrity. If available, the MD5 fingerprint is a particularly good way to verify a program's identity (see Chapter 7). You can compare the fingerprint listed in the online documentation with the MD5 fingerprint obtained from the newly downloaded software. If the two don't match, there's a problem. Of course, for this system to work, you must trust that the online documentation itself is legitimate, something that you can't always take for granted.

Some software developers have begun to use the PGP system to digitally sign their code. If you have the PGP system installed, you can use this signature to verify both the integrity of the code and the identity of the author.

Backups

Even if your system is not attacked by a hostile applet or an evil plug-in, there's still the chance that it will be struck by lightning, dropped, or be at ground zero when a mug of coffee drops. Get backup software and use it.

Barring the Gates

As noted at the beginning of this chapter, active content has security implications both for the unfortunate user who gets burnt and for her employer. Many corporations have attempted to keep active content out by barring the gates at the firewall. Chapter 14 explains how some firewall systems can be configured to scan all incoming HTML documents for <APPLET> and <OBJECT> tags. The tags are quietly removed or commented out before sending the HTML document on to the user who requested it. The user's browser will now display a blank space where the applet or control was supposed to be.

Although this goes a long way toward keeping out unwanted active content, the remedy is not 100 percent effective. There are more ways than one to fetch active content, and if users really want to get at it, they will. The following are just a few ways that determined users can sneak active content past the firewall.

1. They can use FTP or Gopher to fetch pages that contain active content. Most firewalls check only documents transferred via HTTP for forbidden tags.
2. They can contact the remote server using SSL. Because the entire session is encrypted, the firewall can't know if applets and controls are coming in.
3. They can refer to applets and controls from within their personal HTML pages. Firewalls can only monitor HTML pages coming in from outside.

4. They can receive HTML pages that refer to active content via e-mail or Usenet. Several automated Internet servers make it easy to request URLs by e-mail.
5. They can hook a modem up to their office computer and dial in to their own ISP.

Another approach taken by some organizations is to ban their employees from using Java, JavaScript, or ActiveX by policy fiat. However, there is currently no easy way to enforce this policy short of searching everyone's office machine. This may change, however. Both Netscape and Microsoft have announced that future versions of their products will allow system administrators to create and enforce organization-wide browser policies. The new "security-zones" feature announced for Microsoft Internet Explorer (see below) should also offer system administrators some measure of relief.

Changing Active Content Settings

Both Netscape and Microsoft browsers offer a number of options to control the behavior of ActiveX, Java, JavaScript and VBScript. This section reviews the relevant settings in Netscape Navigator 3.02 and in a beta release of Internet Explorer 4.0.

Internet Explorer

Internet Explorer allows you to

- Turn ActiveX, Java, and the scripting languages on and off
- Control ActiveX's security level
- Examine software publisher certificates

Most of the settings related to ActiveX can be found in the security options window, accessed through *View->Options->Security* (Figure 5.1). Four relevant settings are found in checkboxes at the bottom of the screen in the section labeled "Active content."

1. **Allow downloading of active content.** If this checkbox is selected, both ActiveX controls and Java applets will be downloaded to disk and stored in the browser's cache. Whether they are then executed depends on other settings. This checkbox does not affect JavaScript and VBScript
2. **Enable ActiveX controls and plug-ins.** If this checkbox is selected, ActiveX controls will be executed if they meet the signing requirements set in the security level (see page 117).

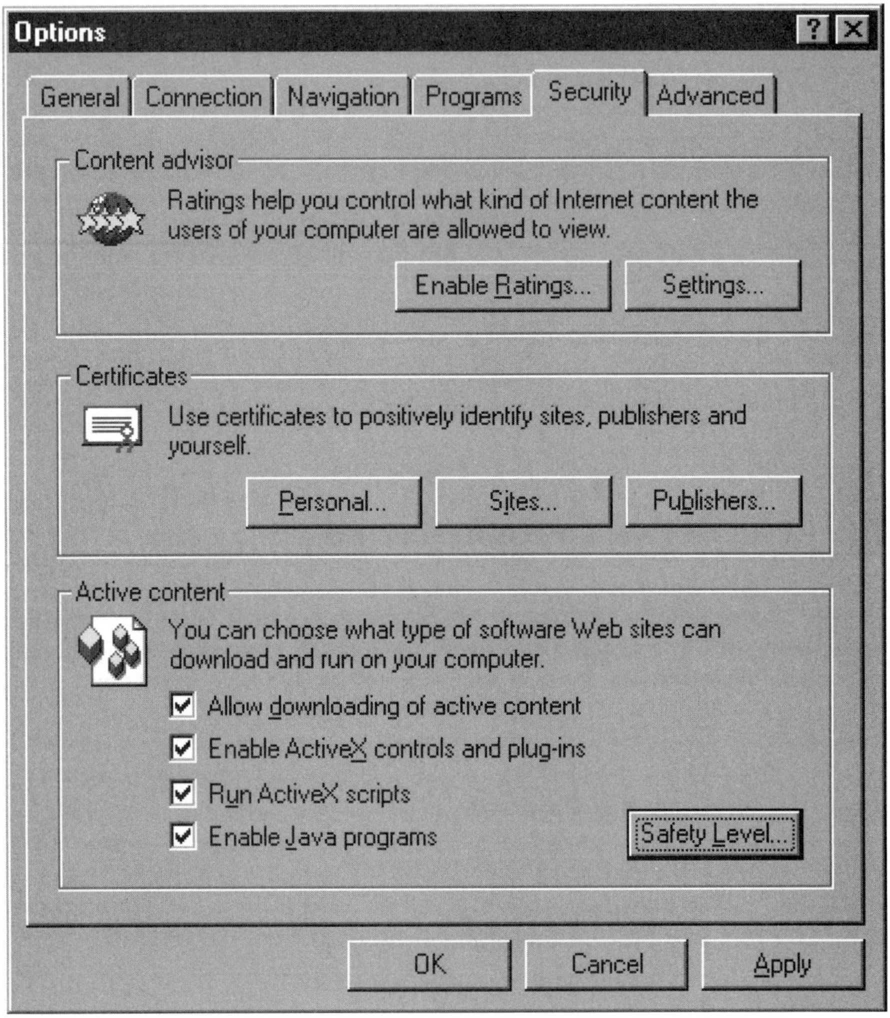

FIGURE 5.1 Internet Explorer's active content settings are found under *View–>Options–>Security.*

3. **Run ActiveX scripts.** This checkbox will turn on the scripting languages. Despite the misleading name, both VBScript and JavaScript are activated.
4. **Enable Java programs.** This activates the Java interpreter.

In the same section, the "Safety Level" button controls the browser's policy with regard to signed ActiveX controls. When you select this button, you will be presented with three radio buttons, "High," "Medium," and "Low."

1. **High (default)** ActiveX controls can run only if they are signed, the signature is valid, and either the vendor's software publishing certificate or the certificate of the certifying authority that signed it is on the list of certificates trusted by the browser (see below). Under any other circumstance, IE will present an alert box warning that it has averted a "potential security problem."
2. **Medium** ActiveX controls meeting the signing requirements for high security are run immediately. Otherwise, a dialog box appears warning you of the problem and giving you the choice to execute the control or abort.
3. **Low** All ActiveX controls are run, signed or not.

The high and medium settings are recommended for daily use. The low security setting is appropriate only in environments in which the browser can access company intranet sites exclusively, and all ActiveX controls were produced in-house. To review the list of certificates of publishers recognized by your browser, select the "Publishers" button in the middle panel of the security options window. This will display an Authenticode window containing a scrolling list of the vendors and certifying authorities that your browser trusts to sign ActiveX controls.

Although you might expect Internet Explorer to come with a preloaded list of trusted vendors, this wasn't the case in the spring of 1997, during a chaotic period when Microsoft was migrating from Authenticode version 1.0 to 2.0 and many publisher's certificates had expired. If you find that the list is empty, then no ActiveX control will run when the security level set to High. One way to repopulate the list of certificates is to accept an ActiveX control that you have reason to believe is safe. Change the security level to Medium and then visit Microsoft's gallery of ActiveX controls (select the "Web Gallery" icon from the main toolbar). When you go to view a page that contains an ActiveX control, you will be presented with a dialog box that warns you that the control is signed with an unrecognized certificate. The dialog box asks you to make several decisions (Figure 5.2).

1. Do you want to run this control?
2. Do you want to trust the individual vendor that signed it?
3. Do you want to trust all vendors whose certificates are signed by this vendor's certifying authority?

For ActiveX controls located on Microsoft's site, it is presumably safe to answer "yes" to each of these choices. The certificates of the vendor and the certifying authority will now appear in the list of trusted certificates in the Authenticode window. After accepting the certificate shown in the screenshot (which happens to belong to a control that updates IE to use Authenticode version 2.0), you will find two certificates in your list of trusted vendors: one the certificate that VeriSign Corporation uses to sign commercial software

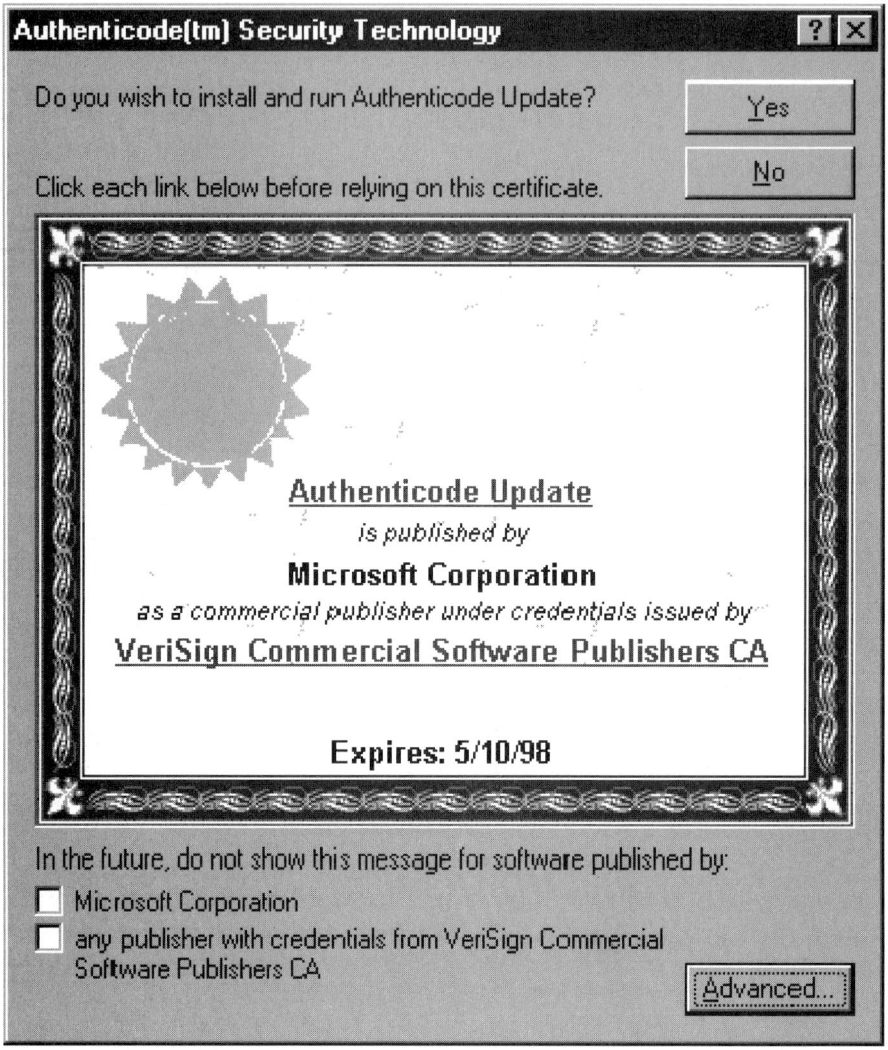

FIGURE 5.2 When Internet Explorer is asked to download and run an ActiveX control signed by an unknown software publisher (and security is set to Medium), it displays this dialog box.

publisher's certificates, and the other belonging to Microsoft Corporation. In order to automatically accept controls signed by developers holding personal publisher's certificates, you will have to leave the security level at Medium, find an ActiveX control at a reliable site that is signed with one of these certificates, and repeat the process. This procedure leaves much to be desired, and I trust it will be unnecessary in future releases of the browser.

Although you cannot view the contents of publisher certificates the way you can with server certificates, you can delete them by selecting them and clicking the "Remove" button. This window also contains a checkbox which, when selected, automatically trusts all vendors holding a commercial publisher's certificate.

Two Java-related options are buried among Internet Explorer's advanced options, available by choosing *View->Options->Advanced.* Look for the section labeled "Java VM."

1. **Java Logging Enabled** If this checkbox is selected, Internet Explorer will keep a log of Java operations, including a record of any error messages that applets have printed and (in 4.0 only) the list of Java classes that have been loaded and executed. The location of the log file is operating-system-dependent. On Windows systems, it can be found at *C:\WINNT\Java\javalog* or *C:\WINDOWS\Java\javalog*. This feature should be activated, as it can be used to track down Java-related problems.
2. **Java JIT Compiler Enabled** This refers to the "just-in-time" compiler, which speeds the execution of Java applets considerably. No security problems are known to be associated with the JIT compiler, but if applets crash with it enabled, you might wish to try again with the setting turned off.

What do you do if you think you have been the victim of an ActiveX attack? In principle, Authenticode allows you to track down the malicious control and discover its author. In practice, you'll need to do some detective work.

First, you'll need to determine which control caused the attack. This may be obvious if the damage occurred while viewing a particular page, but it may not be clear if the damage is discovered later or the effects were delayed somehow. Unlike the Java interpreter, which keeps a written record of which appplets were executed, Internet Explorer doesn't log the ActiveX controls it executes. Microsoft recommends that you examine the browser document cache to see what controls have recently been run. The location of this cache is system-dependent. Look for a directory named Temporary Internet Files in *C:\WINDOWS, C:\WINNT,* or *C:WINNT\Profiles\Username*. Within this directory you will find copies of all the recently viewed pages, among which are any ActiveX controls (usually identifiable by the *.cab* extension). If searching the cache is unsuccessful, system administrators may be able to reconstruct events by examining the firewall log, if there is one.

Once the problem control has been identified, you'll need to discover its author. Unfortunately, Internet Explorer does not provide a way to view the signature of an ActiveX control. To do this, you will need the *chktrust* program, part of Microsoft's ActiveX development kit. This utility is freely available at the URL given at the end of this chapter.

As this book was going to press, Microsoft had just announced future support for a security zones feature, which allows end users to divide the

Web into distinct zones of trust, each associated with a different combination of security settings. Zones can be based on the domain name of the remote Web site or on some combination of its site and publisher certificates. For example, the end user might grant unqualified trust to all ActiveX controls issued by Web servers within the corporate local area network but require that controls from Internet sites be signed by developers with commercial publishing certificates. System administrators will be able to distribute predefined security-zone definitions from a central server and update them dynamically. The security-zones concept also extends to SSL and cookie settings. Overall, it sounds like a helpful feature, and I look forward to seeing it in use.

Netscape Navigator

Netscape Navigator through version 3.02 offers two options for active content.

1. You can turn the Java interpreter on and off.
2. You can turn JavaScript on and off.

These settings are available under *Options->Network Preferences->Languages*.

Netscape also offers a command under *Options->Show Java Console* that will show the Java console window. When a Java applet is activated, the window records all messages the applet prints to its standard output. This is useful for figuring out what an applet is doing, and it is routinely used by developers to debug applets. The console also records error messages, including security exceptions. There is no need to keep the console open continuously. The messages are stored and displayed even when the console window is closed.

One of the early problems with JavaScript was its ability to send e-mail messages without the user's knowledge. Under Netscape's *Options->Network Preferences->Protocols,* there is a checkbox to warn before submitting an e-mail message in response to a fill-out form. This will prevent a number of exploits that seek to recover your e-mail address by tricking you into sending mail.

In the beta release of Netscape Navigator 4.0, these options can be found in a redesigned preferences window available by selecting *Edit->Preferences ->Advanced.* In addition to enabling and disabling JavaScript and Java, you have the option of enabling the AutoInstall feature. If activated, this option will automatically locate and install certain plug-in applications when you try to view a document that the browser can't display. Although convenient, this facility is *not recommended.* There is no way to control what plug-ins do once they're running on your system; installing them should always be something that you do deliberately.

Navigator 4.0 also provides hooks for the new Java and JavaScript code signing scheme. Under *Security->Java/JavaScript,* you will find a list of code signing certificates from trusted software publishers. This feature, which was not functional in the beta versions I examined, allows you to examine the certificates of each software publisher and edit the privileges of applets and scripts signed by them.

Checklist

1. What plug-ins and helper applications are installed in your browser? What do they do?

   ☑ No plug-ins are installed.

   ☑ A few essential plug-ins are installed.

   ❍ I don't know. I just download them when the browser tells me to.

   Plug-ins are untrusted bits of software that can contain viruses, Trojan horses, or bugs. You should limit the number of installed plug-ins to the bare minimum. Only install plug-ins that you are likely to use more than once, and only those written by vendors you trust. In particular, don't use programs that contain macro languages, like Microsoft Word, as helper applications.

2. Do you scan for viruses?

   ☑ Yes

   ❍ No

   A virus checker is a good idea, particularly if you are running a Windows or a DOS system.

3. Do you ever browse the Web while logged on as administrator on Windows NT systems, or as root on UNIX systems?

   ❍ Yes

   ☑ No

   Multiuser systems were designed to protect against attacks by viruses and other malicious software. However, if you run the browser as a privileged user, you lose all benefits of this protection.

4. Do you keep up to date on your browser's security issues?

   ☑ Yes

   ❍ No

It's too bad, but Web browsers are being "improved" so rapidly that it's impossible for all their security-related bugs to be caught and fixed before the browsers are released to the world. It's up to you to read vendors' security alert pages and act on them. URLs for Microsoft's and Netscape's security pages are given below.

5. Do you really need to view active content?

   ☑ Yes

   ☑ No

   ❍ Why not?

   Active content will be essential for the next generation of intranet software and groupware applications. Today, though, it's more often used for cute animations, eye-catching ads, and neat special effects. No active content is free of risks. If your need for active content outweighs the risks of running it, go right ahead. If you don't really need active content, the safest course is to disable it.

Resources

Internet Scams

The Electronic Scams Page

http://www.rcmp-grc.gc.ca/html/scams.htm

Java Applets

Sun's Documentation and White Papers

http://www.javasoft.com/

Java Security FAQ

http://java.sun.com/sfaq/

Edward Felten's Pages on Java Security

http://www.cs.princeton.edu/sip

Netscape's description of signed Java applets

http://developer.netscape.com/software/signedobj/index.html

ActiveX Controls and Authenticode

Microsoft's Authenticode page

http://www.microsoft.com/INTDEV/security/misf8.htm

The World Wide Web Consortium's Digital Signature initiative

http://www.w3.org/pub/WWW/Security/DSig/Overview.html

VeriSign's Software Publishers' Certificates Pages

http://digitalid.verisign.com/software_publishers.html

Microsoft's ActiveX Gallery

http://www.microsoft.com/gallery/default.asp

Microsoft's ActiveX Development Pages

http://www.microsoft.com/activex/

Virus Checkers

McAfee VirusScan

http://www.mcafee.com/

Symantec AntiVirus

http://www.symantec.com/

Norton AntiVirus

http://www.symantec.com/

Virex

http://www.datawatch.com/virex.shtml

IBM AntiVirus

http://www.av.ibm.com/

Dr. Solomon's Anti-Virus

http://www.drsolomon.com/

Security Holes in Microsoft Internet Explorer

Description of how LAN passwords can be intercepted in NT versions

http://www.ee.washington.edu/computing/iebug

A similar hole in Windows 95 versions

http://www.security.org.il/msnetbreak/

A similar hole that works across firewalls

http://www.efsl.com/security/ntie/

Description of the "shortcut" bug

http://www.cybersnot.com/iebug.html

The Unofficial Microsoft Internet Explorer Security FAQ

http://www.nwnetworks.com/iesf.html

Browser Security Pages and Alerts

Microsoft Security Advisor

http://www.microsoft.com/security/

Netscape Security

http://home.netscape.com/info/security-doc.html

Chapter 6

Web Privacy

Web surfing feels like an anonymous activity. In the privacy of your home or office, you jump from site to site, query search engines, peruse Web pages freely, add your favorite sites to bookmarks. You may welcome this feeling of anonymity. Perhaps you visit adult-oriented sites, search job-finding services, read radical political literature, plan your vacation on company time, or engage in other surfing activities that you would not want to become widely known. Or perhaps you would just like to be left to browse in peace without worrying that your habits will be used to stuff your inbox full of junk e-mail.

Although the Web feels anonymous, it isn't. In fact, browsing an online store may be far less anonymous than browsing the real thing in a shopping center.

What Web Surfing Reveals

Everything you do on the Web can be monitored automatically, and much of it is. You can't know when information is being collected, and you have no control over what purpose it is put to. Your name may or may not be associated with your actions.

For an impressive demonstration of the problem, visit the Center for Democracy and Technology's Web site at *http://www.cdt.org/*, where you will find a link to a page that gleans as much information about you as it can and displays the results. When I tried it (Figure 6.1), it correctly deduced my full name, my employer, my geographic location, the name and make of my home computer, the brand of my browser, and the URL of the last page I visited. My full name was available to the page only because I work at a UNIX

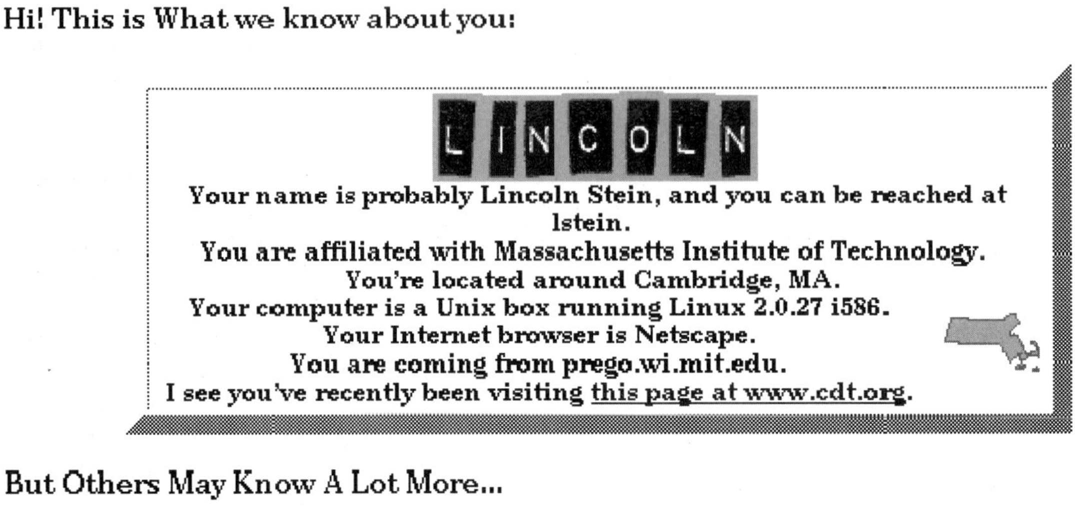
Hi! This is What we know about you:
LINCOLN
Your name is probably Lincoln Stein, and you can be reached at lstein.
You are affiliated with Massachusetts Institute of Technology.
You're located around Cambridge, MA.
Your computer is a Unix box running Linux 2.0.27 i586.
Your Internet browser is Netscape.
You are coming from prego.wi.mit.edu.
I see you've recently been visiting this page at www.cdt.org.
But Others May Know A Lot More...

FIGURE 6.1 The Center for Democracy and Technology runs a demonstration of the personal information available to Web servers.

computer with the *finger* daemon enabled, but the demo could have derived the other fields no matter what operating system I was using. Later, when I tried the demo from my office computer, it correctly identified several Usenet postings I had made and echoed their subject line back to me!

There are several potential locations where the record of all the URLs you've requested may be stored for posterity.

1. In your browser's history file and document cache
2. On your organization's firewall
3. On your ISP's firewall or proxy server
4. On each of the remote servers you've visited

What information can be recovered from these source? It depends. If someone has access to your personal computer and chooses to browse your document cache, they know exactly what sites you've visited and what pages you've looked at, including documents located on the organizational intranet. However, they can't know the contents of any fill-out forms you've submitted or Web searches initiated.

If your organization or ISP runs a firewall or proxy server, someone with access to the firewall logs is able to determine the name and IP address of your computer and the identity of each URL you request. In some cases, the keywords used in Web searches and other types of queries is available. Although your name and e-mail address do not usually appear in firewall and proxy logs, it is frequently possible to match a desktop machine's IP address to its owner.

A remote Web server records only your accesses to its own site. The URL you access and the IP address of your computer are logged, along with the time of access. Although it would seem logical that a remote Web server cannot know anything about other sites you visit, this isn't quite true. Each time you select a link on a page that jumps to a new site, your browser sends the site the URL of the page you were *previously* viewing. Known as the "referer" field, this allows sites to keep track of which Web pages point to them. In some cases, the referer field will contain residual information from Web keyword searches and other fill-out forms. Again, your name and e-mail address are not usually recorded by remote Web sites, but the IP address of your computer may give the remote site a strong hint of your geographic location or the company you work for, as the Center for Democracy and Technology's demo shows. Individual Web sites are also responsible for creating and collecting "cookies," which are used to tag browsers so that the server can identify them when they return. As a later section describes, cookies can be used by colluding sites to collect accurate click-trails of your Web-browsing sessions.

The greatest risk to privacy is information that you voluntarily provide to a remote Web site. User feedback forms, requests for further information, online orders, and posts to discussion groups all may be stored for an indefinite period of time and put to any use the site desires. If your name and e-mail address are associated with this information, you may soon find yourself receiving junk e-mail from unexpected sources. If you provide your postal address, phone number, or other personal data, you may find that information being shared as well.

The Other Side of the Story

Market researchers, advertisers, and Web merchants have a different take on the issue. For them, the Web offers an unprecedented way to learn about the customer's likes and dislikes, allowing them to improve the overall Web browsing experience while maximizing their business goals.

Web advertising agencies want to record which banner advertisements generate the most clicks and what demographic groups find them most compelling. With this information, companies can fine-tune their ads so that incoming users are presented with offers that are mostly likely to appeal to them.

Market researchers would like to know what Web sites people visit, what pages they view, how long they spend on each page, and where they go next. Using this information, researchers can help Web sites make their content more compelling and make them stand out from the increasingly noisy crowd.

Web site operators need the ability to customize sites according to users' tastes. Some customization might be done automatically. For example, if a user has shown a marked preference in the past for sites with flashing logos, heavy metal background music, and scrolling marquees, this is what that user will get. If the user prefers Bach and William Morris prints, the site can satisfy those tastes too. Other customization might be done manually. Various sites now offer users the ability to choose the background color for the sites' pages and which links appear on their home pages. However, in order for this to work, the site must be able to uniquely identify the user when he or she returns.

Vendors of artificial intelligence technologies want to be able to record a user's tastes and habits in order to create sophisticated "smart agents." Using an increasingly refined model of the user's personality, vendors such as Firefly claim that agent technologies will soon be able to plum the Web's depths and net pages on subjects that the user doesn't even suspect she'd be interested in.

Market-based research has been around for years, particularly in the United States, where there are few legal restrictions on the sharing of marketing data. Credit card purchases, magazine subscriptions, airline reservations, direct marketing responses, car rentals, and even chargecard purchases at grocery stores are all routinely recorded, collated, and traded among commercial enterprises. The Web offers marketers an even richer vein of data. When you enter a real-life store and browse among the shelves, no one records which things you passed by and which ones you lingered over. Only your actual purchases are recorded. On the Web, this can happen.

Another point of view holds that good identification makes for good net citizens. In order to make online commerce, electronic financial transactions, and virtual business deals possible, all the parties involved must be strongly identified. Without identification, there is no motivation for users to act responsibly. Without the possibility of reprisal, slander, vandalism and other antisocial acts will proliferate.

The need for strong identification is one of the justifications for the current push to give everyone on the Web a personal certificate (see Chapter 4). A Web where everyone is anonymous will remain much as it is today—a frontier town with all of the excitement of the Wild West but none of the commercial opportunities.

Clearly there are two sides to this story. For the Web to succeed, the providers of Web content and its consumers must find a comfortable balance that neither infringes on users' expectation of privacy nor dampens the prospect for Web commerce.

Server Logs

Much of the information that is recorded during a Web browsing session ends up in the log files of the remote servers. The following log excerpt from one of the MIT Genome Center's servers shows the browsing activities of one user over a two-minute period.

```
ppp.bu.edu - - [09/Dec/1995:20:31:56 -0500] "GET / HTTP/1.0" 200 4029
ppp.bu.edu - - [09/Dec/1995:20:31:57 -0500] "GET /www/bigwilogo.gif HTTP/1.0" 200 620
ppp.bu.edu - - [09/Dec/1995:20:32:00 -0500] "GET /usage/usage.graph.gif HTTP/1.0" 200 154
ppp.bu.edu - - [09/Dec/1995:20:33:22 -0500] "GET /cgi-bin/wwwwais?hemoglobin+gene HTTP/1.0" 200 527
```

Each line in the log file contains information about a separate request for a URL, the exact format of which is explained in detail in the Web Server Logs section in Chapter 8. This example shows four requests by the user at *ppp.bu.edu*. In the first transaction, the user requested the site's home page by downloading the / URL. This page contains two inline graphics, one called *bigwilogo.gif* and another called *usage.graph.gif*. The next transactions show requests for these graphics as the user's browser loads and displays them. The last line shows a keyword search. The user has invoked the *wwwwais* CGI script to search the site for the keywords *hemoglobin* and *gene*.

What can we learn from these log entries? More than you might think. From these transactions, we can deduce that the remote user is affiliated with Boston University (located in Boston, Massachusetts) and is probably working from home. We guess this because of the time (8:30 PM) and because the remote address indicates the use of one of the university's PPP lines. Because the Web site deals with biomedical research, we can deduce that the user is probably a student or faculty member at the university's biology department. The contents of the text search indicate that the remote user is interested in the hemoglobin gene. By looking at subsequent log entries, we could find out what other pages the user requested, gleaning more information about the user's interests.

Notice that none of this information has revealed the user's actual identity. In fact, if we were to see log entries from *ppp.bu.edu* on subsequent days, we could not be sure whether this were the same user or a new one. This is because dial-in IP addresses are often allocated dynamically on a first-come first-served basis. Similarly, if the user were a commercial user who is connecting through a corporate firewall system, it is likely that we would not see the address of the user's desktop machine, but the address of the corporate firewall instead. Despite this limitation, however, we have managed to learn some interesting information.

The information that server log files record is customizable. In addition to the information shown here, server logs can record

- The URL of the referer document, showing the page the user was viewing prior to requesting the current one.
- The browser's manufacturer and version number, which usually includes information about the user's operating system. For example, my version of Netscape Navigator provides this identification string: *Mozilla/3.02Gold (X11; I; Linux 2.0.27 i586)*. From this, one can learn something about my computer system.
- The amount of time taken to process the request.

- The list of MIME types that the browser supports, which sometimes gives information on which plug-ins are installed.

Referer Logs

An important source of interesting server log information is the referer field, recorded by many servers into a separate log file, or "referer log." To get a feeling for the significance of the referer log, consider the user who is viewing the hypothetical page located at URL *http://www.xyz.com/animals.html*.

This page contains a number of links to interesting pages around the world, including one to URL *http://www.capricorn.org/zebras.html*. When the user selects this link to jump to the zebras page, the server at *www.capricorn.org* records the following information in the referer log:

```
user1.abc.com  http://www.xyz.com/animals.html -> /zebras.html
```

The line above indicates that the user, from a computer located at *user1.abc.com*, has requested the document */zebras.html* via a link located at *http://www.xyz.com/animals.html*.

Browsers send referer information when the user selects a link, views an online image, or downloads an applet. If the user types the URL directly into the browser "location" field, no referer information is sent. Older browsers also send referer information when the user picks a URL from her Bookmarks or Favorites list; newer versions generally don't.

The original intention of the referer field was to enable Webmasters to learn who was linking to their sites so that they could catch dead links, typographical errors, and alert remote sites in advance of planned changes of address. In practice, the referer field has proven to be both powerful and problematic.

Uses and Abuses of Referer Logs

A personal anecdote will illustrate the power of the referer field. A few years ago, the Web site I help administer saw an overnight doubling of its hit rate. We found this puzzling as the site is mainly of interest to biomedical researchers, and we hadn't published any earth-shaking results recently. On examination of the server logs, we discovered that a single Web page accounted for the entire increase in the number of hits. This was a home page belonging to one of the laboratory's women technicians.

My site doesn't routinely log referer information, but in order to explore the problem further, we briefly activated referer logging. The source of the phenomenon immediately became clear. An HTML page entitled *Women of the Internet*, located on a server at a large eastern university, had recently incorporated the technician's home page into its list of interesting links. Our naive technician had made the grievious error of placing on her page a (relatively tasteful) photograph of herself at belly dancing class. This had attracted unwanted interest. We advised her of the situation and she removed the photograph, replacing it instead with a photograph of her boyfriend practicing on the rifle range. Since then, the number of hits to the site has returned to normal (although the technician still occasionally receives e-mailed marriage proposals from strangers).

In this case, the referer field helped diagnose and solve a potential problem. Other cases are not so amusing. During the preparation of this chapter, I activated my site's referer log briefly and scanned it for interesting references to pages that I've written. The following is a sample of the entries that turned up.

A Bookmark Referral

This entry is interesting because it shows that someone named "klein," located behind a firewall at a German company has placed a link to my home page in his bookmark file.

```
gate.swm.de     http://ws084242.swm.de/~klein/bookmarks.html ->
                /~lstein/
```

Even though the IP address of the machine the browser is running on is hidden from view behind the firewall gateway (*gate.swm.de*), we still have managed to learn the name of one of the machines protected by the firewall, *ws084242*. We might surmise that *ws* stands for *workstation*. A quick check for a *www.swm.de* site associates a name with the IP address. The company involved is Stadtwerke Munchen.

A Search Engine Referral

This entry shows that a user whose machine's IP address is not listed in the domain name system has used the Excite Web search engine to search for documents containing the keywords *netscape*, *cookies*, and *FAQ*.

```
200.10.239.68 http://www.excite.com/search.gw?
              search=netscape+cookies+FAQ&collection=web ->
              /WWW/faqs/www-security-faq.html
```

He located the WWW Security FAQ, an excellent choice.

A Local File

This entry demonstrates that the referer document need not be located on a Web site. It can be an ordinary file.

```
scilib-153.brown.edu file:///cs2/social%20impact/security.html ->
              /WWW/faqs/www-security-faq.html
```

In this case, someone at Brown University, probably working from a computer in the science library, accessed the FAQ via a link in a file on the machine's hard disk. The file is named */cs2/social impact/security.html*. CS2 sounds like a computer science course. Perhaps some professor at Brown has put together a course curriculum that lists the FAQ among its references?

A Web Site Referral

This one makes me a bit nervous. Why is an organization called *www.trouble.org* interested in the FAQ?

```
194.117.215.97 http://www.trouble.org/survey/introduction.html ->
               /WWW/faqs/www-security-faq.html
```

Of course, it's easy enough to check the indicated Web site and find out. The site is run by a security consultant who has compiled a list of sites his clients might be interested in.

A Referral From a Software Developer

This is a reference to some online documentation for a Perl module that I wrote.

```
janice.informatik.uni-dortmund.de
          http://webreference.com/programming/perl.html ->
          /ftp/pub/software/WWW/cgi_docs.html
```

Interestingly enough, a German software developer has seen fit to include it in a programming reference.

Referer Log Scenarios

Because of the potential for the referer field to leak information from one Web site to another, referer logs can lead to some serious infringements of privacy. A recent case involved the leakage of users' credit card numbers from one site to another. The problem manifested itself in the following way.

1. The user browsed a merchant's Web site and decided to place an order.
2. The user entered her credit card number into the fill-out form and submitted it after dutifully examining the page and confirming that its contents were protected by SSL.
3. The user received a page that confirmed her order.
4. The confirmation page happened to contain an advertisement that points to another site. The user clicked on it to jump to a new site.
5. The following showed up in the referer logs of the *new* site:

```
pressrm.dp.com  http://www.merchant.com/cgi-bin/order?name=Lois+Lane&
                address=Daily+Planet,Gotham+City&item=digital+altimeter
                &quantity=1&credit+card=4128113311838302&-> /index.html
```

What happened? How did an SSL-protected form leak the user's name, address, credit card number, and purchase? The problem is that the designers of the merchant's Web site used the GET rather than the POST method for submitting the contents of the fill-out form to the CGI script that handles it. The main difference between these two methods is that in the former case, the fill-out form fields are appended to the URL of the script that processes the request. Whereas in the latter, they are detached and submitted separately. As a result, when the unsuspecting user filled in the form and submitted it, the form's field values were incorporated into the URL of the confirmation page. When she jumped to the new site, the entire URL, complete with personal information, was duly forwarded in the referer field.

Here's a second scenario, which, unlike the previous one, remains hypothetical. A small software company whose stock has been sinking recently in the stock market starts to see entries like this in its Web server logs.

```
ks8023.xyz.com file:\\SRVR1\HOT\stocks2sellshort.html -> /index.html
```

This entry indicates that a document named *stocks2sellshort.html* located on an internal file server at the XYZ company contains a link to the software company's home page. This pattern of accesses might indicate that XYZ is planning a corporate takeover. Notice that the presence of a firewall system around the XYZ file server would be entirely ineffective at preventing this information leak unless it were specifically configured to strip the referer field from outgoing Web requests.

Keep an eye on the contents of your browser's *Location* or *Netsite* text box. If you ever see any personal or confidential information in the URL displayed there, you can safely assume that it has already been disclosed to a remote site.

Proxy Logs

Web proxies are modified Web servers that act as middlemen between the user and the remote Web server. When a proxy is in use, all requests for documents are indirect. Instead of going directly to a remote Web site for a document, the user's browser asks the proxy to fetch it on the browser's behalf. The proxy fetches the document and returns it to the browser.

Proxies are used by large Internet service providers to reduce network bandwidth. Recognizing that the majority of users request the same popular documents repeatedly, these proxies cache documents locally on the ISP's local machine. When requests for URLs come in, the proxy looks for it first in its local cache. If the requested document is not already present in the cache, the proxy goes out and fetches it. If the requested document is already in the cache (and hasn't gone out of date), the proxy returns the document directly, reducing network usage and improving response time.

Web proxies are also necessary ingredients of many firewall systems. Some firewall architectures prevent requests for Web documents from passing directly through the gateway. In this case, a proxy is installed on the firewall machine to forward requests between the internal network and the outer one.

Proxies are generally transparent to the end user. After the initial step of configuring the browser to use the proxy, all Web accesses occur normally. In fact, newer versions of Netscape and Microsoft browsers support automatic proxy configuration. The system administrator creates a network-accessible configuration file that all browsers on the network use to adjust their proxy settings when they first start up (set up instructions for system administrators are given in Chapter 14). The user may not even know that a proxy is in use.

Proxy servers log everything that a conventional Web server logs and much more. Every URL requested by every user is logged, along with the time and date. Referer information is also sent through the proxy server, and this can be logged, as well.

The implication of this is that the proxy log from a corporate firewall can be used to tell who is reading Dilbert cartoons on company time, who is accessing Usenet newsgroups, and who is spending time reading job postings on a competitor's Web site. Internet service providers can compile detailed statistics on what sites their customers browse, or they can associate customers with specific sites.

Proxy servers can also help preserve privacy. Firewall proxies routinely hide the address of the user's browser by making it seem as if the request originated at the firewall machine. Specially designed "anonymizing proxies" (see below) strip all identifying information from Web requests, making it impossible to trace the request back to its source.

Cookies

As we've seen, server logs record the IP address and/or name of the user's machine, but they don't routinely provide enough information to trace the request back to a specific person. Individual server logs also don't provide sufficient information to trace the user's path through the Web (often called a "click trail"). At most, the referer information allows a site to look back one step only. Browser cookies change that by allowing individual users to be tagged and their Web-surfing sessions monitored.

Cookies were designed with the best of intentions to solve a vexing problem for Web developers. The HTTP protocol is stateless. A browser connects to a server, fetches a URL, and closes the connection. The next time the browser needs to fetch a document from the same server, it opens up an entirely new connection and repeats the process from scratch. Although, from the user's point of view, the sequence of connecting to a site's welcome page and browsing through its pages is a continuous stream of events, the server sees it only as a discontinuous series of requests for URLs. Each request for a document, even if it's an embedded graphic within an HTML page that was retrieved just a second ago, is treated as a whole new request.

Although this stateless behavior gives the HTTP protocol advantages in reduced ovehead, it causes headaches for Web developers who want to do more than create a set of static HTML pages. Consider the problem of creating a Web interface to a database. In a typical database application, you establish a connection to the database software, identify yourself, pose a query, view the result, refine the query until you're satisfied, then generate a summary report. To make this work over the Web, a developer would have to come up with a way to maintain the continuity of the database session across many separate requests. This requires the application to keep track of a particular session on a particular browser, something that's not easy to do in a stateless protocol.

To solve this problem, Netscape introduced the "cookie protocol" with version 2.0 of Netscape Navigator. The idea proved so popular that it has now been made into part of the proposed HTTP/1.1 specification. Cookies extend the HTTP protocol by allowing the Web server to hand the browser a bit of information, the cookie, the first time the browser connects. If the browser is cookie-savvy, it stores the cookie in a small internal database. The next time the browser connects to the server, it searches through the database, finds the cookie, and returns it to the server.

Cookies come in many shapes and sizes. They can contain a large amount of information, such as the entire contents of a shopping cart, or just an arbitrary identification number that the Web server can use to distinguish one user from another. Like the ones found in real life, cookies also have a shelf life. They can be set to expire as soon as you quit the browser, or they can be given an expiration date at some point in the future. Cookies that disappear when you quit the browser are called "transient" while those that remain around between browsing sessions are called "persistent." The latter are saved to disk for long-term storage.

Cookies have names. A server can hand a single browser several cookies to juggle, each with a different name and the browser will return all applicable cookies to the server when it connects. Cookies can also be restricted to certain parts of a site's document tree, or they can be made so that they are only transmitted across the Internet when SSL is in use. Unless you have warnings turned on (see below), browsers send and receive cookies silently. You've probably already collected quite a few without knowing it.

If you use Netscape Navigator, you can see what persistent cookies you've collected by viewing the text file named *cookies* or *cookies.txt*. This file is found in various locations, depending on how Navigator was installed. On Windows systems, try looking under *C:\Program Files\Netscape\Navigator\Program*. On UNIX systems, look in your home directory in the hidden *.netscape* directory.

To view the persistent cookies stored by Microsoft Internet Explorer, look for a directory named *Cookies*, located either in *C:\Windows* or in *C:\WINNT\Profiles\username*. Here's an excerpt from my Netscape *cookies* file:

```
# Netscape HTTP Cookie File
# http://www.netscape.com/newsref/std/cookie_spec.html
# This is a generated file!  Do not edit.
www.wi.mit.edu      FALSE   /  FALSE   898779562  GeneBrowser     Organ+Recital
www.lpf.org         FALSE   /  FALSE   946515599  SpinnerUserID   7032
ad.doubleclick.net  FALSE   /  FALSE   942195540  IAF             d2bbd5
.netscape.com       TRUE    /  FALSE   946684799  NETSCAPE_ID     1000e010,1056503a
.focalink.com       TRUE    /  FALSE   946641600  SB_IMAGE        #29.4.portables_ed.4::pz51.gif
.hotbot.com         TRUE    /  FALSE   937396800  ink             IU0GQ7WP96E57E9E5437F
```

The interesting fields are the first column, which contains the name of the Web site or domain that issued the cookie; the sixth column, which contains the name of the cookie; and the last column, which contains the cookie's value. Other columns give the cookie's expiration date and other attributes.

Most of the cookies shown here appear to be anonymous user IDs, but a few of them contain human-readable information, including a notation from the *focalink.com* site that seems to recall that I once searched that site for information about portable computers.

Cookie Abuse

Used properly, cookies improve the Web browsing experience by allowing developers to add features to their Web pages that would otherwise be extremely difficult to accomplish. Cookies can actually protect your privacy by storing personal information locally on your hard disk rather than on a remote server. Used improperly, cookies threaten your privacy.

The cookie protocol was designed to prevent leakage of information from one site to another. In addition to the ability to designate secure cookies that will be transmitted only when SSL is in use, there is a fundamental restriction on the ability to share cookies among sites. Although a Web site can create cookies that are valid for several different servers within its own domain, such as *www.xyz.com* and *ftp.xyz.com*, it is impossible to make a browser return a cookie to a foreign domain. *www.xyz.com* and *www.abc.com* cannot share cookies, despite press reports to the contrary.

Because cookies are generated by the Web server, not by the browser, a cookie cannot hold any information that you haven't voluntarily given to the remote site. For example, a cookie cannot hold your e-mail address unless you gave the address to the remote site at some point.

So what's the problem? Web sites can collude to share cookie information with one another. To see how this is done, consider the third entry in my cookie file, the one from *ad.doubleclick.net*. The DoubleClick Corporation is a Web advertising agency. For a fee, Web sites join the DoubleClick Network and enter their advertising banners into a pool of ads maintained at DoubleClick's Web site. DoubleClick members are authorized to add an <IMG> tag to their HTML pages that points to a URL on DoubleClick's server. When you browse a page on a DoubleClick member site, your browser sees the <IMG> tag and contacts DoubleClick's server to retrieve the graphic. The DoubleClick server invokes a CGI script to pick a DoubleClick member site's advertising banner at random and return it.

You've seen the DoubleClick advertisements. They're the large, brightly colored ads for Web sites that change, seemingly at random, every time you access the page. Unless you actually view the HTML source code for the page, they look no different from any other inline graphic. You can't tell the graphic is being generated by DoubleClick rather than the site that owns the page.

So far, the story is relatively benign. What worries people is that DoubleClick uses cookies to track individuals' Internet usage. The first time your browser downloads one of DoubleClick's graphics, the DoubleClick server hands your browser a cookie containing a randomly generated customer ID. From then on, every time you contact a site that carries one of DoubleClick's advertisements, your browser happily returns your customer ID to DoubleClick, along with the URL of the page you're accessing in the referer field. This allows DoubleClick to record each of the member sites that you visit. If you click on the banner ad and jump to the advertising site, DoubleClick can record that fact too.

Over a period of time, DoubleClick can compile a very accurate profile of which member sites you visit and then use this information to tune the advertisements it displays. Although the first DoubleClick graphic the server picks for you is random, later selections are tuned to sites that are likely to appeal to you based on your Web browsing history. Digested browser statistics are also made available to the DoubleClick member sites to aid them in focusing their appeal to certain segments of the market. The DoubleClick Corporation can, in effect, follow your movements around the Web, at least so long as you remain on DoubleClick client sites. A similar strategy has been pursued by other Web-based advertising and marketing firms.

It is important to realize that even though DoubleClick-style schemes allow participating sites to learn a lot about you, it still doesn't enable them to identify you. All the system knows is the customer ID that was randomly assigned to you when you first received the cookie. However, if you voluntarily give your name or other identifying information to any one of the participating sites (in an order form, user survey, or guestbook), then it is technically possible to associate your identity with your user ID. As an aside, there is a disturbing trend by certain "family-oriented" sites to entice children into revealing demographic information about their parents.

The bottom line is that the majority of cookies are innocuous things that enhance the Web browsing experience and present no threat to privacy. Some cookies, however, do present a threat. There is no easy way to distinguish between the two types, although persistent cookies are more likely to be a threat than transient ones.

PICS

PICS stands for Platform for Internet Content Selection, and is a WWW Consortium-sponsored standard for labeling the content of Web pages. PICS is widely used for rating Web pages and is the basis of several products that filter pages considered unsuitable for children.

Although PICS isn't strictly related to Web security, it is often included in security discussions, partly because the PICS standard is being extended to label documents with such things as authorship and copyright information, and partly because Internet Explorer prominently features a PICS filter among its security options.

The PICS scheme distinguishes between PICS "rating systems" and PICS "rating services." A rating system is a formal way of describing document content according to one or more quantitative dimensions. For example, the most widely used rating system is one designed by the Recreational Software Advisory Committee (RSAC). The RSAC system uses four dimensions, language, nudity, sex, and violence, each of which can have a values from 0 (none) to 4 (lots).

The Ararat Corporation's rating system, in contrast, rates Web content for commercialism using such dimensions as commercial content and downloading information. Under PICS, a dimension can be a collection of discreet values, a floating-point number, or a multivalued entity such as a set of keywords. You can attach the PICS labels from multiple rating systems to a single document; the filtering software will pick among the PICS labels for the rating system that it cares about.

A rating service is an organization that rates Web pages. The service will typically surf the Web, rate sites and individual pages using its own or someone else's rating system, and store the results in a database. When a piece of PICS-compliant filtering software is asked to fetch a particular URL, it can send a query to a CGI script running on the organization's Web server. The script looks up the URL in the database and returns its PICS labels, if any. A rating service may charge a subscription fee for this service, or it may provide it free. For example, the SafeSurf Corporation provides a PICS-based subscription service that parents can use to block sites they consider unsuitable for children. A Web site can also act as the rating service for its own material; its Webmaster need only add PICS labels to its documents or home page.

In PICS's current incarnation, most pages are self-rated. The labels are placed in the headers of HTML documents, in a special <META> tag. A typical label might look like this.

```
<META http-equiv="PICS-Label" content='
    (PICS-1.0 "http://www.rsac.org/ratingsv01.html"
       l gen true
         comment "RSACi North America Server"
         by "lstein@genome.wi.mit.edu"
         for "http://www.genome.wi.mit.edu/"
         on "1997.04.16T08:15-0500"
         exp "1998.07.01T08:15-0500"
         r (n 0 s 0 v 0 l 0))
'>
```

The label contains details such as the URL for the rating system, the expiration date for the label, the URL being rated, and the e-mail address of the person who performed the rating. The most interesting part of the label is the last bit:

```
r (n 0 s 0 v 0 l 0))
```

The *r* begins the rating field. The rating consists of numeric values from 0 to 4 for each of the RSAC's four dimensions: nudity, sex, violence, and language. In this example, the site is pretty tame; all the dimensions are zero, meaning that there is very little of any of these characteristics. Although not shown here, a PICS label can also incorporate an MD5 fingerprint of the document, preventing the document from being tampered with after the label is attached.

Microsoft Internet Explorer can be set to filter Web pages based on their PICS labels. To turn on filtering, select *View->Options* and select the *Security* tab. At the top of the page, you will see the Content Advisor section. Click the Enable Ratings button.

You will now be asked to provide a supervisory password, which will be used as a lock to prevent children from changing the settings. When this has been entered, you will be presented with a page similar to that shown in Figure 6.2. The central panel shows the four dimensions of the RSAC's rating system. Click on each dimension in turn and use the slider control to set

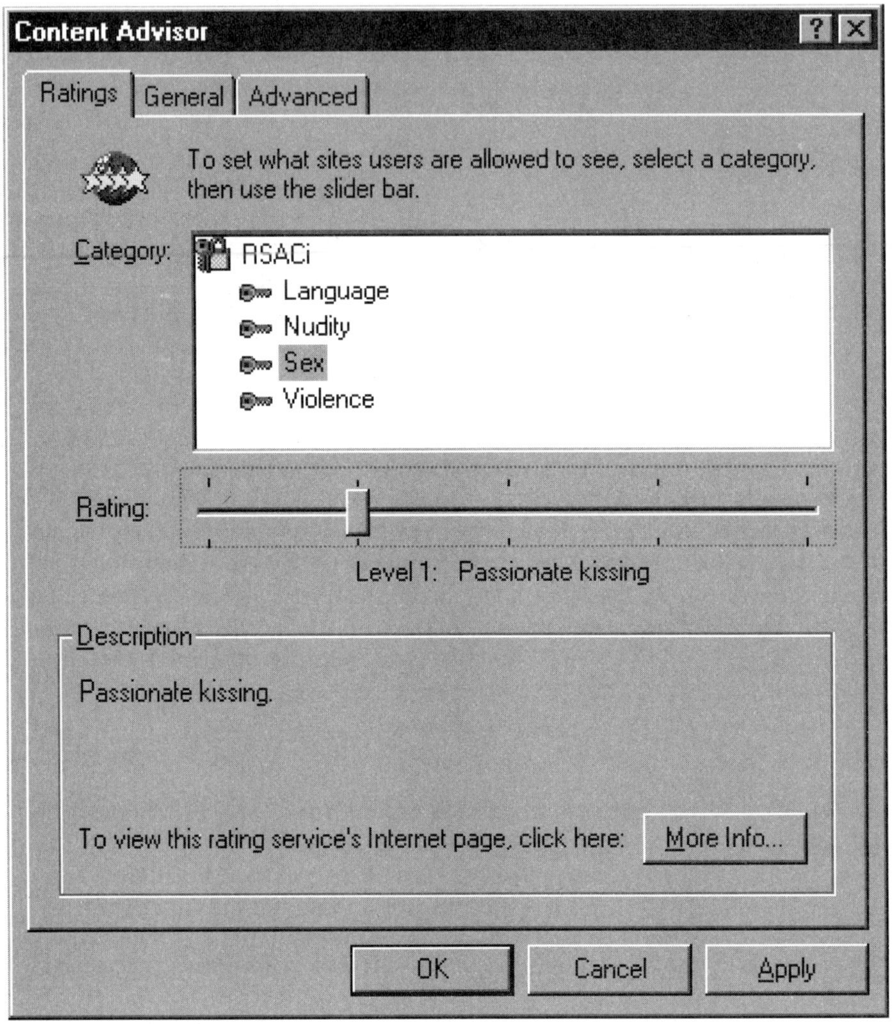

FIGURE 6.2 Internet Explorer's PICS filter allows you to prevent children from viewing pages that might be inappropriate.

its maximum accepted value. When you're finished, the browser will refuse to display pages that exceed these values.

Other settings in this window allow you to install new rating systems, adjust whether the browser will display unrated pages, and the browser to connect to a rating service's Web server in order to retrieve the PICS labels that have been externally rated.

How useful is PICS? Realistically, it is useful only for preventing younger children from accidentally wandering into sites containing sexual or violent subjects. It won't stop children who are actively looking for such material. By the time kids are old enough to be curious about forbidden subjects (approximately age 10) they are also sophisticated enough to find a way to disable the PICS controls, either by editing the system registry or by just downloading and installing a fresh version of Internet Explorer. PICS is more difficult to defeat if the filter is located on a firewall such as one run by a public library or school. Indeed, certain foreign governments are exploring ways of installing PICS filters on national gateways, where they can be used to keep unsuitable sexual, cultural, and political material out of the hands of their citizens.

The real significance of PICS labels is that they are a general mechanism for describing Internet content. They can be used to attach untamperable copyright and authorship information to a document and to describe a Web site's privacy policy regarding information collection and distribution. More information can be found in the World Wide Web Consortium's pages and in the Parental Control FAQ. Both URLs are listed at the end of this chapter.

Advice for Users

Remote Web sites can collect extensive information about users' viewing habits, particularly if the sites collude. Although all sites log access information, most of them do nothing more with this information than crunch it into overall hit rates or search it for signs of technical problems. Some sites do more than this, however, and it is difficult to know which ones they are.

There are a few technical solutions that can increase your chances of remaining anonymous. None is foolproof, and all have their trade-offs.

Anonymizing Proxies

Anonymizing proxies are specially designed Web proxy servers. Like other proxies, your browser sends its URL requests to the proxy, which then forwards the request to the remote Web site on your browser's behalf. Unlike ordinary proxies, which pass through identifying information, anonymizing proxies are careful to scrub all identifiers from the transaction. Referer fields, cookies, and the IP address of your machine are removed before the request is sent to the remote server. The anonymizing proxy is also careful to make no record of your access in its log file.

Advantages

- Anonymizing proxies are effective.
- Once the browser is correctly configured, using the proxy is essentially transparent.

Disadvantages

- An anonymizing proxy will slow the Web response time, sometimes noticeably.
- Sites that depend on cookies may no longer behave correctly.
- Proxies may not support SSL connections.
- Java applets and ActiveX controls can violate anonymity despite the use of an anonymizing proxy.
- You have to trust the anonymizer.

Anonymizing proxies are easy to use. You simply configure your browser to direct requests to the proxy (detailed directions are given in Chapter 14). The proxy can be located on the Internet in your organization's firewall, or at your ISP. The most widely used Internet-based anonymizing service is *www.anonymizer.com*. This site charges $15 for three months of service. (Although the site offers a free trial, a mandatory 60-second delay on each page retrieved makes it effectively unusable.) Other public anonymizers may be available by the time you read this.

The biggest question you should ask yourself before using an anonymizer is whether you trust its maintainers to play fair. Because the anonymizer sees all the traffic that passes through it, there's nothing to prevent it from recording detailed statistics on your usage patterns or even from modifying pages on the fly in order to trick you into sending it confidential information. It is even possible for an anonymizing proxy to play with your mind, creating a "virtual Web" of doctored information that you could peruse for days without suspecting. In the case of *www.anonymizer.com*, the service is jointly sponsored by C2Net and Cyber Pass, two well-known organizations that sell security products and have been involved in Internet privacy issues for years. They claim not to store usage information and nothing has appeared yet to suggest otherwise. Other anonymizer services' reputations may not be so immaculate, however.

Instead of placing your faith in someone else's anonymizer, you might want to roll your own or even convince your organization or ISP to do so. Several software packages make this task easier.

The Internet Junkbuster Proxy is a freeware UNIX-based proxy distributed in source-code form. In addition to blocking cookies and referer information, it can be configured to block advertising, background sounds, animated GIFs, applets, ActiveX controls, and other Web features that some people find annoying or threatening. If you install Junkbuster on your local machine, it will be able to anonymize everything but your IP address. In order to obfuscate your IP address, you'll need to install it on a central machine somewhere, such as a server maintained by your organization or ISP. A Windows version has been announced.

InterMute is similar in conception to Internet Junkbuster, but it is a Java applet that runs within the browser itself. It will block cookies and referer information, as well as filter advertising, animated GIFs, and other annoyances. Because it runs on the same machine as the browser, however, it cannot disguise your computer's IP address. The proxy, currently in beta release, is available for Windows, Macintosh, and UNIX systems.

System administrators who are concerned that employees' worktime Web browsing may leak confidential information should determine whether their existing firewall systems offer any form of outgoing Web-request filtering. If not, they should look into installing Junkbuster or another anonymizing proxy on the firewall.

Cookie Cutters

Both Internet Explorer and the Netscape browsers can be configured to warn before the browser accepts a cookie. You then have a chance to refuse or accept the cookie (Figure 6.3). In the Netscape browsers, the option can be found in the Protocols page of *Options->Network Preferences*. Locate the checkbox labeled "Show an alert before accepting a cookie" and activate it. In Internet Explorer, the option is under *View->Options* on the Advanced page. Scroll down to the section labeled "Warnings" and *uncheck* the confusingly named setting "Do not warn before accepting Cookies."

Unfortunately, having the browser warn before accepting a cookie is problematic. So many sites offer cookies that the warning dialog quickly

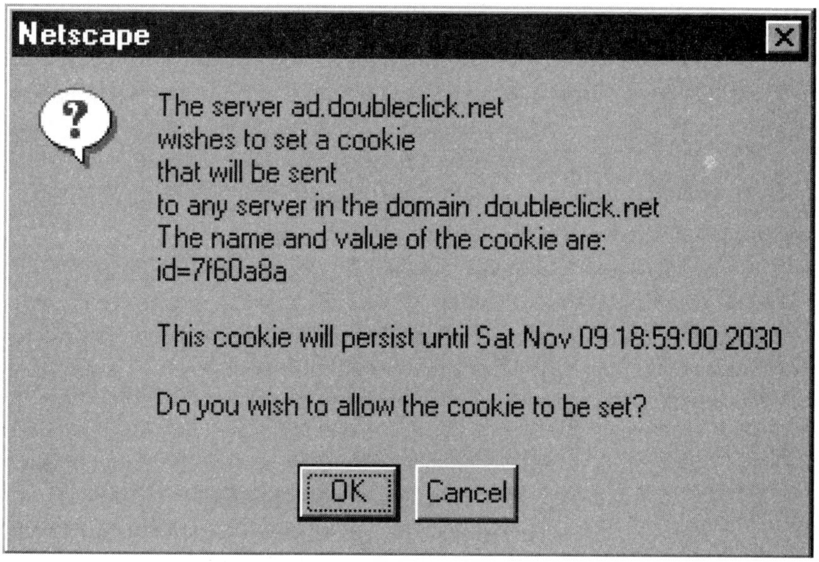

FIGURE 6.3 Internet Explorer and Netscape Navigator (shown here) can be set to warn you before accepting a cookie from a site.

becomes a nuisance. Some sites will also insist on repeatedly offering the cookie even after you've refused it. You can avoid this problem by using one of the anonymizing proxies described in the previous section. Because the cookie is silently filtered by the proxy, the browser doesn't even realize a cookie has been offered.

Unfortunately, if you refuse to accept cookies, you may find that certain Web sites will not work correctly. In the case of Web-based intranet applications and front ends that rely on cookies to maintain state, you may find the programs don't work at all.

An alternative to refusing a cookie entirely is to accept it but not save it to disk. This will eliminate the persistent user ID cookies that advertisers use to tag individuals but still allow the browser to accept the transient cookies that are used by Web-based applications to maintain state.

On UNIX systems, you can prevent the browser from saving cookies to disk by replacing the cookies file with a link to */dev/null*. On Windows and Macintosh machines, commercial programs called NSClean (for Netscape) and IEClean (for Internet Explorer) promise to sweep cookie files clean. These products can also be set to clear periodically the cache and history files, preventing your browsing habits from being disclosed if your computer is compromised.

A better solution to the cookie dilemma would be settings within the browser itself that allowed you to selectively enable cookies from certain trusted sites and disable them for others. The security-zones feature recently announced by Microsoft for Internet Explorer 4.0 (see Chapter 5) seems to offer this capability.

Additional relief is on its way in Netscape Navigator 4.0, which offers many more options for controlling the behavior of cookies. You can choose to accept all cookies, reject all cookies, or warn before accepting cookies. A fourth option is even more interesting. You can choose to accept only those cookies that are submitted by the site that owns the page that is displayed on the screen. Cookies submitted by sites owning graphics, sounds, or other inline elements are quietly rejected. This foils DoubleClick-style schemes. These options can be found under *Edit->Preferences->Advanced*.

Other Ways to Remain Anonymous

E-mail and news article postings leave a record of your return address. You should bear this in mind when posting any fill-out form that sends its results by e-mail or by sending feedback to a Web site. Netscape browsers, but not Internet Explorer, have an option that will warn before sending e-mail in your name (see Settings for Active Content in Netscape and Microsoft Browsers in Chapter 5). Some privacy advocates advise you to enter a phony return address under your browser's e-mail settings. However, this affects all outgoing e-mail and a phony return address is considered antisocial by many.

Another approach is to use an anonymous remailer gateway for outgoing mail and news postings. The gateway receives your mail or posting, strips out identifying information, and posts it using an anonymous account number and a return address that points back to the remailer. E-mailed replies are sent to the remailer, which forwards the mail back to you. These systems provide anonymity, but they can be inconvenient to use and, like anonymizing Web proxies, you have to trust the remailer. A comprehensive listing of anonymous remailers can be found at the *Galactus* site.

Anonymous FTP is, interestingly, one of the back doors that sites occasionally use to recover e-mail addresses from browsers. When an older browser fetches an FTP URL (*ftp:....*) it logs into the remote FTP server with the user name *anonymous* and a password consisting of your e-mail address. Sites can recover your address simply by showing you a page that contains an inline image stored at an FTP site. Recent versions of Microsoft and Netscape browsers avoid this problem. Internet Explorer always sends a phony e-mail address of IE40user@. Netscape Navigator will do the equivalent, but only if the option "Send Email Address as Anonymous FTP Password" under *Options->Network Preferences->Protocols* is *unchecked*. Because of its confusing wording, many people have mistakenly turned on this option.

Advice for Webmasters

Privacy issues are also of concern for Webmasters and system administrators. A Web site that violates users' trust may face adverse publicity. In certain parts of the world, there may even be legal consequences. The following advice gives some rules of the road for Web sites concerned about preserving users' goodwill.

Draft a Privacy Policy

Given the volatile and emotional nature of the Internet privacy debate, it is wise to draft a written policy for your site and display it prominently. Privacy policies can be short and succinct.

Example 1. Complete anonymity

> This site routinely logs all accesses, including user's IP addresses, for the purposes of quality control and statistics gathering. After gathering statistics, the logs are compressed and stored for four days, then deleted. No attempt to correlate your IP address with your identity will be made. This site uses transient cookies to maintain state while using our shopping

card program. These cookies will not be used to identify you or to share personal information with other organizations.

Example 2. User's identity recorded for in-house use only

In the course of using this site, you may be asked to volunteer personal information. This information will enable us to improve your experience at this site. This information will be held in the strictest of confidence at all times. Under no circumstances will it be shared with other organizations or persons.

Example 3. Information shared with selected sites

In the course of using this site, you may be asked to volunteer personal information. This information will enable us to improve your experience at this site. From time to time your name and e-mail address will be shared with other tropical fish and aquarium suppliers in order that you may be alerted to offers that might interest you. If you do not wish to take advantage of this opportunity, please send mail to *webmaster@aquaria.org* and we will remove your name from our lists.

Example 4. Cookies used to track users anonymously

This site uses anonymous cookies to track your use of this and other sites that are members of the XYZ telemarketing network. This information is used to customize our advertisements to match customers' tastes. Under some circumstances, the information gathered from this activity may be shared with other organizations. However, no attempt will be made to correlate cookies with customers' identities.

Example 5. Big Brother is watching

The XYZ Corporation has a firm policy that forbids employees from using the Internet for personal purposes. All Internet accesses from employee's workstations are monitored and routinely scanned for violations. Please refer to the *Employee Handbook* for further details.

A Strictly Anonymous Policy Is the Default

A user's expectation, reasonable or not, is that his or her Web accesses are strictly anonymous. Unless you have an explicit policy that states otherwise, you should observe this expectation.

Cookies should not be used unless they are essential to the operation of your site. Users are sensitive to cookies and may be scared away from your site if they find your site offers them. Some servers generate cookies automatically unless the feature is explicitly turned off. Check yours to be sure.

Server logs should be treated as confidential data. The server should be configured so that server logs are available only to authorized individuals. Log files should be regularly crunched into summary statistics that do not include records of individual Web accesses. The raw logs should then be deleted. If you need to store logs for archival purposes, you should compress and encrypt them with a file encryption program before committing them to long-term storage. Chapters 9 and 10 have more advice on handling server logs.

Personal information provided by users should also be treated as confidential data. File permissions and/or access control lists on files containing personal information should restrict access to authorized administrators. Databases should be restricted by the appropriate authorization measures. Financial information, including credit card numbers, should be treated with the utmost care.

Legal Issues

If you are a U.S. government site, you may be required by law to protect the privacy of your readers. For example, by law, U.S. federal agencies are not allowed to collect or publish many types of data about their clients.

In most states, it is illegal for libraries and video stores to sell or otherwise distribute records of the materials that patrons have checked out. Although the courts have yet to apply the same legal to electronic information services, it is not unreasonable for users to have the same expectation of privacy on the Web. Both federal and several state legislatures are currently debating Internet privacy issues, and it is likely that by the time you read this, bills will have been introduced and possibly passed into law. A discussion of the Clinton administration's thinking on Internet privacy issues can be found in a discussion paper prepared in the spring of 1997 by the National Information Infrastructure Task Force (see Resources at the end of this chapter).

In other countries, such as Germany and France, laws already strictly forbid the disclosure of online access lists and the sharing of personal information among databases maintained by organizations. It is likely that other countries will follow suit.

Policy Initiatives

In response to both widespread public concern about Internet privacy issues and to the growing enthusiasm of lawmakers to do something about it, the software industry has recently undertaken several voluntary programs to regulate the use of personal information on the Web. One approach is exemplified by the TRUSTe Organization (formerly known as eTrust). In the

TRUSTe system, Web sites sign a licensing agreement with TRUSTe. The license binds them to restrict their information gathering and sharing activities to one of three explicit privacy policies.

1. **No Exchange** No personal information is collected by the site except for the IP addresses recorded to server logs. The IP addresses are never linked to other information or used by the site.
2. **One-to-One Exchange** Personal information that the user voluntarily submits will be kept solely within the organization in order to facilitate one-to-one interactions. The information will not be shared with other parties.
3. **Third-Party Exchange** Personal information provided to the site may be shared, transferred, or sold to other parties.

By agreeing to these terms, the site receives the right to use an inline image that displays the TRUSTe trademark and a small icon indicating the privacy policy. A single stick figure indicates no exchange, two stick figures indicate a one-to-one exchange, and so forth. Users can click on the image to bring up a page that gives full information about the site's policy.

TRUSTe intends to use existing trademark and copyright laws to enforce their agreements with Web sites. Web sites that use an inline image without licensing it or that violate the terms of the license will be prosecuted. The hope is that users will learn to recognize and trust sites displaying the TRUSTe logo.

Another approach, recently announced by Netscape, Microsoft, VeriSign, FireFly, and other large Internet vendors, is the Open Profiling Standard (OPS). This technology fits into framework set up by the WWW Consortium, called Platform for Privacy Preferences (P3, not to be confused with PPP).

The P3 specifies a standard vocabulary for describing a Web site's privacy policy. For example, one site might use a user's e-mail address only for the purpose of system administration while another might disclose this information to marketing companies. P3-enabled software products can display a site's policy in human-readable form and can also collect a user's privacy preferences by displaying a detailed questionnaire. When the system finds a mismatch between the user's privacy preferences and those of a site she is attempting to browse, the system warns about the problem and offers the user the choice of overriding the preferences temporarily, editing the preferences, or just accepting the site's policy.

OPS proposes an implementation for the P3 in which the Web site's security policy is distributed as a cryptographically signed, unforgeable certificate. The user's personal information and privacy preferences are likewise stored in signed unforgeable documents. After authenticating themselves to each other, Web browser and server compare the site's policy with the user's preferences in order to negotiate what information, if any, can be shared.

Under the OPS system, a certifying authority is responsible for issuing and signing Web sites' privacy certificates. A site that violates its privacy policy may have its certificate revoked. Not too surprising, VeriSign will be the first CA to offer this service. OPS is expected to be incorporated into the final release of IE 4.0, and it will probably be part of Netscape Navigator 4.0, as well. However, the system will not be of much practical use until it is incorporated into Web servers and wins widespread acceptance from Web site operators.

Although measures such as TRUSTe and OPS are all for the good, they remain strictly voluntary. A Web site doesn't have to buy into the system, and naive users may not realize the difference. Despite these initiatives, it seems likely that lawmakers will ultimately step in to establish national policies to regulate the use of personal information on the Internet and elsewhere. We can only hope that when they do so, their decisions will be wise ones.

Checklist

For Users

1. If your ISP or corporate firewall uses a Web proxy, what is its policy regarding proxy logs?

   ☑ Record nothing
   ☑ Record nothing, anonymize the outgoing request
   ☑ Record everything, use nothing
   ☑ Record everything, use everything
   ❍ Don't know

   As we've seen, Web proxies can diminish privacy by logging amazingly detailed information about a user's personal browsing habits, or it can enhance it by stripping identifying information from the URL request. If your browser is configured to use a proxy, make sure you understand the proxy administrator's policy regarding its logs.

2. Do others have access to your browser's history and cache files?

   ☑ No
   ❍ Yes

   Browsers record to the desktop's disk lots of information about your browsing habits. Make sure that the history and cache files that the browser maintains cannot be read by someone with physical or network access to your system. The same, of course, applies to other personal files and documents.

3. Do you accept cookies?

   ❍ No

   ❍ Yes

   There's no right answer to this one. Most cookies are benign, but some are not so innocent. There's no way to tell the difference between them. Netscape Navigator 4.0's option to reject cookies sent by sites that own the inline graphics on a page closes one of the main sources of cookie abuse.

4. Do you use an anonymizing service?

   ❍ No

   ❍ Yes

   Again, no right answer. However it's important to know that such services exist.

For Web Administrators

1. Does your Web site or proxy have a published privacy policy?

   ❍ No

   ✓ Yes

   It doesn't so much matter what your privacy policy is so long as you have one. If it deviates from a policy of strict anonymity, you should make sure that all users are aware of this fact.

2. Are server log files protected against snooping?

   ❍ No

   ✓ Yes

   Don't treat server logs casually. They are confidential and, sometimes valuable documents. Protect them against unauthorized eyes, and delete them when they're no longer needed.

3. Do you use all the log information you collect?

   ❍ No

   ✓ Yes

   If you don't need the information, don't collect it. For example, many sites collect sensitive referral information but never examine the information.

Resources

Cookies

Netscape Cookie Specification

http://cgi.netscape.com/newsref/std/cookie_spec.html

HTTP/1.1 State Management Specification

http://www.ics.uci.edu/pub/ietf/http/rfc2109.txt

NSClean, IEClean

http://www.nsclean.com/

Anonymizing Proxies

Internet Junkbuster Proxy (UNIX)

http://internet.junkbuster.com/

InterMute (Windows, Macintosh, UNIX)

http://www.intermute.com/

The Anonymizer

http://www.anonymizer.com/

Anonymous Remailers

A good list of remailers and information on using them

http://www.stack.nl/~galactus/remailers/

A comprehensive, but cryptic, list of remailers

http://www.cs.berkeley.edu/~raph/remailer-list.html

Information on anonymizing mail and news gateways

http://students.cs.byu.edu/~don/mail2news.html

A full-service provider of anonymizing services

http://www.cyberpass.net/

Electronic Privacy Resources

The Electronic Frontier Foundation

http://www.eff.org/

Electronic Privacy Information Center (EPIC)

http://www.epic.org/

Center for Democracy and Technology

http://www.cdt.org/

Web Privacy Policy Initiatives

The National Information Infrastructure Task Force's Report on Internet Privacy

http://www.iitf.nist.gov/ipc/ipc-pub.html

W3C Platform for Privacy Preferences (P3) Project

http://www.w3.org/Privacy/

Open Profiling Standard (OPS) Proposal

http://www.w3.org/Submission/1997/6/Overview.html

TRUSTe Project

http://www.truste.org/

PICS

PICS Home Page

http://www.w3.org/pub/WWW/PICS/

Recreational Software Advisory Committee (RSAC)

http://www.rsac.org/

SafeSurf

http://www.safesurf.com/

The Parental Control FAQ

http://www.vtw.org/

Listings of PICS filtering software

http://www.microsys.com/pics/software.htm

http://www.n2h2.com/pics/proxy_servers.html

PART III

Server-Side Security

Don't let the bad guys break in! The rest of this book discusses ways to avoid Webjackings, denial-of-service attacks, breaches of confidentiality, and other nasty surprises.

Chapter 7

Server Security

Installing a Web server is seductively simple. Load the software, adjust a few configuration settings, flip the switch, and, viola, your welcome page is on the Web! Although the mechanics of this operation are simple, the implications are profound. If the server is connected to the Internet, your organization has just become a Web presence, a place where clients, customers, and partners come to learn more about your organization, to shop, to exchange ideas, or to find learning and amusement. Even if the server is restricted to an intranet, you've added a dimension of usability and interest that wasn't there when the network was limited to e-mail and file sharing.

Unfortunately, this increased visibility can have the unwanted side effect of attracting unwelcome attention. As your organization's electronic front door, the Web site host is a natural target for attack. Some attackers may attempt to circumvent the Web server's access restrictions in order to view confidential documents that are intended for internal use only. Others may attempt to Webjack your site and modify its content for thrills or to deliberately embarrass your organization.

Webjackings are not uncommon. It doesn't matter who you are, there's someone who doesn't like you. Sites that have been vandalized during the past year include:

- U.S. Department of Justice
- CIA
- U.S. Air Force
- Nation of Islam
- Kriegsman's Furs of North Carolina
- American Psychoanalytic Association
- National Aeronautics and Space Administration (NASA)
- The Lost World: Jurassic Park
- Republic of Indonesia

- British Labour Party
- Nethosting ISP (all 1,500 clients' home pages vandalized)
- Telia (a large Swedish telecommunications company)

Although the immediate damage was often noticed and repaired in a matter of hours, the effects of Web-site vandalism linger. In each of the above cases, Web surfers noticed the vandalism before the sites' Webmasters did and preserved copies of the Webjacked sites for posterity. You can still see what the Department of Justice or CIA's sites looked like just after they were vandalized (see *http://hem.passagen.se/awesome/index4.htm* for some examples). For some organizations, site vandalism may merely be embarrassing. For others, such as financial institutions, the public knowledge of a break-in may permanently damage their reputations.

Web-site vandalism is, of course, just the tip of the iceberg. A worse threat is someone who breaks into the Web server as a prelude to an attack on other computers in the local area network. In this case, the Web server has provided a portal of entry to confidential information stored on file servers, databases, and accounting systems.

This chapter explains why security holes in Web sites are so common, answers some frequently asked questions, and outlines the steps needed to make your site as secure as possible. Later chapters walk you through the steps at length.

Why Are Web Sites Vulnerable?

Web sites are broken into on a daily basis. A few of the high-profile Webjackings are reported, but most of the break-ins are unpublicized. A substantial number of sites that have been hacked into may not even have noticed the problem. The intruders stole the information they were after and left without a trace, or made subtle modifications to the system that may be discovered accidentally if at all.

The problems that open up security holes in Web sites are various, but they all spring from a handful of root causes, the "eight deadly sins" of Web site security.

Bugs in System Software

A secure piece of software is one that does what it's supposed to and nothing else. In other words, it must be free of bugs. This definition fits a disappointingly small number of programs. As anyone who has worked with computers for any length of time has discovered, software bugs in even the simplest programs are common. Most bugs are inadvertent programming errors, but some are "back doors," bits of code deliberately placed in the program by the software developer in order to aid debugging, then forgotten about by the rollout date.

Bugs become more frequent as programs get larger and more complex. They appear when least expected: in software from vendors both large and small and in programs written for all operating systems. Despite the well-known adage to "avoid version 1.0 software," bugs can be found in release 1.1 or 3.2.

When a bug occurs in an application program, the consequences are annoying. The program crashes, the user's word processor document gets corrupted, or the printer formatting is screwed up. When a bug occurs in a program that acts as a network server, however, it can lead to the compromise of the server's host machine. Typical server software bugs appear when the server is exposed to a condition that its developers didn't anticipate. For example, a server that listens for short commands of less than 100 characters may malfunction when fed a command 10,000 characters long. Other bugs appear when software subsystems interact in unexpected ways, such as a server that behaves strangely when the domain name system becomes inaccessible.

Computer crackers are on the constant lookout for bugs in server software because each bug represents a potential portal of entry. By carefully crafting the input fed to the server or by manipulating the server's environment in a controlled way, the wiley cracker can trick the software into performing some action that no one, including its developers, ever imagined. Often, but not always, the actions are designed to give the cracker access to some part of the system.

Although the basic Web server can be quite small—it needs only listen for incoming requests for URLs, retrieve the corresponding files from disk, and send them across the network—modern Web servers are anything but simple. They come with numerous configuration options; interface to a variety of databases; provide support for advanced Web protocols, such as proxying; have many performance optimizations; and are extensible with programmer's API interfaces and CGI scripts. The executable for a typical Web server is three to five times the size of the executable for an FTP or Gopher server.

Because of the competition among Web vendors, Web servers are being released and updated at a furious rate. This means that the Web server you install on your system takes a double whammy where security is concerned. It's a large and complex program and, therefore, likely to contain security-related bugs. It's young and untested and, therefore, the bugs haven't been shaken out yet. Furthermore, bugs in any systems that interact with the server, such as databases, CGI scripts, and server API modules, may also open security holes.

Table 7.1 lists some of the known security holes in Web servers and CGI scripts. If you use any of these pieces of software, your system has a gaping hole that the bad guys already know about. Some of the holes were discovered within weeks of the time this chapter was written, and the pace of discovery doesn't seem to be slackening. The table will be out of date by the time you read it.

Table 7.1 Known Server and CGI Script Holes

Software	Versions	Description
UNIX Web Servers		
NCSA *httpd*	1.0-1.5a	Remote users can execute UNIX commands with server's privileges.
Apache	1.0-1.1.1	Remote users can execute UNIX commands with server's privileges; remote users can obtain directory listings even when the feature is turned off.
Windows NT Web Servers		
Netscape Communications Server	1.0-1.12	Remote users can execute NT commands with server's privileges.
WebSite Server	1.0-1.1b	Remote users can execute NT commands with server's privileges.
Microsoft IIS	1.0	Remote users can execute NT commands with server's privileges.
Microsoft IIS	1.0-3.0	Remote users can obtain CGI script contents.
CGI Scripts and Server Extensions		
Mindshare Out Box *webdist.cgi*	1.0-1.2	Remote users can execute UNIX commands with server's privileges.
Microsoft FrontPage Extensions	1.0-1.1	Unauthorized users can overwrite and/or append to existing files. If server side includes turned on, users can execute commands with server's privileges.
Selena Sol's Guestbook Scripts	All versions	If server side includes turned on, users can execute commands with server's privileges.
nph-test.cgi	All versions	Remote users can obtain file listing of any directory on Web server machine.
nph-publish.cgi	1.0-1.1	Remote users can overwrite files outside document directory provided that Web server permissions permit.
PHP extensions	Various versions	Remote users can execute commands with server privileges (CGI script version only; module versions seem unaffected).
AnyForm	1.0	Remote users can execute commands with server privileges.
FormMail	1.0	Remote users can execute commands with server privileges.
phf phone book	All versions	Remote users can execute commands with server privileges.

System Software Is Incorrectly Configured

Even if the Web server and all its supporting software are free of bugs, a Web site won't be secure unless the server, all other network servers, and the underlying operating system itself are correctly configured. Although network-ready operating systems were designed to be securable, it often requires some effort to achieve this goal. When vendors ship a shrink-wrapped system, their primary goal is not to make it secure but to make the system easy to install and use. As a result, most systems ship in their most permissive mode. Popular network services are turned on by default, remote configuration facilities are enabled, and the policy for accessing system files is very liberal. Just plug in the system, and you may find yourself running a Web server, a Gopher server, a login server, and an FTP site without even knowing it! Running a network server that you don't know about is a major vulnerability. If you haven't configured the server yourself, chances are that it is not configured the way you want it.

Another vulnerability is default user accounts that some operating systems create as an installation convenience, but fail to delete when no longer needed. In the past, some systems have even come with a preinstalled Guest user account that allows anyone to log into the system and rummage around without providing a password.

The default configuration of Windows NT Workstation is particularly promiscuous, although the server version is less so. Many dialects of UNIX come with all the bells and whistles activated, and it takes some effort to achieve a system that does just what you need it to do and nothing else.

A widespread problem is misconfigured file permissions. Multiuser operating systems, UNIX and Windows NT included, use account privileges as their fundamental security mechanism. Each registered user has a different login account. Each account is associated with a different set of privileges, granting or denying it the ability to read and write certain files, open network connections, and access device drivers. This mechanism gives trusted users, such as system administrators, the ability to make necessary adjustments in the system configuration while preventing others from making unauthorized changes. If a configuration file that should be modified only by system administrators is inadvertently made writable by untrusted users, a malicious user can exploit this fact to modify the system and possibly expand her access to the system.

Like users, network servers and other programs also have distinct privileges. Many servers, in fact, log into the system using accounts that were set up especially for them. In theory, a server should have only the privileges that it needs to do its job. In practice, many sites give their servers much broader access to the system than they need. When this is the case, the server becomes a particularly tempting target for attack. The system cracker will seek to exploit holes in the server software to execute commands of his choosing.

When she succeeds, the commands will be executed with the server's privileges, allowing her access to confidential information and other sensitive parts of the system. Some sites have even made the mistake of running the Web server under an administrative account, effectively giving the subverted server limitless powers. Unfortunately, the default configuration of certain Web servers encourages this practice.

Single-user operating systems that weren't originally designed to support network services, such as Macintosh and Windows 95, have a different set of issues. Unlike their big brothers, these systems do not come with a default suite of network services—you must install and configure the software yourself. Some people argue that this fact makes these systems more secure than their big brothers. However, these systems appear to have an increased vulnerability to denial-of-service attacks that crash or cripple the system. An attack that makes the Web site unavailable may be just as devastating to a mission-critical application as a break-in. More seriously, however, single-user systems do not have a concept of account privileges. This means that a compromised Web server or CGI script has unrestricted access to the entire system, giving it the power to do extensive mischief.

The Server Hardware Isn't Secure

If the server hardware isn't secure, nothing is. This almost goes without saying, but it's ignored surprisingly often. If the server isn't physically secured, then you can forget about all other security measures. If the Web server is located in a computer lab, lounge, unlocked telephone closet, or other common area, it isn't secure. If it doubles as a general-purpose workstation, it probably isn't secure either. Even if the machine requires a user name and password to log in locally, it's both simple and quick for someone with a floppy disk to reboot the machine in permissive mode and steal or modify data. Even if your organization has strict rules against unsupervised outsiders gaining access to the building, you still have to worry about insider threats.

Networks Are Not Secure

Until we all start using IPS (see Chapter 3), all transmissions across the Internet and most local area networks are unencrypted, and anyone with access to the network and the right software can intercept messages with packet sniffers. This means that Web documents, e-mail, and interactive login sessions are all vulnerable to eavesdropping.

At particular risk are account names and passwords, which can be intercepted using specially designed password sniffing programs. Although statistics aren't available, it's likely that, of all the techniques in the system cracker's armamentorium, the password sniffer has contributed to the greatest number of successful break-ins.

Some security-conscious Web sites have focused on system security to the exclusion of network security. This is a mistake. Crackers need only find the weakest link in the system. If a cracker can't break into the machine that hosts the Web server, she will attack a less hardened computer on the same segment of the network. Once in, she can eavesdrop until she recovers a Web server login password transmitted by an unsuspecting author or administrator. From here, it's a simple task to get into the Web host itself.

If the cracker doesn't care about breaking in, but is looking to steal confidential documents transmitted across the network, her job is even easier. She need only set up a sniffer somewhere along the path between server and browser and wait for the document she wants to happen by.

Remote Authoring and Administration Tools Open Holes

Web servers require care and feeding. Log files need to be examined, performance parameters need tweaking, new disks and directories must be added from time to time. The content of the site is always being changed, updated, and renewed.

If you perform these tasks by sitting down in front of the server machine, logging in, and running the administration utilities locally, there's a good chance that what you're doing is safe from prying eyes. However, this isn't always feasible, particularly when many authors and administrators need simultaneous access to the machine. For this reason, many sites use authoring and/or administration tools that support remote updating. Some sites are updated from other machines on the local area network, sometimes from across the Internet. But as we know, networks aren't secure.

Although convenient, remote administration and authoring raises a number of issues. By making it easier for legitimate users to make changes to the Web site, you may inadvertently be making it easier for the wrong people to get in, as well.

Insider Threats Are Overlooked

Although most of the publicity about computer crime comes from dramatic system break-ins by outsiders, most threats are from people who have a legitimate reason to use the system. There are many reasons why a user would want to tamper with his own organization's computer system, ranging from idle curiosity to industrial espionage to the disgruntled employee who wants to bring the walls down with him when he goes. You can't assume that everyone who has a right to access the system is nice or will play by the rules.

A large organization may maintain multiple Web servers. There may be a public server for Internet users, as well as intranet servers for each of the accounting, engineering, marketing, sales, and administration departments. The public server faces threats from the outside, as well as from the inside. The departmental servers each face threats from within their respective departments, as well as from other departments (consider the member of engineering hired by a competitor to obtain information maintained on the sales server). The same attention to security that would be given to an Internet server should be lavished on an intranet site. Some would argue that intranet servers require more attention.

Denial-of-Service Threats Are Often Ignored

What's the good of a state-of-the-art, well-designed, properly configured, secure operating system if any high school student armed with a personal computer and a modem can crash it on a moment's notice? That's the lesson that Microsoft learned in late June 1997 when it was discovered that Windows NT and Windows 95 systems would hang when sent a ICMP ping packet in which the packet size specified in the header didn't match the actual packet size. Computers attacked in this way became unresponsive and had to be manually rebooted.

Although this problem was patched quickly, it illustrates the vulnerability of many systems to simple attacks that make the system unavailable. Sometimes, this is just annoying, but for mission critical applications it can be a serious concern.

You Don't Have a Security Policy

If you don't have a security policy, you can't know if your site is secure. A Web site should have a written security policy. Nothing fancy, just a list of what is and is not permissible. It should reflect your organization's political realities and whatever trade-offs between risk and convenience you are willing to accept. Example 7.1 is a simplified security policy from a hypothetical corporate Web site.

Notice that there's very little technical detail in this security document. It simply says what should be done, not how to do it. The importance of a security policy is that it gives you something concrete against which to design and evaluate your security measures. For example, the restriction on access to the FTP server could be implemented using a firewall system. How effective will that measure be? What advantages might it offer over other technical approaches?

You can also use the security policy to evaluate proposed changes to the system. For example, you might be asked to install a remote authoring package on the Web site. Would this change violate any of the policy's prohibitions? What other changes need to be made in the system to accommodate this modification?

EXAMPLE 7.1 MegaComm Security Policy

PERSONNEL

Access Levels

The Web site grants five levels of access:

1. *The public*—read-only access to all URLs with the exception of the */private* directory.
2. *Employees of MegaComm Corporation*—read-only access to all parts of the site, including the */private* directory.
3. *HTML authors*—ability to create, modify and delete HTML files in the document tree.
4. *Site administrators*—ability to modify Web server configuration files, install CGI scripts, and start and stop the Web server.
5. *System administrators*—ability to modify the Web server host configuration, and start and stop the host machine.

Authorization Procedure

For access levels 3, 4, and 5, personnel must obtain written authorization from the Director or Deputy Director of Information Systems. The written authorization must be presented to a system administrator, who will set up the appropriate account and privileges. Access level 2 is granted automatically to all new employees when they receive their e-mail account and LAN password.

Revocation of Authorization

For access levels 2 through 5, authorization may be revoked without warning at the discretion of the Director or Deputy Director of Information Systems. In case of emergency, a system administrator may also revoke access. This action must be reviewed and confirmed within 24 hours by the Director of Information Systems or her deputy.

ACCESS PRIVILEGES

Local Login

Local (console) login to the Web server host is allowed for system and site administrators only. Logins are for the purpose of site maintenance only.

Network Login

All forms of network login are forbidden, including file sharing.

Authoring Access

HTML authors and site administrators have the right to make changes to the document tree. All authorizing access is via FTP from machines located within the *.megacomm.com* domain. Modifications are timestamped and logged. Except in emergencies, direct modifications to the document tree via local login are forbidden.

Remote Server Administration

Not allowed. All server administration is done locally.

EXAMPLE 7.1 MegaComm Security Policy *(continued)*

Browsing Access

With the exception of the */private* URL, anonymous Web browsing is allowed throughout the site. */private* is restricted to computers within the *.xyz.com* domain.

CGI Script Installation

CGI scripts can be installed by site administrators after at least two members of the site administrators group have reviewed and approved the code. CGI scripts for which source code is unavailable cannot be installed without prior approval by the Director or Deputy Director of Information Systems.

Access to the */private* Directory

The */private* directory contains information that is confidential to the MegaComm Corporation. Access is restricted to host computers in the *.megacomm.com* domain.

NETWORK SERVICES

Web

The Web site will serve static HTML documents and the output of CGI scripts. Incoming Web data is limited to customer feedback and discussion groups, whose scripts deposit their information in isolated databases. Neither CGI scripts nor the server itself are to make connections with other databases, file systems, or services on the LAN without prior written authorization by the Director of Information Systems.

FTP

Incoming and outgoing FTP is provided for the purpose of updating Web pages only. FTP access is restricted to HTML authors, site and system administrators, and only to computers located within the *.megacomm.com* domain. Anonymous FTP and all access from outside the *.megacomm.com* domain is forbidden.

Other Services

No other network services are provided by the Web host.

MAINTENANCE

24 × 7 Operation

The site should be accessible 24 hours a day, 7 days a week, except for a 2-hour maintenance period between 7 AM and 9 AM on Sundays. System administrators should be prepared to switch to a backup server in a timely manner in case the primary server develops hardware problems.

Backups

A complete backup of the Web server host will be done weekly, and incremental backups daily.

EXAMPLE 7.1 *(continued)*

Monitoring

A system administrator is responsible for monitoring the Web server host system logs for errors and other unusual activity. A site administrator has similar responsibility for the Web server logs. Any suspicious activity should be brought to the attention of the Director of Information Systems immediately. A system or site administrator who detects suspicious activity and has reason to believe that the integrity of the system or MegaComm confidential information is imminently threatened is authorized to take the Web server off-line.

Frequently Asked Questions About Web Server Security

Here are answers to a few of the most frequently asked questions about Web security. I give them here because they explode several popular myths and misconceptions.

Which Operating System Is Most Secure?

Without question, of all the operating systems in use for Web servers today, the Macintosh OS is the most secure. This is because Macintoshes don't have a command interpreter and don't, in general, run any network services. A Macintosh would rather crash than let someone break in.

In February 1996, a consortium of Macintosh Internet software development companies, including StarNine, the developer of the WebStar server, posted a $10,000 reward to anyone who could read a password-protected Web page on a Macintosh running WebStar software. After tens of thousands of unsuccessful attempts, no one stepped forward to claim the prize and the contest was eventually closed.

Of course, the main reason that the Macintosh is secure is because its default capabilities are limited. Start adding special services to it—CGI scripts, an FTP server, fancy server extensions—and it rapidly becomes a more risky venture.[1] And the Macintosh is not immune to denial-of-service attacks, as shown by Apple's extended delay in providing a fix for the Ping

---

1. These words were prophetic. Although the first Crack a Mac contest closed without anyone claiming the prize, the second such contest, sponsored by a Swedish consulting firm, announced a winner just as this book was going to the typesetter. The vulnerability proved to be a third-party extension that provides remote administration services. This extension wasn't installed on the server used in the original contest.

of Death attack, a vulnerability similar to the ping attack that brought down Windows systems in the Spring of 1997. This problem was known for many months before Apple was able to provide a fix.

Of the other two contenders, UNIX and Windows NT, the verdict is a toss-up. Both systems have had their share of security problems, and the fact that there have been more security incidents involving UNIX only reflects the fact that UNIX has been around longer. Both operating systems are reasonably secure if configured correctly, but sievelike if not.

At the bottom line, it's the experience of the people running the server host and software that is the most important aspect in system security. If you are most comfortable with a UNIX system, then UNIX will be most secure. If you are an experienced Windows NT administrator, than that system is less likely to produce unpleasant surprises.

Are "Secure" Servers Really Secure?

"Secure" servers are simply those that can protect documents in transit with encryption. From the broader standpoint, secure servers are just as vulnerable to break-ins as any other server.

What Web Server Is Most Secure?

The simpler the server, the more secure it is likely to be. Web servers that do nothing but retrieve static HTML pages are far less likely to contain bugs than are fancy ones with bells and whistles. For example, John Frank's WN server for UNIX systems has a reputation for security and reliability. However, it does not run CGI scripts, offer server-side includes, allow for Java servelets, or support sophisticated authentication schemes. Therefore, it is unsuitable for many sites.

A few Web servers are designed specifically for high-security applications. Hewlett Packard's VirtualVault server is a turnkey system that consists of the Netscape Commerce Server running on top of an extensively modified version of the HP-UX operating system. This operating system, which is said to exceed the U.S. military's B1 security rating, divides the system into an "inner," trusted area, where databases, privileged CGI scripts, and other sensitive information live, and an "outer," untrusted zone, where the Web server runs. All communication between the inner and outer zones is heavily regulated and audited. The system was designed for use by large financial operations and has, in fact, been adopted by at least one online banking operation.

The WebCompare Web site provides up-to-date comparisons among a large number of Web servers for various operating systems and hardware platforms.

Will a Firewall System Make a Web Server Secure?

A firewall system is just one component of an integrated security strategy. By itself, a firewall won't make the server any more secure and may in fact make it less so. If the server is configured well, you may not need to use a firewall system at all. If you don't have a well-thought-out security policy and implementation strategy, the firewall may make the situation worse by lulling you into a false sense of security. More information on firewalls can be found in Chapter 14.

How Do I Prevent Users From Copying HTML Documents?

Webmasters frequently ask whether there is any way to prevent browser users from printing HTML documents, saving them, peeking at secrets stored in "hidden" fields, or obtaining the names of CGI scripts and private links. There is no way to prevent this sort of thing. For the browser to display the HTML document, it must download its source code, then render it. The user is then free to do whatever she likes with the HTML code. If you are considering implementing a security system based on information hidden inside the HTML document, think again. A sophisticated user will be able to circumvent the system in no time.

In contrast, the source code to CGI scripts is not transmitted to the remote browser, only the script's output. The same applies to server side includes ("active server pages" in Microsoft parlance). Only the HTML that is produced after the CGI script or server side include is processed gets relayed across the network.

Overview: Steps to Securing a Web Site

So much for the risks. What can you do about them? The remainder of this chapter presents a seven-step plan for securing a new or existing Web site. Later chapters flesh out the details.

1. **Secure the Operating System and Web Server.** Make the operating system as secure as possible by installing the vendor's security-related patches, removing unnecessary services, and fixing the default configuration to make it less permissive in a process known as "hardening." When the operating system is secure, you can install the Web server software itself.

   Advice for hardening the operating system and Web server is given in Chapters 8 (UNIX) and 9 (Windows NT).

2. **Monitor the Server for Suspicious Activity.** Some attacks are obvious. Others are not. The vast majority of server attacks go unnoticed. Chapters 8 and 9 also give advice on monitoring the Web and system log files for signs of suspicious activity.

3. **Control Access to Confidential Documents.** Not all parts of the Web server are public. Many sites have private areas that only registered users are allowed to visit. In an intranet environment, you may wish the entire site to be open by invitation only. Chapter 10 introduces the basic mechanisms that Web servers use to authenticate and authorize remote users.

   SSL-capable servers go two steps further in protecting confidential information. They can encrypt Web documents as they pass over the network, and they can use client certificates to provide reliable user authentication. Chapter 11 gives guidance on using these features.

4. **Write Safe CGI Scripts.** Even if the server, operating system, and all the support programs are secure, the very next CGI script or server module that you or someone else installs may leave the site open to attack. Chapter 12 discusses where CGI script problems come from and what to do about them.

5. **Set Up Remote Authoring and Administration Facilities.** Chapter 13 reviews the tools available for administering Web sites safely across a network and shows how to allow Web authors to update the site without letting everyone do the same thing. The problems (with solutions) of running the FrontPage Web authoring package figure prominently.

6. **Protect the LAN Against the Web Server.** Before connecting the Web server to the Internet, you should ensure that it can't be used as a springboard for attacking other mission-critical machines within your organization. The same applies to large intranets in which one department doesn't trust another. This can often be achieved by carefully hardening the server and removing trust relationships between it and other members of the LAN. Sometimes, however, you'll need to go further and erect a wall between the server and the LAN. Chapter 14 describes how firewalls can help you do this.

7. **Keep Up on Security Issues.** Security holes are discovered every day. A site that seems secure today may not be so tomorrow. Periodically check the Web sites of your operating system vendor and the manufacturers of all the third-party software you have installed. If you see a security-related patch or advisory, be sure to take action as soon as you can.

Several organizations provide security advisories to the community in the form of Usenet postings and e-mailed notifications. Although these advisories aren't guaranteed to be timely or complete, you can't afford to ignore them. The bad guys subscribe to the mailing lists too. There are also several

Usenet newsgroups and mailing lists that are devoted to discussions of computer security. Sometimes the advice is good—sometimes it isn't.

A list of good general sources for security information follows.

Resources

Operating System Security Information and Alerts

CERT (Computer Emergency Response Team) Coordination Center

This is a part of the Software Engineering Institute at Carnegie Mellon University. To subscribe to its security advisory mailing list, send an e-mail message to *cert-advisory-request@cert.org* with a *subject* line of "SUBSCRIBE *your-email-address.*"

Advisories are also published in the Usenet newsgroup *comp.security.announce* and archived at *ftp://info.cert.org/pub/*

Linux-alert

This is a moderated mailing list run by the RedHat company. It carries alerts specific to the Linux operating system. Many of the alerts that appear here are applicable to other UNIX dialects. Subscribe to it by e-mailing a letter to *linux-alert-request@RedHat.com* with a *subject* line of "subscribe."

Archives of the mailing list can be found at *http://www.redhat.com/linux-info/security/linux-alert/*

Bugtraq

This is an unmoderated mailing list devoted to finding, exploiting, and fixing UNIX security holes. Note that the information on unmoderated lists should always be treated with some caution: The poster may be misinformed. To subscribe, send e-mail to *bugtraq-request@fc.net* with the message "subscribe bugtraq."

An unofficial archive of the mailing list can be found at *http://www.geek-girl.com/bugtraq/archives.html/*

NTBugtraq

This is similar to the Bugtraq but devoted to Windows NT security issues. To subscribe, send e-mail to *listserv@rc.on.ca* with the message "SUB NTBUGTRAQ *your name.*" Use your full name, not your e-mail address.

An online archive is available at *http://ntbugtraq.rc.on.ca/archives/ntbugtraq.html*

NT Security Mailing List

This mailing list is devoted to security issues in Windows NT. To subscribe, send mail to *majordomo@iss.net,* with the message "subscribe ntsecurity *your e-mail address.*"

An archive is available at *http://www.iss.net/lists/*

RISKS forum

This is a moderated forum for the discussion of risks to society from computer systems. It is distributed as a weekly posting to the Usenet group *comp.risks*. Archived postings are available at *ftp://crvax.sri.com/risks/*

Forum of Incident and Response Security Teams (FIRST)

FIRST is a coalition of computer emergency response teams from more than 50 software vendors, academics, and government organizations. From its Web site, you can find pointers to security-related information about your system, as well as information about who to contact if you think you have a problem.

Hardened Web Servers

HP VirtualVault Web Server

http://hpcc995.external.hp.com/gsy/security/virvault/

John Frank's WN Web Server

http://hopf.math.nwu.edu/docs/security.html

WebSTAR WebServer

http://www.starnine.com/

WebCompare Web Server Comparison Site

http://www.webcompare.com/

Chapter 8

UNIX Web Servers

This chapter is devoted to the issues of installing and configuring a UNIX-based Web server. Although I assume that the reader has a basic grasp of the UNIX command shell, user account system, and file system, I do not assume the reader has an advanced knowledge of UNIX.

Although most of this chapter will be irrelevant to Windows NT administrators (skip forward to the next chapter), the section on Web server log scanning is well worth reading because both UNIX and NT Web servers use similar log file formats.

Hardening a UNIX Web Server

The UNIX operating system was designed in the days of mainframes, when no one could imagine having a computer devoted to the needs of a single person. One of the most basic aspects of UNIX is that it is a multiuser system. A single machine supports several (or hundreds) of users. Each has a unique home directory and environment, and each is protected against interference from the others by a system of access permissions. Files, programs, devices, and other system resources are all protected by access control. A user cannot modify or even read a particular resource unless her account has been granted the ability to read or write it. To simplify things, users can be placed into groups that have certain access rights and privileges in common. When a group as a whole is granted permission to access a resource, the permission is automatically extended to all users within the group.

User and group access rights are the basis for UNIX security. Every program that runs on a UNIX system, including those that provide Internet services, runs with the permission of some user or another. A typical UNIX server system will run several services to handle such things as remote login, the printer, incoming FTP, and e-mail. Each of these services runs under a user account. For example a user named *lp* is used for the printer server, *ftp* for the FTP server, and *daemon* for various other services.

The *root* user, also known as the superuser, is a single all-powerful administrative account that has unrestricted access to all parts of the system. Users that have logged in as root have broad powers (to do good, as well as to do damage) because no part of the system is protected from them. The same applies to services that run with superuser privileges, which is why this practice is strongly discouraged.

When you first unpack a UNIX system, it is set up as a general purpose machine and may not be particularly secure. You will need to harden the system before you can safely host a Web site with it. Most of the messy work in setting up a UNIX Web server secure involves just four tasks.

1. Apply vendor operating system patches.
2. Turn off unessential services.
3. Add the minimum number of user accounts.
4. Get the file and directory permissions right.

Ideally you should take these steps off-line *before* you physically plug the system into the network.

Apply Operating System Patches

All software contains bugs, and the operating system is no exception, even if it is well-tested and comes from a venerable and respected vendor. Bugs pop up in all OS versions, not just those that have a zero at the end. Most vendors provide a Web page for distributing patches and upgrades to the OS. Bookmark the page and check it every so often. When a patch appears, read its release notes. If it seems to have anything to do with security, download and apply the patch. Be aware that in order to get the benefit of a particular patch, you may have to download and apply the whole series of patches that proceeded it. Before applying any patches to your system, make sure that you have a backup. Also be aware that many patches will require that the server be taken off line. If the server is currently providing Web services, perform the upgrade at a time when the interruption won't be disruptive.

The details of installing system patches are varied. Often you need only replace one executable with an updated one. However, sometimes you may need to rebuild the kernel if the security hole is a particularly low-level one. You will find full instructions with the patch file.

Security Scanners

"Security scanners" are programs that probe your system for known security holes and configuration weaknesses. Scanners include the freeware COPS and TAMU systems, which run locally and can detect such problems as incorrect permissions on directories, as well as programs that will scan your machine across the network looking for holes in server software. SATAN and the Internet Security Scanner (ISS, both freeware and commercial versions) are the two most popular network-based scanners.

Although a security scanner is no substitute for a careful personal check of the system, it is good to check your system with at least one of these tools—preferably with several. In particular, SATAN and ISS have been widely used by potential intruders to scan other people's systems for vulnerabilities. If you don't run them on your system, someone else will. Information on obtaining these tools can be found at the end of this chapter.

Disable Extraneous Network Services

A typical out-of-the-box UNIX installation comes with all the fancy extras turned on. To give a popular example, a newly booted RedHat Linux distribution comes with FTP, Gopher, Web, mail, POP, NFS, and even Windows NT file-sharing servers up and running. Many of these servers won't be needed for your purposes, and some pose a security risk unless configured carefully.

On UNIX, there are two types of network servers. There are "daemons" that are launched at system start-up time. Daemons lurk silently in the background until an incoming network request comes in on their assigned network port. They handle the request and then resume their brooding watchfulness. There are also servers that are launched on request by *inetd,* the super-daemon. The *inetd* program waits for incoming connections on any of a number of network ports. When a request comes in, it launches the specific server that knows how to handle the request. When the server is finished with the request, it simply exits. *Inetd* will launch it again to handle subsequent requests.

A simple way to obtain a definitive list of what Internet services are running on your system is to use the *netstat* program to find all ports that are in the "listening" state—ones for which a server process has registered itself with the operating system. The arguments to *netstat* vary slightly from system to system. On the Linux system that I do most of my server testing on, the command to obtain information about listening ports is shown on the next page.

```
lstein> netstat -atu
Active Internet connections (including servers)
Proto Recv-Q Send-Q Local Address          Foreign Address         (State)      User
tcp        0      0 prego.wi.mit.edu:1256  prego.wi.mit.edu:7001 ESTABLISHED   root
tcp        0      0 *:666                  *:*                   LISTEN        root
tcp        0      0 *:auth                 *:*                   LISTEN        root
tcp        0      0 *:6000                 *:*                   LISTEN        root
tcp        0      0 *:sunrpc               *:*                   LISTEN        root
tcp        0      0 *:pop3                 *:*                   LISTEN        root
tcp        0      0 *:7001                 *:*                   LISTEN        root
tcp        0      0 prego.wi.mit.edu:7001  prego.wi.mit.edu:1256 ESTABLISHED   root
tcp        0      0 *:www                  *:*                   LISTEN        root
tcp        0      0 *:finger               *:*                   LISTEN        root
tcp        0      0 *:time                 *:*                   LISTEN        root
tcp        0      0 *:smtp                 *:*                   LISTEN        root
tcp        0      0 *:telnet               *:*                   LISTEN        root
tcp        0      0 *:ftp                  *:*                   LISTEN        root
tcp        0      0 *:chargen              *:*                   LISTEN        root
tcp        0      0 *:daytime              *:*                   LISTEN        root
tcp        0      0 *:discard              *:*                   LISTEN        root
tcp        0      0 *:echo                 *:*                   LISTEN        root
tcp        0      0 *:printer              *:*                   LISTEN        root
tcp        0      0 *:shell                *:*                   LISTEN        root
tcp        0      0 *:login                *:*                   LISTEN        root
tcp        0      0 *:exec                 *:*                   LISTEN        root
udp        0      0 *:xdmcp                *:*
udp        0      0 *:ntp                  *:*
udp        0      0 *:sunrpc               *:*
udp        0      0 *:bootps               *:*
udp        0      0 *:time                 *:*
udp        0      0 *:chargen              *:*
udp        0      0 *:daytime              *:*
udp        0      0 *:discard              *:*
udp        0      0 *:echo                 *:*
udp        0      0 *:ntalk                *:*
udp        0      0 *:talk                 *:*
udp        0      0 *:syslog               *:*
```

This machine runs a lot of servers! The third column of this listing, which shows the local address and port of all network connections, is the most interesting. All the entries that begin with an asterisk correspond to servers that are listening for connections. This system runs Web and FTP servers (*www* and *ftp*), a post office protocol server (*pop3*), and servers that allow the machine to receive e-mail (*smtp*).

The more servers running on a system, the more possible avenues for someone to break in. A Web server system should only be running those services that are essential to its operation. What you consider essential, of course, depends on your needs and how you decide to balance security with convenience.

Servers launched by *inetd* are generally found in the file */etc/inetd.conf*. The format of the file is straightforward and usually well documented. You can disable a server simply by finding the appropriate line in the file and commenting it out by placing a hash mark (#) in front of it. The service will be disabled the next time you reboot the system. If you want the changes to the configuration file to take effect immediately, find the process number of the *inetd* program by using the *ps* command, then send the process an HUP signal

```
lstein> kill -HUP 58
```

Services that run as persistent daemons are launched from shell scripts when the system first boots up. The location of these scripts varies from system to system. On older systems, they're located in */etc* or */etc/rc.d* and have names like *rc.system* and *rc.local*. To prevent a server from being started, you should find the place in the script where the server is launched and comment it out, again by placing hash marks in front of the line or lines that start the server. On newer systems, the scripts are located in a directory called *init.d*, which is sometimes located in */sbin* and sometimes in */etc/rc.d*. There are usually a dozen or so scripts, each of which launches a different server. At boot time, the system looks in specially named directories called *rc1.d*, *rc2.d*, and so forth, for symbolic links that point to the server scripts to launch. To disable a service, just locate and remove its link.

You will find summaries of the various UNIX services in most books on UNIX system administration. Don't be shy about disabling network services. There is little chance that you will render the machine unbootable. If you happen to abolish a service that you need, you can always enable it again later.

Certain services are known to be problematic from a security standpoint. If you disable nothing else, get rid of

- tftp
- finger
- systat
- netstat
- uucp
- exec
- login
- shell

The last three services are used by the Berkeley "r" commands (*rlogin* and so forth) and should not be confused with the TELNET service. In addition, many versions of the *sendmail* program are seriously buggy. Unless the server is doubling as an incoming mail gateway, the *sendmail* program (usually launched at boot time) should be disabled. This will not interfere with your ability to send outgoing mail from the server host. Gopher and FTP services should be disabled unless you wish to provide these services. You should also know that certain versions of the syslog and lp daemons are buggy. Upgrade or disable them if necessary.

After disabling all unneeded services on my newly installed Linux system, *netstat* suddenly got very quiet!

```
lstein> netstat -atu
Active Internet connections (including servers)
Proto Recv-Q Send-Q Local Address          Foreign Address         State
tcp        0      0 *:telnet               *:*                     LISTEN
udp        0      0 *:syslog               *:*
```

Only two services are now running on this machine. The incoming TELNET service, used for network login, and the *syslog* service, which records log entries (strictly speaking, it isn't necessary to run even this service). Incoming TELNET service is now the only remaining portal for entry from the network. Remove this and someone would have to have access to the machine's keyboard and console in order to break in. If you need remote access to the server machine across the Internet, you might consider replacing TELNET with the Secure Shell, or with a password system based on one-time passwords or an access card. These options are discussed in Chapter 13, in Remote Authoring and Administration.

Add the Minimum Number of User Accounts

The major sources of Internet break-ins are intruders who have obtained a valid user name and password and use it to log into the server. Sometimes, they obtain a valid password by stealing the system password file (through some security hole) and running a "Crack" program to discover poorly chosen passwords; sometimes, they do it by sheer guesswork and, sometimes, by other means—for example, by noticing a password that's been written on a scrap of paper and taped to a monitor. Despite all attempts to change human behavior, people continue to choose easily guessed passwords, to write their passwords on pieces of paper, and to give their passwords to official-sounding strangers on the telephone.

For these reasons, you'll want to minimize the number of users who can log into the machine. You need one account for yourself and additional accounts for people who will be administering the Web server. Whether you need accounts for the Web authors—those responsible for the content of the site—will depend on how you arrange for the content of the Web site to be updated. If you have a few authors only, it's easiest to have them log into the server machine from your organization's local area network or use FTP to transfer files. If you need to support a large number of authors, some of whom will be working remotely, you'll need a mechanism for updating the Web site content automatically. See Chapter 13 for strategies.

In addition to the root account, most UNIX systems come with a dozen or so predefined accounts for the use of various servers and daemons. Occasionally, some systems are delivered with well-known passwords attached to these predefined accounts. You should go over the system password file carefully to make sure that none of these built-in accounts can be used for login. The password field of each of the predefined accounts (with the exception of root!) should be disabled by placing an asterisk in the second field of the appropriate line of */etc/passwd.*

```
uucp:*:10:14:uucp:/var/spool/uucppublic:
```

When you add users to the system, take advantage of whatever convenience facilities, such as an *adduser* script, that your flavor of UNIX provides. Although it's straightforward to add users by directly editing the password file, it's easier and less error prone to let the automated script do it for you.

Install the Web Server Software

After hardening the operating system and adding user accounts, the next step is to install the Web server (if it isn't already preinstalled). The details differ from server to server, but usually there will be an install script of some sort. Select a location to install the server, and follow the vendor's directions for unpacking and installing the software. The easy part is now done.

In most cases, the vendor's default setup will create a series of directories and executables that are accessible by anyone who can log onto the system. This provides little in the way of security, either from remote users or from nosy local users. Much of the risk from running a Web server can be avoided by carefully restricting access to the server and its support files. The fewer the accounts with access to the server's configuration files, logs, and documents, the more proof the system is against unauthorized modification. The hard part is to modify the directory and file permissions to grant access to only those who really need it.

Although the details vary from server to server, there are several general types of directory used by the Web server. Each has its own issues of privacy and security.

- **Configuration directory** The configuration directory contains files that control server operations. Everything from the network port on which the server listens to the home page's location is determined by the configuration files. It's important to prevent unauthorized modifications to these files.
- **Webmaster tools directory** This contains a variety of executables intended for the Webmaster's use. There may be utilities for managing the server's own access control system, for generating cryptographic keys, and for creating searchable document indexes.
- **Log file directory** This directory contains logs in which the server records all accesses to it, as well as any errors that occurred during operation. The logs frequently contain information that is sensitive, if not private, and should be protected against prying eyes.

The Crack Program and Shadow Passwords

On UNIX systems, user's passwords are stored in the file */etc/passwd,* along with other information about the user, such as her home directory and preferred command interpreter. A typical line from the password file looks like

```
fred:EYObQtjmjsN0.:504:100:Fred Gallo:/home/fred:/bin/csh
```

The password, stored in the second colon-delimited field of this line, has been processed through a one-way hash function, called *crypt(),* to produce an odd-looking string of letters and numbers. Because of the nature of the algorithm, there's no way to work backward from the encrypted password to the human-readable password. However, the system can still use it to verify that the password the user gives in response to the login prompt is the correct one. It takes the plaintext password, passes it through *crypt(),* and compares the encrypted result with the stored one. If they match, the user's password is valid.

The main weakness of this system is that people pick easily guessed passwords. If an attacker has access to the password file, she can take a large dictionary of common passwords and pass them all through *crypt().* He can then compare these encrypted passwords, one by one, with those in the password file until he finds a match. Several programs that do this are widely available; the most famous one is "Crack." Along with Crack go several dictionaries that encompass English and foreign words, commonly used variants and misspellings, and such series as 12345 and qwertyuiop. Crack typically recovers 20 percent to 25 percent of passwords.

You can attack this problem either by making the passwords harder to guess or by making the password file harder to intercept. Several replacements for the standard UNIX password-changing program reject the user's profferred password if it matches a known word or pattern. You can also run Crack on your own password file at regular intervals. None of these methods is foolproof because the attackers may have better dictionaries than you do.

One of the problems of the UNIX password file is that it must be world-readable—that is, readable by ordinary users as well as by privileged ones. If the attacker can exploit a bug in a network server, such as a poorly written CGI script, she can read the password file even though the server is running as an unprivileged user. If, on the other hand, the password file were readable only by the root user, the attacker would have a harder time of it unless she already had root access (in which case, she wouldn't be bothering with the password file!).

Some UNIX Systems support a "shadow password" system in which users' encrypted passwords are stored in a separate file named */etc/shadow* or */etc/security/passwd.adjunct*. This file is readable only by the root user, and programs that need to access the passwords, such as *login* and *su,* are modified to access this file. The regular */etc/passwd* file still exists in order that programs can find users' home directories and other nonsensitive information, but the password values are replaced with dummy data.

The Crack Program and Shadow Passwords *(continued)*

If your UNIX vendor offers shadow passwords as an option for your system, you should take advantage of them. Otherwise, you may be able to upgrade your system by using John Haugh's freeware shadow password suite. In addition to providing shadow password support, it also provides account aging and protection against simple passwords.

- **CGI directory, server module directory** The CGI directory contains server scripts that are invoked to produce dynamic documents, access databases, and perform interactive tasks. The module directory, if one exists, allows programmers to add their own compiled code functions to the server, thereby extending its functionality. Poorly written CGI scripts and server extensions are major source of Web server vulnerabilities. These directories should be restricted.
- **Document directory** Also known as the "document root," this is the top of the HTML file tree and contains the site's welcome file and all other static documents. The document tree may be spread out among several physical directories. For example, some sites have separate directories named *icons, html,* and *java,* which the server combines into one logical hierarchy.

In addition to these, there is often another type of directory that contains ancillary information that the Web server uses while in operation. The most frequently encountered of these is a "security" directory that holds password files that the server uses for access control.

There are four classes of user that need access to the Web server, its documents, and support files:

1. **Webmaster.** The Webmaster, also known as the site administrator, needs both read and write access to the server's configuration files. She also needs read access to its logs for the purposes of tracking down and solving problems. There may be one Webmaster, or there may be several. Because of their power, it's safer to keep the number of Webmasters to a minimum.
2. **Web author.** This type of user needs read and write access to the document tree in order to install and maintain HTML files and images. Authors don't need access to the log or configuration files (either write *or* read), and shouldn't be allowed to alter CGI scripts or server modules.
3. **Web developer.** This user is a Web author with the added ability to install and modify CGI scripts and server modules. The developer has write permission for the CGI directory in addition to access to the document tree.

4. **Web server.** Like any other UNIX program, the Web server, while running, uses the permissions of a particular user. This virtual user needs read access to the document tree but should be restricted from writing to any of the Web directories. It also must be able to execute any script located in the CGI directory. It must *not* have read access to the server's configuration and log files.

Table 8.1 summarizes these access rights.

Assign a UNIX Group to Each Type of User

The easiest way to enforce rational Web server access restrictions is to create a UNIX group for each type of user. This is true even if most of the maintenance and updating of the Web site is accomplished with remote administration tools and people rarely log in directly.

One way to set this up is to create the following administrative groups.

- **webmaster** The Webmaster and all assistant Webmasters belong to this group. Membership in this group grants write access to the configuration directory and read access to the log directory.
- **webdevel** All programmers with responsibility for creating, installing, and maintaining CGI scripts and server modules belong to this group. Membership in this group grants the user the ability to make modifications in the *cgi-bin* directory tree.
- **webauth** This is a general group for authors. Members of this group can freely read and write to the Web document hierarchy.
- **http** This is a group for the Web server to belong to. As described later, I also like to create an *http* user for the Web server to run as.

Certain users will need to belong to several groups. Developers need write access to the document tree, as well as to the *cgi-bin* directory, so they must belong to *webauth*, as well as to *webdevel*. Webmasters need access to all locations, so they should belong to *webdevel* and *webauth*, as well as to *webmaster*. For example, given a site in which *maria* is the Webmaster, *john* is the CGI script developer, and *joseph*, *clarissa*, and *george* are authors, an excerpt from the system's */etc/group* file might look like

```
webmaster::100:maria
webdevel::101:maria,john
webauth::102:maria,john,joseph,clarissa,george
```

Group Private Directories

The main stumbling block for setting up collaborative group projects on UNIX systems is that whenever a user creates a new file in a project directory, her primary group (usually something generic, like "users") is attached to it by default. The user can explicitly change the new file's group to what-

TABLE 8.1 Access Rights for Web Server Files

User	Configuration	Tools	Logs	CGI	Documents
Webmaster	RW	R	R	RW	RW
Web developer	—	—	—	RW	RW
Web author	—	—	—	R	RW
Web server	—	—	—	R	R

Key: R = Read access; W = Write access

ever is appropriate for that directory, but in practice, most people don't bother to do this. The result is a set of Web directories that would seem to have distinct access permissions but whose contents, in reality, are files whose permissions don't honor the administrative boundaries you've set up.

To avoid this, I like to use a system called "group private directories." In this scheme, the group ownership of each directory is set to be the group that has permission to add to its contents. The directory is now made group-writable and -executable. In addition, its *set-group-id (sgid)* bit is set, causing newly created files to be have the same group as the parent directory. Any new directories that are created will also have the set-group-id bit set. This solves half the problem—that of creating new files and directories with the correct group ownership. The second half of the problem is to make sure that each newly created file is both group-readable and -writable, allowing one member of the group to make modifications to a file created by another. A simple way to do this is to make each users umask mode 002. You can do this by including a command like this one in each user's login script.

```
umask 002
```

This causes newly created files to be group-readable and -writable. We would seem to be done—but there's one last catch.

Files in users' private directories, such as home directories, now don't have any protection against modification by other members of their groups. In most cases, you don't want home directories on the Web server machine anyway, so this isn't an issue. But if you need to do this, you can make users' home directories private by assigning each user a like-named primary group that no one else belongs to. For example, Maria's primary group would be a group named *maria* with a membership of one. This is the "private" part of the group private directory scheme.

Directory Settings for a Generic Server Root

Assuming that you are using the generic directory organization introduced by the NCSA and Apache servers, here's the directory listing that shows the server root set up with the access restrictions I've just described.

```
drwxrws--x   2 root    webdevel      1024 Apr 13 21:56 cgi-bin/
drwxrws---   2 root    webmaster     1024 Apr 22 21:30 conf/
drwxrwx--x   6 root    webauth       1024 Nov 16 23:26 htdocs/
---x------   1 root    bin         197389 Jan 15 16:30 httpd*
drwxrwx--x   2 root    webauth       2048 Nov 16 23:26 icons/
drwxr-x---   2 root    webmaster     1024 May  3 22:03 logs/
drwxrws--x   2 root    webmaster     1024 Apr 22 21:30 security/
drwxr-x---   2 root    webmaster     1024 Apr 22 21:30 support/
```

Let's look at the settings in detail.

htdocs, icons

The document root and any other directories that contain HTML pages, images, Java applets, or other types of multimedia file (but not CGI scripts) are writable by the *webauth* group. Permissions should be set differently, depending on whether you're running a small site in which all authors trust each other and allow other authors to modify their files, or a large site in which authors do not trust each other—and may not even know one another.

If all Web authors trust each other, use the *chmod* command to set the directory mode to 2771 (`drwxrws--x`). This gives all Web authors the ability to add to the document root. Provided that you use the group-private system and the authors' default umask is 002, newly created subdirectories and files will automatically be writable by *webauth*, allowing any member of the group to make changes.

If Web authors cannot trust each other, set the directory mode to 0771 (`drwxrwx--x`). This allows any Web author to create a new subdirectory within the document root, but each new subdirectory is created with the group ownership of the user's private group. The owner can make changes freely, but other authors are excluded. An author who wants to share a file can explicitly change its group ownership with the *chgrp* command.

If some Web authors trust each other and others don't, create additional UNIX groups for each set of collaborators. Set the document root mode to 0771 so that any Web author can add new subdirectories. For each collaborative group, create a subdirectory owned by that group and with mode 2771 permissions. Members of the group can freely add and modify files within the subdirectory, but other other authors cannot. UNIX-savvy authors can also do the dirty work of creating collaborative subdirectories themselves. Notice that in all cases, the permissions are set up in such a way that users that do not belong to the Web authors group cannot obtain a directory listing of the document root. This is intentional. A variety of security breaches have been the result of remote users finding forgotten temporary files and autosave files in the document hierarchy. Removing the listing privilege makes this more difficult.

If you want to take advantage of the Web server's ability to generate directory listings on the fly (not recommended) change the access mode to 2775 (`drwxrwsr-x`) for the desired directories.

cgi-bin

The CGI script directory is owned by user root, group *webdevel*. Its mode is set to 2771 (`drwxrws--x`), which gives members of the *webdevel* group full read/write access. Newly created files and subdirectories will be writable by other developers unless the owner changes its permissions. If you work in an environment in which one developer cannot trust another, set this directory's mode to 0771 instead.

Other users, including the Web server, have execute permission for the directory, allowing them to read and run the programs inside it but preventing them from listing the contents of the directory.

The cgi-bin directory should contain nothing but executables. If the executable is a compiled program that can be executed directly, its mode should be 0771 (`-rwxrwx--x`). This provides an added measure of protection against an unauthorized user obtaining the executable's code and possibly decompiling it. If the executable is written in an interpreted language such as Perl, it will need to be world-readable (mode 0775, `-rwxrwxr-x`).

conf

The configuration directory should be owned by user root, group *webmaster*, and set to mode 2770, which prevents access by anybody other than the root user or a Webmaster. All configuration files within it should be mode 0660 (`-rw-rw----`) to prevent reading or modification by unauthorized users.

Logs

The logs directory is owned by the root user and by the *webmaster* group. Its access mode of 0750 gives Webmasters the ability to read the files contained within it but not to make any changes. Others are completely excluded. The log files within this directory should all have mode 0630 (`-rw-r-----`). Most Web servers will create log files with root ownership.

Security

The security directory, a nonstandard name that I use for the directory that contains the password and group files used by UNIX servers for access control (see Chapter 10), should be owned by root and the *webmaster* group. Its 2771 permissions prevent non-Webmasters from making any changes to its contents and from obtaining a listing of its contents. However, because the Web server needs to be able to read the password and group files contained within, it needs to have execute access to the directory.

Support

This directory holds various Webmaster tools and utilities. The access mode of 2770 allows members of the *webmaster* group to run the programs contained within it. Others are not permitted to use these tools.

The Web server itself, *httpd*, has permissions that make it executable by root only. This reflects the fact that the server will ordinarily be started at system boot-up time by the root user. You probably don't want to make it possible for unprivileged users to start a new instance of the Web server.

Run the Web Server as an Unprivileged User

The Web server will ordinarily be launched by the root user at system boot time. It must be started with root permissions so that it can open HTTP port 80 (on UNIX systems, ports 1 through 1,023 are privileged ports that can be opened only by the superuser) and so that it can open the server log files for writing. After launch, the Web server process relinquishes its root privileges and services all incoming requests as an unprivileged user. This avoids the disastrous consequence of having a rogue root process at large if the Web server is ever compromised by a malicious remote user.

Many Web servers are set up to run as a user named *nobody*, belonging to the group *nogroup*. This configuration works well but has the slight disadvantage that the *nobody* user is shared by other servers—in particular, the NFS server. In order to make the Web server accountable for its actions, I recommend creating special user and group accounts for the Web server's use, both named *http*. Having specially assigned IDs also enables you to selectively grant certain privileges to the Web server. For example, you can give CGI scripts write permission to a dropbox directory by making it group-writable by *http*.

The *http* user should not have a login password or a shell. Its home directory can be whatever you want. You might like to choose the server root as its home directory so that you can refer to it from the command line as *~http*. A typical entry from */etc/passwd* might look like this

```
http:*:20:20:WWW Daemon:/usr/local/etc/httpd:
```

The corresponding entry from the */etc/group* file should look like

```
http::20:
```

The numeric user and group IDs will depend on the numbers already used on your system. There's no particular reason for the user and group ID to be identical. It is important, however, that the *http* user not belong to any other groups, such as *users*. This might result in the server getting more access to the system than you intend.

Once server-specific user and group IDs are created, you should configure the server to use those IDs at start-up time. The details are vendor-specific. On an Apache or NCSA *httpd* server, edit the configuration file *httpd.conf* to contain these two directives.

```
User http
Group http
```

A final small but important detail. At launch time, the Web server creates several files to record logging and status information; some of these files contain sensitive information. Some servers create these files with world-readable permissions by default. If the server configuration file provides this feature, you should change the default permissions to remove world access. If this isn't an option, alter the default file-creation umask before the server is started at boot time. A umask of 027 will make the log and status files completely inaccessible to normal users while granting group-read permission. If you've set the system up so that the log file directory is *set-group-id* to the *webmasters* group, you will be able to read them. A typical excerpt from a boot script might look like

```
if [ -x /usr/local/etc/httpd/httpd ]; then
  echo "Starting Web services..."
  UMASK=`umask`                    # save the current umask
  umask 027                        # mask off world read/write bits
  /usr/local/etc/httpd/httpd
  umask $UMASK                     # restore the umask
fi
```

Configuring the Web Server

The previous section focused on the operating system, directory structure, and other aspects external to the Web server itself. We now look at steps for making the server itself run as securely as possible.

Disable Unnecessary Web Server Features

Modern Web servers come with an amazing variety of features. They can generate fancy directory listings on the fly, perform keyword searches of your site, display casual users' personal home pages, and provide gateways to other information services your organization supports. In the past, some of these fancy features have been found to introduce security holes. Unless you absolutely need a feature, the most conservative approach is to disable it.

Automatic Directory Listings

The first feature you should consider turning off is the server's ability to synthesize directory listings on the fly. During the creation and maintenance of a site, all sorts of detritus can accumulate in the document root: test files, scripts, text editor, autosave files, notes, handy links, and outdated pages. If automatic directory listings are left on, it's possible for the casual user to browse through this stuff, learning more about your system than you might like. You can turn off automatic listings either by putting a "welcome" file in each directory (usually named *index.html*) or by entirely disabling the feature. It's generally easier to turn directory listings off than to try to remember to create a welcome page for every directory in your document tree.

Symbolic Link Following

Another feature you should consider turning off is the ability to use symbolic links to extend the document tree to other parts of the file system. Particularly when a Web site is under the control of a group of people, it's easy for someone to create an inadvertent link to a sensitive place, opening up a private directory tree to the outside world. If you turn off symbolic link following, it is still possible to extend the virtual document tree over multiple physical locations, but it has to be done explicitly in the server's configuration file.

CGI Scripts and Server Modules

Executable scripts pose a potential risk because buggy scripts can be coerced into doing things that their authors didn't anticipate. In the past, several CGI scripts have been the subject of CERT advisories. Some, in particular the *phf* script, have been widely used to break into vulnerable systems. (See Table 7.1 in Chapter 7 for a listing of some other scripts that are known to be problematic.)

CGI scripts and modules should be restricted to a limited number of designated directory trees. Although some servers allow CGI scripts to be scattered freely among static files in the document hierarchy, you should avoid this, if you can. It makes the job of finding and auditing the scripts more difficult, and it opens up the possibility that a malicious individual can steal a script's source code. To see how this happens, consider a site that writes a lot of its CGI scripts in Perl and has installed a script named *place_order.pl* in its document root.

```
/usr/local/etc/httpd/htdocs/place_order.pl
```

One day, one of your site's programmers makes a change to the script using a text editor that thoughtfully creates backup files. There are now two versions of *place_order.pl* in the document root.

```
/usr/local/etc/httpd/htdocs/place_order.pl
/usr/local/etc/httpd/htdocs/place_order.pl~
```

The backup file is not executable, nor does it have a file extension recognized by the server as belonging to a CGI script. If it's requested, the Web server will treat it as a text file. The savvy remote user can retrieve the script's source code just by requesting the URL *http://your.site.com/place_order.pl~*

Restricting scripts to a designated CGI directory guarantees that the server will never treat them as normal text files and return their source code. You should know which scripts and plug-ins are installed on your server, and you should know what each one does. Demonstration and testing scripts should be moved off-line before you make your server publicly accessible. Think carefully before installing any new CGI script. If its source code is available, have someone who understands network programming go over it carefully. Although I'd like to be able to tell you that scripts and plug-ins from commercial software houses are more trustworthy than freeware scripts downloaded from the Internet, experience suggests that this isn't necessarily so.

Remember to take advantage of the protection that file-system access privileges give you. When the Web server executes a script or module, it does so under the user ID assigned to it in its configuration file. By limiting the access of this user to the system, you can limit the extent of the damage that an errant script can perform.

Server-Side Includes

Server-side includes allow Web authors to create HTML pages that change dynamically, without resorting to full-blown scripts or plug-ins. One type of server-side include allows various variables, such as the time of day, to be incorporated into the HTML page. This is benign and poses no security risk. Another type allows CGI scripts to be executed from within the page. This poses no more of a risk than running the CGI script directly and can also be allowed. However, a third type, the so-called exec include, allows arbitrary system commands to be executed and their output incorporated into the page. Unless the author really knows what she is doing, this type of include can expose the system to substantial risk. This type of include should be disabled.

User-Supported Directories

User-supported directories allow casual users of the system to maintain a set of Web pages in their home directories without mucking around in the server's official document tree. The user's personal pages can be accessed with a URL that contains the ~ character, as in *httpd://your.site/~fred.*

In my experience, many users expose themselves to risk through this facility, sometimes inadvertently placing private documents in their Web-accessible directories or, worse, creating symbolic links that open up private directories to public perusal. Allowing casual users to install CGI scripts in their home directories is generally an invitation to disaster.

A truly secure Web server shouldn't have casual users, and you may want to turn this feature off entirely. If you need this feature to host users' Web pages, however, I recommend that you restrict what can be placed into user-supported directories by excluding symbolic link following, server-side includes, and CGI scripts.

Start and Stop the Server Without Requiring Root

Of necessity the Web server must be started as root. One also requires root privileges to stop the server, or restart it after a reconfiguration. Starting the server is usually not an issue, as most sites start it automatically from a system boot-time script. But stopping and restarting the server can be problematic because the operation requires root access.

A good policy on any UNIX system is to minimize the number of people who have access to the root account, and to use root privileges as rarely as possible. This helps prevent the root password from being disclosed, and makes the transition easier when the time comes to change the password. However, most Web servers have to be restarted after every small change to their configuration file. As a result, some Web sites have given the root password to the Webmaster and Web developers.

A better way to handle this is to eliminate the need to become root in order to administer the server. Set up a *set-user-id* (*suid*) script to start, stop, and restart the server. Make the script *suid* to root, and executable only by members of the *webmaster* group.

Listing 8.1 shows a Perl script to accomplish this task. You will need to modify the path names for the particulars of your site. A single script selects among the tasks of starting, stopping, and restarting the server, by examining the name of the symbolic link used to invoke it.

```
lrwxrwxrwx  1 root  webmaster  10 Sep  9 08:11 restart_http -> start_http*
-rwsr-x---  1 root  webmaster  681 Sep  9 08:09 start_http*
lrwxrwxrwx  1 root  webmaster  10 Sep  9 08:11 stop_http -> start_http*
```

A final note. The script is implemented in Perl rather than in a shell language. This is because *suid* shell scripts are not secure in many UNIX systems and can be abused by local users to gain root privileges. Recent versions of Perl work around this limitation and are safe to use.

Consider Running the Web Server in a Change-Root Environment

Many Internet servers, such as FTP and Gopher, have traditionally limited the risk of running the server by running it in a *chroot* environment. When the server starts up, the operating system places it in a box from which it cannot escape. After the *chroot* operation, the server's start-up directory, which may have been some deep subdirectory of the system such as */usr/local/etc/httpd*, becomes the root directory */*. The operation is irreversible,

LISTING 8.1 Restarting the Web Server Without Root Access

```
#!/usr/bin/perl

# These constants will need to be adjusted.
$PID_FILE = '/usr/local/etc/logs/httpd.pid';
$HTTPD = '/usr/local/etc/httpd -d /usr/local/etc/httpd';

# These prevent taint warnings while running suid
$ENV{PATH}='/bin:/usr/bin';
$ENV{IFS}='';

# Do different things depending on our name
($name) = $0 =~ m|([^/]+)$|;

if ($name eq 'start_http') {
    system $HTTPD and die "Unable to start HTTP";
    print "HTTP started.\n";
    exit 0;
}

# extract the pid and confirm
# that it is numeric;
$pid = 'cat $PID_FILE';
$pid =~ /(\d+)/ or die "PID $pid not numeric";
$pid = $1;

if ($name eq 'stop_http') {
    kill 'TERM',$pid or die "Unable to signal HTTP";
    print "HTTP stopped.\n";
    exit 0;
}

if ($name eq 'restart_http') {
    kill 'HUP',$pid or die "Unable to signal HTTP";
    print "HTTP restarted.\n";
    exit 0;
}

die "Script must be named start_http, stop_http, or restart_http.\n";
```

so even if subverted, the server cannot access any files or directories outside its box. Although this does not completely eliminate all risks—for example, a malicious user could still try to trick the server into probing your firewall via the network—it does close many avenues of attack.

Some servers, such as the Netscape Enterprise server, have a *chroot* feature built in. To enable the feature, you must manually edit the server's *Magnus.conf* configuration file to include a line like

```
Chroot /usr/local/etc/httpd
```

Replace */usr/local/etc/httpd* with the true absolute location of the server root. You must now edit all pathnames in the *obj.conf* file to be relative to the server root. Any files that the server, its CGI scripts, or plug-ins need must be copied into the server root. For example, if some of your CGI scripts refer to the Perl interpreter at */usr/bin/perl*, you must create *usr* and *usr/bin* subdirectories within the server root, then copy the Perl executable into it. On many systems, you may find that some executables will fail at launch time if they depend on dynamically linked libraries and/or device-special files that are not present within the server root. In such cases, you can either recompile the executable with static linking or mirror the entire shared library in an appropriately named subdirectory within the server root. For dependencies on device files, you may have to make a *dev* subdirectory within the server root and then use the UNIX *mknod* program to create a device-special file with the correct name and mode. Once this has been accomplished, just restart the server.

For servers that don't have native *chroot* support, such as Apache and NCSA *httpd*, you'll need to recompile the server with static linking. Otherwise the executable will be unable to run because essential shared libraries are unavailable after the *chroot* operation. All absolute pathnames in *httpd.conf*, *srm.conf*, and *access.conf* must be rewritten to be relative to the new root. For example, a *ServerRoot* directive that had been */usr/local/etc/httpd* becomes:

```
ServerRoot /
```

Any files and executables used by CGI scripts must also be copied into the server root as described above, and references to absolute path names must be fixed, if necessary. For the server to change its user and group IDs after starting up, you either have to change its *User* and *Group* directives to use numeric user and group IDs or create minimal *etc/passwd* and *etc/group* files within the server root. These files need contain no more than the user and group IDs that the server runs under; *no user passwords should be present!*

When you are ready to start the server, launch it using the *chroot* system command, passing it the path to the *chroot* directory and the command to use to launch the server after the *chroot* operation has taken place. For example, if you had been launching the server with

```
/usr/local/etc/httpd/httpd -d /usr/local/etc/httpd
```

change it to

```
chroot /usr/local/etc/httpd /httpd -d /
```

Limit Denial-of-Service Attacks

Denial-of-service attacks are those in which a malicious individual makes your server unavailable for normal use. Some denial of service attacks, such as the TCP/IP SYN attack, or the Ping of Death, cannot be prevented without applying an operating system patch (if one is available) or a firewall system designed for this purpose.

Other denial-of-service attacks are directed at the Web server itself. You can't avoid these attacks entirely, but you can take some actions that will reduce their impact. A typical denial-of-service attack is to flood the Web server with URL requests. The server gets so bogged down servicing these requests that valid requests can't get through. Sometimes things can get so bad that you can't even use the machine interactively and are forced to hit the reset switch.

Both the operating system and the Web server software provide you with ways to keep the Web server's resource usage under control. On the operating system level, you can set resource limits with the *limit* (C shell) or *ulimit* (Bourne shell) commands before launching the server. Among the things you can limit is the Web server's memory usage, the number of files it can open simultaneously, the number of child processes it can spawn, and the amount of CPU time it is allowed to use. The settings for these values depend on your operating system, but it is wise to set some reasonable upper limit on them to prevent the server from monopolizing the machine during a denial-of-service attack. It's also a good idea to set the core dump size to 0. One mode of attack is to force the server to crash and then examine its core dump for passwords and other secrets.

The Apache Web server versions 1.2 and higher provides several configuration directives of its own for controlling resource use, including RLimitCPU, RLimitMem, and RLimitNPROC. You can use these directives to override the operating system defaults or in combination with them. The settings limit the amount of CPU time, memory, and the number of procedures the server is allowed to spawn. They are ordinarily found in *httpd.conf*.

Other important directives for adjusting resource use include MaxClients, Timeout, and KeepAlive. The first directive limits the number of simultaneous incoming requests that the server will attempt to handle. Beyond the limit, the server will refuse new connections. By default, this is set to 150, which is a reasonable value for moderately busy servers. The second directive controls how long the server will allow a browser to keep the connection open. If the time-out value is excessively long, a malicious user could keep many connections open simultaneously, blocking access to your server. The last directive controls how many times the server will honor browsers' requests to keep the connection open. If this value is set too high, a malicious user might exploit it to block connections in the same way.

If you adjust any of the limits downward, be alert to signs that you are denying services to legitimate users. For example, if you set the time-out limit too low, the server may prematurely terminate the download of unusually long documents.

For other servers, check the documentation for similar settings that limit resource consumption.

Monitoring Logs

The log files maintained by the Web server and the files created by the UNIX system itself offer you a rich harvest of information. The logs can reassure you that the system is running smoothly or warn you that something is broken. If you know what to look for, the logs will alert you to suspicious activity and help you prevent a break-in.

UNIX System Logs

The UNIX system keeps a series of log files. Depending on the system you use, they will have various names and be found in different locations. Popular locations include */var/log*, */var/adm*, and */usr/adm*. The standard *syslog* system allows you to customize what does and does not get recorded to the log files. For example, you can choose to record all messages from the mail and login servers but quench all but error messages issued by the printer daemon. Control over what gets logged is kept in the configuration file */etc/syslog.conf* and is well documented in the UNIX manual pages.

Although the location of the log files varies, their format is similar from system to system. Here's a partial excerpt from a log file on a Web server machine named *waldo*:

```
May  2 16:36:20 waldo sshd[388]: Connection from gumbo port 1022
May  2 16:36:23 waldo sshd[388]: Password authentication for will accepted.
May  2 16:36:54 waldo su: will on /dev/ttyp1
May  3 03:30:56 waldo sshd[13615]: connect from limbo port 1023
May  3 03:30:56 waldo sshd[13617]: executing remote command as root: ps auxwww
May  3 03:30:58 waldo sshd[13619]: connect from limbo port 1023
May  3 03:30:58 waldo sshd[13620]: executing remote command as root: ps auxwww
May  3 04:30:08 waldo rdist[16307]: banquo: LOCAL ERROR: Response time out
May  3 18:15:32 waldo in.telnetd[3392]: connect from 148.57.48.133
May  3 18:15:55 waldo login: 2 LOGIN FAILURES FROM h133n48.names.hal.com, q
May  3 18:15:59 waldo login: 3 LOGIN FAILURES FROM h133n48.names.hal.com, quit
May  3 18:16:02 waldo login: 4 LOGIN FAILURES FROM h133n48.names.hal.com, exit
May  3 18:16:10 waldo login: 5 LOGIN FAILURES FROM h133n48.names.hal.com, quit
May  3 18:16:15 waldo login: 6 LOGIN FAILURES FROM h133n48.names.hal.com, l^H^H
May  3 18:16:29 waldo login: 6 LOGIN FAILURES FROM h133n48.names.hal.com, EOF
```

This excerpt starts at 4:30 in the afternoon, when a user named *will* used the encrypting secure shell program to log into *waldo* from a machine named *gumbo*. He provided a correct password and was allowed in. Soon afterward, he used the *su* command to become root.

Because I know that Will is an authorized system administrator who needs to become root from time to time, and that his usual workstation is Gumbo, this doesn't arouse any suspicions. If, on the other hand, we were to see Will logging in from a machine outside the local area network, or if he were logging in outside his usual working hours, this might be cause for concern.

Following this, there's not much activity until 3:30 the following morning, when user *root* on a machine named *limbo* tries to execute the command *ps auxwww* twice. This too is expected—it's part of the automated backup script that runs on limbo.

At 4:30 A.M., there is a time-out error message from the *rdist* program. This machine uses *rdist* to mirror its Web tree to a backup server named *banquo*. There's no response from *banquo*, indicating that it is either down or misconfigured in some way. In this case, *banquo* had been taken off-line for a hardware upgrade, so the error was expected.

At 6:15 P.M. on May 3, there is a more ominous spurt of activity. The incoming TELNET daemon (which has been left running on this machine for emergency use) reports a connection from IP address 148.57.48.133. A few seconds later, this is followed by a stream of login failures, as the person that connected tries a series of invalid user names. While this could be evidence of a break-in attempt, the user names that were tried, *q*, *quit*, and *exit*, point more toward a hapless newbie who accidentally started the TELNET program and then didn't know what to do.

The recommended practice is to log *everything* and to run the whole thing nightly through a script that filters out all the expected patterns. Once that's done, examine what that's left and follow up on any unexpected entries. If there's too much noise in the residue, add more patterns to the filter.

If you prefer not to write your own scripts, you can use Swatch, a configurable Perl script that monitors UNIX system logs and takes actions when certain patterns are seen. Actions include sending mail to a user, ringing the terminal bell, printing out a warning on the system console, or invoking some other program or script. The list at the end of this chapter tells you where to find it.

Because logs record evidence of unauthorized access, intruders often try to delete or cleanse them. If the unauthorized user has gained root access, there's no way to protect anything located on the local file system. However, several versions of the *syslog* facility allows you to redirect log entries to remote machines. If you have another UNIX host that is network accessible to the Web server, you can have the Web server redirect some or all of its log entries to that machine. If this machine is secure, intruders will not be able to alter the log files; at the very least, it will make it more difficult for them to do so. To enable this feature, add a line or two to */etc/syslog.conf.*

```
*.notice                @host1.yourorg.com
*.notice                @host2.yourorg.com
```

These two lines specify that all messages of priority "notice" or higher will be forwarded to the *syslog* facilities in the machines named *host1* and *host2* on your local area network. (For obscure reasons, the white space separating fields in the file has to be tabs rather than spaces. See the *syslog* manual's pages for more information.)

Another way to insure that the logs aren't tampered with is to have some or all of the log messages directed to the server host's serial port. You can then plug the port into an old dot matrix or daisywheel printer. As each log entry is created, it will be spooled to the printer, creating a permanent written record of what's been happening with your system. If you can't find a suitable printer or are adverse to killing trees, an alternative is to use a null modem cable to connect the serial port to that old Macintosh or IBM PC you have sitting about. Then run a terminal emulation program such as ZTerm on the Mac with the "Capture session to file" option activated.

To log to the serial port, add a line like the following to *syslog.conf*.

```
*.notice            /dev/ttyS0
```

Replace */dev/ttyS0* with the appropriate device-special file for your system's serial port.

Web Server Logs

The log files created by the Web server are also very useful for tracking down problems. Most servers create at least two files: the access log and the error log. The access log provides a blow-by-blow accounting of every access to your server and includes such goodies as the host name of the requester, the URL requested, and the date and time the request was made. The error log, as its name implies, logs problems: requests for documents that don't exist, attempts to access protected documents, and internal errors from CGI scripts and the server. Your server may provide additional log files, or it may have options for including extra information in the standard files.

An immediate problem with Web server logs is that these files, unlike the UNIX system logs, grow extremely rapidly. Each week, the access log file for a Web site with a modest 100,000 hits per week will grow by about 10 megabytes. Some sites will see an order of magnitude more hits. If nothing else, you will need to trim or cycle these logs on a regular basis. Otherwise, they will eventually expand to fill the file system, bringing the server down. I like to cycle my log files, keeping copies of the last four handy while permanently compressing and archiving the oldest ones. Here's a simple script to do this.

```
#!/bin/sh
# This script cycles the access log files, keeping four
# versions handy, while compressing the oldest.  Only two
# copies of the error log are kept.
cd /usr/local/etc/httpd/logs
/bin/gzip -c access_log.4 >> old_logs.gz
mv -f access_log.3 access_log.4
```

```
mv -f access_log.2 access_log.3
mv -f access_log.1 access_log.2
mv -f access_log   access_log.1
mv -f error_log.1 error_log.2
mv -f error_log error_log.1
kill -HUP `cat httpd.pid`
sleep 3
chgrp webmaster access_log
chmod 0640   access_log
chmod 0640   old_logs.gz
```

This script is run at regular intervals from the *cron* table. When it first starts up, it changes to the directory where the logs are kept. It next invokes the GNU *gzip* program to compress the oldest access log file and append it to a file named *old_logs.gz*.

After completing the compression, the script cycles the logs, changing the name of *access_log* to *access_log.1*, *access_log.1* to *access_log.2*, and so forth. The next line of the script sends an HUP signal to the Web server's process ID (stored in the file *httpd.pid* in the case of this particular server), which causes the server to close its log files and create new ones. The script now waits for a few seconds, then adjusts the group ownership and permissions of the files so that unauthorized users can't peek at them.

If server log files are going to be archived indefinitely, they should be encrypted to protect the confidentiality of their contents. Some dialects of UNIX come with the *DES* encryption program installed. This provides a moderate level of security. Commercial encryption products and the freeware SSLEay package (see Chapter 10) provide stronger security.

Much of the information about the Web server's operation can be found in the access log file. A typical line from the access log will look like

```
portio.wi.mit.edu - - [15/May/1997:23:46:58 -0500] "GET /index.html
   HTTP/1.0" 200 1523
```

Each line in the log file is a separate request for a URL. The seven fields contained in each line are *host, rfc931, username, [date/time], request, status, bytes.*

1. **host** The host name or IP number of the user's machine.
2. **rfc931** The user's login name on her personal machine, provided by the "identd" protocol. This protocol only runs on some UNIX machines, so the field is usually displayed as –.
3. **username** For password-protected pages, this field holds the account name provided by the user. The field is – if not applicable.
4. **date/time** The local time of the access in 24 hour format.
5. **request** The URL the user requested, including any CGI script parameters.
6. **status** The status code of the server's response (200 for OK).
7. **bytes** The number of bytes transferred, or – if not applicable

The error log has a simpler format in which time-stamped error messages from the server, CGI scripts, and server plug-ins are recorded. A typical excerpt looks like

```
[Tue Feb  7 22:01:53 1995] httpd: malformed header from script
ppmtogif: computing colormap...
ppmtogif: 4 colors found
[Tue Feb  7 22:02:03 1995] httpd: malformed header from script
[Tue Feb  7 22:10:11 1995] killing CGI process 638
[Tue Feb  7 23:22:08 1995] httpd: connection timed out for ti40.nlm.edu
Identifier "main::q" used only once: possible typo at test line 1
Tie: no such file or directory
```

The messages that begin with a date are usually generated by the HTTP server itself and follow a standard format. Everything else, including two messages from *ppmtogif* and a couple from an unidentified Perl program, are warning messages generated by CGI scripts. When a CGI script executes, its standard error output is automatically redirected to the error log. Unless the author has gone to special effort, error messages from CGI scripts don't follow any particular format.

A large number of freeware and commercial software packages allow you to crunch the server log files in various ways to produce usage statistics and colorful graphs designed to impress your management with the popularity of your site (see Table 8.2). Many of them run on NT systems, as well as on UNIX.

The access and error log files can also give you valuable clues that your site is being probed in preparation for an attack. The general log analysis packages weren't designed for this purpose and aren't much help in this respect.

Like the UNIX system logs, the general strategy for scanning Web logs for suspicious activity is to filter out the expected events and examine what's left. In the case of the access log, you can routinely filter out all accesses that result in a successful status code of 200, as well as accesses to unrestricted parts of the document tree. However, certain status codes, particularly 401 (unauthorized) and 403 (forbidden), which appear when remote users

TABLE 8.2 Web Log Analyzers

Product	Manufacturer	OS(s)	Notes
Analog	Stephen Turner	NT/UNIX	Freeware
wusage	Boutell Corporation	NT/UNIX	
wwwstat	Roy Fielding	NT/UNIX	Freeware
Site Tracker	Tucker Information Services	All OS	Subscription service
net.Analysis	net.Genesis	NT/Solaris	

attempt to access parts of the site that are under access control, may represent an attempt to peek at restricted material. Entries with either of these status codes should be summarized and examined.

A number of Web servers and CGI scripts will break when asked to process very long URLs or URLs containing odd characters. Remote users who carefully craft long URLs have been able to break into such systems. Part of your log-scanning efforts should be to detect these URL-based attacks by finding ones that exceed a reasonable length or that contain characters that are not among the standard set.

The error log grows much more slowly than the access log, and all of its entries are worth examining, if only to identify problems at your site. Some of the error messages that you might see in this file include:

- **"File does not exist" or "no multi in this directory."** These messages indicate that somebody tried to access a nonexistent URL. It's usually a broken link in one of your documents or the user's typographical error. Occasionally, it's a URL-based attack.
- **"File permissions deny server access."** The server tried to retrieve a document, but it didn't have sufficient privileges to read it. Documents that you intend to serve over the Web must be readable by the server. This message could indicate that a file in the document tree simply didn't have the correct permissions, or it could be an early warning that the server is misconfigured and that someone is using it to try to get at files outside the document tree.
- **"Password mismatch."** This indicates that a user tried to access a protected document but typed an incorrect password. A series of these may indicate an attempt to gain unauthorized access to system files.
- **"Client denied by server configuration."** Access to a directory was restricted to certain IP addresses, and someone from outside the list of allowed IP addresses tried to gain access. A series of these may also indicate an attempt to gain unauthorized access.
- **"Malformed header from script."** This is a warning that a buggy CGI script is producing bad output that the server can't interpret. Often, there's also some sort of error message from the script immediately before or after this entry in the error log file. You should not have buggy CGI scripts installed on your system.

Although there is no general utility that I know of for filtering the Web access log for suspicious activity, Listing 8.2 gives a small Perl script named *find_status.pl* that you can use as a starting point for your own utilities. You can use it to summarize the URLs or hosts that have produced certain server status codes. For example, to scan the log for evidence that people are trying to break into protected areas of your site, you can search for all entries that

LISTING 8.2 *find-status.pl*—A Web Server Log Scanning Script

```
#!/usr/local/bin/perl
# File: find_status.pl
# Scan log files for URLs & hosts with certain status codes
require "getopts.pl";
&Getopts('L:t:h') || die <<USAGE;
Usage: find_status.pl [-Lth] <code1> <code2> <code3> ...
       Scan Web server log files and list a summary
       of URLs whose requests had the one of the
       indicated status codes.
Options:
       -L <domain>  Ignore local hosts matching this domain
       -t <integer> Print top integer URLS/HOSTS [10]
       -h           Sort by host rather than URL
USAGE
    ;
if ($opt_L) {
    $opt_L=~s/\./\\./g;
    $IGNORE = "(^[^.]+|$opt_L)\$";
}
$TOP=$opt_t || 10;
while (@ARGV) {
    last unless $ARGV[0]=~/^\d+$/;
    $CODES{shift @ARGV}++;
}
while (<>) {
    ($host,$identd,$user,$date,$request,$URL,$status,$bytes) =
        /^(\S+) (\S+) (\S+) \[([^]]+)\] "(\w+) (\S+).*" (\d+) (\S+)/;
    next unless $CODES{$status};
    next if $IGNORE && $host=~/$IGNORE/io;
    $info = $opt_h ? $host : $URL;
    $found{$status}->{$info}++;
}
foreach $status (sort {$a<=>$b;} sort keys %CODES) {
    $info = $found{$status};
    $count = $TOP;
    foreach $i (sort {$info->{$b} <=> $info->{$a};} keys %{$info}) {
        write;
        last unless --$count;
    }
    $- = 0;  # force a new top-of-report
}
format STDOUT_TOP=
TOP @## URLS/HOSTS WITH STATUS CODE @##:
    $TOP,                      $status
    REQUESTS  URL/HOST
    --------  --------

.
format STDOUT=
    @#####    @<<<<<<<<<<<<<<<<<<<<<<<<<<<<<<<<<<<<<<<<
    $info->{$i},$i
.
```

resulted in either the 401 or 403 status codes. The *-L* flag is used in the example below to suppress entries from the local domain while the *-h* flag causes the script to produce an output based on the remote host name rather than by the URL accessed.

```
find_status.pl -h -L wi.mit.edu 401 403 ~httpd/logs/access_log
TOP 10 URLS/HOSTS WITH STATUS CODE 403:
    REQUESTS  URL/HOST
    --------  --------
         4    ts04-ind-4.iquest.net
         4    d168.nb.interaccess.com
         4    sol.ls.nwu.edu
         2    spd-13.ils.nwu.edu
         2    198.104.230.144
         2    magellan.mckinley.com
         2    alcor.twinsun.com
         2    s057n103.csun.edu
         2    homer-bbn.infoseek.com
         1    shepard.his.ucsf.edu
```

In this case, the number of access attempts by any user is so small that it seems unlikely that it represents an attempt to break into the system.

Feel free to rework the basic skeleton of the script, which loops through the access log and parses out the various fields of each entry, to adapt it to your needs.

Redirecting Web Server Logs

The same trick that allows you to spool the system log files to a printer or terminal emulator works for Web log files, as well. Just replace the name of the log with a reference to the appropriate device-special file in the server configuration file, for instance,

httpd.conf:
```
ErrorLog /dev/ttyS0
```

Some UNIX Web servers, including those from Netscape, allow you to send logging information directly through the *syslog* facility. This allows you to collect the logs of several Web servers on a single logging host and monitor them all from a central location.

Newer versions of the Apache Web server also lets you send entries to the system log. To make this work, however, you need to copy the Perl script named *forward_log.pl* (Listing 8.3) and place it in some convenient location in the server root, such as */usr/local/etc/httpd/support/forward_log.pl*.

Now configure Apache to pipe log entries to *forward_log.pl* by adding the following to *httpd.conf*:

```
ErrorLog "| /usr/local/etc/httpd/support/forward_log.pl"
```

LISTING 8.3 A Perl Script to Forward Web Log Entries to the Syslog

```
#!/usr/local/bin/perl
# script: forward_log.pl
# requires perl 5.001 or higher
require 5.001;
$SERVER_NAME = 'Web';
$FACILITY = 'local0';
$PRIORITY = 'warning';
use Sys::Syslog;
openlog ($SERVER_NAME,'nowait',$FACILITY);
while (<>) {
    chomp;
    syslog($PRIORITY,$_);
}
closelog;
```

You can adapt this technique to forward log entries to relational databases, electronic pagers, and so forth.

Monitor the Integrity of System Files and Binaries

If your system is compromised by an intruder, she will very likely attempt to replace system configuration files and binaries with doctored copies designed to make it easier to gain access to the system again or to attack other machines on your network. You might think you could check for this type of activity by looking for unexpected changes in the modification times of system files, but this is far from foolproof—intruders know how to alter files without changing their modification times.

One way to catch this type of tampering is to run a program that generates a unique fingerprint of each essential system file. Store the fingerprints in a secure place. Then, on a nightly basis, rerun the fingerprinting program and compare the current result with the stored result. Any discrepancies indicate that the file's contents have changed and should be investigated.

Many UNIX systems come with a primitive fingerprint program, called *cksum*, which uses a cyclic redundancy check (CRC) to produce a checksum of any file. It was designed to detect files corrupted in transit across a phone line or network, and not to detect malicious tampering. It's possible to forge an executable in such a way that the CRC checksum doesn't change; in fact, there are hackers' toolkits to help people do it. The *sum* program, available in other UNIX distributions, is even less reliable.

A better fingerprinting tool is the *md5sum* program, available in newer UNIX distributions or at one of the sites given in at the end of this chapter. This program uses Ronald Rivest's MD5 algorithm to generate a cryptographic hash of the file. A single bit change in the input file results in a completely changed hash. There is no known way to discover a file that produces a particular hash, making file forgery virtually impossible.

You can use *md5sum* to calculate the fingerprint of a single file.

```
lstein> md5sum /bin/login
6e69fcbad1af617b6df2afd527ded8c9  /bin/login
```

The 32-digit hexadecimal number preceding the file name is the hash. You can use this command as the basis for a simple system-integrity-checking script. Generate *md5sum* fingerprints of all your essential system files and store them on read-only media, such as a CD-ROM. Recompute the fingerprints nightly, and compare them with the stored values. Any files that have been modified will show up with different fingerprints.

A better idea, however, is to use the freeware Tripwire program, written by Gene Kim and Eugene Spafford. You can have it exhaustively fingerprint the contents of files or just have it warn you when the ownership or permissions of a certain file changes, allowing you to detect unauthorized modifications of files whose contents are expected to change from time to time, such as */etc/passwd*. Tripwire is highly configurable and well tested with multiple UNIX dialects. You can get a copy of it at the site listed as the end of this chapter.

Back Up Your System

File systems get corrupted, hard disks crash, and system administrators running as root accidentally type *rm -r ** (don't laugh—this happened at my site). For these reasons alone, you should back up your Web server on a regular basis. The fact that a recent backup can save your skin if your site is vandalized is icing on the cake.

There are a large number of UNIX-based backup systems, ranging from the simple *tar* program that comes with every system to the more complex *dump* and *restore* programs to fancy commercial systems that feature remote administration and graphical user interfaces. I won't say much about these backup systems as they're well covered in UNIX system administration texts, except to add the following few notes.

- **Wait at least a year before trying a new backup media.** I was an early adopter of both WORM drives and magneto-optical disks. Both were exceptionally unreliable when first introduced. I could have saved myself many headaches by sticking to a traditional tape-based backup system. Similarly, the newer tape systems such as DAT and DLT took a year or so to settle down and become dependable.
- **Don't assume that the backup system is working. Test it.** Just because the backup software reports no errors doesn't mean that it's working the way you think it is. Regularly choose a file or directory at random and attempt to restore it from backup. Not only will this reassure you that the system is working as expected, but you'll be able to act more quickly when disaster does strike.
- **Keep a copy of the backups off site.** Your backup tapes are not much good if they are destroyed by the same fire that wiped out your server.
- **Rotate the media.** Magnetic media isn't immortal. If you record over the same tape repeatedly, it will eventually develop defects. Even magneto-optical disks age. Archive the old media and use fresh media on a regular basis, following the manufacturer's recommendations for reuse.

Checklist

1. Have you installed all security-related patches and updates?

   ❍ No

   ✓ Yes

   By the time the vendor has issued a patch for a security problem, the bad guys know all about it. Keep your server up to date.

2. Have you disabled all unnecessary services?

   ❍ No

   ✓ Yes

   Be sure to disable any network service you don't need. Even those that don't appear a security risk now may contain unknown loopholes.

3. Have you run a security scanner on your system?

   ❍ No

   ✓ Yes

   If you don't scan your system for misconfigurations and other potential security holes, someone else surely will. Test your system against one of the freeware or commercial security scanners listed at the end of this chapter.

4. Does the server do double duty as a user workstation?

   ☑ No

   ❍ Yes

   The Web server host machine should have only user accounts that are necessary for the Web site's operation. It shouldn't be available for casual use.

5. Do the Web server's file permissions make sense?

   ❍ No

   ☑ Yes

   The Web server executable, the document root directory, and the server root directory should all have permissions that prevent unauthorized access. Be particularly careful to avoid giving the user ID that the Web server runs under more privileges than it needs.

6. Is the Web server running as root?

   ☑ No

   ❍ Yes

   It is never a good idea to run the Web server with root privileges. If the server needs access to a particular database or directory, run it under a group that has the appropriate privileges.

7. Is the Web server running any unnecessary features?

   ☑ No

   ❍ Yes

   Server-side includes, automatic directory listings, fancy CGI scripts, and server plug-ins all introduce potential security holes. Disable any features that are not essential.

8. Have you established conservative limits for Web server resource usage?

   ❍ No

   ☑ Yes

   Denial-of-service attacks seek to disable a site by saturating its Web server with requests. A basic defense against these attacks is to limit the amount of memory, network bandwidth, CPU time, and other system resources that the Web server is allowed to use.

9. Do you monitor system and Web logs for suspicious activity?

   ❍ No

   ✓ Yes

   System and Web log files can alert you that someone is contemplating attacking your site, actively attacking it, or has already compromised your security. Unless you check the log files, you may never know you've been broken into.

10. Do you monitor the integrity of the host?

    ❍ No

    ✓ Yes

    Utilities like Tripwire are invaluable for catching unauthorized modifications to system binaries and configuration files.

11. Do you back up your system?

    ❍ No

    ✓ Yes

    Back-ups are essential for any system, but particularly so for servers.

Online Resources

System Configuration Tools

COPS (system configuration checker)

ftp://ftp.cert.org/pub/tools/cops/

TAMU (another system configuration checker)

ftp://net.tamu.edu/pub/security/TAMU/

SATAN (network based security checker)

ftp://ftp.win.tue.nl/pub/security/satan.tar.Z
http://www.cs.purdue.edu/coast/satan.html

Internet Security Scanner (ISS)

ftp://coast.cs.purdue.edu/pub/tools/unix/iss/ (freeware version)
http://www.iss.net/ (commercial version)

Integrity Checkers

md5sum

ftp://prep.ai.mit.edu/pub/gnu/

Tripwire file modification checker

ftp://coast.cs.purdue.edu/pub/COAST/Tripwire/

Log File Analyzers

Swatch Unix logfile analyzer

ftp://sierra.stanford.edu/pub/sources/swatch-2.1.tar.gz

Comprehensive List of Web Log Analyzers

http://www.uu.se/Software/Analyzers/

Analog

http://www.statslab.cam.ac.uk/~sret1/analog/

wusage

http://www.boutell.com/wusage/

wwwstat

http://www.ics.uci.edu/pub/websoft/wwwstat/

Site Tracker

http://www.tuckinfo.com/

net.Analysis

http://www.netgen.com/

Miscellaneous

John Haugh's Shadow Password Suite

ftp://ftp.sunsite.unc.edu/pub/Linux/system/Admin/shadow-960129.tar.gz

Printed Resources

Curry, David, *UNIX System Security: A Guide for Users and System Administrators* (Addison Wesley Longman, 1994).

An excellent overview of the subject

Garfinkel, Simson, and Spafford, Gene. *Practical UNIX and Internet Security* (O'Reilly & Associates, 1996).

A lucid exposition on UNIX system security with special emphasis on Internet working issues.

Chapter 9

Windows NT Web Servers

Microsoft has promised that Windows NT will replace UNIX as the operating system of choice for providing Internet services. With its user-friendly graphical front end, point-and-click configuration tools, and excellent software development tools, this certainly seems like a strong possibility. At the time this chapter was written, however, NT was still a relative newcomer to the Internet and a variety of security problems were still being shaken out. This chapter focuses on preparing a Windows NT Server 4.0 machine to be an Internet server. The Web configuration examples are drawn from Microsoft's Internet Information Server, which, coming as it does free with the operating system, is for many NT networks the Web server of default.

NT Security Concepts

The following is a brief overview of the Windows NT security model intended for administrators whose primary background is in UNIX or DOS systems. It is no substitute for an in-depth understanding of the system. The books listed at the end of this chapter are highly recommended for further reading.

Windows NT Server Versus NT Workstation

Windows NT comes in two flavors. Windows NT Server, the more expensive flavor, has complete functionality. It can coordinate the activities of other machines, provide remote access services, run Windows name resolution, and host the Internet Information Server. Windows NT Workstation is a watered-down version of the Server product, with most of the server functions disabled. Microsoft Internet Information Server runs only on NT Server. However, Web servers from other vendors run with the Workstation version of the operating system, as well. From the point of view of system security, the main difference between the two flavors is that NT Workstation comes with an undesirably permissive configuration, while NT Server is stricter.

Users and Groups

Like other multiuser operating systems, user accounts are the basis of Windows NT security. No user, either sitting at the keyboard or accessing the server remotely, can access any system resources unless he or she first logs in by providing a valid account name and password. Users are prevented from interfering with each other by access control lists (ACLs). Every resource on the system, whether it is a file, directory, shared file system, printer, or record in the registry (a system-wide database of configuration information) has an owner. The owner decides who should have access to a resource and what they have permission to do with it by editing an access control list. This is done with the graphical user interface available under the File menu, in *Properties->Security->Permissions* (Figure 9.1). You can add or delete users from the list of individuals who can access the resource. Each user has a set of access permissions: the right to read a file, to write it, to execute it, to delete it, and to create a new file inside a directory; these permissions can be present singly or in any combination.

User passwords are stored in encrypted form on the computer's hard disk, in one of the system registry files. Even if this file is stolen, there is no way to crack the passwords by decrypting them directly. However, because the algorithm to encrypt the passwords is known, a password-guessing program can encrypt all the words in a large dictionary of popular passwords and compare them with the passwords stored in the stolen file. A surprisingly large number of passwords can be guessed in this way. (See The Crack Program and Shadow Passwords box in the previous chapter and Managing Passwords Safely in Chapter 4; an NT version of Crack is now available).

To simplify the management of many user accounts, users can be assigned to groups. Some groups, such as *Users*, *Administrators*, and *Backup operators*, are installed in the operating system by default. Others can be defined to your liking to represent divisions of responsibilities, for example *Web Authors* and *Web Administrators*. ACLs usually grant access permissions to entire groups rather than to individual users. A privilege granted to a group extends to its members. This makes it easy to create a directory that can only be written to by a member of *Web Authors*.

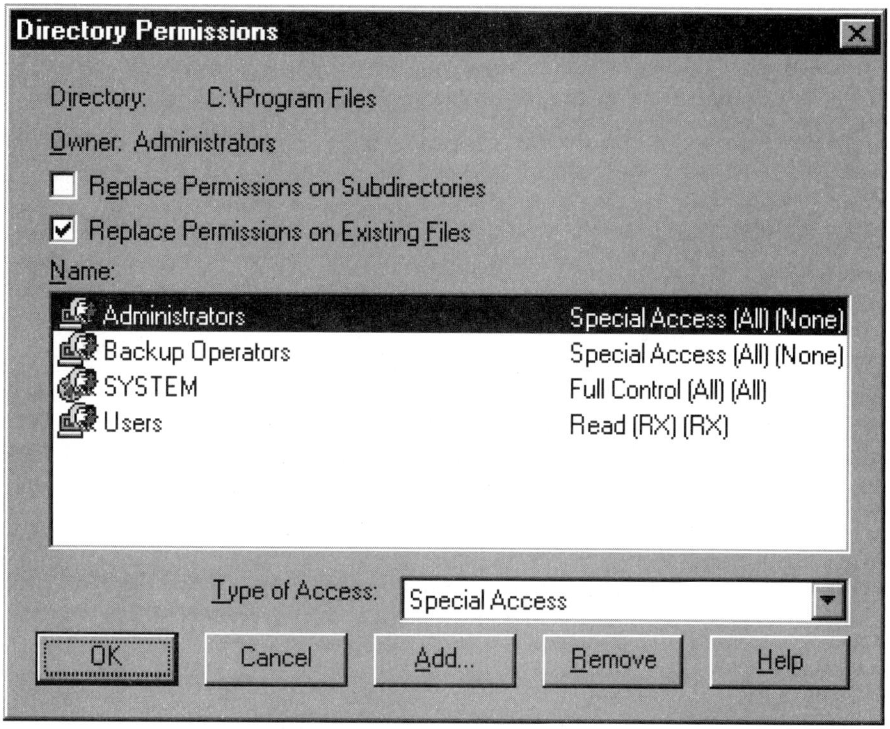

FIGURE 9.1 On Windows NT, file and directory permissions are administered using a graphical user interface.

Domains

Windows NT allows users to share the resources of a set of computers among them by using the idea of a "domain." A domain is a named cluster of computers (they can be physically close or separated by considerable distance) supervised by an NT Server machine designated as their "domain controller." The domain controller maintains a database containing the accounts names and passwords of all users registered for the domain. Once a user has an account with the domain controller, she can log into any of the machines that belong to the domain. This type of domain-based account is called a "global account" to distinguish it from a "local account"—which is recognized only by a single machine. In addition to global accounts, there are global groups. These are groups defined on the domain controller and made available to all machines in the domain.

So far, all this will sound familiar to UNIX administrators who have used the broadly similar Network Information Service. However, there is one twist. In order to allow organizations to build up large networks containing multiple domains, inter-domain trust relationships can be established. For example, an organization might have one domain named *Engineering* and another named *Marketing*. A trust relationship could be set up so that the *Engineering* domain controller trusts the *Marketing* controller and allows any user with a valid account in *Marketing* to log onto a computer in *Engineering*. Trust relationships don't have to be bidirectional, however. The *Marketing* domain controller can be configured so that it doesn't trust users from *Engineering* and will refuse them access.

Built-in Accounts and Groups

In order to prevent unauthorized access or modification, sensitive files such as system binaries and configuration files are usually accessible only to designated system administrators. In addition, the right to execute some commands, such as those to shut the machine down, to add or remove users, or to change the system clock, also require special privileges.

A newly-installed NT system will contain a single built-in account named "Administrator". This account belongs to the built-in local *Administrators* group, which grants its members full access to every nook and cranny of the operating system. Sites that have several system administrators add these users to the *Administrators* membership list. Each member of the group will have the same access rights as the Administrator account. Just to make things interesting, the *Administrators* group, in turn, contains a global group named *Domain Admins*. Users who have been assigned to *Domain Admins* on the controller have full run of every machine in the domain.

Below the omnipotent *Administrators* group are a variety of built-in administrative groups that have more power than ordinary users but less than full administrators. For example, *Backup Operators* can run the backup and restore software, which bypasses security restrictions on certain files, and *Server Operators* can shut down the machine.

Users is a built-in group for ordinary users. Every new account is added to this group by default. Ordinary users have no special privileges, but they can run most programs and create and modify files in their home directories. On NT Server machines, the default group is a built-in global group called *Domain Users*. Because the local *Users* group contains *Domain Users*, the effect of being a member in this group is to have login rights to any machine in the same domain as the server.

There are a few other built-in groups that you need to know about because they can have security implications.

The group *INTERACTIVE* refers to anyone who has logged into the machine locally. Granting exclusive access privileges to the *INTERACTIVE* group ensures that the user is using the host's keyboard and mouse. Conversely, the group *NETWORK*, refers to anyone who has logged into the system from the network—for example, anyone who accesses a file via the file-sharing system.

The built-in *CREATOR OWNER* group is used for shared directories in which members of a group are allowed to create files or directories. You'll sometimes want to give the person who created the file or directory full access to it but restrict access to other members of the group. *CREATOR OWNER* allows you to refer to whoever created the file or directory, without worrying about who, in particular, it is.

A built-in group called *Guests* contains a single user account named *Guest*. This account allows someone to log in anonymously by providing the user name *Guest* and no password. In Windows NT 4.0 and higher, this account is disabled by default, as it should be.

The built-in group *Everyone* is supposed to refer to all valid users and to be roughly equivalent to *Users* (the only difference being that a user can be manually removed from *Users* but not from *Everyone*). However, because of an NT 4.0 peculiarity, this group actually grants limited access to the system for anonymous users. Users (including those on the Internet) can obtain information from the system without providing a user name or a password. I'll give more information about avoiding this problem later.

On systems with service pack 3 or higher installed, the built-in group *Authenticated Users*, corresponds to valid users who have presented a user name and password to the system. If your system has this group, it should be used in preference to *Everyone*.

Finally, a built-in account named *System* is used for programs that run in the background, such as servers, and for the operating system itself. *System* is generally given unrestricted access to all files, directories, and other resources.

You can view, edit, and add to your system's currently defined users and groups using the *User Manager* program (NT Workstation) or *User Manager for Domains* (NT Server). For simplicity, I will refer to this program as *User Manager* throughout this chapter.

Windows NT Security Risks

In theory, the Windows NT system of access control lists, domains, and trust relationships provides a high level of security. In practice, many NT servers on the Internet are not secure. How can this be?

Widespread Misconfiguration Problems

The main problem is that an out-of-the-box Windows NT Workstation installation is not secure. Most of the system's files and directories are read/write by *Everyone*, which means that any local user can tamper with the system to his heart's content. Further, because of the strange properties of the built-in *Everyone* group, there are a variety of ways for unidentified Internet users to view and/or alter the system, as well.

Windows NT Server, in contrast, has a more reasonable set of default permissions when first installed. However, it still contains gaps in its configuration that allow for unwanted mischief. It has also been my experience that many Windows NT Servers were not installed from scratch but were upgraded from previous versions of Windows NT or from Windows 95. In such cases, the access control lists are probably at their least restrictive setting.

An additional problem is that Windows NT actually supports two different file systems, the original FAT file system used by DOS, Windows for Workgroups, and Windows 95, and its native NT file system (NTFS). (Prior to NT 4.0, NT also recognized OS/2's HPFS, but this is no longer true.) Only NTFS provides access control lists. Machines that use an FAT file system have no file protection.

Vulnerability to NetBIOS Attacks

Windows NT uses a family of networking protocols, known collectively as "NetBIOS," to provide Windows file sharing, network printing, and remote system administration. NetBIOS is network-independent. It can run on top of TCP/IP networks as easily as it can across Novell NetWare or IPX. It provides reliable cryptography-based authentication of remote users, and it integrates well with the Windows NT access control system. However, NetBIOS was designed with a local area network in mind, not large networks like the Internet. For this reason, it has certain vulnerabilities.

- **Information leakage.** NetBIOS will advertise information about a system's shared volumes, workgroup name, domain name, and machine name without requiring the remote machine or user to authenticate.
- **Client-controlled fallback to weaker authentication.** In order to be compatible with less-capable operating systems, such as Windows for Workgroups, and Windows 95, NetBIOS will fall back to weaker authentication when a remote client requests it.
- **Anonymous log-in.** NetBIOS allows a limited form of anonymous, unauthenticated log-in. Designed to allow machines on the local area network to exchange information about themselves, this loophole has been used by would-be intruders to gain access to sensitive parts of the system, such as the registry.
- **Vulnerability to man-in-the-middle attacks.** NetBIOS is vulnerable to a variety of esoteric attacks in which it is tricked into sending information to a rogue server that pretends to be part of its domain. In some actual

attacks, Windows NT machines have been tricked into sending users' encrypted passwords to the hostile machine, enabling them to be cracked off-line using a password-guessing program.

For these reasons, Microsoft does not recommend exposing NetBIOS services to the Internet. The company's recommended solution is to block NetBIOS traffic with a firewall system placed between the Windows NT server and the Internet. A less costly solution is to turn off NetBIOS on any machine that's acting as a public Web server.

Future versions of Windows NT are expected to rectify the deficiencies in NetBIOS. In particular, Service Pack 3 has a number of enhancements that lessen the risks posed by the problems listed above. NT 5.0, by adopting a completely different security model based on MIT's Kerberos system, should improve the situation considerably.

Vulnerability to Trojan Horses

Trojan horses, which we met before in Chapter 5, are programs that appears to be benign—a new screensaver perhaps—but, in reality, have a hidden agenda. While the program pretends to be doing something useful, it is modifying files, stealing information, or adding new entries to the system registry. Trojans may lurk in freeware programs downloaded from the Internet or can be created by local users who are intent on gaining more access to the system than they are authorized for.

Although all operating systems are vulnerable to Trojan horses, Windows NT has suffered a disproportionately large number of such attacks in recent years for a number of reasons.

1. There is no standard place to install new software—executables tend to be scattered about the file system.
2. Unprivileged users are frequently allowed to install new software.
3. Users tend to log in with full administrative privileges in order to do nonadministrative work.
4. The NT shell always searches in the current directory for an executable program before searching in the standard locations.

Points (3) and (4) are particularly worth worrying about. If you accidentally run a Trojan horse when you are logged in as an unprivileged user, the amount of damage the program can do is limited. It may be able to erase your personal files, but it can't modify the operating system. If you are logged in as *Administrator*, the Trojan has essentially unlimited access to the system.

If you make a practice of working from the command (MS DOS Console) shell, be aware that NT always looks in the current directory for a command before looking in one of the standard locations. This happens despite the setting of the system PATH environment variable. Consider the following insider attack. A local user named *fred* wants to get write access to the protected Web directory located in *C:\InetPub*. To do this, he creates a batch file named *"NOTEPAD.BAT"* and places it in the world-writable *C:\TEMP* directory. This file contains the code

```
@ECHO OFF
cacls C:\InetPub /E /G fred:F
notepad.exe %1
del NOTEPAD.BAT
```

Fred now only has to wait for you, working as *Administrator*, to try to run the notepad from within *C:\TEMP* (which he can encourage you to do by leaving a file named *README.TXT* there). When you type the *notepad* command, the batch script runs instead of the notepad application. It first invokes the *cacls* command to change the permissions on the Web document tree to give *Fred* full access. It then launches the notepad application and covers its tracks by deleting the *.BAT* file. Fred has write access to the document tree, and you're none the wiser.

Securing a Windows NT Web Server

The recipe for securing a Windows NT-based Web server is similar to the steps for securing a UNIX system.

1. Apply all service patches.
2. Fix the file system permissions.
3. Fix the registry access permissions.
4. Remove or disable all extraneous network services.
5. Add the minimum number of user accounts necessary to maintain the server.
6. Install the server software and adjust file and directory permissions to restrict unnecesary access.
7. Remove or disable unnecessary Web server features, CGI scripts, and extensions.
8. Monitor system and server log files.

Ideally you should take each of these steps *before* you physically plug the machine into the network.

Apply All Service Packs and Updates

Microsoft releases operating system patches called "service packs" at regular intervals. These service packs contain patches for known security holes in the operating system, as well as other bug fixes and feature enhancements. Occasionally, Microsoft also releases "hot fixes," patches for individual problems that do not warrant a whole service pack. Hot fixes are generally much smaller in size than service packs.

The current online list of service packs and hot fixes can be found at URL *http://microsoft.com/NTServerSupport/*. Identify and follow the link labeled "service packs." You'll find a description of the available service packs and instructions for obtaining and installing them. You have the option of ordering the packs on CD-ROM by phone or fax, or you can download them directly from Microsoft's FTP site. One word of warning is that the packs tend to be large: Service Pack 3 is some 15 megabytes in size. Follow the links to an FTP site near you and download the service pack appropriate for your hardware platform (Intel, Alpha, or MIPS) using binary mode. Unless otherwise instructed, you'll need only install the most recent service pack; each pack contains all the fixes that were included in earlier versions. When the service pack has downloaded, you will have a self-extracting executable file named something like *nt4sp3_i.exe*.

Back up your system if it has any valuable data on it. Then transfer the service pack executable to any directory on the target machine if it isn't there already and log in as *Administrator*. Move the service pack into some protected directory, such as *C:\Users\Administrator*, and install it from the NT command line by typing its name.

```
C:\users\Administrator> nt4sp3_.exe
```

If all goes well, the pack will decompress itself and launch a wizard to lead you through the process of updating the operating system.

If you plan to develop software on the system, you will want to download the pack's corresponding "symbols" file. This contains information used by various software debuggers and development environments. Symbols files can be found by following the links from Microsoft's service packs page. See Microsoft's pages for instructions on installing and using symbols.

Fix the File System and Registry Permissions

After applying operating system patches, the next step is to check and adjust the file system and registry permissions. This important precaution is a hedge against a buggy Web server, CGI script, or server module being coerced into viewing or modifying a restricted part of the system.

To get the benefit of file system permissions, you must have formatted Windows NT disk partition as NTFS. The same goes for the disk partition that the Web server and its documents reside on, if different from the NT partition. If the partition is not already NTFS, you can nondestructively reformat it using the Windows NT Setup program. This action will not destroy any data. However, you should be aware that the reformatting is irreversible and will prevent you from dual booting the machine into DOS or Windows 95. Ordinarily this should not be a problem.

Fixing the File System

The following recommendations are borrowed (with small modifications) from those in Stephen Sutton's book *Windows NT Security Guide* (see Printed Resources at the end of this chapter). You should log into the system as *Administrator* and use the *Properties->Security->Permissions* window to change the access control lists to those given here. In some cases, you will be asked to change the permissions of the contents of the directory—its files and/or directories. You can do this automatically by checking one or both of the boxes marked "Replace permissions on existing files" and "Replace permissions on subdirectories" in the Permissions window. I assume that Windows NT is installed in the standard directory *C:\WINNT*; if your system uses a different directory, make the appropriate modifications. Advice on permissions for Web-server-specific files and directories comes later.

Please note that the *Everyone* group has been expressly deleted from each of these access control lists. Use *Users* instead, or, if you have Service Pack 3 or higher installed, *Authenticated Users*. Unlike *Everyone*, a member of *Users* or *Authenticated Users* must present a proper account name and password to gain access to a system resource.

Directory *C:*

Owner	Administrators
Change contents too	files, but not subdirectories
Administrators	Full Control
CREATOR OWNER	Read
SYSTEM	Full Control
Users	Read

Rationale Administrators and the operating system need full access to the top-level directory. Everyone else has read-only access.

Directory *C:\WINNT*

Owner	Administrators
Change contents too	no
Administrators	Full Control
CREATOR OWNER	Full Control
SYSTEM	Full Control
Users	Read

Rationale Administrators and the operating system need full access to the top-level directory. All others have read-only access. To simplify the installation of new software, the owner of any subdirectory has full access to it.

Directory *C:\WINNT\SYSTEM, C:\WINNT\SYSTEM32*

Owner	Administrators
Change contents too	files, not subdirectories
Administrators	Full Control
CREATOR OWNER	Full Control
SYSTEM	Full Control
Authenticated Users	Read

Rationale As above. However, in this case we grant read access to *Authenticated Users* rather than *Users*. This allows the Web server, which runs under a *Guest* account, access to system libraries needed for CGI scripts.

Directory *C:\WINNT\REPAIR*

Owner	Administrators
Change contents too	files, not subdirectories
Administrators	Full Control
SYSTEM	Full Control

Rationale Whenever you create an emergency repair disk, this directory will be filled with copies of the system registry, the password file, and other security-sensitive information. It should be accessible only to administrators and the operating system itself.

Directory *C:\WINNT\PROFILES*

Owner	Administrators
Change contents too	no
Administrators	Full Control
CREATOR OWNER	Full Control
SYSTEM	Full Control
Users	List

Rationale This directory contains the desktop environment and preferences for each registered user on the system, each in its own subdirectory. Users should be able to see what profiles are defined but not allowed to view or change their contents.

Directory *C:\WINNT\PROFILES\DEFAULT USER, C:\WINNT\PROFILES\ALL USERS*

Owner	Administrators
Change contents too	files and subdirectories

Administrators	Full Control
SYSTEM	Full Control
Users	Read

Rationale These two directories contain common preferences shared by all users. Users can view the defaults but not change them.

Directory *C:\WINNT\SYSTEM32\SPOOL*

Owner	Administrators
Change contents too	files and subdirectories

Administrators	Full Control
CREATOR OWNER	Full Control
Server Operators	Change
SYSTEM	Full Control
Users	List

Rationale The spool directory is a temporary holding area for files that are being printed. Users are allowed to view the print queue and to delete jobs that they created but not to interfere with print jobs created by other users. By convention, the *Server Operators* group can control the printer system and, therefore, needs Change access to the directory in order to be able to reprioritize and delete print jobs (on Windows Workstation, this group is called *Power Users*). Sutton recommends that *Users'* access be changed from List to Change if any printing problems appear. I haven't encountered this situation.

Directories *C:\WINNT\SYSTEM32\DHCP, C:\WINNT\SYSTEM32\RAS, C:\WINNT\SYSTEM32\OS2, C:\WINNT\SYSTEM32\WINS*

Owner	Administrators
Change contents too	files and subdirectories

Administrators	Full Control
CREATOR OWNER	Full Control
SYSTEM	Full Control
Users	Read

Rationale This directory holds configuration files for various NT subsystems, including remote access (RAS) and dynamic host configuration protocol (DHCP). Users are allowed to read the directory and its contents but not to make any changes. Any directories or files that the system creates in a user's name is fully under that user's control, hence the entry for *CREATOR OWNER*.

Files *C:\BOOT.INI, C:\NTLDR, C:\NTDETECT.COM*

Owner	Administrators
Change contents too	N/A

Administrators	Full Control
SYSTEM	Full Control

Rationale These three files control the booting process and should be off limits to everyone except the administrator and operating system.

Files *C:\AUTOEXEC.BAT, C:\CONFIG.SYS*

Owner	Administrator
Change contents too	N/A
Administrators	Full Control
SYSTEM	Full Control
Users	Read

Rationale In order to maintain backward compatability with DOS and Windows for Workgroups programs that expect these files to exist, they are user-readable. They are not actually used during the NT boot process and are thus irrelevant.

Directory *C:\TEMP*

Owner	Administrators
Change contents too	subdirectories, if any
Administrators	Full Control
CREATOR OWNER	Full Control
SYSTEM	Full Control
Users	Special Access (RWX)(Not Specified)

Rationale This directory is a world-writable directory for holding temporary files that are generated by user programs, such as word processors. These permissions give users the right to add their own files to the directory but not to peek at others'. (To generate these Special Access permissions, first select "Special Directory Access..." from the pop-up menu and check the R, W and X checkboxes. Then select "Special File Access..." and check "Access Not Specified.")

Directory *C:\USERS*

Owner	Administrators
Change contents too	see below
Administrators	Special Access (All)(Not Specified)
CREATOR OWNER	Full Control
SYSTEM	Full Control
Users	List

Rationale By convention, this directory is the place where local users' home directories are stored. The permissions are designed to make it easy for administrators to create new home directories but hard to poke around inside these directories once created.

Directory *C:\USERS**

Owner	*The user*
Administrators	Read
SYSTEM	Full Control
The user	Full Control

Rationale Each home directory should be owned by the user, who has full control over it. Administrators can read the files within but can't make changes unless they explicitly change file access permissions first. This is a precaution against accidental modification only, not a security consideration.

Directory *C:\USERS\DEFAULT*

Owner	Administrators
Administrators	Full Control
CREATOR OWNER	Full Control
SYSTEM	Full Control
Users	Special Access (RWX)(Not Specified)

Rationale Some systems use this directory as a generic home directory for users who do not have a specific directory assigned to them. I don't recommend that you adopt such a policy, but if you do, this directory should have the same access control policy as *C:\TEMP*.

Create a Standard Location for Third-Party Software

Create a top-level directory to store all third-party software and new executables. The name is up to you, but *C:\Program Files* is being increasingly popular among software vendors as the default install location. Set up access permission as follows.

Directory *C:\Program Files*

Owner	Administrators
Administrators	Special (All)(None)
Account Operators	Special (All)(None)
Backup Operators	Special (All)(None)
Server Operators	Special (All)(None)
SYSTEM	Full Control
Users	Read

The point of this unusual setup is to grant administrators the ability to install new software packages. However, once a package is installed, its executables can't be run (or even read) without explicitly changing their permissions. This discourages administrators from casually running untrusted third-party software.

Once this directory is created, modify the system PATH environment variable to include it (using the *System* control panel). This will allow programs installed in this directory to be run from the command line without specifying their complete path names.

Fixing the Registry

Like the file system, the keys and values of the Windows registry are protected by access control lists. Unfortunately, it is quite hard to configure the registry for maximum security because of uncertainties about when and how various pieces of the operating system and installed software need to access it. A reasonable approach is to keep the default permissions while closing known loopholes and controlling remote access to the registry as a whole.

To fix the registry, you must be comfortable using the registry editor *REGEDT32.EXE*. This program lives in *C:\WINNT\SYSTEM32* and is available only from the NT command line unless you've explicitly added it to the Start menu. See the system documentation for help using this program. Although it's unlikely you'll get into trouble if you follow these directions, manipulating the registry improperly can leave you with an unbootable system. It's recommended that you back up your system before making any registry changes.

Vulnerability Hidden administrative shares

Description Windows NT 4.0 automatically creates a number of hidden, but well-known, file system shares named ADMIN$ and C$. They are intended for remote administration, but have been abused by knowledgeable crackers to gain information about the system.

Solution With *REGEDT32.EXE*, go to the key *HKEY_LOCAL_MACHINE\SYSTEM\CurrentControlSet\Services\LanManagerServer\Parameters.*

Select the *Edit->Add Value* menu command to create the following entry:

- Value Name: *AutoShareServer*
- Data Type: REG_DWORD
- Value: 0

For Windows NT Workstation systems, instead add a value named *AutoShareWks*. If the entry is already present, just check its value and change it to 0 if necessary.

Vulnerability Unauthenticated remote users can access the registry.

Description Completely anonymous users, by using the *Everyone* group, can gain access to the system registry and read various keys. Anonymous users can also make certain additions to the registry.

Solution This solution will work only if you have Service Pack 3 or higher installed. Using the registry editor, go to the key *\HKEY_LOCAL_MACHINE\SYSTEM\CurrentControlSet\Control\LS*. Select the *Edit->Add Value* menu command to create the following entry.

- Value Name: *RestrictAnonymous*
- Data Type: REG_DWORD
- Value: 1

A more extreme solution is to prohibit all remote access to the registry. This is explained next.

Vulnerability Users can access the registry remotely.

Description Windows NT 4.0 allows the registry to be accessed remotely for a variety of purposes, including remote configuration and more mundane services, such as printing. Sensitive parts of the registry are protected only by each key's individual ACLs, which may or may not be correctly configured. You can restrict access to the registry entirely by creating a *winreg* key.

Solution Using *REGEDT32.EXE*, open *HKEY_LOCAL_MACHINE\SYSTEM\CurrentControlSet\Control\SecurePipeServers*. Select the *Edit ->Add Key* menu command to create the following new key.

- Key Name: *winreg*
- Key Class: REG_SZ

Now select this key and use *Edit->Add Value* to add a new value to it.

- Value Name: *Description*
- Data Type: REG_SZ
- Value: Registry Server

The access control list for the *winreg* key controls what users and groups have access to the registry. Select the *winreg* key and choose the *Security ->Permissions...* menu item. Give *Administrators* full control over the key. Remove permissions from everyone else.

If the *winreg* key already exists in your installation, as it should in any recent installation of NT server, just check its permissions to make sure that access isn't granted promiscuously.

WARNING: controlling remote access to the registry may interfere with some services, such as the ability of the system to act as a print server. In the event that you need the Web server to provide these services, see Microsoft's technical support page at *http://www.microsoft.com/kb/articles/q153/1/83.htm* for information on selectively enabling general access to the registry.

Vulnerability Unauthenticated remote users can access system log files

Description The Application and System logs, which may contain sensitive information, can be accessed remotely by the *Event Viewer* program without authentication.

Solution Using *REGEDT32.EXE*, create *two* new values, one under *HKEY_LOCAL_MACHINE\SYSTEM\CurrentControlSet\Services\EventLog\System*, and the other under *HKEY_LOCAL_MACHINE\SYSTEM\CurrentControlSet\Services\EventLog\Application*.

- Value Name: *RestrictGuestAccess*
- Data Type: REG_DWORD
- Value: 1

User Rights Policies

The Windows NT *User Manager* program establishes certain global user rights. Some of the rights on a default installation are inappropriate for a Web server machine; others are simply accident prone. To change these rights, select *Policies->User Rights...* in the *User Manager* program to bring up the User Rights Policy window (see Figure 9.2). In some cases, as noted, you'll need to check the "Show Advanced User Rights" checkbox to see the option.

- **Debug programs** (advanced right) Remove the *Administrators* group from the list of groups authorized to do this. No one should be performing software development while logged in as an administrator.
- **Access the computer from network** Change *Everyone* to *Users*.
- **Log on locally** Windows NT workstation allows all users to log on locally. For Windows NT server, the default is to allow only various types of administrators local access. For a machine that is acting primarily as a Web server, however, you'll want to allow CGI script developers and Web authors to have local access to the machine. I recommend creating special groups for Web authors and administrators and giving these groups local logon rights. This is described in more detail later. If you need to use *Basic Authentication* to password protect directories (see Chapter 10) you'll also need to give local logon rights to all users that will be accessing Web pages.
- **Shut down the system** Remove *Everyone*, *Guest*, and *Users*, if any are present. Only authorized *Administrators* should be allowed to reboot a server!

Security Scanners

If all this seems a bit much to do and check, there are third-party tools that will examine the system for configuration problems and report on any

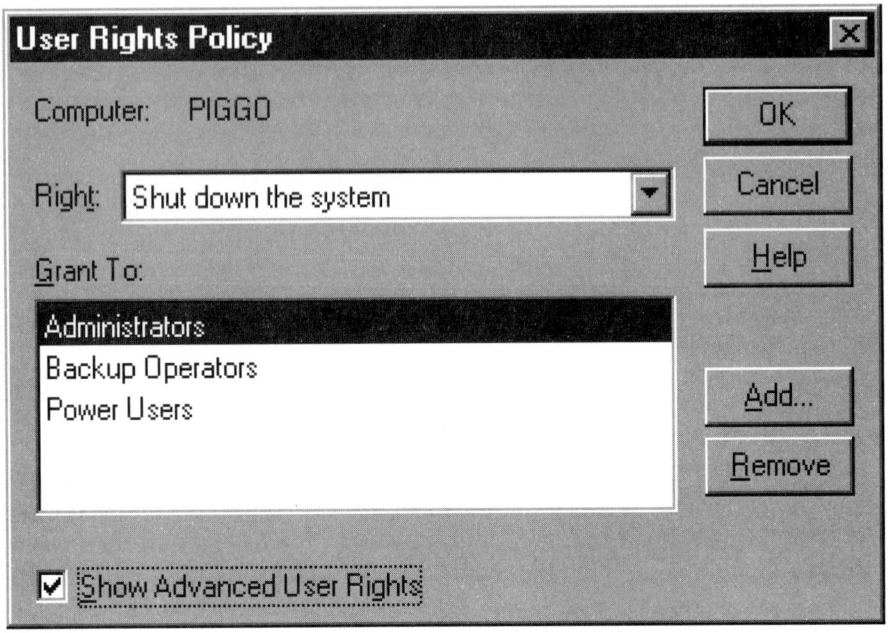

FIGURE 9.2 The User Rights Policy window allows you to grant privileges to selected NT groups.

known security holes. Like their UNIX counterparts, some scanners are designed to be run locally; others scan for problems remotely across the network. NT Security scanners include

- Internet Security Systems *Internet Scanner*
- Midwestern Commerce *Administrator Assistant Toolkit*
- Secure Computing *NT Security Scanner*

Restrict Network Access to NetBIOS Services

The previous sections have focused on closing security gaps in the NT file system and registry configuration. By restricting access to low-level system resources, these measures help protect the system against insider threats (for instance, nosy local users armed with a floppy disk) and network-based attacks.

As a further defense, you can shield the system against many network-based attacks by blocking all TCP/IP access to the NetBIOS services. Native TCP/IP services, such as the Web server, Gopher, and FTP, will continue to work, but the machine will no longer be able to act as a server for domain user administration, file sharing, remote registry editing, remote log file

The System Key

The registry stores a variety of secrets, including account passwords. These passwords are stored in encrypted form but are still vulnerable to dictionary-based guessing attacks. To prevent encrypted passwords from being stolen, NT protects them with registry permissions that allow only members of the *Administrators* group access.

For even greater security, you can elect to add an extra layer of encryption to passwords using the system key. In addition to passwords, the system key is also used to encrypt other secrets, such as the Web server's private key (see Chapter 10). This key can be

1. Stored on an external floppy disk that the system prompts for at boot time.
2. Protected by a pass phrase that the system prompts for during boot.
3. Stored in obfuscated form in the registry itself. The added security depends on the obscurity of the unpublished obfuscation algorithm. This allows for unattended restart, but suffers from the risk that the obfuscation algorithm will some day be disclosed.

The system key is managed using a program called *SYSKEY.EXE,* which can only be run by *Administrators.* This program is available in Service Pack 3 and as a hot fix in pre-SP3 releases. More information can be found in Microsoft technical note Q143475. See the end of this chapter for the appropriate URLs.

viewing, and printing, nor will it be able to use TCP to access these services on other NT machines. Because each of these services provides a potential portal of entry for malicious persons, I recommend that you take this step, particularly if the server has direct access to the Internet.

This belt-and-suspenders approach provides you with two layers of security: even if the file system and registry permissions are not set up quite right, you're protected from NetBIOS attacks. Even if you activate some NetBIOS services accidentally or out of necessity at a future date, you're protected by the file system and registry permissions.

Blocking TCP/IP access to NetBIOS can be done in several ways. If the Web server host is located behind a firewall system, NetBIOS is probably blocked already. To find out, check with the firewall administrator to make sure the system blocks access to ports 137, 138, and 139 (both UDP and TCP). Although this solution prevents Internet users from exploiting NetBIOS services, it may still leave the system open to insider attacks. Consider protecting the server behind an internal firewall if this is an issue. Chapter 14 has more details.

A cheap but effective alternative to a firewall is to unbind NetBIOS services from the TCP/IP driver. To do this, open the network control panel and choose the *Bindings* tab. Select *all services* from the pop-up menu to display the various services that the machine provides. Now for each of *NetBIOS Interface,*

Server, and *Workstation* headings, expand the heading and select the protocol labeled *WINS Client (TCP/IP)*. Click the "Disable" button. A red "forbidden" symbol should appear next to the entries (Figure 9.3). The machine will now be completely deaf and mute to TCP/IP-based NetBIOS services.

Windows NT can use other networking protocols for NetBIOS in addition to TCP/IP, including Novell NetWare and the NetBEUI protocol used in Windows for Workgroups. You may wish to enable one of these protocols on the Web server. This allows you to share files with other machines that use the same protocol, but does not let Internet users access NetBIOS; they are generally limited to TCP/IP. Figure 9.3 shows the NetBEUI protocol being used for NetBIOS. You should be aware, however, that a configuration like this one does leave the server potentially vulnerable to insider attacks. For greatest security, disable NetBIOS completely.

Another way to block unauthorized network access to the server is to block individual TCP/IP ports with NT's TCP security features. This has the added benefit of allowing you to block TCP/IP-only services, as well. To do this, follow these steps.

1. Open up the network control panel and select the *Protocols* tab.
2. Select the *TCP/IP Protocol* entry and choose *Properties...* to bring up the TCP/IP Properties window.
3. Toward the bottom of this window is the "Advanced..." button. Select it to display the Advanced IP Addressing window.
4. Toggle the checkbox labeled "Enable Security" and press the "Configure..." button.
5. This will display a window containing three scrolling lists (Figure 9.4). The left-most panel lists those TCP ports that are to be allowed to connect. Select the "Permit Only" radio button and click "Add...". A small dialog box prompts you for a TCP port. Type in 80 to allow Web services and press "Add...".
6. Repeat for any other Internet service you wish to provide. To provide FTP services, add ports 20 and 21. For Gopher, add port 70.
7. The middle panel lists the UDP ports that are to be allowed to connect. (UDP is the part of the TCP/IP protocol used for name and time servers, as well as for remote procedure calls.) Select the radio button labeled "Permit Only." Do not add any UDP ports to the list; this prevents all UDP services.
8. Close all windows and reboot the machine.

Install Web Server Software

If the software isn't already preinstalled, go ahead and install it by running whatever install program the vendor provides. The install program will create a server root directory containing log files, configuration and support

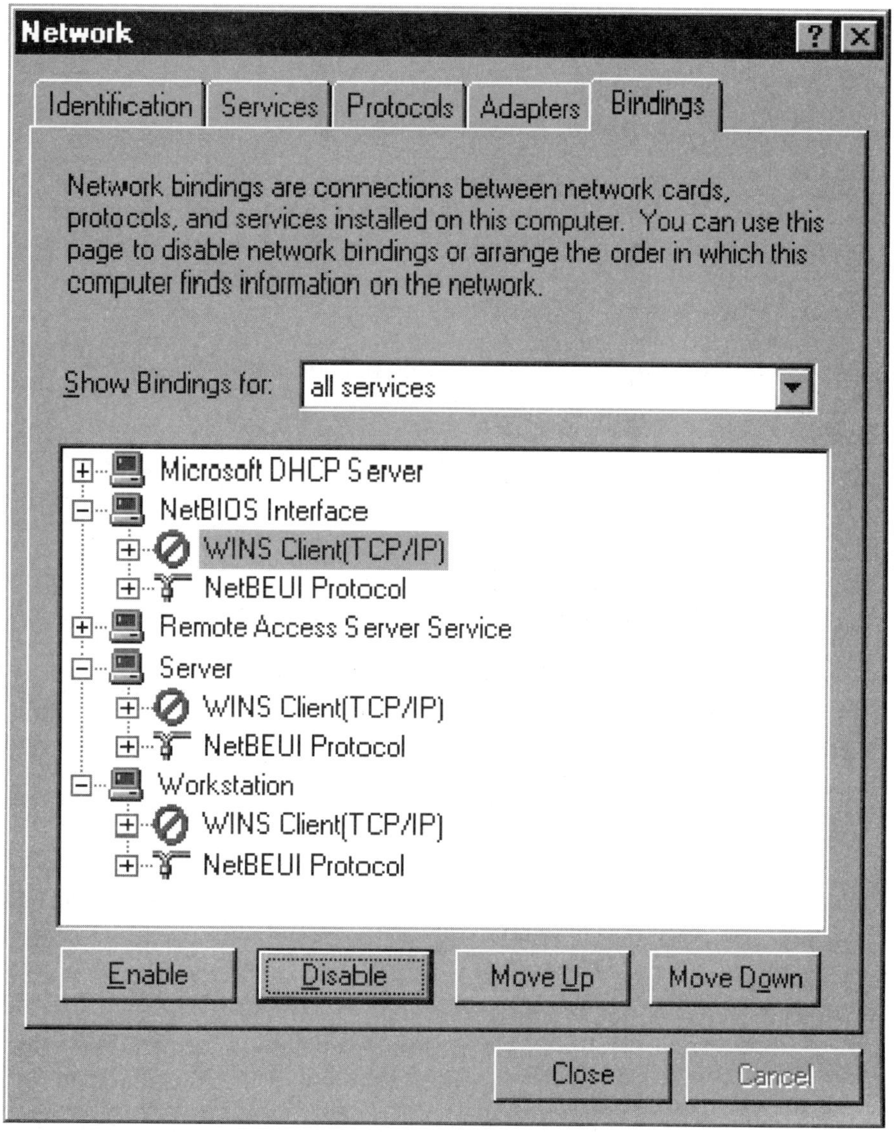

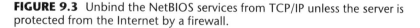

FIGURE 9.3 Unbind the NetBIOS services from TCP/IP unless the server is protected from the Internet by a firewall.

programs, and the document tree itself somewhere on your hard disk. Details vary slightly from server to server, but the default permissions for the server root are usually set up so that members of the *Administrators* group have read-write access to the contents while ordinary users have read-only access. The main task at this point is to tune the directory permissions so that

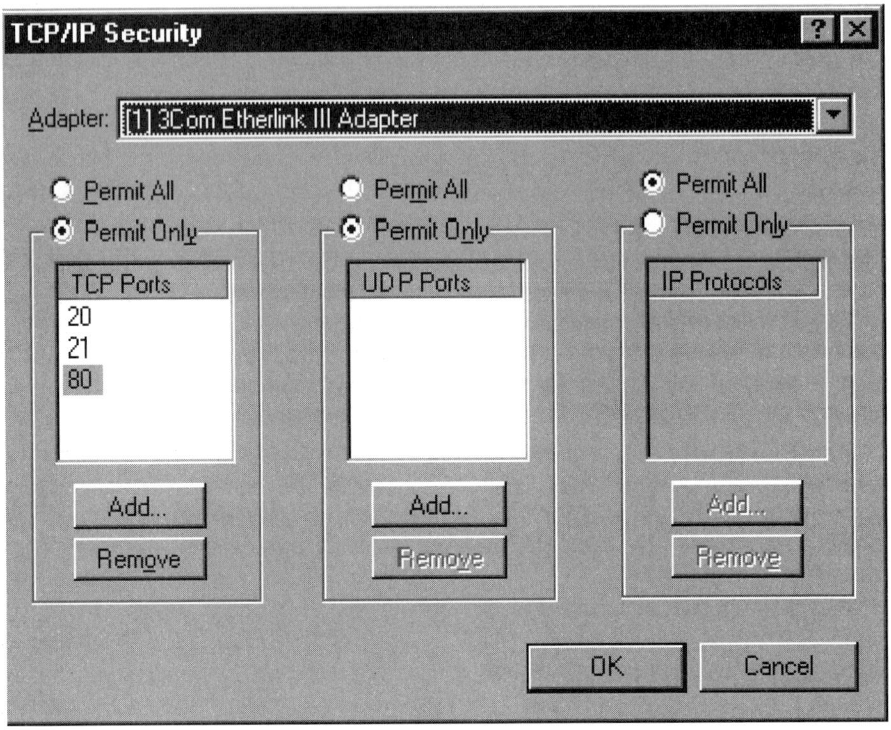

FIGURE 9.4 An "advanced" option in NT's TCP/IP configuration is a feature that allows you to restrict network access to selected ports and protocols.

authorized users can make changes to the Web tree without having to become full administrators to do so.

Users and Groups for Web Server Access

The only people who should be able to log into the Web server host are those who are directly involved in the administration of the Web server software or the contents of the Web site. This means that the server machine should not be part of an NT domain at all, in which case only users who are registered locally will be recognized, or it should be configured so that it will refuse login (both local and network-based) to all but users and groups described in this section. You can do this from within the *User Manager* application by selecting *Policies->User Rights*, and adjusting the groups that are granted the *Log on locally* and *Access this computer from network* privileges.

There are two, sometimes three, classes of users who need access to the Web server and its support files.

Defeating the Floppy Disk

The most dangerous physical threat to a server machine is the humble floppy disk. Armed with a floppy and a few minutes of privacy, someone with physical access to the machine can reboot it and rapidly defeat all the security measures you've put in place.

I'll give one scary, but little known, scenario. The entire Linux operating system fits easily onto a single floppy disk and comes complete with a read-only NTFS driver. An intruder equipped with such a disk is free to reboot the server with Linux, mount the server's main disk, and read its restricted files. Because NT access control lists aren't honored by Linux, all your carefully configured access control restrictions are for naught.

To defeat this risk, you can

1. Lock the server in a cabinet.
2. Put a lock plate on the floppy disk opening. Such plates are available at many computer mail order houses.
3. Pull the internal cable out of the floppy drive and lock the case.
4. Set the CPU to request a password at power on (in certain recent systems).

In addition to these measures, some systems allow you to throw a jumper or switch on the mother board in order to prevent booting from the floppy. It is not usually adequate to disable the floppy from within the BIOS *Setup* program, because the intruder can simply restore the settings.

1. **Webmasters** These are users responsible for the maintenance of the software itself. They need access to the server's log and configuration files and should have the ability to turn the software on and off. Webmasters have full access to the Web document tree, as well as to script and plug-in directories.
2. **Web authors** These users are responsible for the content of the site. They should have read and write permission to all files and directories within the Web server document tree.
3. **Web developers** (optional) These users have all the rights and privileges of Web authors, as well as the ability to install new scripts and plug-ins.

In addition to these user groups, the Web server itself needs to use an account to access the file system. Some servers use a single account to access the file system. Others, such as Microsoft Internet Information Server, use an anonymous account for accessing publicly available documents and individual users' accounts for accessing confidential or restricted documents. More information on access restrictions is given in Chapter 10.

It's important that the account the Web server uses for anonymous access should have only the minimal privileges it needs to operate. If the server is subverted, the damage it can do to the system will be limited to what this account can do. A few servers don't support the concept of an anonymous account at all—they run with System or Administrator privileges. This is an unsafe design because a subverted server or CGI script will have the ability to modify any file on the system. Check with your vendor to see if there's a fix for this problem.

Create or review the server's anonymous user account. If you are using Microsoft Internet Information Server, the install program will have created a special account named IUSR_*computer name*. The special account is used whenever the Web server accesses files and directories in anonymous mode—that is, without requesting a user name and password from the remote user. The anonymous account is a member of both the built-in *Guests* group and the built-in *Domain Users* group, a design that gives the server read-access to much of the file system. A more conservative arrangement is to remove *Domain Users* from the server's group membership, leaving it in *Guests* only. If you do this, you'll need to change the default permissions on the document tree to allow read-access for *Guests*. I describe this scheme below.

You may also wish to choose a more meaningful name for the server account, such as *WebServer*. Because the Web, FTP and Gopher services all use the IUSR_*computer name* account, you might want to do this in order to better distinguish between the various servers. When you create a new user for the Web server, choose a long, hard-to-guess password and make sure that the "User cannot change password" and "Password never expires" checkboxes are selected in the *User Manager* program. Remember this password because you'll need it to configure the Web server. Add the Web server user to the *Guests* group and remove it from the *Domain Users* group. Under *User Rights*, make sure the Web server user is allowed to log in locally.

If you've changed the Web server account name, you'll need to configure the server to use it. For Microsoft Internet Information Server, open the *Internet Manager* program and double-click the Web server status line to display the Web Service Properties windows (Figure 9.5). Replace the default login name and password with the name and password that you've selected. If you want the server to honor requests from the general public, make sure that the "Allow anonymous login" checkbox is checked. Otherwise, the server will require the user to type in an account name and password to access any pages.

Next create the users and groups for the various Web administrators. I like to use three groups, named *Web Masters*, *Web Authors*, and *Web Developers*. From the User Rights page of the *User Manager* application, give the members of each group the right to log in to the server locally.

You'll now set the access permissions for the various Web-related files and directories. Although the details vary from server to server, the general idea is as shown in Table 9.1.

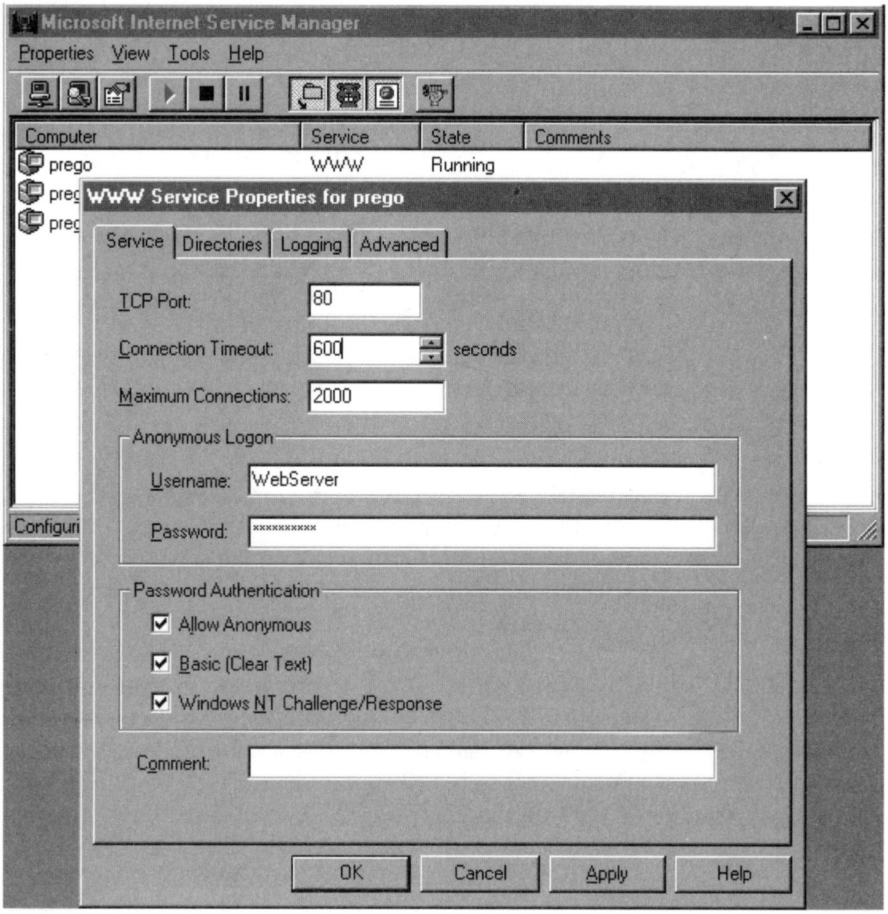

FIGURE 9.5 The IIS Service Properties window is used to change the Web server login account name.

TABLE 9.1 Access Rights for Web Server Files

Group	Admin Tools	Logs	Scripts	Documents
Web Masters	R	R	RW	RW
Web Developers	—	—	RW	RW
Web Authors	—	—	R	RW
Guests	—	—	R	R

Key: R = Read access; W = Write access

For Microsoft Internet Information Server, the permissions I recommend are

Directory *C:\InetPub\wwwroot*

Owner	Administrators
Change contents too	all files and subdirectories
Administrators	Full Control
CREATOR OWNER	Full Control
SYSTEM	Full Control
Web Masters	Full Control
Web Authors	*(see below)*
Web Developers	*(see below*
Users	Read
Guests	Read

Rationale This directory is the top of the tree for all HTML files, images, and other documents. The permissions give Web Masters and full administrators unrestricted access to the directory. The permissions for *Web Authors* and *Web Developers* depends on whether your security policy assumes that authors can trust each other to work on the same documents.

If all *Web Authors* trust each other, give *Web Authors* and *Web Developers* Full Control. Any file created within the document root can be modified or deleted by all members of these groups.

If *Web Authors* cannot trust each other, set the access permissions to Special Access(RWX)(Not specified). This allows *Web Authors* and *Web Developers* to add new files and subdirectories. Once added, they have complete control over their files, but one *Web Author* does not have permission to edit another's files unless its creator specifically grants permission to do so.

If some *Web Authors* trust each other and others don't, create an additional NT group for each set of collaborators. Within the document root, make a subdirectory for each collaborative group that grants it full control.

Domain Users and *Guests* have read-only permission for the directory. This allows the server to read the directory's contents when running in anonymous mode.

Directory *C:\InetPub\scripts*

Owner	Administrators
Change contents too	all files and subdirectories
Administrators	Full Control
CREATOR OWNER	Full Control
SYSTEM	Full Control
Web Masters	Full Control

Web Developers	Special Access(RWX)(Not specified)
Users	Read
Guests	Read

Rationale By default, this directory is where CGI scripts reside. The permissions give *Web Masters* and full administrators unrestricted access to the directory. Web script developers are authorized to add new files and subdirectories, but the scripts generated by one author can't be modified by another unless permission is granted to do so. *Domain Users* and *Guests* have read-only permission for the directory and its contents. This allows the server to run scripts inside the directory when running in anonymous mode.

If all your scripts are compiled *.exe* files, you can achieve a modicum of additional security by making the contents of the *Scripts* directory executable (X) but not readable (RX). This will avoid any chance of the *contents* of the executable being downloaded and decompiled, something that has happened with misconfigured servers. However you cannot use this technique for interpreted CGI scripts, such as Perl and Java programs.

Directory *C:\WINNT\SYSTEM32\LogFiles*

Owner	Administrators
Change contents too	all files
Administrators	Full Control
SYSTEM	Full Control
Web Masters	Read

Rationale This directory is where the Web server logs all accesses. Log files frequently contain information of a sensitive and/or personal nature. Access to this directory is restricted so that ordinary users cannot read the logs. The logs are also protected against accidental deletion by Web administrators. You may wish to modify this policy to suit your needs.

Directory *C:\WINNT\SYSTEM32\inetsrvr*

Owner	Administrators
Change contents too	all files and subdirectories
Administrators	Full Control
SYSTEM	Full Control
Web Masters	Read

Rationale This directory contains executables and support utilities for the Internet Information Server. Only *Web Masters* should run these tools, and the permissions reflect this fact. *Web Masters* are not given the ability to modify the software because changing software usually requires write-access to the system registry, something that only full administrators should have.

Configuring the Web Server

The previous section focused on the operating system, directory structures, and other factors outside the actual operation of the server. We now look at ways of making the server itself run as securely as possible.

Turn off Unnecessary Features

Microsoft IIS and other servers support a few optional features that potentially can be used by unscrupulous individuals to gain information about your system. Unless you really need these features, you should turn them off.

Directory Browsing

If a remote user requests a URL that corresponds to a directory rather than a file, IIS will look first for a default file to display, usually called *Default.htm*. If this file is not present, it will automatically generate a directory listing and allow the user to browse the listing in the same way that FTP directories behave. Unfortunately, it's not uncommon for *Web Authors* to leave files lying around that contain information not intended for public consumption. To reduce the risk of this happening, turn off directory browsing for the document root and other directories by unchecking the appropriate option in the Directories page of the Web server properties window.

Read-Access to the Scripts Directory

The contents of the *Scripts* directory should be marked executable but not readable. Otherwise, a recurring bug in various versions of IIS permits knowledgeable remote users to download the contents of a script (its source code in the case of interpreted scripts; its compiled code in the case of executables). To prevent this, open the Directories page of the Web server properties window, double-click the entry for /Scripts, and uncheck Read access. Note that this is not the same as adjusting the directory permissions from within NT itself.

Execute-Access to Non-Scripts Directories

The root directory and all other directories that are not intended to hold executable scripts should have read-access enabled, and execute-access disabled. In general, there is never a reason to have these access modes enabled simultaneously.

Active Server Pages

Active server pages are HTML files enhanced by nonstandard tags that are processed by the server before returning the document to the browser. Similar to, but more versatile, than server-side includes, active server pages are an add-on for IIS version 3.0, but may become a standard feature in future versions.

The security risks of active server pages are unknown. However, because these pages can run small programs (including BASIC and Perl), it is prudent to deactivate this feature unless you absolutely need it.

Limiting Denial-of-Service Attacks

Denial-of-service attacks are those in which a malicious individual makes your server unavailable for normal use. Some denial-of-service attacks are directed at the operating system. Examples include the TCP/IP SYN attack and the ICMP ping attack (see Chapter 7), both of which can bring NT servers down. To fix such problems, one needs to patch the operating system itself. A patch for the ICMP ping attack can be found at Microsoft's security site.

Other denial-of-service attacks are directed at the Web server itself. You can't avoid these attacks entirely, but you can take some actions that will reduce their impact.

A typical denial-of-service attack is to flood the Web server with URL requests. The server gets so bogged down servicing these requests that valid requests can't get through. Things can get so bad that you can't even use the machine interactively and are forced to reboot it.

IIS provides several mechanisms for putting a cap on the amount of system resources that the Web server will use. The first can be found in the Service page of the Web server properties window.

The text field labeled "Maximum Connections" contains the number of simultaneous connections that the server will handle. If the number exceeds the limit, the server sends a "service unavailable" message. By default, this value is set to 100,000, which is much higher than any ordinary Web site will see. (It's probably set that way for the same reason that some sports cars' speedometers go up to 250 mph.) A more reasonable value would be 200 simultaneous connections, which still allows for a very busy site. Note that the attacker can still deny service to legitimate users by occupying all 200 slots, but at least the system will be usable, giving you a chance to trace the attack back to its source and blocking further attacks.

On the same page, you'll also find a text field labeled "Connection Timeout." This is the number of seconds that IIS will allow an incoming browser to hold the connection open before it times-out. The default is 900 seconds, or 15 minutes. One way to make the system unavailable is to open up 200 simultaneous connections and keep them all open until the server times out. You can make life a little more difficult for the attacker by reducing the time-out to a smaller value, such as 180 seconds (three minutes).

A final option can be found in the Advanced page of the properties window, in the text field labeled "Maximum network use." This field limits the amount of network traffic the server is allowed to produce, expressed in kilobytes per second (not kilobits per second, the more usual measure). The default value of 4 megabytes per second approaches the effective limit of a 100BT network and is much greater than a T3 line. You can protect your LAN from a denial-of-service attack that attempts to saturate your network by activating this limit and lowering it to a more realistic value. The value you choose depends strongly on your network type and topology.

After changing any usage limits, be on the watch for legitimate users who find themselves locked out of your system. For example, if users begin to complain that your server closes their connection before large documents download, you've set the time-out value too low.

Monitor the Web Server and Event Logs

Both the Web server and Windows NT itself are capable of performing extensive logging. Although the Web server logs are turned on by default, NT event logging (aka "auditing") is turned off. Even though there is some performance and administrative overhead associated with NT event logging, I recommend that you enable it.

You can enable NT logging from within the *User Manager*, under *Policies ->Audit...* There are seven categories of events that can be logged, including login events and system shutdowns. You can choose to log the event in case of a successful outcome, a failure, both, or neither.

Figure 9.6 shows a screenshot of the Audit Settings window with the settings that I prefer. You can adjust these settings according to your preferences, but at the minimum, you should log any attempts to change the list of authorized users and groups, any change in security policies, and all logins (successful and unsuccessful). I like to record attempts to read or manipulate files that are refused because of insufficient privileges, as well. Although most of these attempts are innocent user errors, repeated attempts to access a privileged file or directory may be the sign of a break-in attempt.

Once you enable system logging, you have committed yourself to monitoring the logs on a regular basis. The log files will grow steadily at a rate proportional to server activity. If left unattended, they will eventually expand to fill the entire file system. The system log files are kept in a binary format that is browsable through the *Event Viewer* application. Although its interface is spartan, it does allow you to filter and sort events in various ways. You should inspect the logs on a regular basis for suspicious activity. After determining that nothing untoward has happened, truncate them by

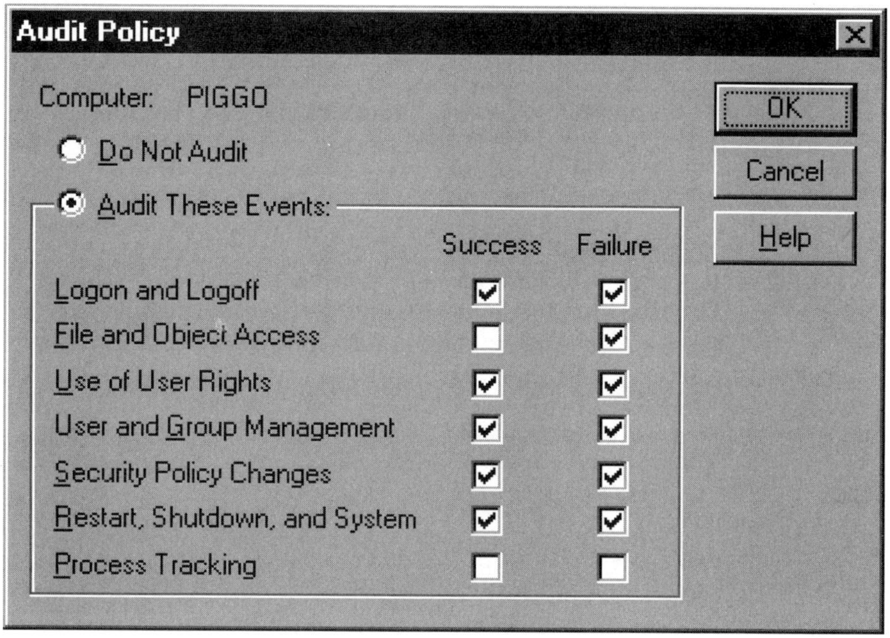

FIGURE 9.6 NT event auditing is crucial for detecting possible break-in attempts.

choosing the *File->Clear* menu item. The *Event Viewer* also gives you the option to save the logs in text-only form so that you can archive them or scan them with tools such as Perl and Visual Basic. The previous chapter gives some general guidelines on how to write log file scanning tools.

Suspicious activity is any activity that is unexpected.

- A service or driver that has previously functioned correctly fails to initialize properly
- A user logs in at an unusual hour or from an unusual location (for example, you see a remote login from a user who usually logs in locally)
- Multiple failed login attempts
- Multiple failed attempts to access a restricted file or directory
- An unauthorized change (or attempt to change) a user rights policy
- An unauthorized change to a user's group membership, or the addition of a new user

Be particularly alert to unusual activity by the Web server account. Ordinarily, the server account should be quiet except for a login event when the server comes on line during system boot, and a logout event just before the system shuts down. Other login attempts or repeated attempts by the server account to access restricted files or directories outside the Web document tree may signal the compromise of the server or one of its scripts.

A number of third parties offer tools for processing the event log. Some, such as *DumpEvt*, dump out the event log in a form suitable for incorporation into a relational database. Others scan logs and warn of suspicious activity. Third-party tools include

- Sunbelt Software *SeNTry*
- Somarsoft *DumpEvt*
- Serverware *SeNTry ELM* (no relation to Sunbelt SeNTry or the UNIX Elm mail program)

The Web server itself performs extensive logging. Depending on the server software, there may be one or several log files. Every server keeps an access log in which each URL request is recorded, along with the DNS name or IP address of the remote machine, the time and date, and the outcome of the request. The access log is usually in plain text format and follows the standard format given in the previous chapter. Some servers also keep an error log to record problems encountered by the server software and CGI scripts. This log's format varies considerably from server to server, if present at all. A few servers, such as O'Reilly's WebSite, maintain a third log that records major server events, such as initialization, shutdown, and system crashes.

Microsoft Internet Information Server's logging is configured from the Logging page of the Web Server Properties window (Figure 9.7). Here you can change the location of the access log file (*C:\WINNT\SYSTEM32\LogFiles*) and customize its format. An important feature in this window is the ability to cycle the logs on a regular schedule. With this option enabled, the server automatically rotates the logs and throws out the oldest one on a regular basis. You should enable this feature. Otherwise, the access log will eventually fill up the disk and bring down the server.

IIS also gives you the ability to send log entries to any SQL/ODBC database. You can use this feature to have log entries sent across the network to a database on a separate machine. This will sharply reduce the likelihood that someone who has broken into the server will be able to tamper with its logs, a common tactic for preventing discovery.

Because NT Web servers, by default, create access logs with the same format as the servers' UNIX cousins, you can use the Perl-based log file analysis tools described in the previous chapter to scan for suspicious activity. Suspicious patterns of activity to scan for include

- Requests for very long URLs and/or URLs containing odd characters. In the past, such URLs have been used to break into systems running buggy servers.
- Requests for URLs that contain *perl.exe* in the path. Because of bad vendor advice, some NT server Webmasters have placed the Perl executable in the *Scripts* directory, with unfortunate results (see Chapter 12).

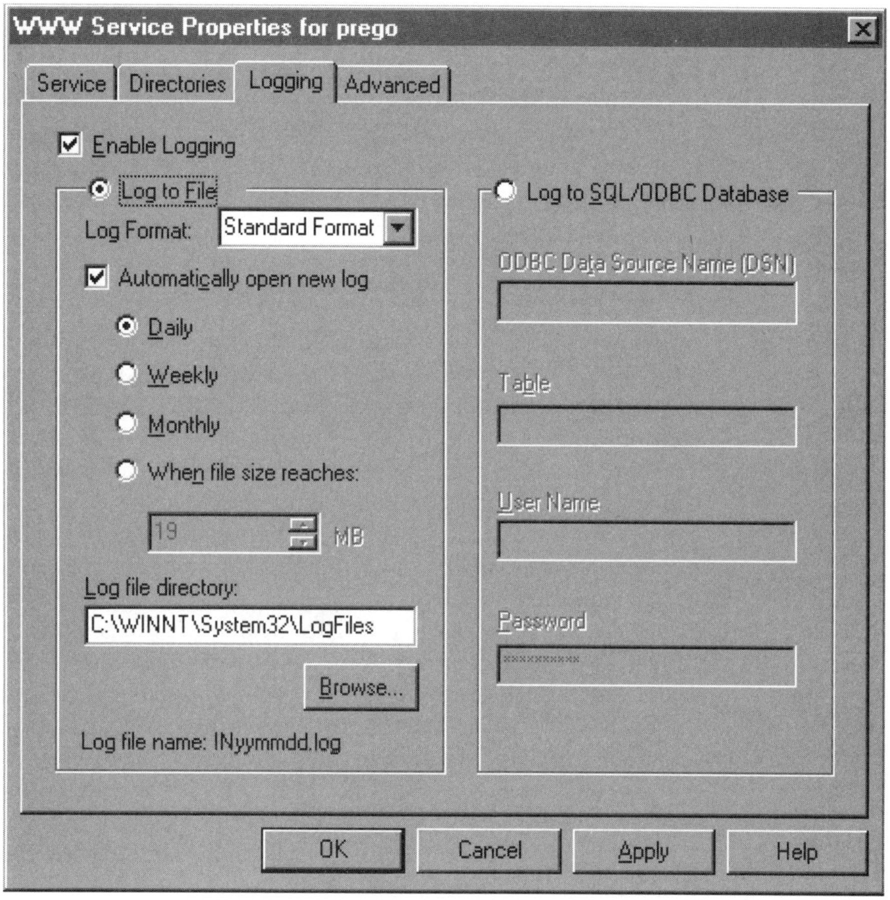

FIGURE 9.7 Microsoft Internet Information Server can log to a file or to a table in an ODBC database.

- Repeated 401 (Authorization Required) or 403 (Access Denied) status codes from the same remote IP address. This could indicate a determined attempt to access confidential information.
- Access to the URLs of documents that you thought were secret. Many sites attempt to reserve a portion of the document tree for documents that are private or in development by simply not linking to them from any public pages. Secret URLs rarely remain secret for a variety of reasons. A longer discussion of this issue can be found in Chapter 10, in the Secrecy Through Obscurity box.

There are many third-party tools for analyzing server logs. See Table 9.2 for a short listing. Also see Table 8.2 in the previous chapter for tools that run on both UNIX and NT systems.

TABLE 9.2 Web Log Analyzers

Product	Vendor	OS
Hit List	Marketwave	Windows NT/95
WebTrends	E.G. Software	Windows NT
IIS Assistant	MediaHouse Software	Windows NT

Create a Backup System and Use It

A recent and complete system-wide backup is essential for recovering from a break-in. Even if your system isn't broken into, a backup will allow you to recover from disasters, ranging from hard disk crashes and overly enthusiastic sprinkler systems to the accidental deletion of an essential file.

Windows NT comes with a plain but serviceable tape backup program called *NT Backup*. There are also many third-party backup systems of varying complexity and functionality. Whatever backup system you use, be sure to test it at regular intervals by choosing a file at random and attempting to restore it. Be aware that magnetic media, such as tape, degrades with multiple uses. Be sure to rotate tapes according to the manufacturer's recommendations.

If your system is broken into, it's possible that core parts of the operating system have been compromised in order to make it easier for the intruder to break in again or to attack other machines on your network. The safest approach is to wipe the system clean and restore from a backup that you trust. Another approach is to scan the system files for changes in modification date, size, and/or content. A number of commercial virus scanning utilities offer this feature. You'll find a listing of the most popular ones in Chapter 5.

Checklist

1. Have you installed all security-related patches and updates?

   ❍ No
   ✓ Yes

   By the time the vendor has issued a patch for a security problem, the bad guys know all about it. Keep your server up to date.

2. Have you disabled all unnecessary services?

   ❍ No
   ✓ Yes

   Be sure to disable any network services you don't need. Even those that don't appear to present a security risk may contain unknown loopholes.

3. Have you disabled NetBIOS services?

   ❍ No

   ☑ Yes

   Convenient as they are, file sharing, remote registry editing, remote Web server administration, and other NetBIOS tools are potential security holes on NT systems. Run them only if the server is on an intranet protected by a properly configured firewall, and only then if you are not overly concerned by insider threats. Definitely disable these services on a server that is connected directly to the Internet.

4. Do the Web server's file and directory permissions make sense?

   ❍ No

   ☑ Yes

   The Web server executable, the document root directory, and the server root directory should all have permissions that prevent unauthorized access. Be particularly careful to avoid giving the user ID that the Web server runs under more privileges than it needs.

5. Is the Web server running under the *System* account?

   ☑ No

   ❍ Yes

   You should be sure that the Web server runs as an unprivileged user when it is serving anonymous requests from the Internet. Some servers are preconfigured to log themselves in under the *System* account, which gives them unlimited access to the system.

6. Have you put maximum caps on the Web server's use of resources?

   ❍ No

   ☑ Yes

   Resource usage caps are essential for avoiding certain denial-of-service attacks. If you can, place limits on the number of incoming Web connections, the length that a connection can be held open, and the amount of bandwidth the server uses.

7. Is the Web server running any unnecessary features?

   ☑ No

   ❍ Yes

   Server-side includes, automatic directory listings, fancy CGI scripts, and server plug-ins all introduce potential security holes. Disable any features that are not essential.

8. Do you monitor the Web server and system event logs?

   ❍ No

   ✓ Yes

   The event and Web log files can alert you that someone is contemplating attacking your site, actively attacking it, or has already compromised your security. Unless you check the log files, you may never know you've been broken into.

9. Does the server perform double-duty as a general purpose machine?

   ✓ No

   ❍ Yes

   The Web server host should be restricted to Web-related work only. Other work should be carried out on a different machine.

10. Do you back up your system?

    ❍ No

    ✓ Yes

Online Resources

NT Configurations

NT Security Alerts

http://www.microsoft.com/security/

Microsoft's Secure NT Installation recommendations

http://www.microsoft.com/security/guidesecnt.htm

Microsoft NT Server Support Pages

http://www.microsoft.com/ntserversupport/

NT Service Packs and "hot fixes"

ftp://ftp.microsoft.com/bussys/winnt-public/fixes/usa/nt4/

Security Scanners

Internet Security Systems Internet Security Scanner (ISS)

http://www.iss.net/ (commercial version)

Midwestern Commerce Administrator Assistant Toolkit

http://www.ntsecurity.com/

Secure Computing NT Security Scanner

http://www.lanwan.fi/turva/nt/ntscan.html

Log Analyzers

SeNTry

http://www.ntsoftdist.com/sentry.htm

DumpEvt

http://somarsoft.com/

SeNTry ELM

http://www.serverware.com

Hit List

http://www.marketwave.com/

WebTrends

http://www.webtrends.com

IIS Assistant

http://www.go-iis.com/

Printed Resources

Russel, Charlie and Crawford, Sharon, *Running Microsoft Windows NT Server 4.0* (Microsoft Press, 1997).

A comprehensive reference guide to Windows NT that explains many aspects of the system's security model.

Sutton, Stephan, *Windows NT Security Guide* (Addison Wesley Developers Press, 1997).

This tutorial on Windows NT security is short and to the point.

Chapter 10

Access Control

By default most Web servers give the public unlimited access to every nook and cranny of the document tree. Often, however, you'll want to restrict areas in which sensitive or confidential information is kept so that only limited numbers of users have access.

The two ingredients of access control are "user authentication" and "user authorization." These are related, but slightly different, concepts. User authentication is the process by which you identify the person who connects to your Web site. Once authenticated, user authorization determines which files, scripts, and directories the user has permission to access.

This chapter shows you how to limit access to all or part of your Web site based on the IP address of the remote browser or a username/password combination. In this chapter, we talk about the strengths, limitations, and pitfalls of these techniques.

The next chapter discusses advanced authentication techniques based on cryptography and digital certificates.

Types of Access Control

Web servers offer many types of access control, ranging from very simple methods to extremely complex ones. Not all browsers and servers offer all types of access control. The following listing is in rough order of complexity.

Access Control Based on IP Address

In this type of restriction, the server examines the incoming connection and grants or denies access based on the browser's IP address. Virtually all Web servers provide this method, and it doesn't rely on the browser for cooperation.

Access Control Based on Domain Name

This is like the previous type, but the server uses the browser host's domain name to decide whether to accept the connection. This type of access control is also nearly universal.

Access Control Based on User Name and Password

Each user is assigned a user ID and a password. In order to access a restricted part of the site, the user has to authenticate herself by entering the correct name/password pair. This type of access control comes in several flavors and is available, in one form or another, in all modern browsers and servers.

Access Control Based on Client Certificates

The remote user is issued a cryptographic certificate to use as a digital signature. The certificate may be provided by either a trusted third party or your own organization. When the user's browser attempts to contact your Web server, it attaches an unforgeable digital signature to its request. The server grants access to the user if her certificate is both valid and authorized. Recent browsers from Netscape and Microsoft support this type of authentication, but only a few servers can handle it. This type of authentication is discussed in more detail in the next chapter.

Access Control Based on Network Security Protocols

A variety of secure protocols have been invented to handle the general problem of authentication and authorization across local and wide area networks. These protocols, which include MIT's Kerberos and DCE authentication, can be used with Web software products, as well. Only Web servers and browsers that have been specially customized can support these protocols, so they're only practical for use in intranets where the protocols are already in use.

Access Control Based on IP Address or Host Name

The most basic type of Web access control is based on the DNS name and/or IP address of the remote browser. Browsers calling from authorized addresses are allowed in. Others are refused. You can use this type of access control to limit your site to a small number of trusted hosts. As an alternative, you

Restricting Robots

Robots, also called "Web crawlers," "spiders," and "agents," are automated programs that crawl across the Web, downloading one document after another. Each time an HTML document is downloaded, the robot scans its text for links to documents that it has not seen before. This process is repeated until the robot has examined every document that is reachable from a public Web site.

Robots serve essential functions on the Internet. They power large text search engines like AltaVista and Lycos, and they allow organizations like Netcraft to compile statistics on the size and makeup of the Web. Most public sites openly welcome robots because they help bring new customers into the site.

In some circumstances, however, you may not want to give robots unrestricted access to your site. One common scenario is when a part of the site contains information that changes constantly. By the time a Web indexing engine adds a document to its index, it will be out of date.

Another common scenario is when a site uses CGI scripts to deliver its information. A robot that wanders into the scripts directory may thrash about in it, attempting to traverse an infinite set of dynamically generated URLs. This type of activity can slow a site to a crawl as CGI scripts designed to accommodate human surfing habits struggle to keep up with the robot's pace.

You can control robots in several ways. Because an access by a robot is no different from an access by a human surfer, all the access control restrictions described in this chapter are valid for robots. If a portion of your site is restricted by IP address or by user name and password, you can safely assume that robots will not be able to enter it. If an internal Web site is protected from the Internet by a firewall, it's also protected against robotic crawlers.

For finer grained control, you can take advantage of "robot rules," an informal etiquette agreed upon by the major robot programmers several years ago. When a polite robot first enters a site, it checks for a file named *robots.txt* at the top of the site's document hierarchy. If it finds the file, it will download it and follow the rules contained within it.

A simple *robots.txt* looks like

```
# robots.txt for http://www.genome.wi.mit.edu
User-agent: *               # match any robot name
Disallow: /cgi-bin/         # don't allow robots into cgi-bin
Disallow: /tmp/             # no need to index temporary files
Disallow: /private/         # don't enter the private directory
```

The file consists of human-readable text. Comments begin with the # symbol. Two different directives are recognized. The first directive, *User-agent:* gives the name of the robot you are sending instructions to. Because you usually don't know robots' names in advance, you can use the wild-card character * to specify any robot. The second directive, *Disallow:* gives a path that the robot shouldn't enter. In the above example, we are telling all robots that they should not enter the *cgi-bin, private,* or *testing* directories.

> **Restricting Robots** *(continued)*
>
> Less frequently used directives allow you to control the behavior of individual robots by name. See the Robots Page at the URL given at the end of this chapter for the complete list of *robots.txt* options.
>
> Not all robots are compliant with the robot rules. If part of the site is to remain truly secret, you should not rely on *robots.txt* alone.

can open your site up to all hosts except for certain ones that are known to be nuisances. You can refer to specific hosts, to whole domains, or to networks and subnetworks.

IP-based authorization has strengths and weaknesses. Its major strength is that it's easy to set up and not likely to be misconfigured. Its major weakness is that it's not very flexible. This type of authorization doesn't work well when you want to grant access to people who are moving around from machine to machine, such as a mobile sales force or employees who frequently work from home. It doesn't accommodate multiuser machines in which several people share the same IP address. Nor does it handle dynamically allocated IP addresses or Web proxies well. For example, you can't use IP-based access control to grant Web access to just a subset of America Online users, because AOL uses a Web proxy that makes all members' accesses appear to come from a single machine.

How secure is this type of access control? Access restrictions based on the host name of the connecting browser is vulnerable to a technique known as "DNS spoofing" in which an unscrupulous individual temporarily assumes control of a portion of the DNS host-name lookup system. The server thinks that it's being contacted by a trusted host but, in fact, the machine at the other end of the connection is something else entirely.

There are two ways to minimize the risk of DNS spoofing. If the Web server supports it, you can configure it to perform "paranoid" DNS checking. When an incoming connection comes in, the server pulls the IP address of the browser out of the TCP/IP header information, then makes not one, but two, calls to the DNS system. First, the server asks the DNS to return the host name registered for the IP address. Next, it asks the DNS system for the IP address of the host name it just returned. For technical reasons, it's easy to spoof the part of the DNS that translates IP address into host names, but hard to subvert the part that translates host names into IP addresses. If the IP address that's returned by the DNS system in the second lookup matches the original browser's IP address, the chance that the remote browser is an imposter is small (it's about the same as the chance of being tricked by IP address spoofing, see below). The Apache and UNIX Netscape servers both provide this type of paranoid DNS checking. Check with your vendor to determine if your server provides this option.

Another way to avoid DNS spoofing is available to you if your organization uses a firewall system and the firewall provides reliable DNS lookups that are immune to such shenanigans. Simply configure the Web server to trust the firewall's DNS server only. Check with your firewall administrator or vendor to see if this is an option.

Access restrictions based on the IP address of the remote browser are more secure and more efficient than host-name restrictions because the DNS system is not involved at all. On heavily loaded servers, DNS lookups may account for the bulk of CPU time. Many sites turn DNS lookups off for performance reasons if not for security concerns.

Unfortunately, IP-based restrictions are not entirely foolproof because of "IP spoofing," a technique that takes advantage of an obscure feature in the TCP/IP protocol, known as source routing. By taking advantage of this feature, an incoming connection from a remote host could pretend to be from an IP address within your own local area network. It takes considerable technical expertise to mount an IP spoofing attack. A very few such attacks have been reported in recent years, but they're reportedly becoming more common. For static HTML pages, IP spoofing offers little risk because the server will return the page to the computer that the spoofer is pretending to be and the destination machine will just ignore the unsolicited page. A more significant risk is that the spoofer will run a restricted CGI script, which may have a side effect such as updating a database.

Many routers and firewalls can be configured to reject connections that use source routing. Some flavors of UNIX, including Linux, Solaris, and HP-UX, also provide the feature of rejecting connections that use source routing.

Last, don't forget that restrictions based on IP address and host name provide no guarantee that the *user* of the remote machine is authorized to access your server. There is always the possibility that the remote host or network has been subverted by the bad guys and is now being used as a staging location to gain access to your Web server.

The details of setting up an IP-address-based access control vary from server to server. In the next sections, I show how to configure this kind of restriction for the UNIX Apache server and the Microsoft IIS server.

Restricting by Host Name and IP Address Restriction in the Apache Server

Apache and other NCSA *httpd* derivatives use a global access configuration file, */usr/local/etc/httpd/conf/access.conf*, to set directory access policies for each part of the directory tree. Optional per-directory access control files (usually named *.htaccess*) can be placed inside the directories themselves in order to fine-tune access policies without having to edit *access.conf* and restart the server. If you run a site with multiple virtual hosts, each host can have a different *access.conf* and a completely different set of access control rules.

Access.conf is divided into a set of directory control sections using the *<Directory>* directive to place access control on a physical directory. The Apache server (but not NCSA *httpd*) also recognizes *<Location>* and *<Files>* directives.

Access.conf is only read once when the server starts. If you make any changes to it, you must restart the server (by sending it a HUP signal) before your changes take effect. This warning does not apply to per-directory access control files, which are re-read every time the server needs to access a file in a protected directory.

To protect a directory based on the IP address or host name of the connecting host, use this model to create a directory section declaration in *access.conf*.

```
<Directory /local/web/private>
  <Limit GET POST PUT DELETE>
    order deny,allow
    deny from all
    allow from .host.domain1
    allow from .host.domain2
    allow from 128.123.7
  </Limit>
</Directory>
```

The example uses several of the directives listed in Table 10.1.

<Directory>

The *<Directory>* and *</Directory>* directives begin and end a directory control section. The format is `<Directory path_name>`, where *path_name* is an absolute physical path to a directory in the Web document tree. All documents located within the indicated directory or in a subdirectory will be

TABLE 10.1 IP Address Restriction Directives in Apache

Directive	Example Parameters	Description
<Directory>	`<Directory /local/web/private>`	Begin a physical directory section
</Directory>	`</Directory>`	End a physical directory section
<Location>	`<Location /private>`	Begin a virtual directory section
</Location>	`</Location>`	End a virtual directory section
<Files>	`<Files */private*>`	Begin a file section
</Files>	`</Files>`	End a file section
<Limit>	`<Limit GET POST>`	Begin an access restriction section
</Limit>	`</Limit>`	End an access restriction section
order	`deny,allow`	Order in which to evaluate other directives
deny from	`.cracker.ltd phreaks.com`	Deny access to some domains
allow from	`.capricorn.org`	Allow access to some domains

protected by the access control restrictions contained within the section. The Apache server (but not the NCSA server) allows the directory name to contain the wildcard characters "*" and "?", which match zero or more characters and a single character respectively. This directive is not allowed in *.htaccess* files.

<Location>

<Location> and *</Location>*, recognized by the Apache server only, are similar to *<Directory>* but apply to a virtual directory rather than to a physical one. For example, if the document root is located at */local/web*, the directives `<Directory /local/web/private>` and `<Location /private>` are equivalent. Like *<Directory>*, this directive is not allowed in *.htaccess* files.

<Files>

The *<Files>* and *</Files>* directives can be used to filter access to files based on their names. The directive's argument is a pattern match for the server to apply to the physical path of a requested document. If a match is found, the access restrictions are applied. For example, you can restrict access to all files named *secret.html* using a directive like `<Files */secret.html>`. In addition to standard wildcards, newer versions of Apache support matching based on regular expressions. Unlike the preceding directives, *<Files>* can also be used within a *.htaccess* file. When used in this way, the server strips off the portion of the path up to and including the current directory before attempting to apply the pattern match.

<Limit>

The *<Limit>* and *</Limit>* directives establish the access policy for this directory. The format is `<Limit meth1 meth2...>`, where each of the parameters is one of the HTTP access methods GET, POST, PUT, or DELETE. Clients that try to use the listed method will be restricted according to the rules listed within the section. GET is the method commonly used to retrieve normal documents, POST is used for sending data to certain executable scripts, and the others are not widely used. Ordinarily, you'll need to restrict only GET requests. You should restrict POST, as well, for directories that contain executable scripts. Because it doesn't hurt, I recommend limiting everything, including PUT and DELETE, in the interest of avoiding nasty surprises when these methods become commonly used at some future date.

Deny From and Allow From

Within each *<Limit>* section, you can put any number of *order, deny from,* or *allow from* directives. To deny access to one or more hosts or domains, use the *deny from* directive (yes, the *from* really is part of the directive):

```
deny from host1 host2 host3 ...
```

Each listed host can be a fully qualified host name, such as *monkey.zoo.org;* a domain name, such as *.zoo.org;* a full numeric IP address, such as *18.128.12.1;* a partial IP address such as *18.128.12;* or the word *all.* Hosts can be listed on one long line or in multiple short directives. Apache matches numeric IP addresses and domain names in slightly different ways. When you give it something that looks like a partial IP address, the server tries to match it from left to right. The address *18.128.12* will match *18.128.12.1* and *18.128.12.2*, but not *192.18.128.12*. Something that looks like a domain name will match from right to left: *.zoo.org* will match *monkey.zoo.org* and *tapir.zoo.org*, but not *monkey.zoo.org.edu.*

The *allow from* directive has the opposite effect, granting access to the host or hosts listed. The order in which the *allow* and *deny* directives are processed is important because later directives override earlier ones. The *order* directive, which comes in three forms, controls this.

```
order deny,allow
order allow,deny
order mutual-failure
```

The first form processes the *deny* directives first, followed by the *allow* directives. Use it when you want to deny access to a number of hosts (such as *all* or an entire domain), and then selectively turn access back on. Unless you specify *deny from all,* all hosts not specifically mentioned are allowed access. This form is the default when order is not specified.

The second form does the opposite, processing all the *allow* directives first, then the *deny* directives. Use it for cases when you want to allow access to most members of a domain and then exclude particular hosts. Like the previous form, hosts not mentioned in either the *allow* or *deny* list are allowed access by default.

The third form, *mutual-failure,* requires a host to be mentioned either in the *allow* list or the *deny* list. Any host that does not appear on one list or the other will be denied. This is probably the form that is safest to use, because there's no chance of a host slipping through the cracks.

Use this template when you want to allow everyone in except a few people who've been giving you trouble (for variety, this example uses *<Location>* rather than *<Directory>*).

```
<Location />
  <Limit GET POST PUT DELETE>
    order mutual-failure
    allow from all
    deny from .crackers.ltd .phreaks.com dorm3.bigU.edu
    deny from 18.157.5
  </Limit>
</Location>
```

And here's one to use when you want to deny access to everyone except for a few trusted hosts.

```
<Location />
  <Limit GET POST PUT DELETE>
    order mutual-failure
    deny from all
    allow from .capricorn.org
    allow from 18.157.0.5 18.157.0.22 192.235.1.3
  </Limit>
</Location>
```

Some systems have trouble retrieving the fully qualified host name for the server host itself and other local machines. If this affects you, you may have to use the numeric partial IP address of your domain in order to allow access by local hosts. On some systems, adding the line *allow from localhost* will allow you to access a protected directory using a browser running on the server machine itself. Also note that in order for DNS-based access control to work at all, the server must be performing DNS lookups on incoming connections. Many sites have turned off DNS lookups for performance reasons.

When an access restriction is applied to a directory, it applies to all its subdirectories as well, unless *access.conf* contains a more specific entry. Access restrictions can also be modified by per-directory *.htaccess* files located in the directory itself. These files should be world-readable and contain whatever you would ordinarily put within a *<Location>* or *<Directory>* section.

For example, to arrange restrictions so that only browsers connecting from hosts in the *.capricorn.org* domain can gain access to the */local/web/confidential* directory, you might create a file named *.htaccess* in that directory containing

```
<Limit GET POST PUT DELETE>
   order mutual-failure
   deny from all
   allow from .capricorn.org
</Limit>
```

Although *.htaccess* files are convenient to use because you can change a directory's access restrictions without restarting the server, they complicate matters if overused. Instead of being centralized in a single configuration file, your site's access control policy is scattered among dozens of files. Another problem with the files is that they're created in the same directories as HTML files. This means that the web authors at your site will have the ability to add and modify access control policies. If this is not what you want, you can eliminate the ability of *.htaccess* files to override access control policies by adding an entry like this to the main *access.conf*

```
<Location />
   AllowOverride FileInfo
</Location>
```

This allows authors to use *.htaccess* files to tweak the MIME types of files within their directories and perform other innocent customizations, but does not give them permission to change access control policies.

There's also an odd security loophole in both Apache and other derivatives of NCSA httpd. Remote users can fetch and view the contents of *.htaccess* files simply by requesting their URLs. This is undesirable since these files may contain the names of confidential files and addresses of internal hosts. To prevent this, add the following to the main *access.conf* file:

```
<Files */.htaccess>
   <Limit GET POST PUT DELETE>
      order mutual-failure
      deny from all
   </Limit>
</Files>
```

After changing DNS or IP address restrictions, you should be sure to test them, if you can, by attempting to gain access to the server from allowed and forbidden machines.

IP Address Restriction in MS IIS

Microsoft Internet Information Server is not as flexible as some other servers in regard to IP address restriction. You can restrict access to the server as a whole, but not to individual subdirectories. IIS does not provide host-name restriction at all.

To use IIS's address restrictions, launch *Internet Service Manager* and open the properties window for the Web server. Select the *Advanced* tab to display the window shown in Figure 10.1. At the top of the window are a pair of radio buttons that select IIS's default access policy. You can toggle them to select whether all computers will be granted access by default or denied access. Select the first option if you want everyone except for a few known bad actors to have access to the server. Select the second option if you want to restrict access to a finite list of trusted machines.

Once you've set the default action, you will create exceptions to the default. In the common case, in which the default action is to deny access, you'll list machines that are granted access. To add a new trusted host or network to the access list, press the "Add..." button. You'll be prompted to enter the IP address of a single machine or the network address of a group of machines. In the latter case, you'll also be asked to provide a subnetwork mask in the standard format. In the example shown in the screenshot, all machines are denied access except those in the class C network address *18.157.1*.

After setting the IP address restrictions, test them if you can by attempting to gain access to the server from allowed and forbidden machines.

Secrecy Through Obscurity

Some sites attempt to restrict access to certain documents by keeping their URLs secret. A Web programmer creates a new subdirectory for use while testing CGI scripts, or a Web author puts up pictures of her grandchildren and gives the URL to friends and family only. If there aren't any links to these URLs from the site's home page, they're safe, aren't they?

Sadly, the answer is: No. Obscure URLs rarely remain secret for long for any of a host of reasons.

- Someone makes a link to the page from a bookmarks file or home page. A Web crawling robot run by some search engine site finds and follows the link.
- The secret URL shows up in some remote server's referer log (see Chapter 5).
- The site's own document search engine finds the hidden document and adds it to its index.

Some day, for fun, go to your favorite Web search site and look for documents with URLs containing the words *secret, confidential,* or *private.*

Secrecy through obscurity is never an adequate solution. It takes a little more work, but make sure that private documents are protected by the server's formal access control system.

Other Servers

Netscape's servers provide a browser-based interface that is run by the separate administrative server. Fill-out forms allow you to add new IP addresses and host names to the list of hosts allowed to access different parts of your site. The logic is similar to that used by Apache and Microsoft IIS, allowing you to deny all by default or allow all by default.

O'Reilly & Associates' WebSite server provides a graphical user interface to IP and host-name restrictions through its *Server Properties* application. Because WebSite was derived from NCSA *httpd*, the configuration options are almost identical to those in Apache.

Access Control Based on User Name and Password

Most Web servers allow you to protect a directory or individual file in such a way that the user has to provide a user name and password in order to gain access. This has certain advantages (see list on next page) over restrictions based only on IP address or host name.

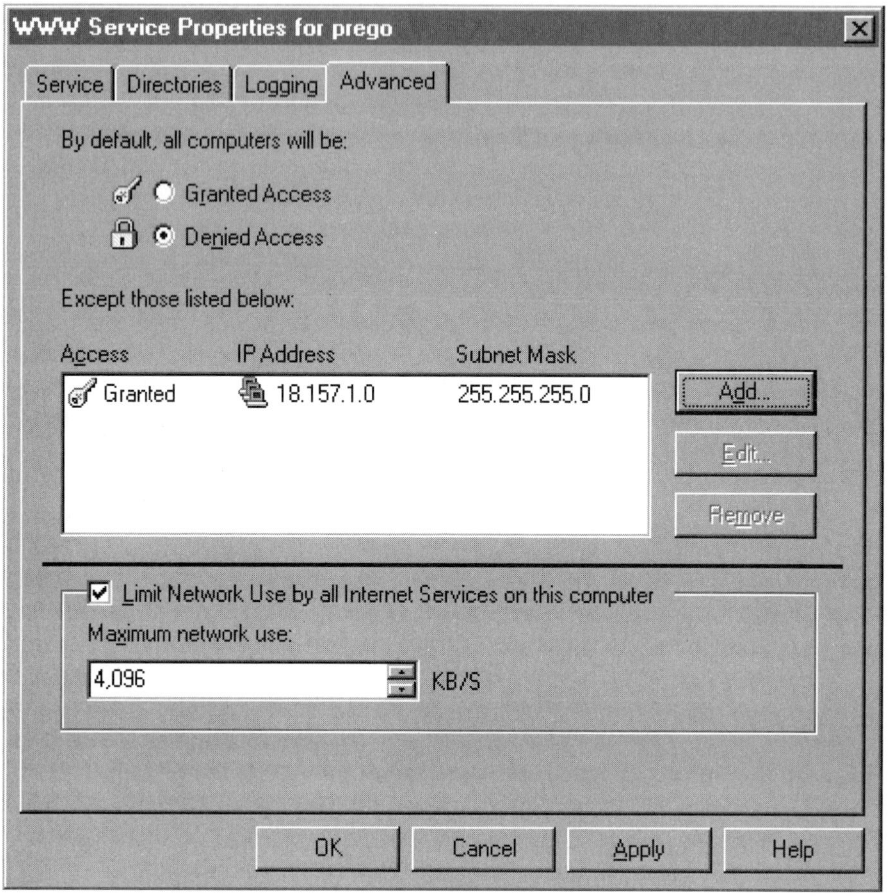

FIGURE 10.1 Microsoft IIS's "advanced" properties allow you to restrict access by IP address—but only globally to the entire site.

- Because you're authenticating the user, not just a machine, you have more assurance that the person behind the browser is who you think it is.
- Users are free to move from machine to machine and still have access to the Web pages they are authorized to read.
- There are no problems associated with dynamically allocated IP addresses or Web proxies.
- Most users are comfortable with account name and password because it is a familiar technology.

Unfortunately, there are also drawbacks to user passwords. For example:

1. Users share passwords with their friends.

2. Users forget their passwords and require customer support to recover them.
3. Users write their passwords down on slips of paper and stick them to their computer monitors.
4. Users choose poor passwords, such as their first names, telephone numbers, or names of favorite pets. Poor passwords are easily guessed.
5. The most widely used implementation of password restriction transmits the password in the clear where it is easily intercepted by a network eavesdropper armed with a packet sniffer.

Problems 1 through 4 can be reduced with proper user education. Users should be encouraged to pick good passwords and to change their passwords on a regular basis. Advice on picking good passwords is given in Chapter 4. Changing passwords may be more problematic. While some Web servers come with scripts that allow users to change their passwords, others are sadly lacking in this regard. A script that works with the NCSA, Apache, and Netscape servers is described in the following sections.

The Problem of Password Sniffing

The problem of password sniffing is the biggest issue in access control based on user names. Some of the password implementations are vulnerable to network eavesdropping. Others are not.

Basic Authentication

Part of the original HTTP/1.0 protocol was a simple system for password authentication, now built into all modern browsers and servers. It's unfortunately a very weak system (some people jokingly call it basically awful authentication). To see how basic authentication works, see Figure 10.2. When a browser first attempts to download a page that's protected by this scheme, it sends a request like this one.

```
GET /protected/index.html HTTP/1.0
```

Because the page is protected, instead of returning it in response to the request, the server generates a response like this.

```
HTTP/1.0 401 Unauthorized
Date: Monday, 02-Jan-96 00:30:29 GMT
Server: Apache/1.1.1
MIME-version: 1.0
WWW-Authenticate: Basic realm="private"
```

This HTTP header begins with a 401 status code, indicating that the browser has requested a page for which it needs authentication. Later, a

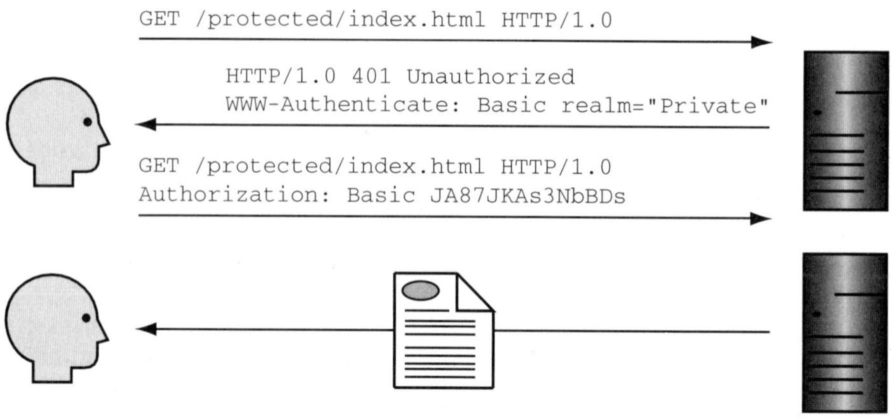
GET /protected/index.html HTTP/1.0
HTTP/1.0 401 Unauthorized
WWW-Authenticate: Basic realm="Private"
GET /protected/index.html HTTP/1.0
Authorization: Basic JA87JKAs3NbBDs

FIGURE 10.2 Although basic authentication appears to be encrypting user names and passwords, it is really transmitting them in the clear.

WWW-Authenticate header tells the browser to use *basic* authentication. The realm name that accompanies this field is there only to provide a label that the browser can display when it requests the user's password.

The browser responds to this by putting up a dialog box requesting the user's name and password. After she types this information in, the browser sends the server a second request.

```
GET /protected/index.html HTTP/1.0
Authorization: Basic a2FyZW5nOmxhbW1hczk3
```

The "Authorization" field holds the user's authentication information. The word *basic* tells the server that basic authentication is being used. The garbled text that follows holds the user's name and password.

Although this information *appears* to be encrypted in some way, it's actually not. It's just encoded using the Base64 algorithm that the MIME system uses for e-mail enclosures. Anyone who intercepts the request from the browser to the server can obtain the user's name and password and go on to use the information to access all protected pages on the server. If the password is used to protect scripts that update a database, the intruder can change the database in the user's name or do other damage.

Because the HTTP protocol is stateless, the browser must reauthenticate itself to the server every time it accesses a protected page, not just the first time it enters a protected directory. In order to make this palatable to the user, browsers remember the name and password used to access a page and retransmit them automatically whenever the user accesses a page in the same directory hierarchy. This gives network sniffers many chances to intercept passwords.

Fortunately, there are a growing number of alternatives to basic authentication that solve this problem.

Digest Authentication

Because of basic authentication's severe problems, the HTTP/1.1 protocol, introduced in the spring of 1997, provides an improved technique, known as digest authentication (Figure 10.3). Digest authentication uses a challenge/response technique to confirm that the user knows the proper account name and password without actually transmitting the password information across the network.

Digest authentication begins in much the same way as basic authentication, when the browser attempts to fetch a URL with the standard GET request. However, the server's response now looks like this.

```
HTTP/1.1 401 Authorization Required
Date: Sun, 08 Jun 1997 01:38:42 GMT
Server: Apache/1.2b10
WWW-Authenticate: Digest realm="private", nonce="865733922"
```

Aside from the fact that the header now specifies the HTTP/1.1 protocol (and that it's a year later), the main difference here is that the *WWW-Authenticate* header specifies the digest authentication scheme. It also provides a "nonce" with a value of 865733922.

What's a nonce? It's an arbitrary challenge value that the server sends to the browser. It can be a random number, as used here, or a longer value that

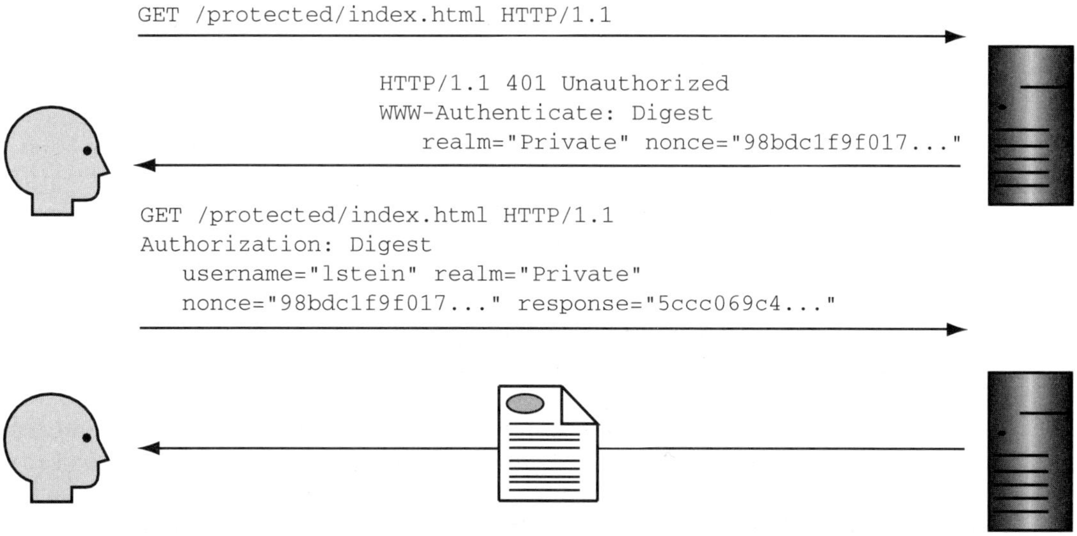

FIGURE 10.3 Digest authentication, part of HTTP/1.1, never transmits passwords in the clear.

contains information about the current transaction. Longer nonces typically contain the IP address of the browser, the URL requested, and a time stamp.

In response to the challenge, the browser again displays the user name and password dialog. When the user enters the information this time, however, the browser concatenates the values and uses the MD5 algorithm to generate a one-way hash value. This hash value is now concatenated to the nonce and the requested URL. Finally the whole thing is again hashed with MD5. The result is a response value that is returned to the server.

```
GET /protected/index.html HTTP/1.1
Authorization: Digest realm="private", nonce="865733922",
                      username="lstein", uri="/protected/index.html",
                      response="48e58853bb70284cf7b98fc757a0f3e1"
```

When the server receives this request, it looks up the user's name in a file and retrieves the user's hashed name and password. It concatenates this hash value to the nonce and to the requested URL, hashes them both, and compares this value with the response returned from the browser. If they match, the server knows the browser knows the password.

The strength of this scheme is that passwords are never sent over the network, just hashed values. Provided that the user has picked a good password, it's impossible to derive the password from the hash value. For further protection, the user's password is not stored in plaintext on the server side, where it could be stolen by someone with access to the server host. Only the hashed value is stored in the file (this is similar to the way that NT and UNIX systems store users' passwords).

As a final precaution, the requested URL is part of the hashed response value. If the response is intercepted by an eavesdropper who attempts to play it back to gain access to the server, he'll be able to get access only to that single URL. He'll be unable to generate new responses to gain access to other parts of the directory hierarchy. Servers can further minimize the playback risk by adding a time stamp to the nonce so that responses expire after a short period of time.

Digest authentication is far superior to basic authentication. If it's available to you, use it. Several servers support it, including the Apache 1.2 server. Although none of the commercial browsers had been modified to use this protocol at the time this chapter was written, I hope it will be a widespread feature by the time you read this.

NT Challenge/Response Authentication

Windows NT uses a challenge/response authentication mechanism conceptually similar to digest authentication. When a Microsoft Web browser is used in combination with a properly configured Microsoft server, it can use NT challenge/response to authenticate itself. The advantage of this is the same as digest authentication: The user's password never passes over the network in the clear.

Unfortunately, NT challenge/response differs in detail from digest authentication and so the two are incompatible. Internally, NT challenge/response uses the DES cryptographic algorithm, whose export is restricted by U.S. munitions control regulations. This means that NT challenge/response is unlikely to become an Internet standard in the near future. This type of authentication is most useful in intranet environments in which you can require everyone to use the Microsoft Internet Explorer browser. It's probably not useful for Internet applications.

Encrypted Communications

If the browser and server are communicating with an encrypting protocol, such as SSL, the problem of password sniffing goes away. The encrypted channel is set up *before* any HTTP headers pass across the network, so the user name and password are part of the encrypted data stream. They cannot be sniffed.

Restriction by User Name and Password in Apache

Like the accounts on UNIX and NT systems, Apache allows you to create authorized users, give them passwords, and place them in groups. You then grant Web access to individual users or to groups as a whole. It's important to understand that the user accounts known to Apache have nothing at all to do with UNIX accounts. Having a UNIX account on the server host doesn't automatically grant a user access to a restricted Web directory, and having an Apache account doesn't allow a user to log in to the server. This is probably the way you want it.

Apache uses a variety of file formats to store lists of users, groups, and passwords.

- **text** User information is stored in human-readable text files. You can view and edit the information with a text editor. However, the format is suitable only for sites with fewer than a hundred or so user accounts. Beyond that, server performance suffers.
- **DBM** User information is stored in database files managed with the DBM or NDBM libraries that come preinstalled on most UNIX systems. User names and groups are stored in a binary format, so you can't edit the files directly. They have the advantage, however, of being able to store thousands of user accounts without performance degradation.
- **DB** User information is stored in UNIX database files managed by the Berkeley DB library. This library is similar to DBM and NDBM but has better performance.
- **MSQL** User information is stored in the MSQL freeware SQL database. This allows Web access and authentication to be run from the same data-

base in which you store other user account information, such as billing information.

On top of these multiple file formats are the two types of authentication currently defined in Apache: digest and basic authentication. Because of the many possible combinations, Apache offers a dizzying array of directives for configuring user authentication. For historical reasons, the command-line tools have grown up in a haphazard way that makes them difficult to describe and confusing to use.

I recently put together a Perl tool called *user_manage* that provides a high-level, unified interface to Apache's user management system. In addition to providing a command-line interface to Apache's users and groups files, it can be used as a CGI script to provide a Web-based graphical front end. You can add, edit, and delete users from the convenience of a browser window. An added benefit is that it allows remote users to change their own passwords conveniently and safely.

Although the script was designed for use with Apache, many of its features work with other NCSA-derived Web servers, including NCSA *httpd* and Netscape's UNIX servers. This section shows you how to set up password restrictions using *user_manage*. For details on Apache's lower-level tools, including *htpasswd* and *dbmmanage*, see Chapter 4 of my previous book, *How to Set Up and Maintain a Web Site*.

Obtaining and Installing user_manage

The list at the end of this chapter gives the URL for the *user_manage* package. The package consists of a Perl script plus a set of Perl modules for manipulating Apache's password and group files that were written by Doug MacEachern. If you use digest authentication, you also need to obtain the Perl MD5 module, available at CPAN, the Comprehensive Perl Archive Network.

Follow the instructions in the package for installing the Perl modules and the *user_manage* script itself. I like to place the script in the server root's *support* directory, but you can place it anywhere you prefer. If you wish to use *user_manage* as a CGI script, you'll need to place it in the scripts directory and to designate a group that will be granted administrative access to the script, such as *Webmasters* (an Apache group, not the similarly named UNIX group). There are also issues of file permissions and ownerships when *user_manage* is used as a CGI script. These are described in detail in the documentation.

realms.conf

user_manage works from a configuration file called *realms.conf*, which is usually stored with Apache's other configuration files in */usr/local/etc/httpd/conf*. A *realms.conf* file might look like this.

```
# realms.conf
<Realm main>
        Type            text
        Authentication  Basic
        Users           /usr/local/etc/httpd/security/passwd
        Groups          /usr/local/etc/httpd/security/group
</Realm>

<Realm development>
        Type            DBM
        Authentication  Basic
        Users           /usr/local/etc/httpd/security/devel.passwd
        Groups          /usr/local/etc/httpd/security/devel.group
</Realm>

<Realm members@capricorn.org>
        Type            DB
        Authentication  Digest
        Users           /usr/local/etc/httpd/security/passwd2
        Groups          /usr/local/etc/httpd/security/group2
</Realm>

<Realm subscriptions>
        Type            MSQL
        Authentication  Basic
        Database        web_accounts@localhost
        Users           table="user_records" uid="UserID" passwd="Password"
        Groups          table="user_records" group="Group"
</Realm>
```

realms.conf is made up of one or more *realm* sections, each of which defines a password protection scheme. You may protect multiple directories with the same scheme, or partition the site up into several realms, each with a different administrator responsible for maintaining the user database.

The opening *<Realm>* tag must contain the realm's name, which can be any set of non-whitespace characters. Each section contains directives that tell *user_manage* what type of authentication to use for the realm, what type of database to use, and where to find the files or database tables used for the realm. The users and groups defined in one realm are independent of those defined in another, giving you a lot of flexibility in setting up access control for your site.

The example shown here defines four security realms. The first, named *main*, uses human-readable text files and the basic authentication protocol. The second, *development*, also uses basic authentication but stores users and groups in DBM files rather than in text files. The realm named *members@capricorn.org* uses digest authentication on top of DB database files. By convention, digest realms look like e-mail addresses, but this doesn't have to be the case. The last realm definition uses basic authentication on top of an MSQL database.

TABLE 10.2 *user_manage* <Realm> Directives

Directive	Example Parameters	Description
Type	`DBM`	Database type (text, DBM, DB, MSQL)
Authentication	`Basic`	Authentication scheme (basic, digest)
Users	`/etc/httpd/passwd`	Path to users and passwords
Groups	`/etc/httpd/group`	Path to groups
Database	`www@capricorn.com`	Location of MSQL database (MSQL only)
Server	`NCSA`	Type of server (Apache, NCSA, Netscape)

The directives allowed within a <*Realm*> section are listed in Table 10.2. Descriptions of them follow.

- **Type** This directive specifies the database type. It can be any of text, DBM, DB, or MSQL. Although these are the only databases currently recognized by Apache, other UNIX DBM-like formats, including GDBM and SDBM, are recognized for future compatibility.
- **Authentication** This directive specifies the type of authentication to use. It can be either basic or digest.
- **Users** This is the path to the file or database table that holds user names and passwords. For everything but MSQL databases, it's a physical path to a file on your system. If the file doesn't exist, *user_manage* will create it the first time it needs to. For MSQL databases, the value of the directive should have the format

  ```
  table="table" uid="user field" password="password field"
  ```

  The value of *table* is the name of the table in which to look for the user. The value of *uid* and *password* are the fields in which Apache will look for the user ID and password. For lookup efficiency, the *uid* field should be defined as the primary key field in the table.
- **Groups** This is the path to the file or database table that holds group assignments. If you don't need groups, just leave the directive out. For everything but MSQL databases, the argument is the physical path to a file on your system. If the file doesn't exist, *user_manage* will create it the first time it needs to. For MSQL databases, the directive points to a previously defined table and field in the database in the format

  ```
  table="table" group="group field"
  ```

  The value of *table* is the name of the table in which to look up the user. The value of *group* is the field in which Apache can find the group the user belongs to. Apache will look for the user name in the same field as declared in the <*Users*> directive, so don't declare another `uid=` field here. You can use the same table for both *users* and *groups*, or a different one. In the latter case, you can have several records for each user allowing the same user to belong to multiple groups.

Using user_manage *from the Command Line*

The command line syntax for *user_manage* is

```
user_manage [-r realm] command argument1, argument2...
```

The optional *-r* flag indicates the security realm to operate on. If it isn't specified, the first realm in the *realms.conf* file will be assumed. This is followed by a command and optional arguments. Here's a command summary:

realms Summarize the realms defined in *realms.conf* in tabular form.

add *user_name password group1,group2,group3...* Add the user named *user_name* to the current realm with the password and groups listed. If any of the arguments are not listed, the script will prompt for them. If the user is already defined, her password and groups will be changed. For example:

```
lstein> user_manage add Alice yow2wow members,authors
```

Groups can be separated by commas, as shown here, or by white space. Both forms also work when the program prompts you to enter a list of groups interactively.

edit *user_name password group1,group2,group3...* This command is identical to *add* but is intended to be used for modifying existing entries.

groups *user_name group1,group2,group3...* Change the named user's group membership without changing the password. If no groups are specified, the program prompts for them. It is an error to use this command on a user who isn't already in the database.

delete *user_name1 user_name2...* Delete the named users from the database. If a user is removed from a group that has no other members, the group itself is deleted.

view [*user_name*] Print out information on the user. If no user is given, dump out the entire database (use this with care on large databases!).

directives Apache doesn't interact directly with *realms.conf* (although it ought to). This command will print out a set of Apache directives suitable for pasting into *access.conf* or *.htaccess* files. For example, here's how to generate a template for the *development* realm given in the example configuration file at the top of this section.

```
lstein> user_manage -r development directives
AuthName  development
AuthType  Basic
AuthDBMUserFile /usr/local/etc/httpd/security/devel.passwd
AuthDBMGroupFile /usr/local/etc/httpd/security/devel.group
<Limit GET POST PUT DELETE>
```

```
order deny,allow
allow from all
require valid-user
</Limit>
```

You would now cut and paste this template into *access.conf* or *.htaccess* and modify the *<Limit>* section to your tastes. Later in this chapter, in Apache Authorization Directives, I'll describe how to customize the template.

Using user_manage's *Graphical User Interface*

When *user_manage* is installed in the *cgi-bin* directory, you can use it to add, edit, and delete users from your browser window. Ordinary users can use it to change their Web (*not* UNIX) passwords.

To distinguish between ordinary users and those who have administrator privileges, *user_manage* checks whether the user belongs to a special administrative group. The group is named *administrators* by default, but you can change it to whatever you prefer by editing a definition in the source code. In preparation for using the script in CGI mode, you should use the script's command-line mode to add yourself and any other authorized administrators to the realms you wish to manage, making sure to place yourself in the administrative group. No administrative group is required if you never intend to run *user_manage* remotely.

To link to *user_manage* from a Web page, create a link like this.

```
<a href="/cgi-bin/admin/user_manage?realm=development">Change
your password</a>
```

The script expects a single CGI parameter named *realm* with the value of the security realm that you want to modify. If this parameter isn't present, *user_manage* will default to the first realm defined in *realms.conf*. You will be asked to authenticate yourself by providing a user name and password. By default *user_manage* does its own authentication and requires you to produce a valid password for the relevant realm. If you like, you can place the script itself under access control in the manner described in the next section, but this won't ordinarily be necessary.

If you are successfully validated, the system checks whether you are a member of the special administrative group (*administrators* by default, you can change it via a definition in the *user_manage* source code). If you're not a member of this group, you are presented with a simple fill-out form that prompts you to enter your old and new passwords. For members of the administrative group, a screen like the one shown in Figure 10.4 appears. To the left is a scrolling list of the users who are currently members of the realm. To change a user's entry, select the name from the list and press the "Edit/Add" button. You are prompted to enter and confirm the user's new password.

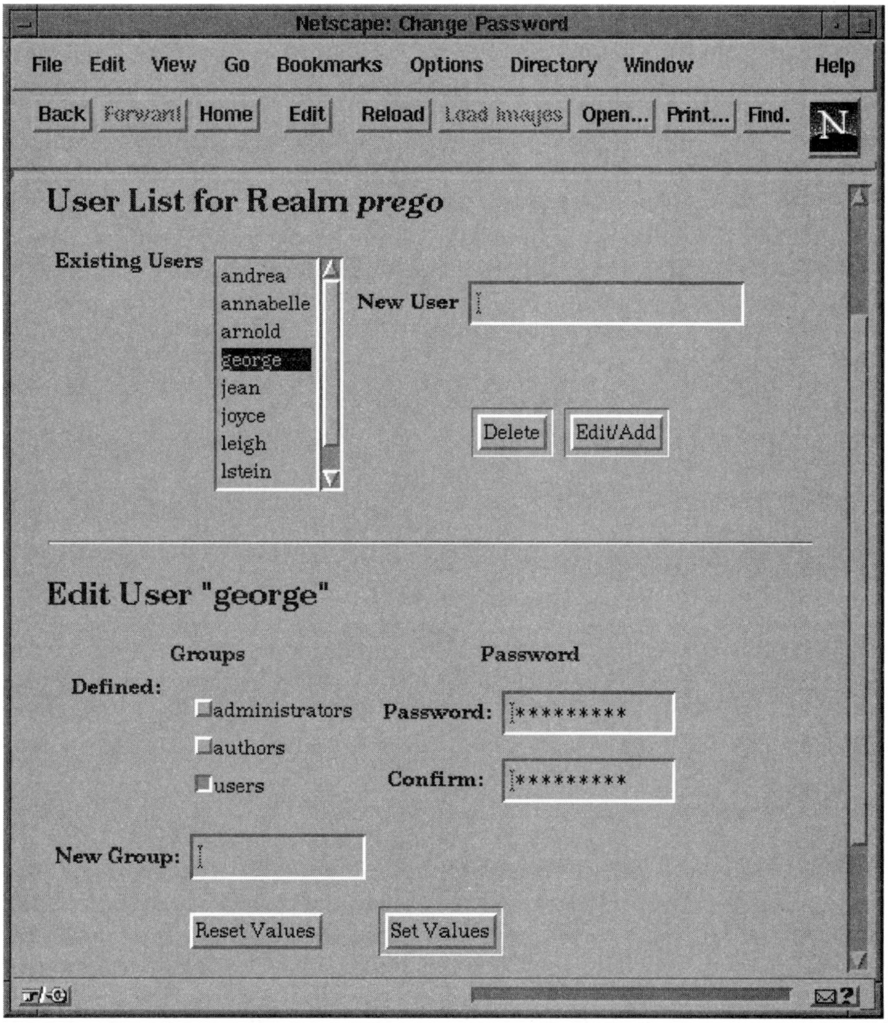

FIGURE 10.4 When installed as a CGI script, *user_manage* can be run by administrators to add and edit users.

You can change the user's group membership by selecting one or more check boxes (which will be replaced by a scrolling multivalue list if the number of groups grows large) or define a new group by typing its name into the appropriate field.

To add a new user, just type the new account name into the field labeled "New User" and press "Edit/Add." You can delete a user entirely (along with any groups in which she is the sole member) by selecting her account name and pressing "Delete."

There is an important caveat on using this script. Just like basic authentication, the script passes user names and passwords across the network in the clear. If the information you're trying to control access to is important, you should force users to access the script via SSL by using an SSL-enabled version of the server software and using an *https* link to enter the script (see the next chapter). If you place the script in a directory that is itself protected by digest or basic authentication, *user_manage* will use the account name provided by authentication and skip the initial sign-on phase. However, user's passwords will still be passed in the clear whenever they're changed—it's an unavoidable problem of using HTTP.

Fine-Tuning Access Restrictions

Although the *user_manage* script simplifies managing Apache's various user and group files and outputs templates suitable for pasting into Apache's access control files, you still need to understand the directives in order to use them effectively. When you give the command-line version of the *user_manage directives* command, it will print out something like this.

```
AuthName  development
AuthType  Basic
AuthDBMUserFile /usr/local/etc/httpd/security/devel.passwd
AuthDBMGroupFile /usr/local/etc/httpd/security/devel.group
<Limit GET POST PUT DELETE>
    order deny,allow
    allow from all
    require valid-user
</Limit>
```

At the top of the output, the *AuthName*, *AuthType*, and other *Auth* directives tell Apache the name of the realm, what type of authentication to use and where to find the password and group files. You should be able to paste these into a *.htaccess* file or into the *<Directory>*, *<Location>*, or *<Files>* section of *access.conf* without modification. The section within the *<Limit>* section may need to be modified, however. By default, the contents of this section will restrict access to the directory to any user who is a member of the realm.

To change this restriction, you can replace the line "require valid-user" with any of the forms of the *require* directive listed here.

1. `require user` *name1 name2 name3...* Only the named users can access the contents of this directory using the method specified in the enclosing *<Limit>* section.
2. `require group` *group1 group2 group3...* Only users belonging to one or more of the named groups can access the contents of this directory using the method specified in the enclosing *<Limit>* section.
3. `require valid-user` Any user who can produce a valid username/ password combination, as described before.

Basic and digest authentication can both be combined with IP/host name restrictions. Simply combine a *require* directive with the appropriate *allow from* or *deny from* directives. The following example restricts access to authorized users who are connecting from machines in the *capricorn.org* domain.

```
<Location />
  AuthName  development
  AuthType  Basic
  AuthDBMUserFile /usr/local/etc/httpd/security/devel.passwd
  AuthDBMGroupFile /usr/local/etc/httpd/security/devel.group
  <Limit GET POST>
    order mutual-failure
    deny from all
    allow from .capricorn.org
    require valid-user
  </Limit>
</Location>
```

By default, incoming connections must satisfy both IP address restrictions *and* user authentication restrictions. To allow users in if they satisfy either one or the other criterion, insert the phrase *Satisfy any* within the *<Limit>* section. This is valid only for Apache 1.2 or higher.

Apache 1.2 also offers an anonymous authentication mode similar to anonymous FTP. In this mode, users are allowed access to a restricted directory if they log in as a user named *anonymous* and provide an arbitrary password, often an e-mail address. This allows users the option of providing you with voluntary identification information and may be useful for some applications in which reliable authentication isn't needed.

Restriction by User Name and Password in Microsoft IIS

Microsoft IIS, unlike most other Web servers, does not distinguish between Web-based users and other users of the system. All Web users must have active accounts on the system, either as locally registered users on the Web server machine or as global users on the server's domain controller. This design has both good and bad aspects, as we shall see.

To set up access control properly, you have to understand the sequence of events that occurs when a user tries to access a Web page on an IIS server.

1. The user's browser requests the URL of a document.
2. IIS translates the URL into a physical path to a file or directory.
3. If IIS is configured to allow anonymous access to its pages, it assumes the identity of the anonymous user (by default this is *IUSR_machine_name*. I like to change it to the more meaningful name *WebServer*.)
4. As the anonymous user, IIS attempts to read the file or directory. If the operation succeeds, IIS returns the document.

5. If the operation fails, IIS sends the browser a *401 Authorization Required* message. If the user is running Internet Explorer from an NT machine, the browser pulls the authentication information right out of the user's current login account. Otherwise, the browser pops up the user name and password dialog box, and the user types in the information. The browser returns the authentication information to IIS.
6. IIS verifies that the user name corresponds to a known account and that the password is correct. If everything checks out, the server now assumes the identity of this user and again attempts to access the file or directory. If successful, the document is returned; otherwise, IIS repeats step 5.

To restrict access to a file or the contents of a directory, therefore, use Windows NT's *Properties* command to adjust the access control list in exactly the way you would if users were logging in locally. To give a concrete example, when IIS is first set up, the contents of its document tree are readable by members of the *guests* group. Because the anonymous user is a member of *guests*, the entire document tree is available to remote users without providing any additional identification information. To change this policy for a specific directory, simply remove *guests* from the access control list and add the users and/or groups that you want to grant access to. IIS will take care of the rest.

Details

There are a few details to worry about. IIS can authenticate Web users using either the standard basic authentication or the Windows NT challenge/response protocol. The latter is more secure, but it is only available when IIS is used with a browser that understands the protocol, currently only Internet Explorer. You have the option of choosing whether the server allows basic authentication, challenge/response, or both. You can also decide whether to allow anonymous access at all.

To adjust these parameters, use *Internet Service Manager* to open the Web server properties window. Under the Service page you'll find the authentication options in a section labeled "Password Authentication" (Figure 10.5). If you are using IIS in an intranet environment where everyone is guaranteed to be using Internet Explorer to access the server, you can safely select challenge/response authentication and leave basic authentication unchecked. In a heterogeneous environment or for a server connected to the Internet, however, you'll probably need to select basic authentication as well. If both authentication methods are available, the browser will choose the more secure one. *Internet Service Manager* will complain each time you select basic authentication—don't let it rattle you. If you wish *all* Web accesses to be authenticated, uncheck the box labeled "Allow Anonymous."

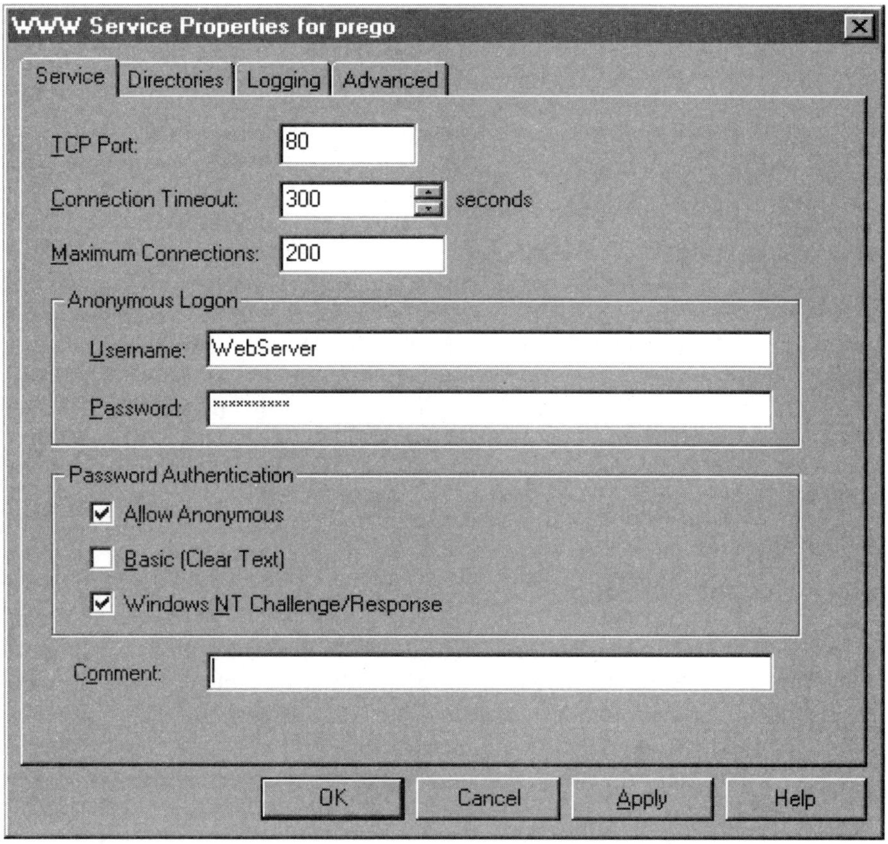

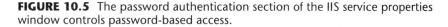

FIGURE 10.5 The password authentication section of the IIS service properties window controls password-based access.

The other important detail is the privileges of the accounts that are used to access Web pages. For challenge/response authentication, all such accounts must have the right to *Access this Computer from the Network* (set by the *Policies->User Rights...* menu command in the *User Manager* application). However, for basic authentication, these accounts must have the right to *Log in Locally*. In order to support both authentication methods, you'll have to give the accounts both privileges.

You may feel uneasy about using NT user accounts for Web access control and then giving them the ability to log in to the server. This is another good reason to physically secure the server machine and to turn off all network services other than the Web server.

I know of no CGI-based tool that allows remote users to change their IIS passwords. Since IIS uses NT accounts for access control, intranet users can use the standard Task Manager tool to change their domain password. The Front Page program (see Chapter 13) includes user management among its remote administration facilities.

Other Types of Access Control

The next step beyond access control by IP addresses, host names, and passwords is client-certificate-based systems. These systems rely on the remote user possessing a cryptographically signed certificate of identity. Client certificate systems promise strong, reliable, trouble-free authentication. Whether they deliver on this promise is another story. See the next chapter for details.

There are also a number of specialized access control schemes. While not suited for general Internet use, they may be ideal for controlled intranet environments.

Kerberos

This authentication and access control system was invented at MIT in the 1980s for use in the University's Project Athena experiment in distributed computing. Kerberos relies on a secure "key server" to authenticate users when they first log in. During a login session, users remain authenticated and are free to use any host machines, printers, and other services that participate in the Kerberos network. All authentication and authorization transactions are encrypted, thereby avoiding password sniffing.

Kerberos runs on top of many operating systems. However, in order to participate, all server and client software must be modified to make calls to the Kerberos library, a process known as "kerberizing." Kerberization is straightforward, but you need access to the software source code in order to do it. Pre-kerberized versions of NCSA Mosaic, NCSA *httpd*, and Apache are all available. If your organization already uses Kerberos for access control and you can live with the limitation of using freeware Web servers and clients, you may wish to consider this option.

It is interesting that Microsoft NT 5.0 reportedly will replace the current NT security model with one based on Kerberos. If this is the case and if the Microsoft Kerberos implementation is compatible with the standard MIT libraries, Kerberos-based Webs may become common in the future.

Distributed Computing Environment

Distributed Computing Environment (DCE) is a product designed by the Open Software Foundation in Cambridge, Mass., that provides homogeneous, integrated network services on top of a network of heterogeneous computers and operating systems. Among its features is single sign-on security service that is conceptually similar (but different in detail) to the Kerberos scheme.

OSF is reportedly developing Web servers and browsers that take advantage of the DCE security architecture. It may be worth following the development of this software if your intranet already uses DCE-based authentication.

Proprietary Protocols

A handful of vendors have introduced Web products that use proprietary protocols to secure communications and authenticate users. Among these are Siemans Nixdorf's TrustedWeb, a system that combines elements from both Kerberos and Sieman's SESAME security architecture. TrustedWeb has three main selling points.

1. Because it was developed in Europe, it is free from U.S. export licensing restrictions and, therefore, can use strong encryption to secure communications between browser and server.
2. The system relies heavily on "role-based" authorization, meaning that the process of verifying the identity of a user is separate from the process of deciding what resources a user can access. This simplifies administration and avoids many potential pitfalls.
3. It uses specialized proxies at both the server and the client sides, allowing unmodified Web browsers and servers to take advantage of the TrustedWeb security model.

TrustedWeb runs on UNIX Solaris, Windows NT, and Windows 95 systems.

Access Control and CGI Scripts

As a last word, it's worth mentioning that even the most sophisticated, state-of-the-art access control system can be easily circumvented by a poorly written CGI script. Because CGI scripts are run as external processes with the user privileges of the Web server, they can read any file that the Web server can read, including restricted documents. Typically, CGI scripts do not know anything about server-based access control. Scripts that read HTML files and process them in some way (such as scripts that process server-side includes) are particularly vulnerable; a knowledgeable remote user can fool them into retrieving documents that the server would refuse to return if asked directly. This is one situation in which the IIS method of basing Web access control on the file system's access control lists is a definite advantage—because CGI scripts cannot circumvent the restrictions.

For more information on safe CGI scripting, see Chapter 12.

Checklist

1. How do you keep unauthorized people from reading private files on your Web site?

   ☑ We restrict access to IP addresses from machines within our organization.

   ☑ We restrict access to users who can produce valid account names and passwords.

   ❍ The URL for the private area is secret. No one will ever figure it out.

   Within the limitations described above, access control by IP address, host name, or user name and password are all effective ways to keep private documents out of the hands of unauthorized people (remembering, always, that unless the connection is encrypted, passwords and the documents themselves can be intercepted). Restricting access to documents by keeping their URLs secret is not a secure practice, but it is practiced by a surprising number of people!

2. If you rely on user names and passwords for access control, how do users change their passwords?

   ☑ There's a Web page that allows them to do this.

   ☑ They log in to the server and run a program.

   ☑ They call up the system administrator, who changes it for them.

   ❍ They don't.

   In order for passwords to remain secure, users should be encouraged to change them periodically. The longer the same password is in use, the more likely it is to be compromised. Unfortunately, many Web servers provide inadequate password-changing services. You can have the system administrator change the password for the user, but this is inconvenient and unsafe—the system administrator ends up knowing everyone's password. Nor do you want users to have login privileges to the Web server. The best solution is to obtain a CGI script or server extension that allows users to securely change their passwords from their Web browsers.

3. If you rely on user names and passwords for access control, how do you protect them from interception?
   - ☑ The site uses SSL for all its password-protected pages.
   - ☑ The site uses digest authentication rather than basic authentication.
   - ☑ The site uses NT challenge/response authentication.
   - ❍ Our network is protected by a firewall.
   - ❍ We don't.

   It's important to realize that passwords can be intercepted by a packet sniffer anywhere along the connection between the browser and the server. If your Web server handles requests from Internet users, their passwords can be sniffed even if you've protected your server with a firewall. SSL, digest authentication, and NT challenge/response all take care to avoid transmitting user names and passwords in the clear. Basic authentication takes no such precaution and should be avoided for any truly sensitive application.

Online Resources

user_manage Administrative Tool for Apache

http://www.genome.wi.mit.edu/~lstein/user_manager/

Perl MD5 Module

http://www.perl.com/CPAN/modules/by-module/

DCE and the Web

http://www.osf.org/tech/dce/
http://octavia.anu.edu.au/~markus/DCE-WEB/papers/Conf_94.html

TrustedWeb

http://www.trustedweb.com/

Web Robots

The Robots Page

http://info.webcrawler.com/mak/projects/robots/robots.html

Chapter 11

Encryption and Certificate-Based Access Control

Web servers that support the SSL protocol have two features that other servers do not have.

1. They can encrypt their communications.
2. They can use client certificates to authenticate users and control their access to the site.

Combined, these features greatly increase the chances that confidential documents will remain that way. Certificate-based access control ensures that only authorized people can download restricted documents, while encryption prevents the documents from being intercepted en route.

This chapter describes how to install and configure an SSL-capable server. It then moves on to the more complex topic of using client certificates for access control.

SSL-Enabled Web Servers

Most commercial Web servers now support SSL—either version 2.0 or the improved version 3.0. SSL-enabled servers are available for UNIX, Macintosh, Windows, and OS/2 operating systems, among others. The list of specific servers is long and will be out of date by the time this book is printed. For a current list of servers that support SSL, check the *WebCompare* site at the URL given at the end of this chapter.

The ready availability of SSL servers in the commercial domain contrasts with the freeware and public domain servers, which do not, as a rule, support SSL. The main reason for this is patent restrictions on the RSA public key algorithm. In the United States, this patent is held by Public Key Partners, a partnership between Caro-Kahn, Inc., and RSA Data Security, Inc. It is illegal to use software that implements RSA cryptography without purchasing a license. The purchase price of commercial Web software includes such a license, explaining the fact that servers that support SSL tend to be more expensive than those that don't.

It is interesting that the RSA patent is not recognized beyond U.S. borders because of differences in U.S. and international patent law. For this reason, Eric Young, an Australian, was able to develop a freeware implementation of SSL named SSLEay. Ben Laurie, a British citizen, then developed a patch kit for the Apache Web server that incorporates the SSLEay library. If you are not a citizen of the United States, you may combine these ingredients with the standard Apache distribution to create Apache-SSL, an SSL-capable version of this UNIX server (Windows NT versions of SSLEay and Apache-SSL are reportedly in preparation). If you are a U.S. citizen, you must license RSA before using SSLEay software. The SSLEay documentation gives advice on how to do this.

Apache users who are not committed do-it-yourselfers should consider purchasing Stronghold, a commercial version of Apache-SSL. In the United States, it can be purchased from C2Net Corporation. Outside U.S. borders, Stronghold is available from C2Net's South African partner, Thawte Communications, Ltd. Both versions support full-strength encryption, making Stronghold one of the very few strongly encrypting Web servers available to overseas users.

At press time, the WWW Consortium (W3C) had announced that it had successfully incorporated SSL v3.0 into Jigsaw, its freeware Java-based Web server. See the W3C's Web pages for more information.

Installing an SSL Web Server

In order to use SSL with a Web server, you must obtain and install a site certificate signed by a well-known certifying authority (CA). Some commercial Web servers come with signed certificates included in the purchase price. In most cases, however, you will have to go through the application process yourself. Although the details vary for different servers and CAs, the basic steps for obtaining a site certificate are as follows.

1. Select a CA.
2. File a certificate application form with the CA and pay the appropriate fee.
3. Generate a public/private key pair and submit an electronic certificate request to the CA.
4. Wait for the CA to sign your certificate and return it to you.
5. Install the signed certificate.

Signed certificates are good only for a limited length of time. You will need to renew the certificate on a regular basis (usually annually). There is, of course, a renewal fee.

Selecting a Certifying Authority

To enable most users to connect to an Internet Web server, you must select a CA that is widely recognized and whose certificates come preinstalled in the browser software. Netscape Navigator versions 3.0 and higher recognize a large number of certifying authorities (you can review the list by selecting *Options->Security...->Site Certificates*). Microsoft Internet Explorer (currently at version 4.0) recognizes only a subset of these CAs. IE choices include VeriSign, AT&T, MCI, and Keywitness Corporation of Canada. Your choice of CA will also depend on its fee schedule and its requirements for certification. In addition, some CAs are particular about which server software they support.

For historical reasons, VeriSign Corporation is the most widely used CA, and I'll use it in the examples below.

Filing the Application Request

Application requests are generally filed electronically via Web-based forms. The requests are encrypted using SSL in order to protect the privacy of your organization, as well as to prevent tampering en route.

VeriSign's application procedure is straightforward. Using an SSL-compatible Web browser, connect to its site *(http:/www.verisign.com/)* and follow the links to *digital server IDs*. You are presented with a series of colored icons for the various secure Web servers. Choose the one appropriate for your server software (for instance, *Internet Information Server).*

You are next led through a fill-out application form. You are asked to enter a "Distinguished Name" for your server, which consists of your organization's name, the Web server's domain name, and your organization's address. An important part of the distinguished name is the "Common Name" field, which should contain your Web server's public host name—for instance, *www.capricorn.org*. It is important that this is correct, as browsers complain if they find the certificate's common name does not match the site name exactly. You are also asked to provide information to be used to confirm your organization's identity, as described below.

At the bottom of this form is billing and payment information, which you must fill out.

When you submit this form, VeriSign's server will create an application letter for you and present it to you for your review. If you approve, you can submit it, and it will be entered into VeriSign's application queue. You'll be given a tracking number to use to check on the progress of your application. Keep a copy of the application letter by choosing your browser's *Save* command. Among other things, it contains the distinguished name that you entered. You'll need this information later to generate a valid key pair. A typical distinguished name looks like this.

```
Common Name          www.capricorn.org
Organizational Unit  Community Outreach
Organization         The Capricorn Organization
Locality / City:     Boston
State:               Massachusetts
Country:             US
```

The application letter also contains an e-mail address to send the server's certificate request to. You need this information to complete the process.

VeriSign needs sufficient information to verify the identity of your organization. For U.S. corporations, a Dun & Bradstreet (D-U-N-S) number is sufficient. Organizations that do not have such information will be required to produce other information, such as hard copies of articles of incorporation, partnership papers, a business license, or a notarized confirmation of a federal tax ID. Academic users and noncommercial entities need to contact VeriSign in order to determine what proof of identity is sufficient. The verification process may take a week or longer.

VeriSign also offers free trial server certificates for Netscape and Microsoft servers only. No verification process is needed, but they have a limited lifetime of two weeks and are recognized only by browsers that have a corresponding test certifying authority certificate installed. You will find a description of the test certificates at *http://digitalid.verisign.com/test_intro.html.*

Generating the Certificate Request

After submitting the certificate application, you must generate a public/private key pair and submit the public key to the CA. The key pair is generated by the server software and it takes the form of a *certificate request* that is e-mailed directly to the CA.

The certificate request is generated by your server software. UNIX servers based on SSLEay, such as Stronghold, use a shell script called *genkey*. *genkey*, which resides in the *ssl/bin* directory under the server root, should be invoked using the host name of your server as its argument. The name you give it should be identical to the common name used for the certificate application, for example:

```
lstein> cd /usr/local/etc/http/ssl/bin
lstein> ./genkey www.capricorn.org
```

genkey will now take the following actions:

1. It prompts you for the desired length of your site's public key. It's recommended that you use at least 1,024 bits. Higher values are more secure but slow the server's performance.

2. It prompts you to type random letters on the keyboard. The intervals between keystrokes are used to seed a random-number generator.
3. It prompts you for the name of the CA to submit the request to. You have the choice of several built-in CAs, or you can choose to send the request to the e-mail address of your choice (you might want to send the request to yourself so that you can examine it before forwarding it to the CA).
4. It prompts you for the organizational unit, state, country, and other fields of your site's distinguished name. These fields should be filled out exactly as they were for the certificate application.
5. It prompts you for a pass phrase, which will be used to store the private key in encrypted form on the server's hard disk. Choose a long, hard-to-guess password. Remember it! You'll need it every time you start the server.

In addition to sending the certificate request, *keygen* will store the encrypted private key in a file named *your_site_name.key*. This file is located beneath the server root in the *ssl/private* subdirectory.

Netscape servers use a similar command-line key generating function, except in this case the command to generate the public/private key pair is called *sec-key*. After the key pair is generated, you will use the Netscape administrative Web server's graphical user interface to generate the certificate request and install the signed certificate.

Microsoft Internet Information Server uses the graphical *Key Manager* program to generate certificate requests. When you first launch the program, you are presented with a hierarchical view of all the Web servers in your domain. To generate a new request, select the icon for the server you wish to generate a certificate for and choose *Key->Create New Key...* from the menu bar. You will be presented with the dialog box shown in Figure 11.1. At the top of the dialog are three fields that control the key's properties.

1. **Key Name** This is a nickname for the certificate that will be displayed in the hierarchical list of servers and certificates. Choose anything you like.
2. **Password** This key is used to encrypt the server's private key before it is stored to disk. This extra encryption step helps prevents the private key from being compromised. Pick a long, hard-to-guess password. Don't forget it!
3. **Bits** This is a pop-up menu that selects the length of the key. Choices are 512, 768, and 1,024 bits on domestic versions of the software, 512 bits on the crippled export version. You should choose the highest value available.

Below these fields is a section labeled "Distinguishing Information." This section contains the various fields for your server's distinguished name. You should give the same information you used for the certificate application.

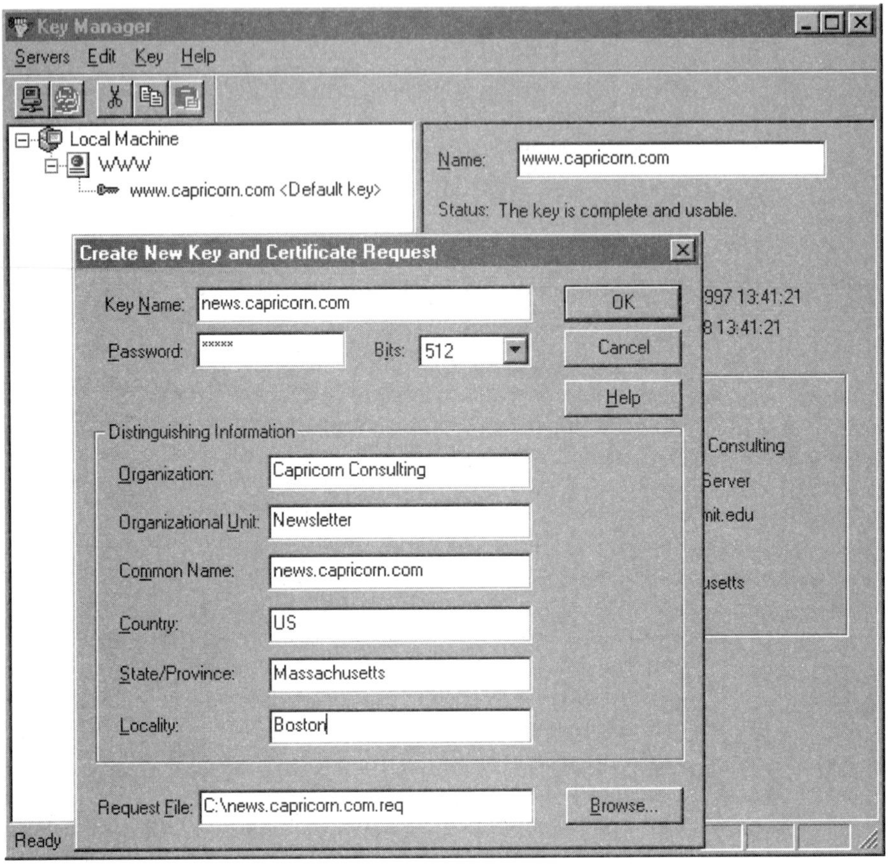

FIGURE 11.1 The IIS key manager program allows you to create new key pairs and install signed certificates.

The last field to fill in is at the bottom of the dialog box, labeled "Request File." When *Key Manager* is finished generating the key pair, it will leave the certificate in the file indicated by this field. You can accept the default of `C:\`*nickname*`.req`, or change it.

When you are satisfied, select "OK." The certificate request will be left in the file you indicated. You should send a copy of this request to the e-mail address indicated by your CA.

Installing a Signed Request

If all goes well, you'll eventually receive a signed certificate by e-mail. The certificate itself is a block of characters bracketed by the phrases *BEGIN CERTIFICATE* and *END CERTIFICATE*. To install this on your site, save the entire block of characters, including the BEGIN and END lines, to some convenient location on your hard disk, such as */tmp/certificate*. You now install it on the server.

For servers that use SSLEay, such as Stronghold, run the *getca* script with a command like

```
getca www.capricorn.org < /tmp/certificate
```

You will be prompted for the pass phrase that you used to generate the certificate request. If all goes well, the certificate will be validated and installed in a file named *your_site_name.cert*, located beneath the server root in the *ssl/certs* subdirectory. You can now delete the temporary certificate file if you like.

The next time you launch the server from the console, it will ask you to type in the pass phrase to unlock the private key. It will then start up as usual.

To install the new certificate in Microsoft Internet Information Server, open the *Key Manager* application once again. You'll see an icon for the submitted request with the notation "pending" next to it. Select this icon, then choose the menu command *Key->Install Certificate....* You'll be presented with a file browser. Select the certificate file and click "OK." You will now be prompted for the key's pass phrase. If all goes well, the certificate will now be installed into the system registry for use by IIS.

Unlike most encrypting servers, Microsoft IIS does not require you to unlock the certificate with a password in order to launch the server.

Certificates and Virtual Hosts

Many servers, Stronghold and Microsoft IIS included, support virtual hosts, multiple Web sites run from a single Web server program. Stronghold and other Apache derivatives allow multiple hosts to be assigned to a single IP address. Microsoft IIS requires a different IP address for each virtual site.

If you wish to use SSL for several virtual Web sites, you need to repeat the process of submitting a certificate application, generating a key pair, and installing the certificate for each one. Each certificate must have a different common name corresponding to the virtual site's home URL.

When you install the certificate, you must indicate which virtual host it corresponds to. In Microsoft IIS, you can do this with the *Key Manager* application. After installing the certificate on the Web server, double-click its icon to open its properties window. Select the radio button labeled "IP Address" and type in the IP address of the virtual host the certificate should be used with.

For Stronghold and other Apache-SSL servers, you must point the server to the correct private key and certificate files by entering *SSLCertificateFile* and *SSLCertificateKeyFile* directives in the appropriate *<VirtualHost>* section. See the next section for details.

Configuring SSL

In most cases, once the certificate file has been installed, you do not have to do anything special to use SSL. If your site is accessed using an *https:* URL, the server will use SSL; it will use unencrypted HTTP if accessed with an ordinary URL.

This default behavior may not be desirable. For example, you may want a directory containing confidential documents to be accessible via SSL only. Most Web servers can be configured to require that SSL be used to access a portion of the document tree. If you wish, you can put the entire document root under SSL protection, although there will be a performance penalty if you do so. Most sites choose to protect only their most sensitive documents, such as the fill-out forms that allow users to place electronic orders.

For Microsoft Internet Information Server, the SSL options are simple. To require an SSL connection for a particular Web subdirectory, open the *Internet Service Manager* application, select the Web server, and open its properties window. Select the Directories page and define a new or existing virtual directory. Open this directory's properties sheet and select the checkbox labeled "Require secure SSL channel." If you wish to use SSL to access the entire site, repeat this process for the document root home directory and all other defined virtual directories.

Other SSL options in IIS allow you to use client certificates for access control. This facility is described later in this chapter.

In contrast, Stronghold and other versions of ApacheSSL support a large (and sometimes bewildering) array of SSL-related directives that give you exquisite control over SSL's behavior (Table 11.1).

SSL Activation Directives

The three directives *SSLFlag, SSLProtocol,* and *RequireSSL* allow you to control SSL's basic operation. *SSLFlag* recognizes the parameters "on" and "off" (the default). If turned "on," the server will recognize incoming SSL connections. Otherwise, it will refuse them. This directive can be placed among the main configuration directives or within a *<VirtualHost>* section. A typical Stronghold configuration is to run SSL and non-SSL servers side by side with a configuration that looks (in part) like the following.

```
Port 80       # This is the standard HTTP port
Listen 443    # This is the standard SSL port
# virtual host at port 80
<VirtualHost www.capricorn.org:80>
SSLFlag off   # do not run SSL on this server
</VirtualHost>
# virtual host at port 443
<VirtualHost www.capricorn.org:443>
SSLFlag on    # run SSL on this server
</VirtualHost>
```

TABLE 11.1 Stronghold Configuration Directives

Directive	Example Parameters	Description
SSL ACTIVATION		
SSLFlag	`on`	Turn SSL "on" or "off" for entire host
SSLProtocol	`all`	Set which version(s) of SSL to accept
RequireSSL	`on`	Require SSL to be used in a directory
CIPHER SUITE		
SSLRequiredCiphers	`MEDIUM:HIGH`	List of allowable cipher methods
SSLRequireCipher	`HIGH`	Require named cipher to be used in this directory
SSLBanCipher	`LOW`	Don't allow named cipher to be used in this directory
SSL CONFIGURATION AND LOG FILES		
SSLRoot	`/usr/local/ssl`	Location of SSLeay files
SSLCertificateKeyFile	`private/www.capricorn.org.key`	Your private key
SSLCertificateFile	`certs/www.capricorn.org.cert`	Your server's certificate
SSLLogFile	`logs/ssl_log`	Log file for SSL messages
SSLErrorFile	`logs/ssl_error_log`	Log file for SSL errors
SSLCertificateLogFile	`logs/ssl_certs`	File for logging client certs
CLIENT AUTHENTICATION		
SSLVerifyClient	`0`	Require client certs (0=no, 1=optional, 2=required)
SSLCACertificatePath	`certs`	Location of server certificates
SSLCACertificateFile	`CA/rootcerts.pem`	Trusted CA certificate file
SSLVerifyDepth	`10`	Depth to which certificate chains are followed
SSL_Require	`"ou EQ 'Accounting'"`	Limit access by client cert attribute(s)
SSL_Group	`Accounting "ou EQ 'Accounting'"`	Define groups to use with *SSL_Require*

The *SSLProtocol* directive controls which versions of SSL the server will accept. Possible values are *SSLv2* for version 2, *SSLv3* for version 3, and *all* to accept both SSL versions. The server defaults to *all* if this directive is not specified. Certain combinations of encryption algorithms are not available in SSL version 2. This directive can be placed either among the main configuration directives or in a <*VirtualHost*> section.

RequireSSL can be used to force browsers to use SSL to access the contents of a particular Web directory. If they try to use unencrypted HTTP, they will be met with a "forbidden" message. Possible arguments to *RequireSSL* are "on" and "off." The directive can be placed in a per-directory access control file, *.htaccess*, or in a <*Directory*>, <*Files*>, or <*Location*> section.

Cipher Suite Directives

The confusingly named *SSLRequiredCiphers*, *SSLRequireCipher*, and *SSLBan Cipher* can be used to adjust which cipher suites browsers are allowed to use to access the server. You refer by name to any of the cipher suites indicated in Table 3.2 (see Chapter 3).

To simplify things somewhat, Stronghold supports cipher suite aliases that allow you to refer to suites by more meaningful names. Among the aliases are "LOW," "MEDIUM," and "HIGH." LOW is a catchall for symmetric encryption algorithms that use keys less than 128 bits in length (56-bit DES and the 40-bit crippled versions of RC2 and RC4). MEDIUM corresponds to 128-bit-key symmetric algorithms; HIGH denotes algorithms that use key lengths larger than 128 bits (currently only the 168-bit triple-DES algorithm). Notice that Stronghold's definitions of low, medium, and high don't correspond exactly to those in Table 3.2.

SSLRequiredCiphers is used to control which cipher suites will be accepted for the site as a whole. It belongs among the main configuration directives or within a *<VirtualHost>* section. Its argument is a colon-delimited list of the cipher suites or aliases that the server will accept. You can use this directive to set the overall SSL policy for the server. If this directive is not present, all SSL cipher suites will be accepted.

SSLRequireCipher (notice the absence of the *d* in *Require*) is used within a per-directory access control file or inside a *<Directory>*, *<Files>*, or *<Location>* section to specify that a particular cipher suite must be used to access the contents of the directory. You can specify several allowable cipher suites by repeating the directive. In this example, the */private* URL can be accessed only by SSL connections using high- or medium-grade keys.

```
<Location /private>
# SSL must be used here
RequireSSL on
# use high or medium strength encryption
SSLRequireCipher MEDIUM
SSLRequireCipher HIGH
</Location>
```

The opposite effect is provided by *SSLBanCipher*, which specifies a cipher suite or alias that is not allowed to be used in a particular part of the directory hierarchy. Using the alias "EXP" to indicate export-crippled cipher suites, we can forbid SSL connections from export version browsers.

```
<Location /private>
# SSL must be used here
RequireSSL on
# Forbid crippled export ciphers
SSLBanCipher EXP
</Location>
```

SSL Configuration and Log File Directives

The *SSLRoot* directive gives the location of the top of the SSL directory tree, where various SSL libraries, binaries, and configuration files are stored.

SSLCertificateKeyFile and *SSLCertificateFile* specify the location of the private key and certificate file for the main server or virtual host. Each virtual host that is to provide SSL services will need a pair of these directives. Two virtual hosts cannot share the same certificate. The private key is generally stored under the server root in the file *ssl/private/your_site_name.key*. The certificate can be found in *ssl/certs/your_site_name.cert*.

SSLLogFile, *SSLCertificateLogFile*, and *SSLErrorFile* point to files in which to save various SSL logging information. These logs are distinct from the ordinary access and error logs; the first two logs record information about the cipher suite used by incoming connections and the client certificates presented by the browsers. The error log records information that can be useful for debugging failed SSL connections.

Like other log files, they will need to be trimmed on a regular basis.

Client Authentication Directives

These directives are used to control access based on the browser's client certificate and are discussed in more detail in the second half of this chapter.

Key Management

It is essential that your server's private key remain confidential. Anyone gaining access to it will be able to eavesdrop on your server's SSL sessions. Possibly more serious, someone with access to the private key could impersonate your Web site, publishing fraudulent pages and fooling people into sending confidential information to it. A more prosaic problem is the risk of the private key being corrupted by a disk crash. If this happens, your Web site cannot run in SSL mode until a replacement certificate can be obtained from a certifying authority.

On UNIX systems, the private key should be stored on disk in encrypted form. This is the default for most servers. To further protect the key from compromise, the private key file and the directory containing it should be readable by the superuser only. Make sure to keep a backup copy of the private key on tape or floppy, and keep the backup in a secure place. The signed certificate should be backed up, as well, but there's no reason to go to any effort to protect the certificate from prying eyes. The certificate is a public document.

The Microsoft IIS *Key Manager* has an option for creating a backup copy of the key and its certificate. Select the key you wish to back up and choose *Key->Export Key->Backup File*. You will be prompted for the location of a file to save the key to. Save the key to a floppy disk, then store the disk in some safe location. You can restore it later using the *Key->Import Key* menu command.

While the server is executing, the unencrypted private key is stored somewhere in RAM. You should take precautions to prevent someone with local or network access to the machine from pulling the private key out of memory. On some UNIX systems, a special device file named */dev/mem* gives access to physical memory. It should be readable by the superuser only. Likewise, if your system uses files or disk partitions as swap devices, the swap device should be accessible only to the superuser. You should make sure that it is impossible for a user to spy on a running server with a debugger. Finally, you should make sure to limit the core dump size to zero prior to launching the server, using the shell's *limit* or *climit* commands. Otherwise, if the server core dumps, spontaneously or deliberately, it may be possible to recover the private key from the core file. This last caveat also applies to NT based systems: Make sure that *Dr. Watson* trace files are protected against prying eyes.

You may wish to change the private key's encryption password from time to time. To do this on systems based on the SSLEay library, use the *change_pass* command, which you will find in the *bin* directory of the ssl/ directory tree. The command takes the domain name of the Web site as its argument. It prompts you first for the old pass phrase, then for the new one (twice).

Certificates will expire after a period of time, usually a year. The server will warn you as the expiration date approaches. In order to renew a certificate, you must fill out a certificate renewal application at your certifying authority's Web site, pay a renewal fee, then run a program that generates a certificate renewal request. On ApacheSSL systems, the program is named *renewal* and behaves much like *keygen*. When the signed, renewed certificate arrives, you will install it with *getca* as before.

With Microsoft IIS, the *Key Manager* application has a *Key->Create Renewal Request* command. Select the key you need to renew and choose the command. It will generate a renewal request file that you should mail to the certifying authority.

The pass phrase presents an interesting challenge for Web server management, because if the server crashes for any reason, someone has to relaunch it in person in order to enter the pass phrase from the command line. Although Web server software is generally stable, power losses, brownouts, disk errors, and network outages do occur. If there is a transient system crash and the Web server host reboots automatically, the boot sequence will hang until someone types the pass phrase at the console. This may be unacceptable to a 7x24 operation.

One way to get around this is to store the private key in unencrypted form. For SSLEay servers, the *decrypt_key* command, called with the name of the Web site, will do this. If you do take this route, be extremely careful that the private key is stored in such a way that only the superuser can read it.

Another option is to write a script that will monitor the Web server and relaunch it if it goes down for some reason. When the script is first started, it prompts for the pass phrase and reads it into memory. It then uses this pass phrase as many times as needed to launch and relaunch the server. Listing 11.1 gives a Perl script that does this sort of thing. It demonstrates the most difficult part of the process, that of tricking the server (Stronghold in this case) into thinking that the pass phrase is being typed in interactively (in order to prevent the pass phrase from being echoed to the screen, the server reads the characters directly from the terminal device rather than from standard input). Every five seconds, the script checks that the server is still running by sending a signal to its process ID. If the server has crashed, the script relaunches it and sends an e-mail message to the Webmaster.

This script's main limitation is that it runs on the same machine as the server, which won't do much good if the machine itself crashes because of a disk error or power outage. A better script would run on a different machine and monitor the Web server from afar by attempting to connect to port 80 or 443 every so often. If the server went down, it would attempt to relaunch via a remote shell command. If, after a certain number of trials, this still didn't work, the script would launch a backup server on a different machine, or it would page the Webmaster.

Microsoft IIS encrypts the private key with the Windows NT system key, then obfuscates the system key by an unpublished method and stores it in the system registry (see Chapter 9). For this reason, IIS does not need operator intervention at boot time. Because it is likely that the obfuscation algorithm will some day be reverse engineered or leaked, you might wish to consider using the *SKEY.EXE* command to store the system key on a floppy disk or to encrypt it with a pass phrase. Although this will require manual intervention every time the server boots, it provides better assurance that the server's private key will not be compromised. See Chapter 9, The System Key, for more details.

LISTING 11.1 A Script to Relaunch an SSL Web Server Automatically

```
#!/usr/local/bin/perl
# restart.pl
# A functional example of how to automatically restart an SSL server
# that requires a pass phrase at launch time.  If the server
# crashes, this script will relaunch it and send the webmaster mail
# indicating when the problem happened.
# To run:
#   1) ./restart.pl
#   2) type your pass phrase when prompted
#   3) put it into the background if desired
#   4) send process signals to control it:
#      a) HUP:  reconfigure http daemon
#      b) TERM: kill http daemon AND script
```

continued

LISTING 11.1 *(continued)*

```
# Known problem: on some systems, HUP will not correctly
# reconfigure the http daemon.  You need to send http daemon
# a TERM signal and let restart.pl reinitialize it.  This
# script has not been extensively tested and may need tweaking
# to work on your system.
# Before calling this program, it is strongly suggested that
# you set the core dump size limit to zero so that someone
# cannot retrieve the pass phrase from a perl core dump.
# CHANGE THESE FOR YOUR INSTALLATION
# Check server every 5 seconds.  Doesn't hurt to make this
# more frequent.
$CHECK_TIME = 5;
# location of the server and ssl roots
$SERVER_ROOT = '/usr/local/etc/https';
$SSLTOP = '/usr/local/etc/https/ssl';
# location of stty program (for turning off terminal echo)
$STTY = '/bin/stty';
# Location of the server executable and its arguments.
$STRONGHOLD = "./httpsd";
@ARGS =  ('-d' => $SERVER_ROOT,
          '-f' => 'conf/httpd.conf');
# Location of the PID file
$PID_FILE = "$SERVER_ROOT/logs/httpd.pid";
# Location of sendmail
$SENDMAIL = '/usr/lib/sendmail';
# E-mail address of person to send restart notification to.
$NOTIFY = 'webmaster';
# Set this to 1 if you want verbose debugging messages
$DEBUG = 0;
# Set this to 1 if you want restart.pl to go into the
# background automatically
$BACKGROUND = 0;
#-------------------------------------
$ENV{IFS} = '';
$ENV{PATH}='/bin/:/usr/bin:/sbin:/usr/sbin';
# NO USER SERVICEABLE PARTS BELOW
require "chat2.pl";
$SIG{HUP} = $SIG{TERM} = $SIG{INT} = 'send_signal';
$ENV{SSLTOP} = $SSLTOP unless $ENV{SSLTOP};
chdir $SERVER_ROOT;
# Prompt for user password
system "$STTY cbreak -echo >/dev/tty" and die "$STTY: $!";      # turn off echo
print "Enter pass phrase:";
chomp ($PASSWD = <STDIN>);
print "\n";
system "$STTY -cbreak echo >/dev/tty";  # turn on echo
die "No pass phrase.  Aborted" unless $PASSWD;
# Enter the background if requested
if ($BACKGROUND) {
    exit 0 if fork();             # parent dies
    exit 0 if fork();             # child dies
    # We're running in background now
}
```

```
$PID = launch_server();
while (1) {
    sleep $CHECK_TIME;
    warn "Checking server" if $DEBUG;
    if ( !server_running() ) {
        $PID = launch_server();
        message("Server died.  Relaunched successfully.") if $PID;
        message("Server died.  UNABLE TO RELAUNCH.") unless $PID;
    }
}
sub server_running {
    return undef unless $PID;
    # by sending a kill(0) to a process, we can find out
    # if it still exists without actually sending it a
    # signal.
    my $result = kill(0,$PID);
    warn "Got $result from kill(0,$PID)" if $DEBUG;
    return $result;
}
sub launch_server {
    my ($handle,$result,$gotit,$pid);
    warn "Launching server with $STRONGHOLD @ARGS\n";
    $handle = chat::open_proc($STRONGHOLD,@ARGS);
    while ($result = chat::expect($handle,2,
                                'pass phrase:'=>1,
                                '(.+)\n'=>'$1')) {
        if ($result == 1) {
            warn "printing pass phrase" if $DEBUG;
            &chat::print($handle,"$PASSWD\n");
            $gotit++;
        } else {
            print "=> ",$result,"\n";
        }
    }
    &chat::close($handle);
    wait or warn "No child processes";
    return undef unless $gotit;
    # Return the httpd pid as the result
    sleep 5;
    open (PID,$PID_FILE) or die "Couldn't open PID file";
    chomp($pid = <PID>);
    close PID;
    warn "Launched https with pid $pid\n";
    return $pid;
}
sub message {
    my $message = shift;
    my $time = localtime;
    print "$time: $message\n";
    open (MAIL,"| $SENDMAIL -t -oi") or die "sendmail: $!";
    print MAIL <<END;
To: $NOTIFY
From: $NOTIFY
Subject: Web server restarted
```

continued

LISTING 11.1 *(continued)*

```
$time: $message
END
    ;
    close MAIL;
}
sub send_signal {
    my $sig = shift;
    $sig = 'TERM' if $sig eq 'INT';
    # Forward the signal to the daemon
    if ($PID) {
        warn "Sending a sig$sig to $PID" if $DEBUG;
        kill $sig,$PID;
    }
    return if $sig eq 'HUP';
    die "Received a sig$sig\n";
}
```

Using Client Certificates for Access Control

Although passwords are a simple and effective way to identify Web users, their security is limited by the combined problems of picking good passwords, password sniffing, and the ease with which people share them. In addition, passwords have scaleability problems. A password system that works well with one Web server and a few hundred users becomes unmanageable across an enterprise of dozens of servers and thousands of users.

For this reason, SSL-enabled servers can authenticate browsers based on client certificates. By using cryptographically secure digital signatures, this technique promises the ability to design intranet and Internet systems that overcome the vagaries of traditional password-based systems. Client-certificate-based systems scale to tens of thousands of users, and allow for systems in which the responsibility for verifying and authorizing users can be spread among multiple departments within an organization rather than maintained centrally.

It all sounds wonderful, but there are some caveats, as you shall see.

Who Issues Client Certificates?

As described in Chapter 2, client certificates, also known as personal certificates, are issued to end users by certifying authorities. The certifying authority may be a public authority whose primary business is certificate issuance, or it may be a private authority run by an organization for the purpose of certifying its employees.

Only a handful of public certifying authorities currently issue client certificates, chief of which is VeriSign, with its personal ID program. We walked through the process of obtaining and installing a personal Verisign ID in Chapter 4. Although the client certificates that VeriSign offers the general public may be useful for subscription-based Internet services and for e-mail, they don't work in corporate intranet environments, where the goal is to use them like name badges to identify current employees. One option is to contract with a public certifying authority to issue client certificates in the company's name, following some procedure to grant the certificate when the employee is hired and revoke it when the employee leaves. Another option is for the company to become its own certifying authority. It can then generate and issue certificates without outside help.

What Are Client Certificates Good For?

In addition to containing its owner's public key, a client certificate contains its owner's name, the name of the certifying authority that signed it, a serial number, and "attributes." Attributes are arbitrary fields that contain various types of textual and numeric information, such as

- E-mail address
- Surface mail address
- Employer
- Title
- Department
- Office number
- Telephone number
- Birth date
- Gender
- Security clearance
- Nationality

Attributes give Webmasters considerable flexibility in designing access restrictions based on client certificates. They can choose to grant access to particular individuals, to anyone carrying a certificate signed by a certain certifying authority, to French nationals, to people who are at least 18 years of age, to members of the sales department, or to people at the director level or higher. Because the information is embedded in the certificate, it's possible to run sophisticated access control systems without having a large centralized database somewhere to keep track of all the information.

Because of the way certification works, organizations that have chosen to create their own certifying authorities can create additional CAs to form a hierarchy of trust. A company can set up a root certifying authority that is trusted by all its departments. This root certifying authority then issues certificates to each of its departments, delegating to them the responsibility for issuing client certificates to their members. The Web server that holds the employee manual and corporate telephone directory can now be configured to accept requests from anyone who holds a certificate signed by any of the departments, and the accounting server can be configured to accept only certificates issued by its own department.

How Reliable Are Client Certificates?

The reliability of a client certificate is limited by several factors.

1. **The strength of the cryptographic algorithm and private key.** The basis of client certificate authentication is that only the holder of the certificate knows the private key that corresponds to the public key contained within the certificate. A message signed with the private key can be checked against the certificate's public key in order to validate the user. If the algorithm used to create this digital signature is weak or if the private key is not sufficiently long to prevent a brute-force guessing attack, the digital signature can be forged. In practice, this is rarely a problem because the considerations below are much greater risks.
2. **The certifying authority's certification procedures.** A client certificate is only as good as the procedures that the certifying authority used to validate the requesting user's identity. For example, VeriSign issues Class 1 IDs to anyone who requests one. Because no identity check is performed, these IDs aren't useful for real authentication. In contrast, VeriSign only issues Class 3 IDs after a thorough check of the requester's credentials. This provides much better assurance that the bearer of a certificate is who the certificate claims she is.
3. **The security of the user's private key.** By design, client certificates themselves are easy to steal. They are offered to any SSL-enabled server that requests them. The security of the system depends on the safety of the user's private key, which is usually stored in encrypted form on the user's personal computer and unlocked by a password whenever the Web browser needs to use it. If a thief can circumvent this system and steal the key, the thief can impersonate the user.
4. **The security of the certifying authority's private key.** If a certifying authority's private key is stolen, the consequences are dire. The thief can forge any certificate in the certifying authority's name, allowing him to impersonate anyone he wants.

What Are the Limitations of Client Certificates?

Client certificates are not a panacea. They have problems, and some of the problems are significant.

Certificates Are Easy to Issue, Hard to Revoke

A certificate may need to be revoked after it is issued. The owner's private key may have been compromised, she may have forgotten the password used to unlock the key, personal information on the certificate may need to be updated, the user's electronic copy of her private key may have been corrupted by a software crash. If an organization grants its employees access to intranet Web servers by issuing them certificates, it will need to revoke an employee's certificate when she leaves the organization.

Unfortunately, it is not nearly so simple to revoke a certificate as it is to issue one. To handle revocations, certifying authorities maintain certificate revocation lists (CRLs), which are lists of the serial numbers of invalid certificates. Just putting revoked certificates on a CRL, however, does little good. In order for a CRL to be effective, a server that uses client certificates for authentication must check the CRL each time a request comes in to ascertain that the certificate is still good. For intranet applications, this means that the organization must maintain a centralized database that each Web server checks every time there's an access, effectively annulling much of the simplicity and scaleability of client-certificate-based access controls. For Internet applications, there is as yet no standard mechanism for checking a third-party certifying authority's CRL.

Netscape has proposed that "certificate revocation" and "CA revocation" URLs be incorporated into each certificate. By fetching these URLs, a Web server would be able to determine whether the client or CA's certificates have been revoked. Aside from performance issues with this scheme, it's not clear whether the server would be immune to DNS spoofing attacks. For its part, VeriSign had announced a revocation list management framework to be incorporated into its products during 1997.

In the absence of working CRLs, the only way to revoke a client certificate is to let it expire naturally. Because this may be as long as a year, the delay will be unacceptable for many applications. Certificate revocations are the public key infrastructure's Achilles' heel.

Client Certificates May Be a User Support Nightmare

Anyone who has worked at the computer help desk of a large organization knows that a large fraction of support time is devoted to helping users who have forgotten their login passwords, have locked themselves out of their account, or are otherwise unable to log in. If there are so many problems with the simple password-based systems that people have used for decades, what happens when users are asked to juggle client certificates? Failure modes for client certificates include the following.

- The user forgets the pass phrase she uses for decrypting her private key.
- The user's computer crashes, corrupting her certificate or private key.

- The user updates her Web browser software, wiping out her previous certicates.
- The user accidentally deletes a certificate.
- The user can't figure out which of several personal certificates to use to access your service.
- The user's laptop is stolen and her private key is compromised.
- The user shares her private key and certificate without realizing the implications.

In most of these cases, the only solution is to revoke the old certificate and start the whole process over again with a new certificate request.

Using Client Certificates for Web Server Access Control

When a browser contacts an SSL v3.0 server that has been configured to request client certificates, the browser is required to produce its certificate and prove that it is the rightful owner. The server scrutinizes the certificate for validity, in the manner described in Chapter 3, and either approves it or rejects it.

Provided that the authentication phase is successful, the server is now ready to move on to the authorization phase and determine whether this client should be granted access to the requested resource. This is the interesting part, because it is the point at which Web servers diverge. There are two different philosophies on the market.

1. Base access control solely on the information contained within certificate attributes.
2. Use the certificate for identity checking only, and base access control on external information contained within an enterprise database.

Both philosophies have their advantages and disadvantages. The first is simple to set up, has good performance, and is easily scaleable. It works well across organizational boundaries and allows you to mix and match certificates signed by different CAs. However, it provides no way to check for revoked certificates unless you add a centralized database to the mix, eliminating many of its advantages.

Another problem with the first scheme is that it confuses users' identities with their privileges. If an employee is transferred from accounting to sales, the certificate that grants her access to accounting's Web server no longer reflects her new role.

In the second philosophy, the certificate is used only to establish the user's identity. The combination of the certificate's "Common Name" field (CN, see page 298) and the CA's common name is, in theory, unique across the Internet (certificates also have a unique serial number field that you can use for this purpose). This combination is used as a key into a database in which the user's access rights are stored. This provides a clean way to distinguish between users' identities and their privileges and throws in certificate revocation lists, to boot. However, set up and administration of a database that is shared across a large organization can be problematic.

At press time, the following servers were offering client certificate-based authentication.

- **C2Net Stronghold (UNIX, NT)** This Apache derivative, available in UNIX and NT implementations, uses the first philosophy to base access control on any arbitrary combination of certificate attributes. Hooks for authorization via external databases are provided for developers. There is no direct support for CRLs.
- **XCert Sentry (UNIX)** This is another Apache derivative that comes bundled with XCert's certificate server and database. Access control models following either the first or the second philosophies are available. CRLs are fully supported.
- **Microsoft Internet Information Server (NT)** IIS 3.0 accepts client certificates and can be configured to require that users present valid certificates in order to gain entry to a directory. However, there is no simple facility to make access control decisions based on the contents of the certificate. To do this, you need to create customized access control rules using Microsoft's ISAPI library or wait for Microsoft to release modules of its own.
- **Netscape Enterprise Server (UNIX, NT)** Netscape's Enterprise Server 2.0 uses client certificates in combination with the Netscape Directory Server database to provide access control support along the lines of the second philosophy. The system is integrated with Netscape's Certificate Server product.
- **OpenMarket WebServers (UNIX, NT)** Various OpenMarket Web servers provide client-certificate-based authentication and access control. Access control uses the second philosophy in conjunction with a relational database.

Certificate-Based Access Controls in Stronghold

To give you an idea of what you can do with client certificates, let's use the Stronghold server as a concrete example. Unlike other commercial offerings that rely on an external database to determine when to allow a certificate bearer to access a protected document, Stronghold allows you to base access control decisions on attributes contained within the certificate itself.

Figure 11.2 shows the text representation of a client certificate. The certificate has two parts, the "Subject" section, which gives information about the person the certificate was issued to, and the "Certificate" section, which gives information about the certifying authority. Both sections contain a series of attributes, each identified with a one- or two-letter abbreviation. Some attributes are standardized; others can be added if needed.

CN	User's name (CN = Common Name)
EMail	User's e-mail address
O	User's organization (i.e., employer)
OU	User's organization unit (i.e., department or division)
L	User's locality, usually a city or town
SP	User's state or province
C	User's country code

Stronghold uses about a dozen new directives to handle certificate-based access control. The four most important of which are:

1. **SSLVerifyClient *0* | *1* | 2** This directive, which can appear in the server's global configuration file or in a *<VirtualHost>* section, controls

```
Subject:
      C=US
      ST=Massachusetts
      L=Boston
      O=Capricorn Organization
      OU=Sales
      CN=Wanda
      Email=wanda@prego.wi.mit.edu
Certificate:
     Data:
        Version: 1 (0x0)
        Serial Number: 866229881 (0x33a19e79)
        Signature Algorithm: md5WithRSAEncryption
     Issuer:
        C=US
        ST=MA
        L=Boston
        O=Capricorn Consulting
        OU=Security Services
        CN=Capricorn Signing Services Root CA
        Email=lstein@prego.wi.mit.edu
     Validity:
            Not Before: Jun 13 19:24:41 1997 GMT
            Not After : Jul 13 19:24:41 1997 GMT
```

FIGURE 11.2 Text form of a client certificate.

whether Stronghold will request a client certificate when a browser connects. Its value can be

- 0—Don't request certificate
- 1—Certificate is optional
- 2—Certificate is required

If either 1 or 2 is specified, Stronghold verifies that the certificate is valid.

2. **RequireSSL *on | off*** This directive controls whether Stronghold will require an SSL connection in order to allow access to a directory. Its values can be either

   - On—Require SSL
   - Off—SSL is optional

   The directive can be placed within a *<Location>*, *<Files>*, or *<Directory>* section or used inside a per-directory access control file.

3. **SSL_Require *any | none | groupname | rules...*** This directive provides general-purpose pattern matching and comparison operations on the attributes within a client certificate. Legal values include *any*, to allow clients bearing any valid certificate access; *none*, to forbid any clients access; a named group created with *SSL_Group;* or a set of certificate attribute matching rules. These rules are discussed below. This directive can be placed within a *<Location>*, *<Files>*, or *<Directory>* section or used inside a per-directory access control file.

4. **SSL_Group *group_name rules...*** This directive is a macro facility that allows you to define commonly used attribute matching rules to be used later in *SSL_Require* directives.

Most of the certificate filtering functions are found in the attribute matching rules used by *SSL_Require* and *SSL_Group*. This directive uses a rich syntax that is too complex to explain in depth here, but a few examples will give you a feel for its style.

1. Accept certificates issued to people with addresses in the United States.

```
SSL_Require 'C EQ US'
```

2. Accept certificates from people with academic or governmental e-mail addresses.

```
SSL_Require  'EM MATCH ".edu" OR EM MATCH ".gov"'
```

3. Accept certificates whose private key length is greater than 512 bits (that is, not export crippled).

```
SSL_Require "size GT 512"
```

4. Accept certificates issued to members of the accounting department.

```
SSL_Require 'OU EQ "Accounting Department"'
```

5. Accept certificates issued by the accounting department.

```
SSL_Require 'IOU EQ "Accounting Department"'
```

6. Accept certificates issued by VeriSign.

```
SSL_Require 'IO EQ "VeriSign, Inc."'
```

The last two examples demonstrate an interesting feature of the *SSL_Require* syntax. By prefixing the certificate attribute abbreviation with an *I*, you refer to the corresponding attribute in the issuing certifying authority's certificate rather than to a field in the client's certificate.

The following code is a complete example in which access to the URL */private/accounting* is restricted to members of the accounting department who have been certified by a private CA known as *Capricorn CA*. It can be placed within the *access.conf* configuration file, or a per-directory access control file.

```
# Certificates are optional by default
SSLVerifyClient 1
<Location /private/accounting>
RequireSSL on     # insist that a secure connection be used here.
<Limit GET POST PUT>
# Limit access to the capricorn domain, for
# extra safety.
order deny,allow
deny from all
allow from .capricorn.org
# Limit access to people who bear client certificates
# from the Accounting department
SSL_Require 'OU EQ "Accounting Department" AND IO EQ "Capricorn CA"'
</Limit>
</Location>
```

Certificate-based access restrictions can be combined with other types of access control, such as IP and host-name-based control, as shown in the example, or even conventional passwords. In addition to filtering by client certificate, Stronghold can be configured to save information about incoming clients' certificates to a log file, allowing you to track who is accessing your site.

For those who would like to restrict access to bearers of either VeriSign Class 1 or Class 2 client certificates, the field to examine is "Organizational Unit" (OU). Look for one of these lines.

```
VeriSign Class 1 CA - Individual Subscriber
VeriSign Class 2 CA - Individual Subscriber
```

The complete list of attributes found in various types of VeriSign certificate can be found at *http://digitalid.verisign.com/verisign-certs-tech.html.*

Becoming Your Own Certifying Authority

If you are running an intranet, particularly an extended one that spans several locations, you may wish to consider setting up a private certifying authority. This will allow you to issue your own certificates—the Web server type, as well as the client type—and to delegate certificate signing authority to departments and other organizational subdivisions.

There are some significant advantages to this approach, as well as some problems. The main advantage is complete control over your organization's certificate issuance policy. Certificates are issued only when individuals satisfy the requirements set down in the policy, and they are revoked when circumstances change. You are free to set the period of time during which certificates remain valid, specify their attributes, and design the way in which access privileges and certificates are linked.

One problem with running a private CA is the need for strong security measures surrounding the machine that generates and issues certificates (the "certificate server"). Because of the pivotal role of this machine, various authorities recommend that it be physically secured, protected from unauthorized network access by a dedicated firewall system, and even placed within a Faraday cage to prevent its radio frequency emissions from being intercepted by eavesdroppers equipped with electronic surveillance equipment. While some of these recommendations might seem like overkill, they reflect the difference between a certificate server and an ordinary Web server. If someone cracks a Web server password, they have gained access to a subset of the documents on the server. In contrast, if the certificate server's private key is compromised, the intruder gains the ability to forge any certificate he wishes and gain free access to all your organization's servers.

Administration is another problem. A certificate-granting service that is fully functional is complex. At a minimum, it consists of two Web servers and a network-accessible database. Each must be properly configured, monitored, backed up, and otherwise maintained. In the real world, the certificate system often needs to interface with other systems in the organizations, such as payroll and personnel. This may require the development of custom software and adds to the administrative complexity.

Last, the certificates signed by your private CA are worthless outside your organization. Unless the certificate that your CA uses for signing is itself signed by a well-known commercial CA, the certificates you create are of no use for accessing other servers on the Internet.

As an alternative to rolling your own Web certifying authority, you should consider contracting with a commercial CA to provide client certificates for your organization. A number of CAs will provide you with "branded" certificates for use by your employees and/or clients.

1. United States and Canada
   - VeriSign
   - GTE CyberTrust
   - Keywitness
   - IBM (announced)
2. South Africa
   - Thawte Consulting
   - BiNARY SuRGEONS
   - CompuSource
3. Europe
   - COST Computer Security Technologies
   - EuroSign (announced)
4. Other
   - SoftForum (Korea)

The Structure of a Certifying Authority

A certifying authority usually consists of the three parts shown in Figure 11.3. Physically, these parts may reside on separate machines or be bundled together on a single server.

1. **Enrollment Server** This is the Web server that handles new requests for client certificates. People who want a certificate connect to this server and fill out an online form. The form contains special HTML tags (see Certificate Servers: Behind the Scenes in this chapter) that cause the Web browser to generate a new public/private key pair and include the public key in the certificate request. The enrollment server must be running the

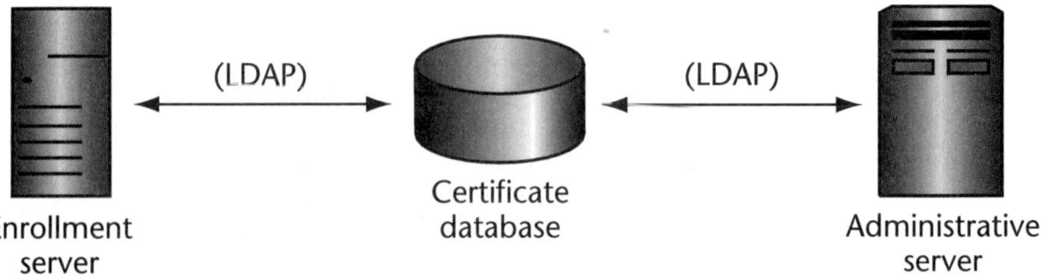

FIGURE 11.3 A typical certificate system uses two servers to control enrollment and authorization, and a database to track issued certificates.

SSL protocol but does not need strong access control because the actual signing of the request is done elsewhere. The enrollment server is also used to process renewal requests.

2. **Administrative Server** When the enrollment server processes a certificate request, it typically places the request onto a queue. Authorized administrators periodically check the queue for pending requests. When a request is approved and the certificate signed, the user is e-mailed (or physically given) a URL at which she can pick up the signed certificate. The administrative server is responsible for queue review and certificate signing. It also handles other administrative functions, such as certificate revocation and renewal. Because this is where certificate signing occurs, the administrative server is under strong access control. Typically, only users bearing administrator certificates are allowed to connect.
3. **Database** This is a network-accessible database that keeps track of certificates. It maintains the public certificate of the certifying authority, as well as all server and client certificates the CA has issued. It's also responsible for maintaining certificate revocation lists and managing the queue of pending requests. There is an industry trend to use databases supporting the Lightweight Directory Access Protocol (LDAP) for this purpose. LDAP was designed to provide a "white pages" style directory of people's names, e-mail addresses, and other information. Since then, it has been extended to support encryption via the SSL protocol. However, a conventional relational database will work just as well for this task.

Your organization will be responsible for maintaining several certificates, each part of a hierarchy of trust (Figure 11.4). At the top of the pyramid is the root CA, the certifying authority that owns the certificate that is used to sign all the others. The root CA's certificate will need to be installed on all your organization's servers, browsers, and other software that uses certificates.

Underneath the root certificate are a variety of certificates that have been signed by the root CA. There are the server certificates used for running Web servers securely, and client certificates. In addition, there may be second- and third-tier CA certificates, certifying authorities that have been certified by the root CA. These subsidiary CAs can issue their own server and client certificates. Any software that trusts the root CA will trust certificates issued by the subsidiary CAs. The ability to create subsidiary CAs allows your organization the flexibility to delegate certificate administration tasks to departments and other subdivisions.

Because compromise of the root CA's private key will cause the entire enterprise to come crashing down, some organizations keep the root CA on a machine that is physically secured and completely disconnected from the network. The root certificate is used only occasionally to sign and renew subsidiary CAs' certificates. The subsidiary CAs are responsible for the daily tasks of certifying client and server certificates.

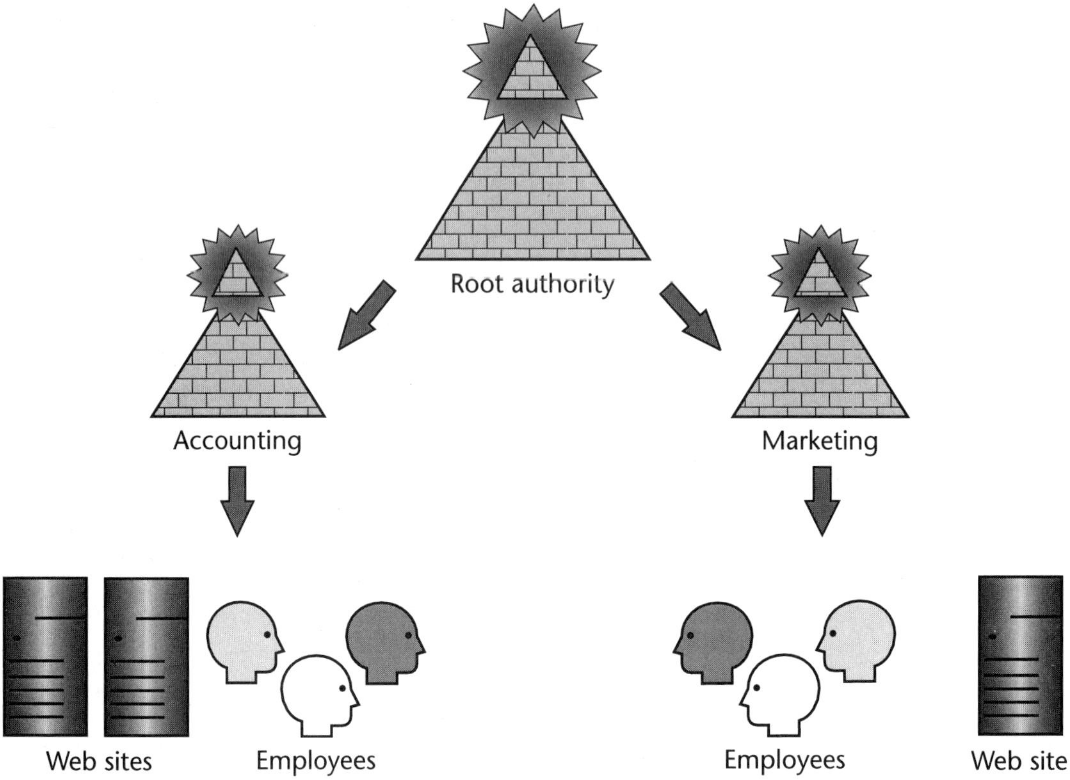

FIGURE 11.4 In-house certificate servers allow organizations to create a certificate-signing hierarchy for departments, Web sites, and individuals.

Certificate Authorities—Behind the Scenes

Generating a client certificate for a Web browser is more complicated than generating the certificate and e-mailing it to the user. The reason is the key-pair-generation step. Before the certificate can be generated, the browser must create a valid public/private key pair. The public half of the pair is sent to the server, along with other identifying information in the form of a certificate request. When the certificate request is approved, the public key is signed with the certifying authority's private key and the signed certificate is returned to the browser in a recognized format.

RSA Data Security has created a number of de facto public key cryptography standards, including the format of certificate requests, *PKCS10;* and the format in which signed certificates are returned to the requestor, *PKCS7*. However, the standards themselves are not sufficient for a Web-based certificate enrollment system because the browser needs additional information in order to create the fill-out form and other aspects of the user interface.

Certificate Authorities—Behind the Scenes *(continued)*

Netscape and Microsoft, not surprisingly, have addressed these problems in completely different ways.

With Netscape browsers, the certificate request process is initiated when the browser sees a fill-out form containing the nonstandard HTML tag

```
<KEYGEN NAME="SPKAC" CHALLENGE="challenge phrase">
```

The challenge phrase is used by certifying authorities to verify a user's request for a certificate revocation. It is generally chosen by the user before the page containing the *<KEYGEN>* tag is generated and sent to the browser.

To work properly, the fill-out form must also contain fields for the client's name, e-mail address, and other certificate attributes. After generating the public key, Netscape will submit it, along with certificate attribute information, to the CGI script pointed to by the form's ACTION parameter. The CGI script is then responsible for turning this information into a valid PKCS10 request. The request is in a binary format that has been encoded with the MIME base64 system to allow it to be transmitted via e-mail. This format, known as *PEM*, will look like this (some lines in the middle have been removed to make it shorter).


```
——-BEGIN CERTIFICATE REQUEST——-
MIIB1zCCAUACAQAwgZYxCzAJBgNVBAYTAlVTMQswCQYDVQQIEwJNQTElMCMGA1UE
BxYcNDQgQm95bnRvbiBTdHJlZXQgIzMsIEJvc3RvbjEdMBsGA1UEChMUQ2Fwcmlj
b3JuIENvbnN1bHRpbmcxGjAYBgNVBAsTEVNlY3VyaXR5IFNlcnZpY2VzMRgwFgYD
+j0m/5zwpkENLdzZs/NcV9JpvnLTtZT9SBUNC2s730CO8TAwrjZK0582AD1mOh/c
VQ/+o5rGZtiwlwy5KpoKbeqcF7efSJ+Dq2jVKAtY9QyvAgMBAAGgADANBgkqhkiG
9w0BAQQFAAOBgQAUQdlTMP+kkuIWOSqSn1vX4jAME7Lxu+ylADXGO9dGfV5V6OrF
AAiFPRQ/1PiP3LRQhdf1A3MSQLi/RkM0aP3Xs34d3c6fqU86qahd8bHEuJPM9f/B
M/OsjXam4Ehtr4JT9V8Bx1x3h0aLYudmA39fMa2XWEJoTLEx4V7/ezOhTQ==
——-END CERTIFICATE REQUEST——-
```


Microsoft Internet Explorer, in contrast, generates PKCS10 requests directly using an ActiveX control named certHelper. IE initiates a certificate request when it sees a tag like the following in an HTML page.

```
<OBJECT
    CLASSID="clsid:33BEC9E0-F78F-11cf-B782-00C04FD7BF43"
    CODEBASE="/controls/certenr3.dll"
    ID="certHelper">
</OBJECT>
```

The attributes in the *<OBJECT>* tag include the serial number of the certHelper control itself, the name of the control, and the URL where it can be found. The page also needs to contain a fill-out form containing whatever fields are appropriate for the certificate, plus a short Visual Basic script to invoke the control's *GenerateKeyPair* function. The certHelper control and a complete example that shows how to use it can be found in a self-unpacking file downloadable from *http://www.microsoft.com/intdev/security/csa/certenr3.exe).*

Certificate Authorities—Behind the Scenes *(continued)*

On the certificate-server side, the software that signs certificate requests generates an X.509 certificate. Again, this is a binary format encoded with base64. It looks like this (some lines in the middle have been removed to make it shorter).


```
—-BEGIN CERTIFICATE—-
MIIC2DCCAkECAQUwDQYJKoZIhvcNAQEEBQAwgdExCzAJBgNVBAYTAlVTMQswCQYD
VQQIEwJNQTElMCMGA1UEBxYcNDQgQm95bnRvbiBTdHJlZXQgIzMsIEJvc3RvbjEd
LQO7Kt0ZnMgHfS/WkoKyf+d3aMDkJHk8sYAgqW4lsyOsGgK6/wERSj/kCK2h0jsx
gfc2P71bt+tA9qtPoTWaHqX5oFBZLgHPCKmJlx0rVCJZjdlG8OnYE+14pZr/PWEU
BfuZlwIDAQABMA0GCSqGSIb3DQEBBAUAA4GBAGIxPwTVpNoqqHvPhmKm2oc9GS9+
vGDg0qlkpZheiB1xdJ7QzG1q0KiEUYlrJmc8utI1sGF82uhtgJT8S7Tli4+tee8M
Gqst2z4TSKXLsHrVkVwF6+vcMOlxJWtkKIpbfW4eJ7UO6z2oKBZR841UtG2BhgOw
gMsUiykymFB6p9X4
—-END CERTIFICATE—-
```


For a browser to install this certificate automatically, the signed certificate need only be made available on a Web site. The Web server should be configured so that the certificate file's MIME type is *application/x-x509-user-cert.* When the browser downloads the certificate, it will check that it matches a previous certificate request. If it does, the certificate will be installed and activated.

If you will be certifying your organization's Web sites, you need to arrange for your CA's self-signed root certificate to be installed on all Web browsers that will contact these sites. The easiest way to do this is again through the Web. Like user certificates, browsers will automatically install new CA certificates when they download a document of type *application/x-x509-ca-cert.*

You need only make the root certificate available on a Web site, give it this MIME type, and instruct users to select the certificate's link. The browser will present a series of dialog boxes that guide the user through the process of installing a new trusted CA.

The main complication of this is that while Netscape Navigator will accept CA certificates in several formats, including the standard PEM format shown above, Microsoft Internet Explorer recognizes certificates only in a binary format known as DER. To support IE browsers, you need to transform your PEM-encoded CA certificate into DER format, using whatever tools your CA software provides. In packages based on the SSLEay library, the *x509* command-line tool does the trick.

```
x509 -in ./ca_certificate.pem -outform DER -out ./ca_certificate.der
```

See the resources at the end of this chapter for documentation on the Netscape *<KEYGEN>* tag and the Microsoft certHelper control.

Private Certifying Authority Products

A handful of vendors currently provide software to enable you to establish a private CA. The number will have grown by the time you read this.

- **Netscape Certificate Server** Netscape sells a certificate server that integrates with its SuiteSpot package of Web server, LDAP directory server, and Web clients. The package is available for NT and UNIX systems and is relatively affordable.
- **Microsoft Certificate Server** Microsoft has announced a certificate server that works hand-in-hand with Internet Information Server version 5.0.
- **XCert Sentry** Sentry is a derivative of the popular Apache Web server, modified to enable it to handle certificate enrollment requests and to issue signed certificates. It is currently available only for UNIX systems, but an NT version is reportedly in development. It comes bundled with the Xudad LDAP server. A simple developer's API gives the system substantial customizability.
- **GTE CyberTrust** GTE, which also provides third-party branded certificates on a contractual basis, sells a high-end CA package. In addition to Web browser X.509v3 certificates, CyberTrust can produce certificates used by the Secure Electronic Transaction (SET protocol; see Chapter 3), making the system suitable for use by banks and other financial institutions. Another feature allows the CA's private key to be stored in a hardware device, substantially reducing the risk of compromise.
- **Entrust Technologies WebCA** This software product, currently available for Windows NT systems, consists of a certificate server, an LDAP database, and CGI scripts and form templates to add to an existing Netscape or IIS Web server. It integrates with Entrust's other security products for secure remote login, e-mail, and file encryption.
- **Frontier Technologies eLock** eLock is a family of products that includes a secure Web server, a certificate server, and software for securing e-mail and files. eLock also supports a variety of hardware key tokens.
- **SSLEay** For the inveterate do-it-yourselfer only, the freeware SSLEay package provides basic support for setting up a certifying authority. However, extensive custom programming is required in order to make the system usable and secure in a production environment. The URLs given in Software Resources provide some guidelines for writing the scripts necessary to make SSLEay work with certificate requests generated by Netscape Navigator and Internet Explorer. Note that U.S. patent restrictions may make it illegal to use this package within the United States without first obtaining a license from Public Key Partners.

Final Words

Because of their technological sophistication, encryption and certificate-based authentication run the risk of providing Webmasters with a false sense of security. In fact, these technologies are only as effective as the weakest link in the system. Even the strongest cryptography won't keep confidential documents secret without the end user's cooperation. A user may send a confidential document to a public printer, e-mail it to herself over an unsecure network, make a copy and store it in an unsafe location, share her private key with a friend, or inadvertently disclose the information in some other way.

On the server side, if confidential documents are stored on a Web site that isn't physically and electronically secure, all bets are off. The secrets will be compromised as soon as someone manages to break into the system. CGI scripts that ignore the site's access restriction policies are also common problems. The next chapter deals with this pitfall, along with other aspects of safe CGI scripting.

Checklist

Encryption

1. How does your server prevent confidential information from being intercepted by packet sniffers?

   ☑ It doesn't. There is no confidential information on the server.

   ❍ No need. There are no packet sniffers on our network.

   ☑ It uses SSL (or another encrypting protocol).

   If you think your network is free of packet sniffers, think again. Even if your organization is protected from the Internet by a firewall, there is always the risk that a nosy insider or an intruder who has managed to find a back door into your network has installed a packet sniffer somewhere. If the Web site is accessible to the Internet, you have to worry about packet sniffers on every ISP, router, and personal computer between your site and the end user's personal computer.

2. What level (export-grade or U.S. domestic-grade) of encryption does your server use?

   ❍ Export-grade SSL (40-bit keys)

   ☑ Domestic-grade SSL (56- to 168-bit keys)

   Forty-bit keys are too weak to withstand a brute-force attack by a determined foe. Forty-bit encryption may be sufficient for personal information, and perhaps even to transmit credit card numbers, but not for major financial transactions, trade secrets, or business plans. Remember, in order to use strong encryption, the server *and* the browser must use domestic-grade encryption to achieve the full benefit.

3. What certifying authority do you use to sign your site's public key?

   ☑ A widely-recognized CA (for instance, VeriSign, MCI, AT&T).

   ❍ We got a real bargain from an Internet outfit called Certs 'R Us.

   If you want browsers to trust your site certificate, it needs to have been signed by a CA whose certificate comes installed in the browser software. Almost anyone can set up a certifying authority and advertise it. Only well-known CAs' signatures are worth much. Also consider the chances of the CA remaining in business for long. If the CA goes out of business and your certificates expire, you're out of luck.

4. Have you backed up your private key and certificates?

   ❍ No

   ☑ Yes

   If the private key is lost or corrupted, your server can't run in secure mode until you go through the whole certificate application process again.

5. How do you protect your private key?

   ☑ It's stored to disk in encrypted form.

   ☑ It's stored to disk in unencrypted form, but with strong access control restrictions.

   ❍ It's stored in unencrypted form, with world-readable privileges.

   Knowledge of the server's private key allows anyone to read the site's encrypted communications and to impersonate it. Be careful to keep the private key secret.

Client Certificates

1. How does your Web server check client certificates for validity?

   ☑ It accepts any certificate that hasn't expired.

   ☑ It accepts any certificate from XYZ certifying authority.

   ☑ It accepts any certificate from XYZ certifying authority that hasn't been revoked.

   ❍ I don't know.

   The answer to this one depends on your access control policies. The first alternative is the weakest. The possession of a client certificate from a recognized CA doesn't mean much unless you know what measures the CA took to verify the bearer's identity. The second alternative is more useful because you are now looking for certificates signed by a CA whose policies you (presumably) know and trust. Better still is to use software that checks the certificate authority's revocation list—if such software is available! The only incorrect answer is ignorance. If you don't know what the software is supposed to do, how do you know it's working?

2. How does your Web server use certificates to authorize clients?

   - ☑ It checks the contents of the certificate for certain attributes.
   - ☑ It checks the certificate's ID against an authorization database.
   - ❍ I don't know.

   Again, there's no best answer to this one. Authorization information can be stored inside the certificate or kept externally in a database of some sort. The first alternative is less flexible and probably suitable only for use within a private CA used by your organization alone. The second alternative is practically a necessity if your access control is based on certificates issued by a commercial CA service.

3. If you run a private CA, where do you keep your CA's private key?

   - ☑ On a secure, access-restricted machine.
   - ❍ On a workstation that doubles as a file server, multiuser dungeon, and news spooler.

   In a private CA setting, everything depends on the secrecy of the private key. You should make every effort to protect the machine from unauthorized access.

4. What do you do when a user has lost or corrupted her certificate's private key?

   - ❍ Tell the user to request a new certificate.
   - ❍ Revoke the old certificate and tell the user to request a new one.
   - ☑ Revoke the old certificate, tell the user to request a new one, and make certain that the servers do not honor revoked certificates.

   Revocation is the most problematic part of certificate-based authentication. It's not enough simply to issue a new certificate or even to revoke the old one first. To be effective, each certificate-accepting server must check the certificate against a network-accessible certificate revocation list. This requirement can be problematic.

5. For how long are your client certificates valid?

   - ☑ One month
   - ☑ Three months
   - ☑ One year
   - ❍ Forever

There's no right answer to this one, but the question is one you should think about. Because certificate revocation is problematic, you may have to rely on revoked certificates expiring naturally. The shorter the certificate's life time, the quicker this will happen. There's nothing magic about the commercial CAs' choice of certificates that expire after a year. For some applications, you may want a shorter expiration time. For others, a longer period may do. It's important that certificates expire after some period of time. Otherwise, certificate revocation lists would grow without limit.

Online Resources

SSL

WebCompare

http://www.webcompare.com/

SSLEay and Apache-SSL

ftp://ftp.psy.uq.oz.au/pub/Crypto/

Stronghold

http://www.c2.net/ (U.S. and Canada)

http://www.stronghold.ukweb.com/ (overseas)

Jigsaw

http://www.w3.org/

Certifying Authorities and CA Products

VeriSign CA

http://www.verisign.com/

Entrust WebCA

http://www.entrust.com/

GTE CyberTrust

http://www.cybertrust.gte.com/

XCert Sentry

http://www.xcert.com/

Thawte Consulting CA

http://www.thawte.com

EuroSign CA

http://eurosign.com

COST CA

http://www.cost.se

BiNARY SuRGEONS CA

http://www.surgeons.co.za/certificate.html

Keywitness CA

http://www.keywitness.ca

SoftForum CA

http://www.softforum.co.kr/

CompuSource CA

http://www.compusource.co.za/

Frontier Technologies eLock

http://www.frontiertech.com/Products/e-Lock/

SSLEay

ftp://ftp.psy.uq.oz.au/pub/Crypto/

Other Information

Tips on creating a certifying authority with SSLEay.

http://www.psy.uq.edu.au:8080/~ftp/Crypto/

Netscape certificate request protocol

http://www.netscape.com/eng/security/certs.html

Netscape *<KEYGEN>* Tag

http://www.netscape.com/eng/security/ca-interface.html

Microsoft CertHelper

http://www.microsoft.com/intdev/securing/csa/certenv3.exe

Printed Resources

Howes, Tim, and Smith, Mark, *LDAP, Programming Directory-Enabled Applications with Lightweight Directory Access Protocol* (Macmillan Technical Publishing, 1997).

A practical introduction to LDAP aimed at the applications developer. Extensive source code examples are included.

Chapter 12

Safe CGI Scripting

Common gateway interface (CGI) scripts, and their cousins, server API modules, give Web developers the ability to extend the Web server's abilities in many ways. CGI scripts can generate pages with dynamic content, provide interfaces to databases, run online games, process customer orders, and even act as front ends for hardware devices.

Unfortunately, bugs in CGI scripts have been a major source of security incidents on the World Wide Web. The scripts are seductively easy to write—but not so easy to write well. One small mistake in a script exposes the Web server and its host machine to attack by malicious intruders. There are many buggy CGI scripts floating around on the Web, some published as misguided examples of the "right way" to do it. Even the big guys, Microsoft, Silicon Graphics, and Novell, to name a few, have published scripts containing serious holes.

This chapter provides some guidelines for writing, testing, and evaluating CGI scripts and server API modules. It also gives advice on other pesky CGI issues, such as how Web site hosting services can minimize the risk of allowing clients to add CGI scripts to their pages.

Introduction to CGI Scripts and Server Modules

CGI scripts are small executable programs that are independent of the main Web server binary. When a remote user requests a URL that points at a CGI script, the server executes the script, passing it various bits of information about the current session. The CGI script processes this information and outputs a document that is often, but not necessarily, an HTML page. This page is then returned to the browser.

Among the information the server provides to the CGI script is a "query string," which contains information originally provided by the remote user and is the user's sole means for passing data to the script. The contents of the query string is arbitrary. It may contain a list of keywords for text search engines or an SQL expression for use by a database gateway.

Query strings are sent to CGI scripts in two ways. One way is to append them directly to the script's URL.

```
http://www.capricorn.org/cgi-bin/do_search?first=George&last=Jetson
```

Everything after the question mark is the query string, in this case the phrase "first=George&last=Jetson." Because it is part of a URL, it has to follow the URL syntax rules, such as replacing spaces with the + character. The CGI script recovers the query string by examining an environment variable. This method uses the standard HTTP GET method for accessing URLs and is typically used by older CGI scripts written before the days of fill-out forms.

Alternatively, the query string may be sent to the CGI script URL using the HTTP POST method. In this case, the Web server sends the query string directly to the script's standard input. The POST method is usually called in response to the user filling in and submitting a fill-out HTML form.

```
<FORM ACTION="/cgi-bin/do_search" METHOD=POST>
First name: <INPUT TYPE="text" NAME="first"> <P>
Last name: <INPUT TYPE="text" NAME="last"> <P>
<INPUT TYPE="submit" VALUE="Search">
</FORM>
```

When this is interpreted by a Web browser, a form that looks something like the one shown in Figure 12.1 appears. If the user types "George" and "Jetson" into the text fields and presses the "Search" button, the contents of the form will be submitted to the URL */cgi-bin/do_search*, as indicated by the HTML form ACTION attribute, using the POST method, as indicated by the form's METHOD attribute. The CGI script will now find the following query string on its standard input.

```
first=George&last=Jetson
```

A baroque set of conventions controls how the browser converts the contents of the form into a query string. The fill-out form is often generated by the CGI script itself, allowing the script to conduct an interactive (if stilted) conversation with the user.

Server modules are conceptually similar to CGI scripts with the important difference that they are compiled and linked directly into the Web server binary itself. As a result, they have access to the Web server's data structures and internal functions. This makes them faster and more powerful than CGI scripts. It also gives them the ability to crash the Web server if they are not properly written. Unlike CGI scripts, user data is sent to server

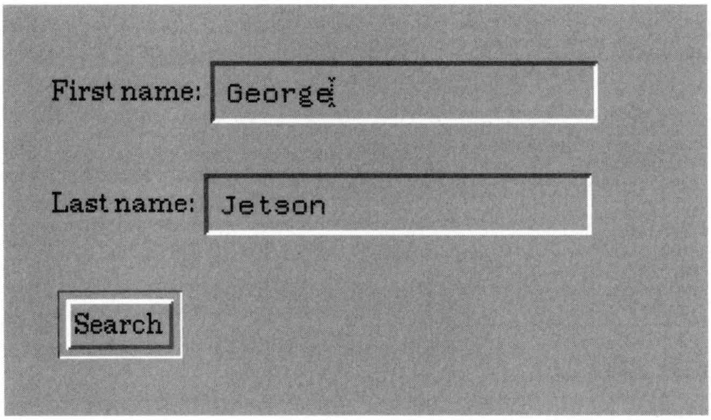

FIGURE 12.1 Fill-out forms are the primary way that users send data to CGI scripts.

modules directly in memory structures rather than through environment variables or standard input.

What Can CGI Scripts and Server Modules Do?

CGI scripts and server modules can do anything they like. They are first-class programs that run on the Web server's host machine, and they have as much access to the file system, network, and hardware devices as any other program. This allows scripts to open up database connections, write customer orders to disk, send e-mail, capture images from a digital camera, and so on. The operating system itself imposes the main limitation on what a CGI script or module can do. When a script executes, it does so with the identity and privileges of the user account the Web server runs under.

What Can CGI Scripts Do Wrong?

There are three categories of risk from buggy CGI scripts.

1. They may unintentionally leak information that will help intruders to break in or gain access to confidential documents.
2. They may be tricked into making unauthorized modifications to files on the Web site or the server host machine.
3. They may be tricked into executing commands on the server host machine.

Carefully designed user privileges are the first line of defense against these bugs. Whatever restrictions apply to the Web server, apply to its CGI scripts and modules, as well. To give an example, if the server runs on a UNIX system that has implemented the shadow password file scheme, the Web server user will be unable to read the password file. As a result, a buggy CGI script cannot be tricked into leaking system passwords. The corollary to this is that the server must never be run with more privileges than it needs. A server running with root (UNIX), Administrator, or System privileges (NT) has unlimited powers, and so does each of its scripts.

Controlling Web server privileges is a good first step, but it cannot protect you against all the ways that scripts can go wrong. To be safe, scripts must be bug free.

Common Failure Modes

Any bug that causes a CGI script or server module to perform in an unexpected manner opens up security holes. Five themes have emerged as common failure modes for CGI scripts.

1. Misuse of interpreters as CGI scripts
2. Flawed memory management
3. Passing unchecked user input to command interpreters
4. Opening files based on unchecked user input
5. Writing unchecked user input to disk

The first problem is an administrative one. The second problem is primarily the domain of compiled programs, such as C and C++ language executables. The second, third, and fourth problems apply to all scripting languages, compiled and interpreted.

Misuse of Interpreters as CGI Scripts

A number of Internet security incidents have been the result of hapless Webmasters who installed a powerful command interpreter in the scripts directory, such as

- The Perl interpreter
- The Tcl interpreter
- The Java interpreter
- The UNIX Bourne/C/Kourne shells
- The NT/DOS *command.com* interpreter
- HTML page preprocessors, such as *php*

In the most notorious of such incidents, Netscape issued a technical note recommending that users of its Windows NT server software place the *perl.exe* executable into the scripts directory. It did this in order to work around a limitation in the server software that causes the server to ignore NT's association of particular file extensions, such as *.pl*, with particular programs, such *perl.exe*. By placing *perl.exe* in the CGI scripts directory, remote users could run Perl CGI scripts by invoking them with URLs such as

```
http://www.victim.com/cgi-bin/perl.exe?search.pl
```

The unfortunate side effect of this configuration, however, is that it allowed *anyone on the Internet* to run arbitrary Perl commands on the server machine. For example, remote users could request the following URL from the victim's Web server.

```
http://www.victim.com/cgi-bin/perl.exe?-e+%27unlink+%3C*%3E%27
```

Following the protocol for unescaping URLs, the Web server obediently transforms this into the shell command *perl -e unlink* '<*>', which Perl programmers will recognize as the command to delete all files in the current directory. Whether the command is successful depends on whether the server's user permissions allow it to make these deletions.

Despite new technical notes from Netscape that warn of this problem, many systems are still misconfigured. Furthermore, the same problem has cropped up in Microsoft servers, because of the complexity of configuring IIS to recognize file suffix mappings. Such sites are easy to find with Internet search engines and easy to exploit. Latro, a freely available demonstration script written by Tom Christiansen, can be used to run arbitrary Perl programs remotely on misconfigured systems (see the end of this chapter for Latro's address).

A more recent episode illustrating the same vulnerability involved the *php* interpreter, a program used to add dynamic elements to HTML pages on both UNIX and NT systems. Webmasters who place this interpreter in their scripts directory open their sites to a number of attacks, including granting remote users the ability to run commands on the server host.

All command interpreters, shells, and language interpreters should be excluded from the scripts directory. Only programs designed to be CGI scripts should be installed there.

Flawed Memory Management

Flawed memory management has been responsible for the opening of security holes in a number of Internet server programs. It was responsible for a hole in older versions (1.3 and lower) of NCSA *httpd*. By requesting extremely long URLs to the server, remote users could execute arbitrary shell commands on the server. More recently, flawed memory management allowed denial-of-service attacks against sites running Microsoft Internet Information Server version 3.0. By requesting URLs of a particular length, malicious individuals could cause IIS servers to crash, making the sites unavailable until the server software was manually restarted. This bug was discovered in late June 1997.

Over the years, the same type of bug has reared its ugly head in non-Web services, as well, including the UNIX *syslog* program, the *lpr* line printer program, and in the *finger* daemon. Among CGI scripts, the widely distributed *count.cgi* script contains a stack overflow bug (November, 1997) that allows remote users to execute shell commands on the server host.

The most common example of a memory management bug is the use of a statically allocated memory buffer, followed by the failure to check the length of a data structure before moving it into the buffer. Here's a bit of C code that shows the problem.

```
char* oops () {
   static char buffer[128];
   return gets(buffer);
}
```

In this example, the function `oops()` is being used to retrieve a string from standard input. A naive programmer might attempt to use this in a CGI script to retrieve the query string from a POST operation. The problem here is two-fold. The memory structure named "buffer" is allocated statically with a length of 128 bytes. The function `gets()` reads a line of input from standard input into the buffer until it finds a new-line character or encounters an end of file condition. `gets()`, however, is one of several C library functions that fails to check for buffer overflow. If the input is longer than 128 bytes, `gets()` will happily overwrite the buffer, destroying any memory structures that happen to be in the way.

In the best case, the program will crash. In the worst, a technically skilled individual can exploit this bug by feeding the program carefully designed data. By overwriting the buffer with just the right number of bytes, the remote user can arrange for the crashing program to leave valid machine-language instructions on its execution stack. When these instructions are executed, they invoke a shell interpreter to run some commands of the user's choosing.

Here's a better way to read data from standard input into a memory buffer. This example shows a way to recover the query string created by a POST operation.

```
char* read_post() {
   int   query_size;
   int   chars_read;
   char* query_string;
   query_size=atoi(getenv("CONTENT_LENGTH"));
   query_string = (char*) malloc(query_size+1);
   if (query_string == NULL)
      return NULL;
   chars_read = fread(query_string,query_size,1,stdin);
   if (chars_read != query_size) {
      free((void*)query_string);
```

```
        return NULL;
    }
    query_string[query_size] = '\0';
    return query_string;
}
```

This function determines in advance how large a memory structure is needed by retrieving it from the environment variable `CONTENT_LENGTH` (the CGI protocol calls for this variable to be set by the server prior to invoking the script). It then calls `malloc()` in an attempt to dynamically allocate a character array large enough to hold this information. If the memory allocation fails, the function returns NULL. Notice that the amount of memory allocated is actually one byte greater than the size of the query string. This is in order to allow room for the null character that terminates all C strings (forgetting this is another common pitfall).

The function next attempts to read the query string from standard input. The `fread()` function call reads in the number of characters we specify, guaranteeing that the buffer cannot be overrun. The function checks the number of characters read. If the number of characters read doesn't match what was expected, the function cleans up and exits. If all has gone well, the function adds the terminating null character to the C string and returns it.

The point of this example is not to show the best way to process POST input in a CGI script, but to demonstrate the need to check sizes carefully before performing any operation that moves memory. In addition, functions should check the result codes every time they make a system call. In the example above, the `fread()` command might return fewer characters than expected if the remote user prematurely terminated the connection. This event should be caught and handled in some reasonable way rather than blindly continuing to process invalid data.

Unfortunately, it's not sufficient to read data into memory safely. Every time the data is manipulated, there is the potential to corrupt memory. Dozens of C library calls move memory around, and many of them have the potential to overflow static buffers. Some C library functions, in fact, use internal static buffers that are not visible to the programmer.

The following functions can overflow static buffers on many systems.

```
gets()          scanf()         sprintf()       realpath()
strcpy()        fscanf()        vsprintf()      getopt()
strcat()        sscanf()                        getpass()
                vscanf()
```

The three functions in the first column all have safer alternatives that take a byte-count argument. Use *fgets()*, *strncpy()*, and *strncat()* in preference to *gets()*, *strcpy()*, and *strcat()*. The others should be avoided, if possible, or used cautiously if not.

Memory management bugs are very difficult to catch and avoid, which explains their frequent recurrence. The best way to avoid such bugs is to avoid memory management completely. Programming languages that perform memory management internally, such as Perl, BASIC, Java, and Python, are immune to this type of problem—provided, of course, the language interpreter itself is free of bugs!

Passing Unchecked User Input to Command Interpreters

Authors of CGI scripts often assume that end users will play by the rules: that they'll type in valid e-mail addresses, that file names will contain legal characters only, that they won't peek at secret CGI parameters contained inside "hidden" form fields.

None of these assumptions is true. Malicious end users will send CGI scripts e-mail addresses that are thousands of characters long and file names containing shell metacharacters. They will view the source of fill-out forms (including the contents of hidden fields) and reverse-engineer the script's calling parameters. They will then craft unanticipated combinations of inputs designed to trick the script into performing some action it wasn't designed for.

The largest class of CGI scripting bug involves failures to perform validity checking on user-supplied input. The invalid input is passed blindly on to subroutines or system calls which then fail with unanticipated consequences.

The most serious ramification of this bug occurs when unchecked user input is passed to a command shell, allowing remote users to execute shell commands on the server machine. This bug has surfaced many times in both commercial and freeware software. It is present in all versions of the *phf* phone book script, long distributed as part of the NCSA and Apache server distributions. It is present in versions 1.0 to 1.2 of *webdist.cgi*, part of Silicon Graphics, *Out Box* package. It's found in version 1.0 of both the *AnyForm* and *FormMail* form-processing scripts. The bug is also found in older versions of the NCSA and Apache Web servers themselves. Needless to say, if any of these scripts is installed on your system, remove them immediately. (You may not even be aware that they're installed; check to be sure.)

A typical example of this bug crops up in Perl CGI scripts designed to send e-mail to an address entered in a fill-out form (some of which have been published in books as examples of how to write good scripts!). In UNIX, it's deceptively easy to do this by opening a pipe to the *mail* command and printing the body of the e-mail to the pipe. Here's the wrong way to do it.

```
$address = param('address');
$subject = param('subject');
$message = param('message');
open (MAIL,"| /bin/mail -s '$subject' $address");
print MAIL $message;
close MAIL;
```

For the sake of simplicity, some of the necessary CGI details aren't shown here. Assume that *param()* is a function that extracts named fields from the CGI query string (there is, in fact, such a function in the standard Perl CGI library).

The code first uses *param()* to recover the e-mail address, subject line, and body of the message. It then opens up a pipe to the *mail* command, using the *-s* flag to specify the subject and passing the recipient's e-mail address on the command line. The script prints the body of the message to the pipe, then closes it. When the pipe is closed, the mail command delivers the message.

This script is intended to be called from a fill-out form that looks like this.

```
<FORM ACTION="/cgi-bin/do_mail" METHOD=POST>
To: <INPUT TYPE="text" NAME="address"> <P>
Subject: <INPUT TYPE="text" NAME="subject"> <P>
Message: <TEXTAREA NAME="message" ROWS=5> </TEXTAREA> <P>
<INPUT TYPE="submit" VALUE="Send Mail">
</FORM>
```

If the user types "bill@microsoft.com" into the Address field, and "NT 5.0 anticipation" into the Subject field, the CGI script will open a pipe to the following command.

```
/bin/mail -s 'NT 5.0 anticipation' bill@microsoft.com
```

In this case, everything will work as anticipated and Bill's e-mail will be delivered.

However, this script has a big problem. It blindly trusts that the e-mail address and subject line provided by the user are valid. But consider what happens when a malicious user types this into the e-mail address field: *bill@microsoft.com; cat /etc/passwd*. The shell command the hapless script now executes looks like

```
/bin/mail -s 'NT 5.0 anticipation' bill@microsoft.com; cat /etc/passwd
```

On UNIX systems, the semicolon character is a metacharacter used to separate multiple commands. The effect of this is to run the anticipated mail command and then execute something completely unexpected, *cat /etc/passwd*. The *cat* command prints the content of the system password file to its standard output, which is transferred intact to the remote user's browser. The remote user is now free to crack the contents of the file using a password-guessing program.

Of course, there's no reason that the same technique couldn't be used to read the contents of any file on the server host, including HTML files normally protected by access control restrictions or SSL. Variants on this exploit can be used to modify files on the host system, read network databases, or play any number of other naughty tricks.

One way to approach this problem in the e-mail script is to perform pattern-match checks on the supplied subject and mail address. E-mail addresses are relatively easy to check. The great majority of Internet addresses consist of one or more "word" characters (the characters a to z, A to Z, 0 to 9, and the underscore character) followed by @ (at sign). This is followed by one or more additional word characters. The dot and hyphen characters are also allowed in e-mail addresses. The basic pattern-matching check looks like

```
$address = param('address');
do_error('Address not in form foo@nowhere.com')
    unless $address =~ /^[\w.-]+\@[\w.-]+$/;
```

do_error() is assumed to be some sort of routine that issues an error message and aborts the script. (Be aware that this particular pattern match may be too restrictive for some sites. It doesn't allow for UUCP-style addresses or any of several other addressing schemes).

The e-mail subject line is harder to check correctly because almost any text can be valid. In addition, there's another subtle bug lurking in the code example given above: If the user provides a subject text that contains a single quote character ('), the piped open will fail when the shell detects the mismatched quote. One way to handle the subject line is to escape all characters that aren't safe. Placing the backslash character in front of an unsafe character tells the shell to ignore it.

What's the list of unsafe characters? The UNIX shell has so many that it's hard to remember them all. It's better to compile a short list of characters you know to be safe and to escape everything else than to try to escape a list of bad characters. It does no harm to escape a character unnecessarily. We know a to z, A to Z, 0 to 9, and the punctuation marks _ (underscore sign), @ (at sign), . (dot), , (comma), and – (hyphen) are safe. This substitution expression will escape other characters efficiently:

```
$subject=~s/([^a-zA-Z0-9_@.,-])/\\$1/g;
```

A nice side effect of this is that we no longer need to put single quotes around the subject variable in the piped open.

With these checks in place, a better e-mailing script looks like this.

```
$address = param('address');
$subject = param('subject');
$message = param('message');
#check the address for correct format
$address = param('address');
do_error('Address not in form foo@nowhere.com')
    unless $address =~ /^[\w.-]+\@[\w.-]+$/;
#remove unsafe characters from the subject
$subject=~s/([^a-zA-Z0-9_@.,-])/\\$1/g;
open (MAIL,"| /bin/mail -s $subject $address");
print MAIL $message;
close MAIL;
```

The script is now safe. Or is it? Its safety relies on the pattern-matching operations working as expected. Unfortunately, it's easy to make mistakes in pattern-match operations, as well as in other routines that manipulate text. A better solution is to avoid passing user input to a shell entirely. In the case of e-mail, UNIX offers an lower-level alternative to *mail* called *sendmail,* which can be called in such a way that the e-mail address and subject line are specified within the message itself rather than as command-line arguments.

```
$address = param('address');
$subject = param('subject');
$message = param('message');
open (MAIL,"| /usr/lib/sendmail -t -oi");
print MAIL <<END;
To: $address
From: Webmaster (webmaster\@capricorn.org)
Subject: $subject

$message
END
close MAIL;
```

In this new and improved example, the address, subject line, and mail message are recovered as before, and the *sendmail* program is opened using flags that tell it to take the address from a provided e-mail header (*-t* means to ignore any address provided on the command line, *-oi* turns off special processing of the . (dot) character, used by some versions of *sendmail* to terminate a message). Notice that no user-provided values whatsoever are passed to the *sendmail* command line. Instead, the address and subject are incorporated into fields of the e-mail message header itself. As an added bonus, this method allows the e-mail return address to be specified explicitly.

A variety of system calls open command shells. Any one of them is vulnerable to the type of bug described in this section. Similar concerns apply to calls within interpreted languages that reinvoke the interpreter to execute commands. Calls that should be treated with care include

C

- *popen()* (open a pipe)
- *system()* (invoke a subshell)

Perl

- *system()* (invoke a subshell)
- *exec()* (invoke a subshell—don't return)
- *eval()* (invoke Perl interpreter)
- " " "(backticks—run subshell and return result)
- *open(S,"| ..."* (piped open)
- *open(S,"... |")* (open pipe)
- *s/.../.../e* (substitution using the eval flag)

Java

- *System.exec()* (invoke a subshell)

Whenever possible, avoid sending any user input through a shell or command interpreter. When this can't be avoided, check the user input thoroughly. Perl-oriented techniques for avoiding being bitten by this class of bug is given later in the Safe Scripting in Perl section.

Opening Files Based on Unchecked User Input

It isn't necessary for a CGI script to send unchecked user input through a command shell to get into trouble. A common class of hole arises when unchecked input is used to derive the name of a file to open for reading and writing. Remote users can exploit this bug to read files that aren't intended for public consumption or to overwrite existing files.

Among the scripts affected by this bug are *files.pl*; part of the Novell Web Server distribution (version 2.0); *print_hit_bold*, a program that displays HTML files with keywords highlighted (all versions); and *nph-publish* (versions 1.0 to 1.1), an Apache PUT handler that enables the server to receive uploaded files.

To show how this bug works, consider a CGI script or API module that acts as a front end for an online role-playing game. The game has a configurable set of options for difficulty level, game character, and so on. As a convenience, the CGI script allows users to save their preferences to a file stored on the Web server host machine. Again assuming a CGI script written in Perl, the fragment of code responsible for opening a preferences file for reading might look like this.

```
$preferences = param('preferences');
$file = "/local/web/parameters/$preferences";
open(P,$file) or errorExit("Couldn't open preferences $preferences");
readPreferences(P);
close P;
```

The assumption here is that users will use simple names for their preferences, such as *prefs1*. The code will translate this name into the file path */local/web/parameters/prefs1* and attempt to process it. This is a poor assumption. Ignoring for the moment the problem of one user overwriting another user's parameter set by picking the same name, what happens if the user enters a name like *../../../etc/passwd*? In this case, the CGI script will attempt to open the path */local/web/parameters/../../../etc/passwd* and try to process the system password file in some way. This is likely to have undesirable results.

Metacharacters are also an issue here, at least for Perl scripts. A wily remote user could append a | character to the end of the parameter set, causing the script to try to execute a piped command. Or he could prepend a > symbol, instructing Perl to truncate the file before opening it.

As in the previous examples, it's crucial to check user input for validity before opening any files. The correct check to perform is operating-system-dependent. On UNIX systems, the following subroutine will check first for the presence of undesirable relative paths in the file name. If it passes this check, it will convert unusual file name components (white space, punctuation characters, and the like) into underscores.

```
sub fix_filename {
   my $file = shift;
   error_exit("File name contains naughty relative path components")
       if $file=~m!^\.\./|/\.\./!;
   $file=~tr/a-zA-Z0-9_.\/-/_/c;
   return $file;
}
```

On Windows NT systems you'll want to replace the relative pathname pattern match check with something that allows for DOS backslashes, for example `$file=~m!^\.\.[/\\]|[/\\]\.\.[/\\]!;`. This routine does *not* handle the problem of one user overwriting another user's preferences file. For that, you need an application-specific solution, such as including the remote user's name or browser's IP address in the file path.

A more subtle manifestation of this bug appears when CGI scripts and server API modules are used to post-process HTML files and other documents. A good example of the problem is the *print_hit_bold* program, a Perl script that is commonly used in conjuction with a site search engine to retrieve documents that contain certain keywords. To understand what this script does, say a user has performed a site search for the word *defenestrate* and the search engine has retrieved the URL */windows/history/accidents.html*. The CGI script that displays the search engine's hits presents the document to the user with this URL.

```
/cgi-bin/print_hit_bold/windows/history/accidents.html?defenestrate
```

This convoluted URL is actually an instruction to *print_hit_bold* to performing the following steps.

1. Open and read the document contained at */windows/history/accidents.html*.
2. Find all occurrences of the word *defenestrate*.
3. Boldface the occurrences by placing <B></B> tags around them.
4. Return the modified document to the browser.

The bug occurs when the Web site contains a mixture of public and private documents. *print_hit_bold* fails to check whether the documents it processes are restricted. If, for example, *print_hit_bold* is asked to process the file */private/confidential/trade_secrets.html*, it will merrily go ahead and do so, despite the fact that the Web server is configured to prevent the general public from gaining access to this portion of the document tree. The situation is not helped by the fact that many popular keyword indexing and search engines also fail to check access restrictions during the document indexing phase. The combination of the two provides a convenient back door for anyone wishing to gain access to restricted portions of your Web site. The remote user runs a keyword search to find the names of confidential documents, then uses *print_hit_bold* to fetch their contents.

If you are writing a document-processing script, you should consider implementing it as a server API module rather than as a CGI script. Modules have full access to the server's access control system, allowing you to check that the server allows a remote user to read a particular document before processing it. With CGI scripts, at least those written for UNIX systems, there is no general solution to this problem. You can't use file permissions to protect confidential documents because all CGI scripts run under the same user ID. You can't use the Web server's built-in access control system because the access control API isn't made available to external programs.

An exception to this advice is for servers running Microsoft IIS. IIS uses the file system's native access control lists to restrict access to confidential Web documents, a mechanism that's difficult for CGI scripts to circumvent. In this case, there is little risk of a well-written CGI script being used to bypass Web server access restrictions.

Writing Unchecked User Input to Disk

CGI scripts that update files in the document tree based on user input can run into problems if they fail to check the input carefully. Programs that are susceptible to this bug include

- Guestbook scripts
- User feedback scripts
- Discussion scripts
- Voting scripts
- Web page publishing scripts

Among the well-known packages that contain this flaw are Microsoft FrontPage extensions for UNIX and NT systems, versions 1.1 and earlier; and Selena Sol's guestbook script, all versions as of 8/1/97. In the case of FrontPage, the bug affects the *Discussion* and *Save Results* "WebBots." A page incorporating either of these WebBots displays a fill-out form that prompts the user for input. The contents of the form are saved to disk in a "results file" that is available to other users for browsing. Unfortunately, vulnerable versions of FrontPage perform no checking on the contents of the fill-out form, allowing a wily user to append raw HTML to the results file. This raw HTML can, in turn, be used to access the FrontPage system, allowing the remote user to create her own *Save Results* WebBot. This WebBot allows the user to replace selected documents on the Web site.

The problem with Selena Sol's guestbook script is similar. In this case, the vulnerability appears only when the guestbook script saves its results to a server-side include file. Because the guestbook fails to check user input for the presence of server-side includes, malicious users can insert their own directives. If the Web server is configured to allow server-side includes to invoke shell commands, then remote users can execute arbitrary commands on the server host machine.

The best way to avoid this class of bug is to deactivate HTML tags in user-provided input. It's wise to do this even if you're not worried about the security implications, as bad HTML in a results file can prevent the page from displaying properly. A straightforward way to deactivate tags is to replace all < (less than), > (greater than), and & (ampersand) characters with their HTML character entities. Instead of being interpreted, HTML tags will be displayed in their source code form. In Perl, this code fragment illustrates the technique.

```
$input =~ s/</&lt;/g;
$input =~ s/>/&gt;/g;
$input =~ s/&/&amp;/g;
```

A more aggressive approach is to remove HTML tags completely. This bit of Perl code will identify and delete anything that looks remotely like HTML.

```
$input =~ s/<[^>]*>//mg;
```

Other Advice

If you take care to close the five holes listed above, you'll have significantly improved the safety of your CGI scripts. However, there many are other lurking pitfalls. Here are more bits of advice, some garnered through unfortunate personal experience!

Log Everything

CGI scripts should record all unusual events to an error log. Unusual events include invalid user input, system calls that fail, and file operations that return an error code. During development, you should use a "debug flag" to turn on verbose logging. When you deploy the script, deactivate the debug flag but keep the debugging code available in case you need it again.

Under most Web servers, when a CGI script is launched, its standard error is redirected to the server's error log. The server's error messages are nicely formatted and time stamped, but your script's messages will not be stamped unless you make them that way. Perl developers should take advantage of the *CGI::Carp* module, part of the standard Perl 5.004 distribution. When this module is in use, error messages are time stamped, labeled with the name of the currently executing CGI script, and written into the server error log.

A few Web servers, Microsoft IIS included, do not handle CGI script error messages gracefully. Error messages are intermingled with the script's normal output or else cause the server to abort the request with an "Internal server error" message. For these servers, CGI scripts should handle their own error logging. In Perl, the most convenient place to do this is at the top of the script in a BEGIN block.

```
BEGIN {
   open (STDERR,'>>C:\WINNT\SYSTEM32\LogFiles\CGI_errors.txt');
}
```

The CGI log file must have been previously created and be writable by the IIS anonymous user before this will work.

On UNIX systems, another option is to log CGI script error messages with the system logging facility, using the *syslog()* function. This offers considerable flexibility at the cost of some processing overhead. Interfaces to *syslog()* are available for C, Perl, and several other programming languages. If you decide to take this route, be sure to use a recent version of the *syslog* library. Some versions of the library contain a bug that can overflow a static buffer.

A similar solution for Windows NT is to use the system event log, interfaces to which are available for both C and Perl.

Trust Nothing

The fewer assumptions your script or module makes about the current environment, the less vulnerable it will be to malicious interventions. Here are the four most common assumptions to avoid.

1. **Current Working Directory** Most Web servers will change the working directory to the location of the CGI script before executing it, but some don't. Do not rely on this behavior. Explicitly set the working directory yourself if you are going to be accessing relative files and paths. In Perl

   ```
   chdir('/usr/local/etc/httpd/cgi/')
       or die "Couldn't set working directory: $!";
   ```

2. **PATH** Do not depend on the PATH environment variable being set to a reasonable value. When shelling out to system commands, either refer to the command using its absolute path or set the PATH yourself. Better yet, do both. In Perl

   ```
   $ENV{PATH} = '/bin:/usr/bin';
   $date = `/bin/date`;
   ```

   Never place the current directory . (dot) in the PATH variable.

3. **IFS** The IFS environment variable is an obscure UNIX shell feature that allows you to change the character that separates arguments on the command line from white space to something else. If this variable is changed, your script could be fooled into doing something unexpected when it invokes an external shell. On UNIX systems, it is best to set this environment variable to an empty string at the top of each script. This will restore the expected behavior. In Perl

```
$ENV{IFS}='';
```

4. **Location of Document and Server Roots** It's best not to hard-code the location of the Web document and server root directories. The script could be moved, the Web server configuration changed, or the script invoked in the context of a virtual server. Many servers provide directory configuration information in environment variables. See your server's documentation for details.

Use Temporary Files with Care

If your CGI script or API module creates temporary files during the course of its operation, you need to handle the file operations with some delicacy. One risk is that the temporary file will be read by some other user (or process) on the server, disclosing sensitive information (remember that CGI scripts all run under the same user ID). Another is that a malicious local user, knowing the type of names your script uses for its temporary files, will set a trap for your script. The malicious user creates a link between some important file and a temporary-file name that your script is likely to use. When the script goes to open this link, it accidentally clobbers the important file.

Create temporary files by opening them with the O_EXCL and O_CREAT flags, causing the open operation to fail if the file already exists. (WARNING: This may not work correctly across NFS file systems.) Before working with a newly created temporary file, you should unlink it in order to make it inaccessible to other processes on the system. Then truncate it to length 0 in order to eliminate the possibility that someone else may have appended to the file in the brief time between creating the file and unlinking it. This small Perl program demonstrates a subroutine that safely creates a temporary file, opens it, and returns a file handle for subsequent I/O operations.

```
#!/usr/bin/perl
use FileHandle;
$TMPDIR = '/usr/tmp';              # location of temporary files
srand();                           # randomize temp file names a bit
$tempFileHandle = tempFile() or die;
[Use the file handle for something]
close $tempFileHandle;             # will automatically be deleted
sub tempFile {
```

```
    my $basename = 'temp';
    my $seq = rand(10000);
    my $filename;
    do {                          # loop until we find an unused name
        $filename = sprintf("$TMPDIR/%s.%05d",$basename,$seq++);
    } until !-e $filename;
    my $fh = new FileHandle $filename,O_RDWR|O_CREAT|O_EXCL;
    unlink $filename;
    truncate $fh,0;
    $fh;
}
```

C programmers should use the *tmpfile()* function found on most POSIX systems. It does the equivalent of the Perl code shown above, returning a FILE pointer to the open temporary file if successful.

Restrict Access to Sensitive CGI Scripts

Some CGI scripts and modules are intended to be available only after the remote user has authenticated herself to the Web server. Typical examples include scripts that act as front ends to databases containing confidential information or those that allow the remote user to make modifications to the document tree. Such scripts are typically placed under Web server access control. On the Apache server, the entry in *access.conf* may look something like this.

```
<Location /cgi-bin/database>
AuthType Basic
AuthUserFile /usr/local/etc/httpd/security/passwd
AuthGroupFile /usr/local/etc/httpd/security/group
<Limit GET POST>
require valid-user
</Limit>
</Location>
```

The important thing to note is that the *<Limit>* directive restricts both GET and POST methods. Many sites have been burnt when they've restricted GET access to a sensitive CGI script, only to have an unauthorized user invoke it using POST.

You may also wish to require remote users to access a particular CGI script using SSL encryption. This will prevent the interaction between user and script from being intercepted by a network eavesdropper. You can do this by placing the directive *RequireSSL on* within a Stronghold/ApacheSSL *<Directory>* or *<Location>* section, or by selecting the "Require secure SSL channel" checkbox in a Microsoft IIS virtual directory properties window. For more information, see Chapter 11.

If a CGI script is intended to run in a secure environment, it should not assume that the server has been configured correctly. Double-check that the expected security restrictions are in place by examining any environment variables that the server makes available. If any inconsistencies are found, the script should log the problem and exit.

If access to a script is restricted by user name and password (basic or digest authentication; see Chapter 10), then the environment variable *REMOTE_USER* will be set to the account name the user gave to the authentication system. If authentication was bypassed in some way, then this variable will be undefined.

```
$ENV{REMOTE_USER} or die "Not running under authentication!";
```

If the script is intended to be used in a secure SSL session, it should check that the *HTTPS* environment variable exists and has the value "on." There are other SSL-specific environment variables, as well, including ones that indicate the key size and cipher suite in use.

```
$ENV{HTTPS} eq "on" or die "Not running under SSL!";
$ENV{HTTPS_SECRETKEYSIZE} >= 128 or die "Not using strong encryption!";
```

Cookies

Cookies are useful for keeping track of users' click trails and can be indispensable for maintaining a continuous virtual session across many HTTP transactions (see Chapter 6). Because cookies are maintained in an insecure location on the user's personal computer, they should contain no confidential information. Instead, cookies should contain an anonymous user identifier that has meaning only for your script or API module.

When you first create a cookie, choose a new unique random identifier and place it in a database record, along with any information you wish to associate with the user or session. When the user's browser subsequently returns the cookie, use the identifier to retrieve the information from the database.

Cookies can be made persistent across browsing sessions, or they can be set to vanish when the user quits the browser application. Unless you really need a cookie to remain available across sessions, you should allow it to expire when the user quits. If you need a cookie to remain persistent, choose a conservative expiration date. The longer a cookie remains on the user's hard disk, the more vulnerable it is to interception or tampering.

You need to be aware that cookies can be sniffed in transit just as any other part of the HTTP session can be. To avoid this, you can set a flag in a cookie that tells the browser to return it only when SSL is in use.

Cookies are also useful for implementing one-time login systems on networks that maintain several Web servers. The first time a user connects to your site, a CGI script prompts her for user name and password, then checks

SSL Environment Variables

SSL-capable servers set several environment variables when SSL is active. CGI scripts are free to use these variables for any purpose. For example, a CGI script that provides access to a database of sensitive information could abort unless a certain type of cipher suite were in use.

Here are the more useful SSL-related environment variables set by Stronghold and other versions of Apache-SSL. Variables that begin with *HTTPS* are relatively standardized and will usually be set by other SSL-capable servers, as well. Check your server's documentation to be sure.

- *HTTPS* "on" if SSL is active; "off" or undefined if otherwise.
- *HTTPS_SECRETKEYSIZE* The effective size, in bytes, of the session key (the temporary symmetric key used for the duration of the communications session).
- *HTTPS_KEYSIZE* The native size of the session key. This is the key size used by uncrippled versions of the encryption algorithm. It will be identical to *HTTPS_SECRETKEYSIZE* unless an export-crippled cipher suite is in use. This variable is mostly of academic interest. Do not use *HTTPS_KEYSIZE* to determine the strength of the encryption session.
- *HTTPS_CIPHER* The exact name of the cipher suite in use as it appears in Table 3.2.
- *HTTPS_EXPORT* "true" if using a browser and/or server that is crippled for export; "false," otherwise.
- *SSL_PROTOCOL_VERSION* The version of SSL in use; currently either 2 or 3.
- *SSLEAY_VERSION* The version of the SSLEay library in use.
- *SSL_SERVER_KEY_SIZE* The size, in bytes, of the server's public/private key pair used for authentication and session key negotiation.
- *SSL_SERVER_KEY_ALGORITHM* The public key algorithm used by the server for authentication, usually rsaEncryption.
- *SSL_SERVER_SIGNATURE* The server's signature algorithm—for instance, RSA-MD5.
- *SSL_CLIENT_KEY_SIZE* The size, in bytes, of the client's public/private key pair used for authentication.
- *SSL_CLIENT_KEY_ALGORITHM* The public key algorithm used by the client for authentication, usually "rsaEncryption."
- *SSL_CLIENT_SIGNATURE* The client's signature algorithm—for instance, RSA-MD5.
- *SSL_SERVER_CN, SSL_SERVER_EMAIL, SSL_SERVER_OU, etc.* These environment variables correspond to similarly named attributes in the server's certificate. For example, *SSL_SERVER_CN* corresponds to the "common name" attribute. See the previous chapter for details.
- *SSL_CLIENT_CN, SSL_CLIENTR_EMAIL, SSL_CLIENT_OU, etc.* These environment variables correspond to similarly named attributes in the client's certificate.
- *SSL_CLIENT_ICN, SSL_CLIENTR_IEMAIL, SSL_CLIENT_IOU, etc.* These environment variables correspond to similarly named attributes in the signature of the certifying authority that *signed* the client's certificate.

these values against an authentication database. If the name and password are valid, the system generates a "passcard" and gives it to the user's browser in the form of a cookie. Until the cookie expires, the browser can use it to gain access to other servers on the network. This scheme can significantly reduce the load placed on the authentication database.

To avoid the risk that a passcard cookie will be intercepted and used by a third party to gain unauthorized access, the cookie should incorporate the IP address of the browser and a time limit over which it is valid. This will make it useless to anyone but the user it was issued to (but beware clients whose IP addresses are allocated dynamically by their ISPs!). The cookie must also incorporate an authentication code to prevent forgery. A simple scheme is to take the contents of the cookie, concatenate it with a secret known only to the site's Web servers, and compute the MD5 or SHA hash of the whole thing. This hash is appended to the cookie before issuing it to the browser, and it is used by the server to check the integrity of the cookie each time it is returned.

```
identification = IP address + expiration time + other info
cookie = identification + MD5(secret + identification)
```

See the end of this chapter for the URL of the cookie specification. The Perl *CGI.pm* module is also a good source for cookie usage and examples.

Use SUID and SGID Scripts with Care

Sometime, you will need to run a CGI script with privileges different from those of the Web server itself in order to access restricted files, databases, or commands. On UNIX systems, the easiest way to do this is by setting the script's set-user-id (SUID) and/or set-group-id (SGID) file mode bits. In the former case, the script will take on the identity of its creator when launched. In the latter, the script will assume the identity of the group that owns it.

Whenever you create a script that runs with the SUID or SGID bits set, take great care that it is running under the conditions that you expect. SUID programs have been a major source of security breaches on UNIX systems. Recommended checks include the following:

- Was the script invoked by the expected user (typically the Web server user)?
- Was the script invoked by the expected group (typically the Web server group)?
- Is the script protected from writing by the user or group that launched it (to avoid the possibility that it was modified in some way before it was launched)?
- Is the user or group ID that the script is running as *not* that of the superuser (ID = 0)?

You may wish to perform other checks, as well. For example, you might not allow the script to be run through a symbolic link.

In Perl, these checks can be accomplished with the following fragment of code. Be sure to change the definitions of *WEB_USER* and *WEB_GROUP* to whatever is appropriate for your site.

```
#!/usr/local/bin/perl
$WEB_USER = 50;
$WEB_GROUP = 50;
print "The script is ", check_suid() ? "OK" : "NOT OK","\n";
sub check_suid {
    my $user_from = $<;           # ID of launching process
    my $user_to = $>;             # ID that we're suid -to-
    my $group_from = $(;
    my $group_to = $);
    # not running suid or sgid, so no checks needed
    return 1 if ($group_from == $group_to) && ($user_from == $user_to);
    do { warn "Can't be suid/sgid root"; return undef }
       if ($user_to == 0) || ($group_to == 0);
    # fail unless we were launched by correct user & group
    do { warn "Not launched by web user"; return undef }
       unless $user_from == $WEB_USER;
    do { warn "Not launched by web group"; return undef }
       unless $group_from == $WEB_GROUP;
    # fail if the script is writable by the user or group
    # of the process that launched it (the real uid/gid)
    do { warn "Writable by uid/gid invoking process"; return undef }
       if -W $0;
    return 1;
}
```

Perl automatically turns on "taint checks" when executing an SUID or SGID program. See *Safe Scripting in Perl* later in this chapter for information on how to work with taint checks.

When launching subprocesses or opening files within an SUID or SGID script, you may want to revert to the original Web server's permissions. Otherwise, the subprocess will inherit the script's SUID/SGID permissions. In Perl, a simple way to do this is illustrated by the following code.

```
# open the "ls -l" command
if (open(LS,"-|")) { #fork a copy of ourselves
   while (<LS>) { #this is the parent process
      # do something
   }
} else {           #this subprocess calls the ls command
   $> = $<;  # reset UID to that of launching process
   $) = $(;  # reset GID too
   exec '/bin/ls','-l';
   die "Can't exec /bin/ls: $!";
}
```

It is not safe to run UNIX shell scripts with the SUID or SGID bits set because of a race condition in most UNIX kernels. Perl is the exception to this rule because it uses a special executable, named *suidperl,* to work around this problem. Perl has to be installed correctly in order for this to work properly, however. If SUID Perl scripts do not seem to be working on your system, you may need to reinstall the Perl distribution.

In general, it is not possible to run a server API module with permissions different from those of the parent Web server. See *CGI Wrappers* later in this chapter for more information on running scripts in SUID mode.

Limit Script Resource Usage

A buggy CGI script may consume system resources rapidly if it goes into an endless loop or tries to allocate too much memory. The system resource limits described in Chapters 8 and 9 can be used to prevent CGI scripts from driving up server load. CGI scripts can also implement their own resource control. For example, two lines like the ones that follow, placed at the top of a Perl script, will cause it to abort if it has been running for more than a minute.

```
$SIG{ALRM} = sub { die "Timed out" };
alarm 60;
```

Manage Your Code Carefully

Many security incidents occur because someone got sloppy. Here's common sense advice for managing your code resources.

Use a Standard CGI Library

Don't reinvent the wheel. If there is a well-tested and debugged library for parsing CGI input and producing valid output, use it. Not only will you improve your development and debugging time, but you may avoid security holes. For Perl, I recommend the *CGI.pm* module, now part of the standard Perl distribution. It is available for both Windows NT and UNIX. C programmers should use either the *cgic* library, or *cgi++,* a CGI class hierarchy for C++.

Don't Use the Shell for CGI Scripts

Although easy to use and often chosen for simple scripting examples, shell scripting languages such as the Bourne, Korn, Bash, and C shells for UNIX, and the *.BAT* command processor for Windows NT, are poor choices for CGI scripting languages. These languages make it impossible to check user input adequately and are hard to debug. Even simple errors can create disastrous security holes.

Review Your Code with Others

Despite the best intentions, some obvious (and not so obvious) security holes inevitably slip through the cracks. Before moving any new CGI script or API module onto a production Web server, sit down with at least one other knowledgeable developer and review the script's source code line by line. Explain what the program is doing at each point. You'll be surprised by some of the things that pop out at you during this process.

Repeat the code review process every time the script is changed substantially. Repeat the review at regular intervals even when no major changes have been made. At the very least, this will keep you and the reviewer on top of the code in case it needs to be changed in a hurry.

Use Source Code Control

Even minor changes can sometimes have unanticipated large effects. Source code control systems keep track of every change made to the source tree. You can review the changes or even back-track to an earlier working version if you have to. Source code control is essential for projects that are shared by multiple programmers.

Use Regression Tests

Regressions tests help ensure that a script still performs in the expected manner after it has been modified. The simplest way to start a core regression test suite is to create a series of test inputs for the script, along with a set of corresponding expected outputs. To run the regression tests, feed each input to the script, capture its output, and perform a "diff" with the expected output. If there's a mismatch, you have a problem.

Old bugs have a way of popping up again. As you find and fix bugs in your scripts, take a moment to create regression tests that detect them. In this way, you can slowly build up a powerful suite of specific tests for your application.

It might seem difficult to run regression tests on CGI scripts and API modules because of the need to test them while they're running under a Web server. Fortunately, the Perl *LWP* library provides a programmatic interface for feeding specific inputs to any running script or module and capturing its output. This library should be a part of any Web developer's tool box. See the end of the chapter for LWP's URL.

Consider Torture-Testing Scripts and Modules

An inefficient, but sometimes effective, way to find bugs in CGI scripts, server modules, and even the Web servers themselves is to torture-test them by repeatedly feeding them long strings of random illegal input. Although this is most effective in picking up memory overflow bugs in compiled programs, it can occasionally detect flaws in interpreted scripts, as well.

Code Listing 12.1 is a simple Perl script that will perform this type of testing. It requires the *LWP* library to run. Select the URL to test, the maximum length of the random data to send, whether to use the GET or POST method, and the number of times to run the test. Generally you will want to test a CGI script several hundred times with random data that is at least 32K long. The testing script pummels the CGI script with random data, waits for a response, then prints out the server's status code. A CGI script that is functioning correctly should return a status code of 200 (OK), 400 (Bad request), or 404 (Not found). If the CGI script crashes, the testing script will report a status code of 500 (Internal server error) that appears for one test only. Sometimes the server itself crashes. If this happens, a long series of 500 errors will appear. Any crashes are evidence of a potential problem.

LISTING 12.1 A Perl program to torture test Web servers and CGI scripts

```
#!/usr/bin/perl

# file: torture.pl
# Torture test Web servers and scripts by sending them large arbitrary URLs
# and record the outcome.

# Examples of usage:

# Fetch http://www.capricorn.org/cgi-bin/search 1000 times,
#       giving it random data of up to 10K bytes in the query string
#  torture.pl -t 100 -l 10000 http://www.capricorn.org/cgi-bin/search

# Fetch http://www.capricorn.org/cgi-bin/search 1000 times,
#       giving it random data of up to 10K bytes in the POST message
#  torture.pl -P -t 100 -l 10000 http://www.capricorn.org/cgi-bin/search

# Fetch 100 random URLs from the Web server up to 10K long.
#  torture.pl -p -t 100 -l 10000 http://www.capricorn.org/

#  The output will look like this:
#  torture.pl version 1.0 starting
#    Base URL:               http://www.capricorn.org/cgi-bin/search
#    Max random data length: 1024
#    Repetitions:            100
#    Post:                   1
#    Append to path:         0
#    Escape URLs:            0

# 200 OK
# 200 OK
```

continued

LISTING 12.1 *(continued)*

```
# 200 OK                \
# 404 File Not Found
# 200 OK
# 403 Bad Request
# ...

use LWP::UserAgent;
use URI::Escape;
require "getopts.pl";

$USAGE = <<USAGE;
Usage: $0 -[options] URL
       Torture-test Web servers and CGI scripts

Options:
       -l <integer>  Max length of random URL to send [1024 bytes]
       -t <integer>  Number of times to run the test [1]
       -P            Use POST method rather than GET method
       -p            Attach random data to path rather than query string
       -e            Escape the query string before sending it
USAGE
    ;
$VERSION = '1.0';

# process command line
&Getopts('l:t:Ppe') || die $USAGE;
# seed the random number generator (not necessary in perl 5.004)
srand();

# get parameters
$URL = shift || die $USAGE;
$MAXLEN = $opt_l ne '' ? $opt_l : 1024;
$TIMES = $opt_t || 1;
$POST = $opt_P || 0;
$PATH = $opt_p || 0;
$ESCAPE = $opt_e || 0;

# cannot do both a post and a path at the same time
undef $POST if $PATH;

# create an LWP agent
my $agent = new LWP::UserAgent;

print <<EOF;
torture.pl version $VERSION starting
  Base URL:               $URL
  Max random data langth: $MAXLEN
  Repetitions:            $TIMES
  Post:                   $POST
  Append to path:         $PATH
  Escape URLs:            $ESCAPE
```

LISTING 12.1 *(continued)*

```
EOF
;

# Do the test $TIMES times
while ($TIMES) {
    # create a string of random stuff
    my $garbage = random_string(rand($MAXLEN));
    $garbage = uri_escape($garbage) if $ESCAPE;
    my $url = $URL;
    my $request;

    if (length($garbage) == 0) { # if no garbage to add, just fetch URL
        $request = new HTTP::Request ('GET',$url);
    }

    elsif ($POST) {             # handle POST request
        my $header = new HTTP::Headers (
                     Content_Type => 'application/x-www-form-urlencoded',
                     Content_Length => length($garbage)
                                       );
        # garbage becomes the POST content
        $request = new HTTP::Request ('POST',$url,$header,$garbage);

    } else {                    # handle GET request

        if ($PATH) {            # append garbage to the base URL
            chop($url) if substr($url,-1,1) eq '/';
            $url .= "/$garbage";
        } else {                # append garbage to the query string
            $url .= "?$garbage";
        }
        $request = new HTTP::Request ('GET',$url);

    }

    # do the request and fetch the response
    my $response = $agent->request($request);

    # print the numeric response code and the message
    print $response->code,' ',$response->message,"\n";

} continue { $TIMES--}

# return some random data of the requested length
sub random_string {
    my $length = shift;
    return undef unless $length >= 1;
    return join('',map chr(rand(255)),0..$length-1);
}
```

This type of test is crude and will not pick up many subtle bugs. However, it would have readily detected the static buffer bug present in older versions of NCSA *httpd*, as well as the bug recently found in IIS 3.0. Do not run the test on a production server because it will adversely affect performance.

Safe Scripting in Perl

The Perl programming language has several unique features that can help you avoid security traps. This section briefly introduces them.

Taint Checks

The most important of Perl's security features is taint checks. When taint checks are turned on, Perl keeps track of all variables that contain information that came from "outside" the program. Such information includes data read from files, from standard input, from external processes, from the command line, and from environment variables. Any variable that comes into contact with a tainted variable itself becomes tainted. If the script later tries to use a tainted variable in any of a variety of unsafe operations, Perl will complain and abort. Taint checks also check for other security holes, such as the failure to set the PATH or IFS environment variables or an attempt to unlink a file based on unchecked user input.

Taint checks are turned on automatically when a script is run in SUID or SGID mode. This is not usually the case for Web CGI scripts, however, so you will have to turn them on explicitly using the *-T* switch. While you're at it, use the *-w* switch to turn on verbose warning messages.

This line at the top of a Perl CGI script will turn both checks on.

```
#!/usr/local/bin/perl -Tw
```

The script will now abort with the error message "Insecure dependency" if you attempt to pass unchecked user input (or any other information from outside) to a shell, pass untested input to an *eval()* statement, or try to use unchecked input to open a file for writing. Additionally, if you attempt to invoke a shell from within the script, you will get the message "Insecure $ENV{PATH}" unless you set the PATH and IFS environment variables at the top of the script.

```
$ENV{'PATH'} = '/bin:/usr/bin';
$ENV{'IFS'} = '';
```

Once a variable is tainted by outside information, it remains tainted forever. The only way to untaint a tainted variable is by performing a pattern match, then extracting the matched substring(s) using Perl's pattern reference variables $1, $2, and so forth. For example, if the variable *$filename* is supposed to contain a UNIX file name (no slashes allowed), the following pattern match will extract the name into a variable named *$untainted_name*.

```
$filename =~ /([\w.-]+)$/;
$untainted_name = $1;
```

$untainted_name can now be used without activating Perl's taint warnings. Note that it is *not* sufficient to perform a string substitution or translation on a tainted variable. Another thing to be aware of is that the taint checks do not apply to strings used to open files for reading, only those opened for writing.

Non-Shell System Calls

Another useful Perl feature is an obscure syntactic variant of the *system()* and *exec()* calls, which allows Perl scripts to invoke subprocesses without going through an intermediate shell. This avoids the possibility that stray shell metacharacters will have unanticipated effects. The difference is subtle. Instead of invoking a subprocess in this way:

```
system "/usr/bin/sort $file1 $file2";
```

invoke it this way:

```
system "/usr/bin/sort",$file1,$file2;
```

When the *system()* and *exec()* functions are invoked with a single string argument, as shown in the first example, it passes the entire string to the shell using */bin/sh -c*. In contrast, when either of these functions is given a list of arguments to execute, the function directly executes the command named in the first argument using the C library *execve()* call. No shell is involved; hence, shell metacharacters have no special significance. When possible, this syntax should be used.

Non-Shell Pipes

A related trick can be used to open a pipe without involving a shell. It uses another obscure Perl syntactical feature, the special `|-` and `-|` file names. Opening `|-` causes Perl to fork and attaches the file handle in the parent process to the standard input of the child process. Opening `-|` causes a fork as well, but this time the child processes' standard output is connected to the parent script's file handle. The idiom for reading from an external command without invoking a shell is

```
open(SORT,"-|") || exec "/usr/bin/sort",$file1,$file2;
while (<SORT>) {
     # do something
}
close SORT;
```

Here's the idiom for writing to an external command.

```
open(SORT,"|-") || exec "/usr/bin/sort",$flag1,$flag2
while $line (@lines) {
   print SORT $line,"\n";
}
close SORT;
```

The Perlfunc and Perlsec manual pages have more information on these features, as does the book *Programming Perl5,* by Christiansen, Schwartz, and Wall.

CGI Wrappers

The fact that all CGI scripts run with the identity and permissions of the Web server process can cause problems for Web site hosting services. Such services may host hundreds of virtual Web sites, each maintained by a different set of authors, none of whom knows about the others. The problem occurs if the hosting service allows authors to add executable CGI scripts to their sites. Because all CGI scripts run as the same user, one author can easily write a script to trash another author's files or to peek at confidential information stored in a different author's Web site. Once the damage is done, it can be difficult to track down the source of the problem because all CGI script processes use the same user ID. A similar problem is encountered by many academic Web servers, in which students' Web pages are stored in user-supported directories accessed by URLs beginning with *~username.*

The simplest solution to this problem is to forbid untrusted Web authors from installing CGI scripts. Alternatively, one could propose a system in which authors submit their scripts for security reviews. The scripts are then installed only after they check out. In many cases, however, neither of these solutions is practical.

On UNIX systems, CGI wrapper programs attempt to circumvent the problem. Scripts are not run directly by the server but, rather, via a small SUID program that changes its identity to that of the script's author prior to running the script. Because each CGI script now runs with its author's permissions, each author is accountable for her script's actions.

The downside of this approach is that CGI scripts now execute with permissions that allow them to make modifications to their authors' files and directories. If the script is poorly written, a malicious remote user might use it to vandalize an author's Web pages.

Sites that use recent versions of the Apache server can use the *suexec* wrapper. It comes in the form of an SUID program that runs externally to Apache. When properly installed and configured, *suexec* will execute CGI scripts with the permissions of an alternative user and group. It will also log the scripts it runs, helping you to track down misbehaving programs.

The *suexec* wrapper is activated in two different circumstances.

1. When the CGI script is associated with a virtual host and the corresponding *<VirtualHost>* section contains *User* and *Group* directives. In this case, the script will be executed with the permissions of the user and group given by the two directives.
2. When the CGI script is in a user-supported *~username* directory—in which case, the script is executed with the user's permissions.

The first scenario is unusual because the *User* and *Group* directives are generally not allowed in *<VirtualHost>* sections. They are associated with the main server's configuration rather than with virtual host's. These directives are legal only when the *suexec* wrapper is in use. A simplified set of declarations for two virtual hosts would look like this.

```
<VirtualHost www.capricorn.org>
   ServerName www.capricorn.org
   ServerAdmin webmaster@capricorn.org
   ScriptAlias /cgi-bin/ /home/web/capricorn/cgi-bin/
   DocumentRoot /home/web/capricorn/htdocs/
   User  capricorn
   Group capricorn
</VirtualHost>
<VirtualHost www.zoo.com>
   ServerName www.zoo.com
   ServerAdmin webmaster@zoo.com
   ScriptAlias /cgi-bin/ /home/web/zoo/cgi-bin/
   DocumentRoot /home/web/zoo/htdocs/
   User  zoo
   Group zoo
</VirtualHost>
```

In this example, CGI scripts for *www.capricorn.org* run as user *capricorn*, and scripts for *www.zoo.com* run as *zoo*.

No special configuration is needed to handle the CGI scripts in user-supported directories beyond the need to enable them. The following *<Location>* section treats all files in URLs of the form */~username/cgi-bin/* as CGI scripts.

```
<Location /~*/cgi-bin>
   SetHandler cgi-script
   Options ExecCGI
</Location>
```

Before *suexec* will run a CGI script in SUID mode, it performs a series of consistency checks.

- The process that launched the wrapper belongs to the Web user.
- The script to be launched is located within the document root.
- The target user and group correspond to valid accounts on the system.
- The target user is not the superuser.
- The script is not itself SUID or SGID.
- The script is not writable by its group or other users.
- The script is owned by the target user and group.

Although most of these restrictions are sensible, the last one may be a problem in virtual hosting environments. The requirement that the script to be launched must be owned by the target user and group means that the script can write to itself and possibly to other files in the virtual site's document tree. This opens up the possibility that a subverted script could be used to vandalize a virtual site's HTML files. A better solution might be to have the virtual host run *suexec* with user and group permissions that do not overlap with those of Web authors. On this book's companion Web site, you'll find a patch to *suexec.c* that relaxes this restriction but adds the new restriction that the script cannot modify itself.

For non-Apache sites, the *cgiwrap* utility, written by Nathan Neulinger, provides similar functionality for NCSA *httpd*, Netscape servers, and CERN *httpd*. Another UNIX wrapper utility, *sbox* (written by myself), adds to *cgiwrap*'s functionality by calling the *chroot()* function to run CGI scripts in a restricted portion of the directory tree. I am unaware of a wrapper utility for Windows NT-based servers.

Checklist

1. What CGI scripts/server modules are installed on your site, and what does each one do?

   ❍ I don't know, there are too many!

   Poorly written CGI scripts are the greatest source of security holes on Web sites. Don't get bitten by that buggy example script left over from the initial installation.

2. Are there any general-purpose interpreters in the scripts directory?

   ☑ No
   ❍ Yes

   General-purpose interpreters, such as Perl, *command.com*, or any of the UNIX shells have no place in the scripts directory.

3. Do your compiled scripts/modules allocate any static buffers?

   ☑ No. All buffers are allocated dynamically.

   ❍ Of course. Is there any other way?

   Memory overflow bugs can compromise a Web site in short order. Avoid allocating static buffers, if at all possible. Check the length of strings and other structures before copying them.

4. Do you check user input before passing it to a shell?

   ❍ No

   ☑ Yes

   All user-supplied input should be checked before passing it through a command shell, an interpreter, or any external program.

5. Do you check file names supplied by users before opening them?

   ❍ No

   ☑ Yes

   File names should be examined carefully before opening them. Strip out absolute and relative path information and funny characters. Be particularly alert for file names that refer to the .. parent directory.

6. Do you check user-supplied input before writing it to disk?

   ❍ No

   ☑ Yes

   Allowing users to write raw HTML to disk is often a bad idea. It's better to strip out HTML tags, server-side includes, and other sources of active content.

7. Do your site's CGI scripts log their actions?

   ❍ No

   ☑ Yes

   Log everything. It's often the only way to track down small problems before they become large ones.

8. Do your site's CGI scripts use a standard CGI parsing library?

   ❍ No

   ☑ Yes

   Learn from other people's experience. If a well-tested CGI library is available for your development language, use it.

9. What language do you use for CGI scripting?

   - ☑ C
   - ☑ Perl
   - ☑ Java
   - ☑ Visual Basic
   - ❍ C-shell

   Almost any language can be used for CGI scripts. Most are equally secure (or insecure), although Perl holds a slight edge by virtue of its taint-check facility. Command shells are the exception. It's difficult to write a secure CGI script in a shell scripting language.

10. How do your scripts/modules handle temporary files?

   - ☑ They create them with care not to clobber existing files or to disclose confidential information.
   - ❍ What, me worry?

   Temporary files can be exploited in a variety of ways by unscrupulous users. Follow the guidelines above for manipulating temporary files.

11. Do your scripts run SUID/SGID?

   - ☑ None of them do.
   - ☑ A few do, but they perform extensive consistency checking before doing anything dangerous.
   - ❍ Some do, but they don't do any special checking.
   - ❍ All our scripts are SUID to root.

   SUID/SGID permissions allow you to give selected CGI scripts more privileges than the Web server itself can give. Such scripts should be used sparingly, and they should check their environment suspiciously before doing anything significant. Do not run any CGI scripts with superuser privileges.

12. Do your Perl scripts use the taint check and warning switches?

   - ❍ No
   - ☑ Yes

   Perl-based CGI scripts should run with taint checks turned on (the *-T* switch). Cautious developers should use the *-w* switch to turn on verbose warnings, as well.

13. If your server hosts multiple virtual Web sites, how do you handle authors who want to install their own CGI scripts?

- ☑ User-supported CGI scripts are not supported.
- ☑ We use a CGI wrapper to run each author's scripts with distinct permissions.
- ❍ Authors are allowed to install CGI scripts without restriction.

User-supported CGI scripts can be a menace to other authors' sites, as well as to the server as a whole. If you allow user-supported CGI scripts, strongly consider using a wrapper script such as *suexec* or *cgiwrap*.

Online Resources

Latro

http://www.perl.com/perl/news/latro-announce.html

php

http://www.vex.net/php/

CGI.pm, CGI::Carp (Perl CGI modules)

http://www.genome.wi.mit.edu/ftp/pub/software/WWW/
These are also part of the standard Perl 5.004 distribution.

Cookie Specification

http://cgi.netscape.com/newsref/std/cookie_spec.html

cgic CGI Library for C

http://www.boutell.com/cgic/

C++ CGI Library

http://sweetbay.will.uiuc.edu/cgi%2b%2b/

LWP Library for Perl

http://www.perl.com/CPAN/modules/by-module/LWP/

CGIWrap

http://www.umr.edu/~cgiwrap/

Sbox

http://www.genome.wi.mit.edu/~lstein/sbox/

Printed Resources

Christiansen, Tom, Schwartz, Randal, and Wall, Larry, *Programming Perl5* (O'Reilly & Associates, 1995).

The definitive book on the Perl programming language also contains much good advice on safe scripting.

Chapter 13

Remote Authoring and Administration

To keep a Web server secure, you have to keep most people out (except for legitimate browsing, of course). However, some people—the site's Web authors, developers, and administrators—have a legitimate right to get into the Web server and make changes. The challenge is to open the doors just wide enough to give legitimate users the level of access they need without burdening them with awkward restrictions.

Most sites have some form of remote authoring and administration facility, whether it be a simple text login, or a fancy Web publishing tool. This chapter focuses on providing this type of service securely, with particular attention to Microsoft's FrontPage product.

Degrees of Trust

The security requirements for remote authoring and administration issues are different from site to site. For simplicity, we'll divide Web sites into three categories.

1. **Few Authors, Complete Trust** The Web server is a small Internet site or designed for in-house (intranet) use only. A small number of authors and Web administrators are responsible for the site. Because they trust each other, security policy allows one author to make modifications to another's documents. The server is protected from untrusted outsiders by a firewall or strong access restrictions.

2. **Many Authors, Read-Only Trust** The Web server is a large intranet or Internet site with many pages. The responsibility of maintaining the site is divided among a large number of authors, each of whom is responsible for a different part of the Web tree, such as a department's pages. All authors are allowed to read each other's pages locally as well as remotely, and to build onto the document tree. However, one author isn't trusted to modify another author's pages. This situation is also typical of many academic situations, where students are responsible for maintaining their home pages.
3. **Many Authors, No Trust** The Web site is large and has restricted areas that are not available to the general public. Authors are not trusted to read each other's pages, let alone modify them. Ideally, one author should not even know that the other authors exist. This situation is typical of Web presence providers who host virtual Web sites. One client's authors shouldn't have access to another client's private pages. This configuration is also sometimes used by corporate intranet servers.

You should enforce your site's security policy at multiple levels. Use the host's login facilities to prevent unauthorized users from connecting to the system. Use the operating system's file system permissions to ensure that authors have read and write privileges only for the parts of the Web document root that they have a right to modify. Use the remote authoring system's tools to exclude those who aren't authors, developers, or administrators.

Controlling Access to the Web Server Host

To do their work, Web authors have to be able to read and write HTML files located within the Web server's document tree, to upload various types of image and sound files, and to move, delete, and rename files with a minimum of hassle. They should not be able to mess with the server's configuration tools (unless they also have Web administrative responsibilities) or have access to parts of the host that are unrelated to the Web.

There are four main ways to give authors access to the server host.

1. Network log-on
2. File sharing
3. FTP access
4. Web server publishing extensions

Network Log-On

If the Web server machine is physically available to an author, she can sit down at the keyboard and start typing. This works well if there's only one author, poorly if there are two authors, and not at all if there are three or more (unless you convince each author to take a different eight-hour work shift).

Network log-on is one option to allow multiple authors to share the same server. On UNIX systems, give each author a login account on the system and let her log in with TELNET to get text-based access to the system. For GUI programs, the ubiquitous X Windows System allows users to run graphics-intensive applications on the server.

Windows NT has similar facilities. Although the NT server has built-in support for incoming TELNET connections, it gives access only to the NT command line. The lack of a graphical user interface severely limits its usefulness (if you need it, incoming TELNET can be found in the *NT Server Resource Kit* available at most software stores and mail-order houses). To run graphical programs remotely, several third-party products allow users to run applications on the server while viewing them on their desktop machines. These products vary dramatically in price and features.

- Symantec *pcANYWHERE*
- Tektronix *WinDD*
- Insignia *NTrigue*
- NCD *WinCenter*
- Citrix *WinFrame*

At the low end, pcANYWHERE offers a simple "remote control" system for Windows clients only. WinDD offers multiuser access from both Microsoft Windows and X Windows clients, and NTrigue offers Macintosh and Java clients. At the high end, WinFrame's WAN product offers a host of features plus data encryption and the ability to run NT applications within a Web browser via an ActiveX control.

While direct network logon has the advantage of simplicity, it has some problems, as well. The most serious of these is that a login account gives the author access to more than Web server documents. Once logged in, a user can look around the file system, run programs, and rattle door handles. Unscrupulous authors may attempt to gain more access than they should have.

Eavesdropping is also a problem. The basic TELNET and X Windows protocols encrypt neither login passwords nor the data transmitted within the session. Passwords are usually encrypted in NT-based remote access systems, but the data stream may or may not be, depending on the product.

It's a good policy to keep the number of login accounts on the Web server to a minimum. If you do allow authors login access to the host machine, make sure the file system permissions don't allow authors to see or change what they shouldn't. If you allow logins across an unsecure network, such as the Internet, it's prudent to use secure variants of the login protocols. On UNIX and NT systems, you can use the Secure Shell (see the Secure Login with SSH box). SSH can also make X Windows sessions secure. On UNIX systems, other good alternatives include SSL-Telnet, part of the SSLEay distribution, and the *stel* program.

File Sharing

An easy way to make the Web document hierarchy available to authors without giving them login privileges for the host is to use the operating system's file sharing facility to make part or all of the document root a network-shared directory. Authors then just mount the shared directory on their desktop machines and work with it as if it were a local disk. Windows NT systems can do this using their built-in file sharing system. UNIX systems will probably use NFS.

The file sharing solution is great for intranets, but it may not be the best idea for Web servers that are connected to the Internet. For one thing, in order for file sharing to work properly, the Web server host must have access to each author's account information. Otherwise, file and directory permissions won't work as expected. This means that each author must either have a local account on the host or the host must be able to find the account information in a network database, such as an NT domain controller or a UNIX NIS server. If the host has access to this database, unfortunately, then the Web server does too, and it's possible that the server can be tricked into revealing it to an outsider.

For another thing, a variety of security loopholes have been discovered in both NFS and Windows NT's file sharing. Many vendors recommend that you turn off sharing in systems that are connected to the Internet, a step I recommend as well.

If your organization uses a firewall system, you may be able to set things up so that the Web server can share files with machines within your local area network while blocking accesses from foreign IP addresses. This technical solution is discussed in more detail in Chapter 14.

If the Web server is on an intranet and the main issue is to allow employees to work on pages from home, you might consider setting up a remote access dial-in service. On Windows NT networks, technical solutions include the Remote Access Server (RAS) and the Point-to-Point Tunnelling Protocol (PPTP). On UNIX networks, it's straightforward to set up a basic Point-to-Point Protocol (PPP) server. Instructions for setting up dial-ins for the two operating systems are given respectively in *Running Windows NT Server 4.0* and *TCP/IP Network Administration* (see Printed Resources). Dial-ins can open up a whole new can of security worms—make sure you understand what you're doing!

FTP Access

FTP, the File Transfer Protocol, is a practical way to provide authors with the ability to upload, download, and rename files in a restricted directory without giving them undue access to the system. It works as well across the Internet as it does across an intranet and is supported by client programs on

Secure Login with SSH

Whenever a Web author logs in to a server across the Internet in order to update a page, there's a possibility that an eavesdropper armed with a packet-sniffer program will intercept and read her user name and password. One way to avoid this risk is to use cryptography to protect the session from prying eyes.

The Secure Shell (SSH), a freeware product developed in Finland, provides an effective way to encrypt network log sessions. SSH uses a combination of public key and symmetric cryptography to authenticate one machine to another and to create an encrypted communications channel between them. Unlike SSL, you do not need to purchase server or client certificates in order to use strong cryptography. And because the product was developed in Europe, it gives users outside U.S. borders access to strong cryptography, unlike SSL-based products whose export versions are crippled to meet U.S. government export restrictions.

Secure Shell's main use is to replace the *telnet*, *rlogin*, *rsh*, and *rcp* programs with secure alternatives. It also automatically encrypts X Windows sessions on the machine on which it's installed. However, it can do more than that. One of the interesting things you can do with Secure Shell is to encrypt arbitrary TCP/IP connections, such as HTTP and FTP channels. This is done by starting a secure proxy program on your local machine and pointing your network client (for instance, the Web browser) at the proxy. The proxy will encrypt the request and tunnel it across the encrypted channel to the real server at the other end of the connection. This allows you to use HTML editors, graphical Web managers, and other products that don't support cryptography directly, and to encrypt communications on a Web server that doesn't have a server certificate installed.

To create an SSH proxy to a remote Web server, first pick an unused high-numbered port on your local machine, such as 1234. Now use the *ssh* program to log in to the machine that runs the Web server, giving it the *-L* option to create a proxy.

```
lstein> ssh -L1234:www.capricorn.com:80 www.capricorn.com
lstein's password: ********
Last login: Mon May  5 12:42:56 1997 from cajun.spice.com
www>
```

The format of the argument passed to *-L* is *localPort:remoteHost:remotePort*. Here we're requesting that the proxy listen to local port 1234 and forward its communications across the secure channel to port 80 on *www.capricorn.com*. Now launch a Web browser on your local machine and have it fetch *http://localhost:1234/*. Things will act exactly as if you'd pointed the browser at *http://www.capricorn.com/* except that the conversation is now safe from sniffing. When you are finished using the browser, log out of the remote machine.

The UNIX incarnation of Secure Shell is freeware. Commercial versions for Windows and Macintosh systems are available from Datafellows, Inc. Contact information is given at the end of this chapter.

all operating systems. An increasing number of WYSIWYG HTML editors and Web site organizers use FTP as their underlying protocol.

The main disadvantage with FTP is that, like TELNET, the unmodified protocol sends user names and passwords across the network in the clear. If authors are working across the Internet, this exposes FTP to the possibility that an eavesdropper will intercept this information and use it to make unauthorized changes to the Web site. Nor is the content of a file page encrypted as it's uploaded with FTP, making it possible for an unscrupulous person to intercept the document or even modify it as it passes by.

The risk of password interception can be mitigated using a variety of one-time password schemes (see the One-Time Passwords box). You can eliminate the second problem by encrypting the document during transit. One software solution is the Secure Shell (see the Secure Login with SSH box in this chapter). Another solution is a modified FTP server that uses the secure sockets layer (SSL). A freeware implementation of an encrypting FTP server is available with the SSLEay distribution. However SSL-aware FTP clients are uncommon.

Specific advice on setting up an FTP daemon to accept incoming files from Web authors is given in a later section.

Web Server Publishing Extensions

The Web server itself can be used to upload and manage files. Some high-end servers understand the HTTP PUT and DELETE commands, which were written into the protocol for the purpose of remote Web publishing. Less savvy servers can be turned into Web publishing engines by installing a CGI script. A properly formatted request directed to the CGI script will allow files to be uploaded, renamed, or deleted. The FrontPage remote Web management and authoring tool uses this approach.

Using the Web server for authoring has several advantages over FTP. One advantage is that you have only one server to worry about, rather than two. Another is that the same access control system that restricts end users from reading protected pages is used for file uploading, as well. Finally, both Web clients and servers speak SSL, allowing authoring sessions to be encrypted.

This chapter provides advice on setting up FrontPage securely and briefly discusses supporting the PUT command used by the Netscape Navigator Gold editor.

Remote Authoring Via FTP

Authenticated FTP is an easy way to allow Web authors to upload new pages to the Web server without giving them full login privileges. Several popular HTML editors, as well as Microsoft's Internet Publishing Wizard, make FTP-based uploads relatively painless.

One-Time Passwords

Passwords are problematic because of their vulnerability to sniffing and guessing. A popular solution to the problem is to use a one-time password system, in which the password changes in an unpredictable way every time it's used. Because the passwords keep changing, they are immune to guessing, and even if a password is intercepted by an eavesdropper, it's valueless because it will never be used again.

Three widely used one-time password systems are Bellcore's S/Key, Security Dynamics' SECURID, and Digital Pathways' SecureNet. S/Key is the oldest and simplest of the systems. For each authorized user, the system administrator runs a program that generates and prints out a list of passwords. The user uses each password in order, crossing it off the list when finished. (A less clumsy version allows the user to run a program on his home computer or laptop to generate the next valid password).

In the SECURID system, users carry around a small device that looks like a digital clock. It displays a password on its LCD screen, which changes every 60 to 90 seconds. When she needs to log in, the user types in the currently displayed password. By using a synchronized clock, the server is able to determine that the user's password is correct for the current date and time.

A slightly more complex login procedure is used by the SecureNet system, in which each user carries a small pocket-calculator-like device. At login time, the remote machine instructs the user to type a random number into the device. Using this number, the device calculates and displays the current password.

The S/Key system is distributed as freeware, while SECURID and SecureNet are commercial products. Check with the vendors for the list of operating systems and server software that their products support.

It's important to distinguish authenticated FTP from anonymous FTP. In anonymous FTP, anyone wishing to connect to your FTP site logs in with a user name of *anonymous* and an arbitrary password. The FTP server takes the remote user to a special anonymous FTP area, where the user can browse and download files. Uploads, deletes, and file renames are forbidden. There's rarely a compelling reason to run an anonymous FTP site these days. All its functions can be done more quickly and easily by a Web server.

In authenticated FTP, the user logs into the FTP server with a user name and password recognized by the host. If the name and password check out, the server drops the user into her home directory. She is now free to do anything that file and directory permissions allow, including file uploads and deletions. This is the type of FTP that you want to use for remote authoring. In the next sections, I'll show you how to set up this type of server for incoming FTP, first for the Microsoft Internet Information Server, and then for the standard UNIX FTP server.

Incoming FTP with Microsoft IIS

The FTP server that comes with the Microsoft IIS is remarkably straightforward. Start by creating accounts for all the Web authors that you wish to have access to the server using the standard *User Manager* application. Each author account should be given the right to *Access this computer from network*, but not to *Log on locally* unless they will occasionally be working at the server host machine itself. If the Web site is on an intranet and your authors are all on the local area network, uncheck the *Password never expires* and *User cannot change password* options. If the authors will be working from remote Internet locations, make sure that *Password never expires* is checked. Otherwise, the password will expire and the user will have no way of changing it. If the Web server participates in an NT domain and these users are already defined globally on the domain controller, you can skip this step entirely.

The groups that you assign Web authors to should reflect your site's security policies. If the Web site is small and you have only a few people with authoring privileges to worry about, create a single local group named *Web Authors*, if you haven't done so already, and add the accounts to the group. If the authors have complete trust in each other, you can give this group full control of the Web document root directory. Otherwise, you should arrange things so that members of *Web Authors* can create new files and subdirectories within the document root but can't interfere with files created by others. Both configurations were described in Chapter 9.

If there are a large number of authors, you may need to create additional groups to reflect the portion of the site they're responsible for. For example, authors who are responsible for the customer support pages could be added to *Support Page Authors*. Then modify the access control list for the subdirectory that holds those pages to give members of this group write access. It's usually simpler in the long run to grant access rights by group rather than by user name, even if the group initially holds a single person only.

If you are hosting Web sites for several organizations, none of which trust the others, create a different local group for each client and set up the permissions on each document root to forbid one client from accessing another client's portion of the tree.

Be aware that every group a user belongs to grants him additional privileges. By default, the primary group for all new user accounts is *Users*. This is appropriate for users who are indeed employees of your organization, but it's not right for Internet-based authors, who need have access only to the document root. For these users, remove them from *Users* and add them to *Guests* instead. This restricts their ability to access sensitive parts of the server host should they ever find a way to log in.

After setting up accounts for the Web authors and adjusting the access control lists on the Web document root to reflect their various privileges, open up the *Internet Service Manager* application. Find the line corresponding to the host's FTP services and double-click it to open up its Properties window (Figure 13.1). When first installed, FTP is configured to allow anonymous FTP; authenticated access is disallowed. This is the exact opposite of what you want. On the page labeled Service, deselect the checkboxes labeled "Allow anonymous connections" and "Anonymous only connections" and click "Apply." An alert will appear to warn you that FTP transmits passwords across the network in unencrypted form. Click "OK." This is an unavoidable risk of using FTP (however, the Secure Shell can be used to work around it).

Like a Web server, the IIS FTP server uses the idea of a document root that all inbound and outbound files are restricted to. By default, the FTP document root is *C:\InetPub\FTProot*. To allow authors to modify the Web document tree, you'll want to change this to be the same as the Web document root.

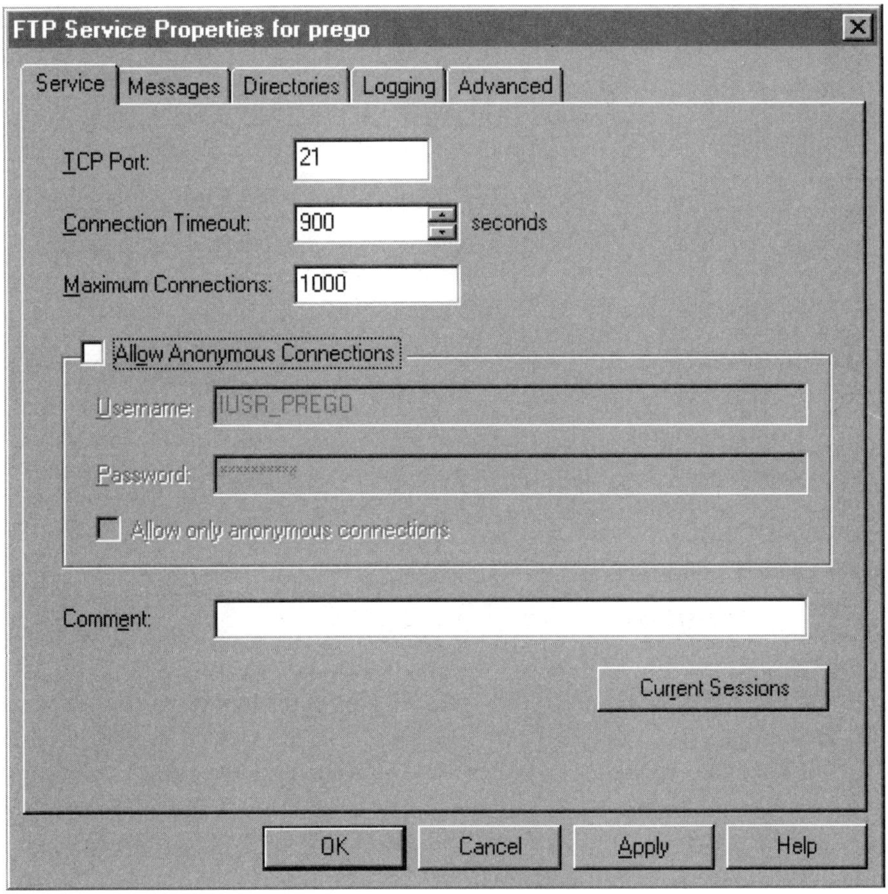

FIGURE 13.1 The Windows NT Internet Service Manager supports incoming nonanonymous FTP.

Choose the Directories page of the properties window (Figure 13.2). A scrolling list at the top of the page lists all the directories that the FTP server has access to, starting with the default directory marked with a "home" icon. Change the home directory to *C:\InetPub\WWWRoot*, or whatever is appropriate for your Web server's document tree. Now select both read and write access by checking the boxes at the bottom of the window.

If the FTP server isn't already configured to do so, arrange for it to be started up automatically at system boot time by opening the services control panel, selecting the FTP server from the list of services, and choosing *Startup...->Automatic*.

From another machine, you should now be able to FTP to the server host and log in using an author's account name and password. Confirm that you can upload new files (using the *put* command) and create new directories (using the *mkdir* command).

Confirm that you can't make alterations to parts of the document tree that should be off limits or see parts of the file system outside the document root. If you attempt to log in as anonymous, you should be denied access.

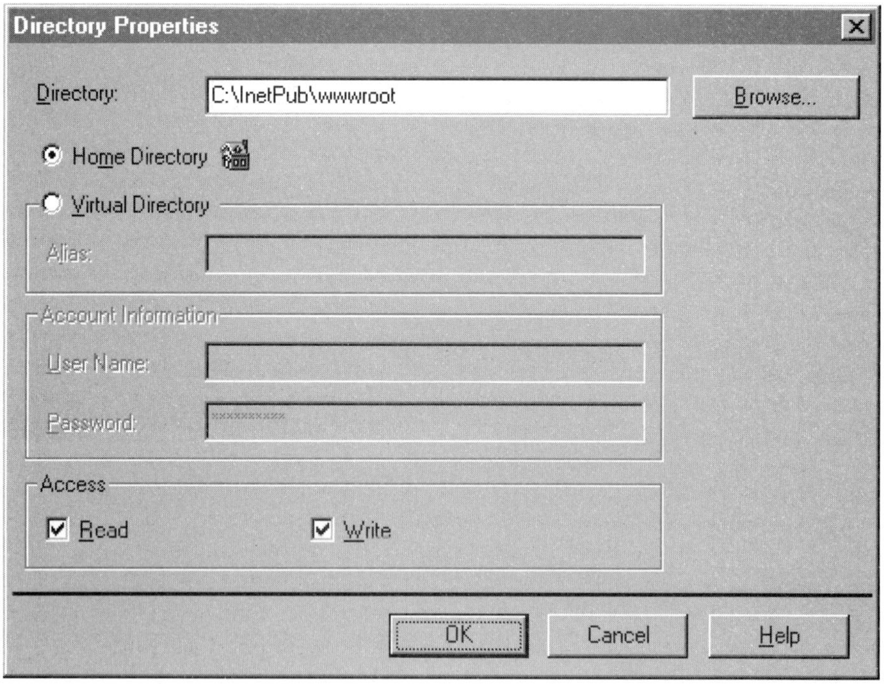

FIGURE 13.2 To allow remote authors to FTP into the Web root, add the Web root directory to the list of directories recognized by the FTP server.

Incoming FTP on UNIX Systems

Setting up incoming FTP on a UNIX box is almost as simple, but there are a couple of interesting twists.

As with Windows NT, you should start by creating user accounts for Web authors if they aren't already defined. Authors' group membership should reflect how much you trust them and whether they trust each other. For a small site with a few authors that trust each other completely, you can add them all to a *webauth* group and make the Web document tree read/write for members of this group. For a medium-size site with many authors, create groups that reflect each author's responsibilities and set the access permissions on the Web subdirectories to grant write-access only to the group responsible for that part of the site.

Unless you're planning to give authors shell access to the host, assign the account passwords yourself. If you have a password aging system installed on your server, be sure to set the expiration time to infinity; otherwise, authors' passwords will expire and they won't be able to change them. For the Web authors' convenience, you should set their home directories to the part of the Web document tree that they have jurisdiction over. This may be the top of the document directory itself or a subdirectory somewhere.

We now come to the first twist: adding user accounts without providing shell access. Unless authors need to have TELNET access to the system, you should make it impossible for authors to log in to the system directly. The easiest way to do this is to set the shell listed in the last field of */etc/passwd* to an executable that doesn't provide a command shell. The */bin/sync* command, which has no untoward side effects, is frequently used for this purpose, but I prefer to set FTP user's login shell to a Bourne shell script named */etc/ftponly*.

```
#!/bin/sh
echo "This account is for FTP only."
exit
```

If the user attempts to log in locally or via the network, he'll receive a warning message and be disconnected. After modifying */etc/passwd* in this way, you should add */etc/ftponly* to the list of valid login shells maintained in the file */etc/shells*. Many FTP daemons refuse to run if the user who's trying to log in doesn't have one of the shell executables listed in this file.

If you find an account named *ftp* while you're adding Web authors, you may want to remove it. When present, this account activates anonymous FTP—which you probably don't need.

The FTP is run under the control of the *inetd* super daemon. Open the *inetd* configuration file */etc/inetd.conf* and add something like the following line, if a similar one isn't present already.

```
ftp     stream  tcp     nowait  root    /usr/sbin/in.ftpd       in.ftpd
```

If you've edited */etc/inetd.cof*, you'll need to restart the inetd daemon by sending it an `HUP` signal.

You should now go to an FTP client on a different machine and confirm that you can FTP to the Web server host and log in with a Web author's user name and password. Confirm that you can upload new files (with the *put* command) and create subdirectories in places where the Web author is allowed. Confirm that such actions are refused elsewhere. From the server side, look at the group ownership and modes of the newly uploaded files. If they are not what you wish (for example, you want the uploaded files to be group-writable, but they're not), you may have to change the FTP server's default umask. On some FTP servers, you can do this by adding a *-u* flag to the *inetd.conf* entry.

```
in.ftpd -u 002
```

If the group ownerships are not what you desire, a handy trick to remember is that turning a directory's set-group-id bit on (*chmod g+s .*) will cause all new files and subdirectories to take the group ownership of the directory.

Unlike the IIS FTP server, when a remote user uses authenticated FTP to access a UNIX machine, she is not restricted to a single document root. She can browse through much of the host's file system on a read-only basis. Though authors cannot make any unauthorized changes, you may be uncomfortable giving them this much information about the host's configuration.

The popular Washington University FTP server, *wu-ftpd*, offers several FTP extensions, including one that restricts users to a subdirectory. Internally, it uses the UNIX *chroot* command, which makes the subdirectory of your choice seem like the / directory to FTP users. This ensures that Web authors cannot gain access to anything outside the Web document root.

wu-ftpd recognizes three types of accounts. "Anonymous," for anonymous FTP; "real," which is what we've been calling authenticated logins; and "guest," authenticated logins that are limited to a specified subdirectory. The last type is the kind we want.

Three steps are involved in getting *wu-ftpd* set up for guest access. First, edit *wu-ftpd*'s configuration file to tell it to treat members of the *Web Author* group(s) as guests. Then modify */etc/passwd* to put *Web Authors'* home directories in a particular format recognized by the FTP server. Finally, add some files to the Web document root directory so that the FTP server can successfully perform a *chroot* operation into it.

The file */etc/ftpaccess* contains most of *wu-ftpd*'s configuration directives. To enable guest access, add a line like the following.

```
guestgroup webauth
```

The *guestgroup* directive tells *wu-ftpd* to treat any individual who belongs to the indicated group(s) as a guest. You can list a single group, as shown in the example, or indicate multiple groups, separated by spaces.

wu-ftpd uses the guest user's home directory to figure out where to *chroot* to. To do this, it looks for a directory path in the format */document /root/./home/directory*. Everything to the left of the dot is the directory that *wu-ftpd* will *chroot* to. Everything to the right of the dot is a subdirectory in which the user will be placed when she first connects via FTP. This is a convenience feature. To give a concrete example, if the Web document root on your system is */web/htdocs* and you wish the author named *mabel* to start out in a like-named subdirectory, her */etc/passwd* entry should look like this.

```
mabel:passwd:520:150:Mabel Webauthor:/web/htdocs/./mabel:/etc/ftponly
```

When Mabel logs in, her / directory will actually be */web/htdocs*. Mabel's home directory will appear to be */mabel* from her point of view and */web/htdocs/mabel* from your point of view.

The final task is to make the Web document root compatible with *wu-ftpd*. In order for *wu-ftpd* to work after performing the *chroot* call, the document root must contain a miniature root file system containing skeletal */etc* and */bin* directories, and possibly */dev* and */lib* directories, as well. This is similar to the directory structure used for anonymous FTP. If your system came preconfigured for anonymous FTP, the simplest way to do this is to copy the relevant parts of the anonymous FTP directory over to your Web document root. If this isn't an option, set up the document root according to the instructions for anonymous FTP given in the *wu-ftpd* documentation. Detailed instructions are also given in Chapters 5 and 6 of the book *Managing Internet Information Services*. See Printed Resources at the end of this chapter.

If you run a virtual hosting service, you can have multiple FTP document roots, one for each client. By setting up each document root in this way, you can use this technique to completely insulate one client's authors from another's.

The Internet location for *wu-ftpd* is given at the end of this chapter. Be sure to obtain version 2.4.2-beta-12 or higher because earlier versions contained a security-related bug in signal handling.

Microsoft FrontPage

Most Web authoring tools use FTP internally in order to upload the HTML files on the author's personal machine to the Web server. The main limitation of this technique is that it prevents certain customizations that authors often want to make, such as password protecting their pages and creating CGI scripts. Web server publishing extensions circumvent this problem by using the Web server itself to provide file upload and manipulation capabilities.

Microsoft FrontPage is currently the major Web authoring and administrative tool in this category. With FrontPage, Web authors can remotely create and upload sophisticated sets of HTML pages using an intuitive graphical editor. By adding any of several "WebBots" (CGI scripts) to their pages, authors can create user comment forms, discussion groups, guestbooks, and other popular types of Web page. Authors can control access to their pages by protecting them with user names and passwords. FrontPage administrators can do everything authors can do and have the additional ability to create new top-level directories ("webs," in FrontPage parlance) and to create authoring accounts.

FrontPage comes in two halves. The client half, contained in the programs *FrontPage Editor* and *FrontPage Explorer*, are used by Web authors and Web administrators to edit documents and remotely administer the Web server. The server half, *FrontPage Extensions*, consists of a series of CGI scripts that run under the Web server's control. FrontPage extensions are available for a variety of popular UNIX and Windows-based Web servers.

FrontPage extensions pose an interesting challenge for secure installation. Together, the extensions are a large, but thinly documented, system that is most happy when it has asserted complete control over the server. The recommended configuration violates some of the common-sense rules for secure Web installation. And it doesn't help to know that earlier versions of the extensions are known to have contained a big security hole (see the A Security Hole in FrontPage box).

This section shows you how to install the FrontPage extensions in a way that minimizes their risk. Even if you don't use FrontPage, the path I follow to assess and remedy the risks should help you do the same when installing other types of Web publishing extensions.

FrontPage Extensions on UNIX

On UNIX systems, the FrontPage extensions are implemented as a series of CGI scripts. Their job is to upload new files to the document root, create new subdirectories within the document root, edit the server's access control files, and change FrontPage's own configuration files. One of FrontPage's CGI scripts is also responsible for implementing the WebBot functions that run discussion groups and guestbooks. FrontPage's scripts and their support files are located within the document root in a series of directories with obscure names like *_vti_bin* and *_vti_cnf*.

The FrontPage security dilemma is this: When its scripts are run, they're run with the permissions of the Web server user. For security, this user is ordinarily not allowed to change the Web's configuration files or modify its content in any way. However, in order for FrontPage to work at all, the Web user must be given write-access to the document root. For FrontPage to carry out its remote administration features, the Web user must be given access to the FrontPage configuration files and, for many UNIX servers, the configuration file for the Web server itself.

A Security Hole in FrontPage

Prior to version 2.0 of the FrontPage server extensions (both NT and UNIX versions), FrontPage contained a serious security hole. The *Discussion* and *Save Results* WebBots were designed to allow authors to create pages containing fill-out forms, which, when submitted, were saved to a file somewhere on the site where the authors and other users could view them. These WebBots were widely used to create guestbooks, chat rooms, and the like.

Unfortunately, neither the *Discussion* nor *Save Results* WebBots checked the contents of the fill-out forms for raw HTML. As a result, an unscrupulous remote user who understood how FrontPage's CGI scripts worked could place his own fill-out form in the file that the WebBot saved its results to. The user could craft the fill-out form in such a way that, when invoked, it saved *its* results to a file of the user's choosing, such as the site's main welcome page. This allowed malicious users to replace pages at will. If the site were poorly configured in other ways, such as having server-side includes enabled or allowing fill-out-form results to be processed by arbitrary programs, unauthorized users could exploit this hole to do even more serious damage to the system.

Since discovering the hole, Microsoft has modified the server extensions to check the contents of fill-out forms and remove raw HTML. This seems to have been effective in closing the hole. If you are running an older version of the FrontPage extensions, be sure to upgrade to the current version.

FrontPage documentation recommends making the entire document root owned by the Web server's user and group and giving all files user and group read/write permission. This configuration gives the FrontPage extensions the amount of control needed to create and edit documents. Unfortunately, it has several bad side effects.

1. If the Web server software is subverted, it can modify the content of any HTML file or CGI script within the document root.
2. If any FrontPage CGI script is subverted, it can modify any file in the document root, including ones that FrontPage didn't create.
3. If any non-FrontPage CGI script is subverted, it can modify the document root, including files and directories managed under FrontPage.
4. Because all files and subdirectories are owned by the same user, one Web author's documents have no file-system-based protection against meddling by another author. As long as all authors publish to the server from the Web, the Web server's access control restrictions (which can be managed through FrontPage) will prevent meddling. However, authors who upload files via TELNET or FTP are not bound by those rules.

5. Rogue programs or malicious actions launched by the FrontPage server cannot be distinguished from those launched by the server or non-FrontPage CGI scripts because they all run with the same user ID. This makes it difficult to track problems to their source.

The fix for these problems is to recognize that the Web server and the FrontPage scripts perform two different functions and need to be assigned to distinct user accounts. Instead of running the FrontPage extensions under the Web server account, create a new user named *fpage* and assign it to a group that has write permission for the document root. If groups are set up in the manner described in this book, the group will be *webauth*. Using the set-user-id and set-group-id bits, we will arrange for the FrontPage scripts to take on the *fpage* persona whenever they execute. Now the Web server and its CGI scripts will continue to run as a user that has read-only access to the document tree. FrontPage scripts, however, will have the write access they need to function correctly.

Back up your server and document roots before installing the FrontPage extensions. The installation procedure changes the contents of your document root and server configuration files, and you may want to return your server to a pristine state if something goes amiss. Following Microsoft's installation directions, use the *fpservadm.exe* program to install FrontPage onto your server, and create a remote administrator's account for your own use. You will probably have to be logged in as the superuser to do this.

Now comes the hard part of fixing up directory ownerships and permissions in the document root. The installation procedure will have created several new files and directories in the document root. There will be six new directories, named *images, _private, _vti_bin, _vti_cnf, _vgi_log, _vti_pvt,* and *_vti_txt*. Several of these directories contain multiple files and subdirectories. There will be a new access control file (named *.htaccess* on most UNIX servers) and two new files named *_vti_inf.html* and *postinfo.html*. Change all of these so that they are owned by user *fpage*, group *webauth*, and have user read/write access, group and other read-only access.

```
root# find _vti* images postinfo.html .htaccess -exec chown fpage.webauth {} \;
root# find _vti* images postinfo.html .htaccess -exec chmod 0755 {} \;
```

The document root should now look something like this.

```
drwxrwxr-x  13 fpage   webauth      1024 May 28 13:18 .
dr-xr-xr-x   7 root    webmaster    1024 May 28 10:12 ..
-rw-r--r--   1 fpage   webauth       341 May 28 11:46 .htaccess
drwxr-xr-x   2 fpage   webauth      1024 May 28 11:46 _private
drwxr-xr-x   4 fpage   webauth      1024 May 28 11:46 _vti_bin
drwxr-xr-x   2 fpage   webauth      1024 May 28 13:15 _vti_cnf
-rw-r--r--   1 fpage   webauth      1819 May 28 11:46 _vti_inf.html
drwxr-xr-x   2 fpage   webauth      1024 May 28 11:46 _vti_log
drwxr-xr-x   3 fpage   webauth      1024 May 28 13:18 _vti_pvt
drwxr-xr-x   2 fpage   webauth      1024 May 28 11:46 _vti_txt
[...]
```

For the FrontPage extensions to add new files to the document hierarchy, the document root must be writable by the FrontPage user. You can accomplish this either by making the document root owned by the *fpage* account or by making the directory writable by the *webauth* group. For reasons explained later, it's beneficial to do both.

The next step is to set the SUID and SGID bits on the FrontPage executables. On a newly installed system, there will be only three executables to modify. If you've already been running the FrontPage extensions for a while, however, there will be more executables to track down—three for each top-level directory managed by FrontPage. Enter the *_vti_bin* directory and set the SUID and SGID bits on the files *shtml.exe, _vti_aut/author.exe,* and *_vti_adm/admin.exe.*

```
root# chmod 6555 shtml.exe _vti_aut/author.exe _vti_ adm/admin.exe
```

An *ls* should now show this.

```
root# ls -lR
total 1500
drwxr-xr-x   2 fpauth   webauth     1024 May 28 11:46 _vti_adm/
drwxr-xr-x   2 fpauth   webauth     1024 May 28 11:46 _vti_aut/
-r-sr-sr-x   1 fpauth   webauth  1525901 Feb 12 07:55 shtml.exe*
_vti_adm:
total 1497
-r-sr-sr-x   1 fpauth   webauth  1524773 Feb 12 07:55 admin.exe*
_vti_aut:
total 1497
-r-sr-sr-x   1 fpauth   webauth  1524773 Feb 12 07:55 author.exe*
```

(You may notice that *admin.exe* and *author.exe* are identical in size. This is no coincidence. At least in version 2.0 of the extensions, they are identical in all but name.)

You can now restart the Web server and test things out. From the *FrontPage Explorer* client, you should be able to log in as an administrator, view the document tree, add new files, and edit old ones. The *Tools ->Permissions...* menu command allows you to add new administrative and authoring accounts, as well as to restrict browsing to certain end users (Figure 13.3). To add a new author to the list, select the "Add..." button, then type in the user's name and password. A set of three radio buttons controls the user's privilege level. You may choose browsing only, browsing and authoring, or browsing, authoring, and administrative privileges.

Confirm that while you are logged in as an administrator you can add new users and authors. Logged in under an author's account, confirm that you can edit and delete pages.

After using FrontPage to create a few files and directories remotely, check that their ownership and permissions look all right on the UNIX side. If all is well, the new files will look like this.

```
-rw-r--r--   1 fpauth   webauth      318 May 28 13:15 index.htm
```

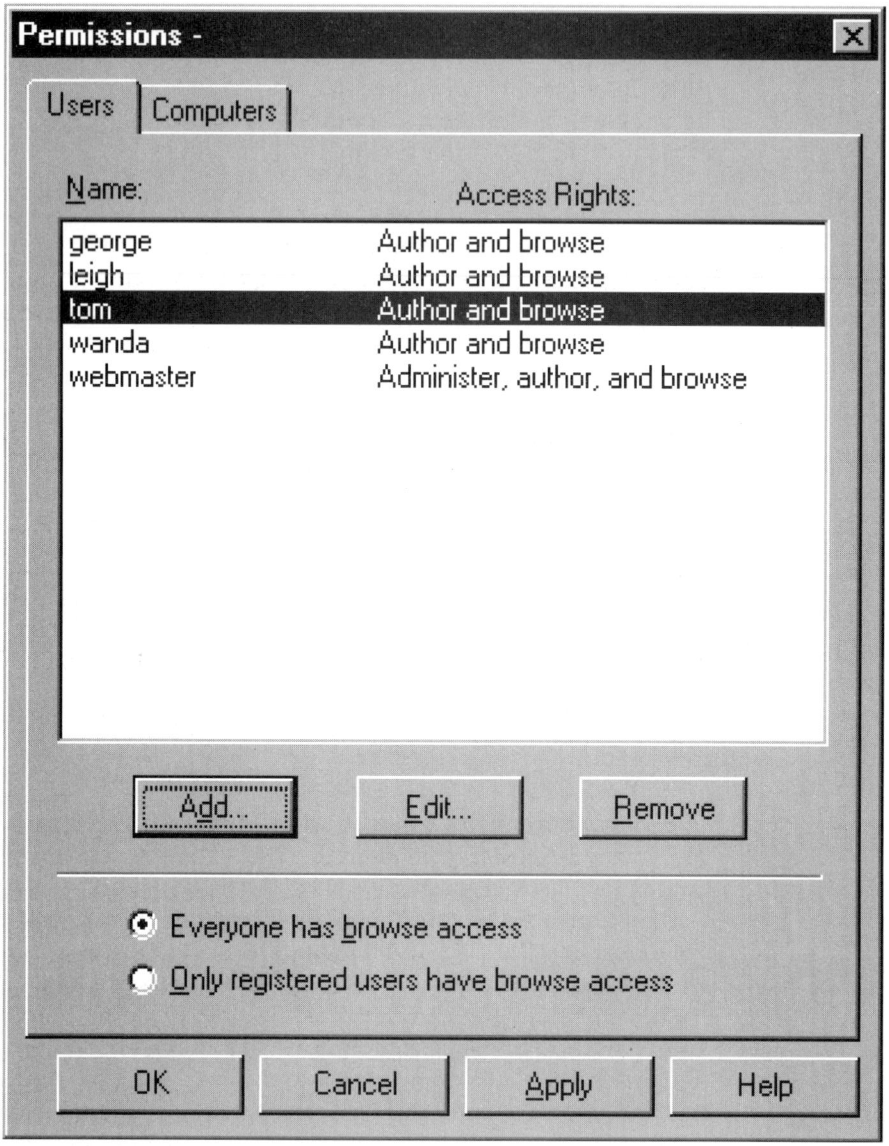

FIGURE 13.3 When Microsoft FrontPage talks to a non-IIS server, authoring and administration permission is granted to users on an individual basis.

Usually, you'll want a file created by FrontPage to be read/write by itself, read-only to group and others. If the *webauth* group had write permission, Web authors who are logged on locally or via FTP will be able to edit the files created by FrontPage, invalidating its internal bookkeeping. If this is not the behavior you are seeing, or it's not the behavior you want, you may need to modify the Web server processes' umask. The umask should be set using the shell's built-in *umask* command just before launching the Web server. Set it to 022 if you wish the files created by the FrontPage user to be read-only by the *webauth* group. Set it to 002 if you want FrontPage-managed files to be writable by *webauth*.

With the configuration given here, you may be unable to create new top-level directories from FrontPage Explorer. The problem is that with some Web servers, FrontPage tries to modify the main server configuration file every time it creates a new top-level directory. The configuration recommended by Microsoft suffers from this problem too. However, when running under the *fpauth* account, the FrontPage CGI scripts don't have write access to this file. If you can, it's safest to live with this problem and simply add new top-level directories manually by running the *fpservadm.exe* program while logged in to the server machine as a Web administrator. If this isn't feasible, here is a workaround.

Find the FrontPage executable *_vti_bin/_vti_adm/admin.exe*. This is the script that's invoked when the FrontPage client is asked to perform an administrative function, such as adding new top-level directories. Change this script's group to the one you use for Web administrators—for instance, *webmaster*. When this is done, reset the user and group SUID bits.

```
root# chgrp  webmaster  _vti_bin/_vti_adm/admin.exe
root# chmod  ug+s  _vti_bin/_vti_adm/admin.exe
```

Now go to the directory that holds the server's configuration files and give it *webmaster* group ownership and make it group-writable. Similarly, make the configuration files contained within it writable by the *webmaster* group.

After you've made these changes, *admin.exe* will run with the permissions of the *webmaster* group, allowing it to make changes to the Web server's configuration files. Because the document root is owned by the *fpauth* user, *admin.exe* will still be able to edit HTML documents. Note that if you use per-user Web directories using the *~username* notation, you'll need to make each user's *public_html* directory owned by *fpauth* and writable by the user's group.

What are the risks of allowing FrontPage to modify the server's configuration files remotely? The main risk is that a bug in the *admin.exe* program might allow someone to make a malicious change to the configuration, such as running the server with root privileges or adding the system *bin* directory to the list of directories holding CGI scripts. Although we cannot rely on *admin.exe* being bug free, FrontPage's access control restrictions allow it to be invoked only by those who know the administrative account name and password. This limits who can get access to the script, and may reduce the risk to an acceptable level—provided that you take steps to prevent the password from being intercepted by network eavesdroppers.

Using FrontPage with Virtual Hosts

If your Web server manages several virtual hosts, you can protect the authors of one virtual host from interference by the authors of another by a logical extension of the scheme described above. Just create a different FrontPage user for each virtual host and assign it to the group used by that virtual host's authors. After installing FrontPage for the virtual host, change the ownerships and *suid/sgid* bits of *shtml.exe, auth.exe,* and *admin.exe* to reflect the user and group that's appropriate for the virtual host.

Microsoft provides a FrontPage "Web Presence Toolkit" that takes a similar approach. The toolkit includes a Perl script that automates the process of changing the ownership and file modes on newly installed FrontPage executables. The most substantial difference from the approach described here is that the scheme set up by the toolkit makes the executables writable by the owner. This is a potential security hole: CGI scripts should not be allowed to modify themselves. If you use the toolkit, I recommend that you fix this manually. You'll find the toolkit at Microsoft's FrontPage site.

Limiting FrontPage Access to Certain IP Addresses

FrontPage's Permissions window (Figure 13.3) also gives you the option of using IP addresses to limit access to the FrontPage extensions. If all Web authors and administrators will be connecting from a predictable location, such as within the organization's local area network, you can limit FrontPage access to these IP addresses.

To establish IP restrictions, select the *Computers* tab from the *FrontPage Explorer* Permissions window (Figure 13.4). With the "Add..." and "Edit..." buttons, create a series of IP address patterns to be granted access. For each, you can selectively grant browsing, authoring, and administrative access. In the example shown in the figure, browsers from all IP addresses have the right to browse and author, but only incoming connections from the 18.157.2 class C subnetwork have administrative access.

IP-based restrictions may not be available for some servers. In particular, because the IIS server does not offer per-directory IP restrictions, this feature does not appear when FrontPage is talking to IIS.

Using FrontPage with Windows NT Servers

This section describes the security issues to be aware of when using FrontPage to remotely manage an NT-based Web server.

Internet Information Server

When used with Microsoft Internet Information Server running under Windows NT, FrontPage is quite a different animal. IIS uses NT's own users

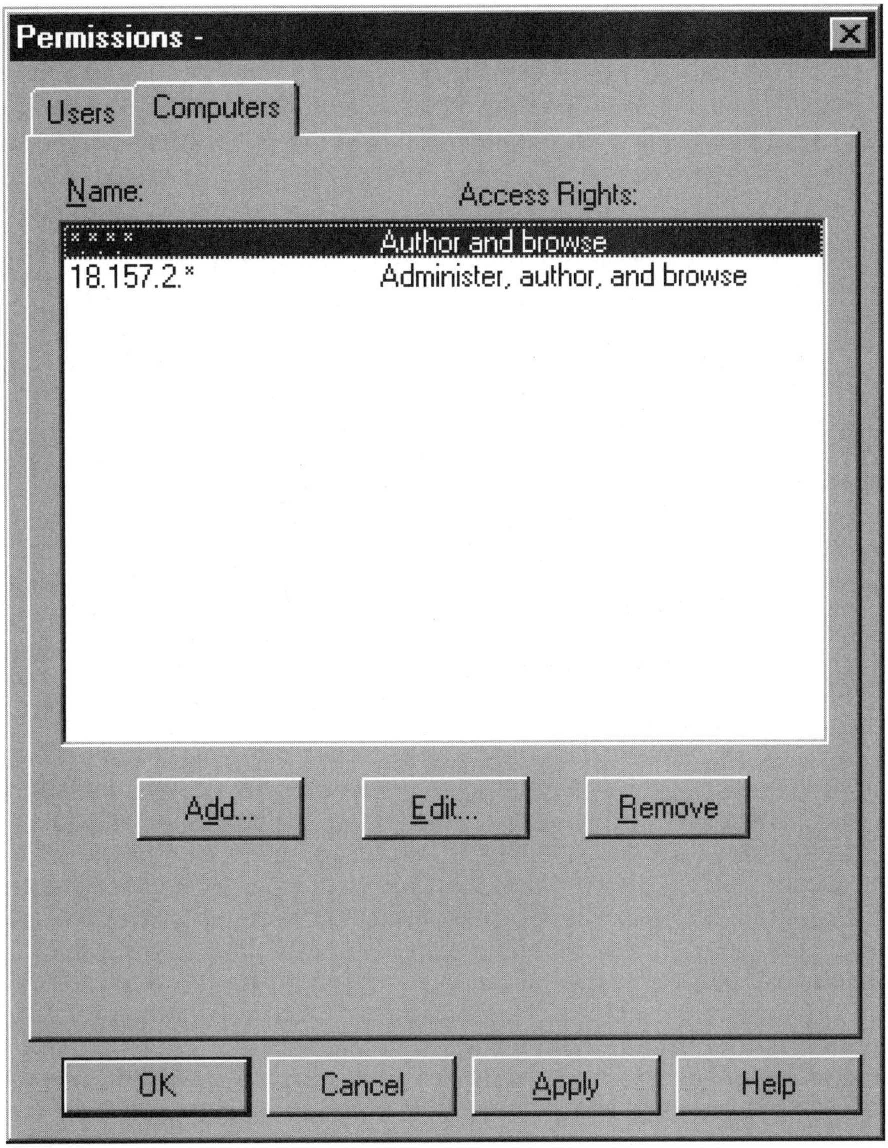

FIGURE 13.4 FrontPage allows administrative and authoring privileges to be restricted to certain ranges of IP addresses.

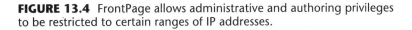

and groups to control access to its administrative and authoring functions. For an author to make changes to a FrontPage-administered Web directory, she must have a login account on the host, as well as write permission for the directory. The server assumes the identity of the remote author before it attempts any accesses to the file system. It can do this because FrontPage's authoring and administrative functions are implemented as server modules rather than as CGI scripts, allowing for much tighter integration with the server and operating system.

This security model provides good assurance that one FrontPage author cannot modify another author's content, provided that the file and directory permissions in the document root are set up correctly. It also allows authors the freedom to work on their documents via FTP, FrontPage, local login, or file sharing. There are no artificial constructions, like a "FrontPage user," to complicate things. Simply set up the Web document root as if the FrontPage authors will be logging in to the Web server host locally.

Unfortunately, there is one annoying complication when FrontPage is run in conjunction with IIS. When the FrontPage extensions are first installed, it modifies the document root and subdirectories so that the Web server anonymous user has full control (RWXD) permissions over the directory tree. This is to allow FrontPage WebBot CGI scripts, which open and write files, to work correctly. The risk of this configuration is that a bug in the Web server or its CGI scripts will enable a malicious user to vandalize the Web site.

After installing the FrontPage extensions, I recommend manually changing the anonymous user's access back to read only (RX). This will also have to be done whenever a remote user with administrative permissions adds a new top-level FrontPage "Web" to the document tree. Remote authors who want to add WebBots to their pages should configure them so that they store their results to designated directories that are writable by the anonymous user. I recommend creating new directories specifically for this purpose rather than using one of the ones automatically created by FrontPage.

When communicating with an IIS server, the security configuration window that appears when you select FrontPage Explorer's *Tools->Web Permissions...* command (Figure 13.5) is a bit more complex than the one used for UNIX installations. When you first open the window, you are presented with lists representing the users and groups known to the NT host. You can assign authoring privileges to users individually or by group membership. To assign authoring privileges to a group such as *Web Authors*, select the *Groups* tab, choose the group to authorize, then select the radio button labeled "Author and browse this web." In a similar way, you can grant FrontPage administrative privileges to certain users or control who has browse access to the system.

Unlike the UNIX version, you cannot add new users to the system with *FrontPage Explorer*. You must do this while logged into the server machine as an NT administrator.

Other Windows NT Servers

Unlike IIS, most other Windows NT-based servers run under a single user account. Access control is supported through user and group accounts that

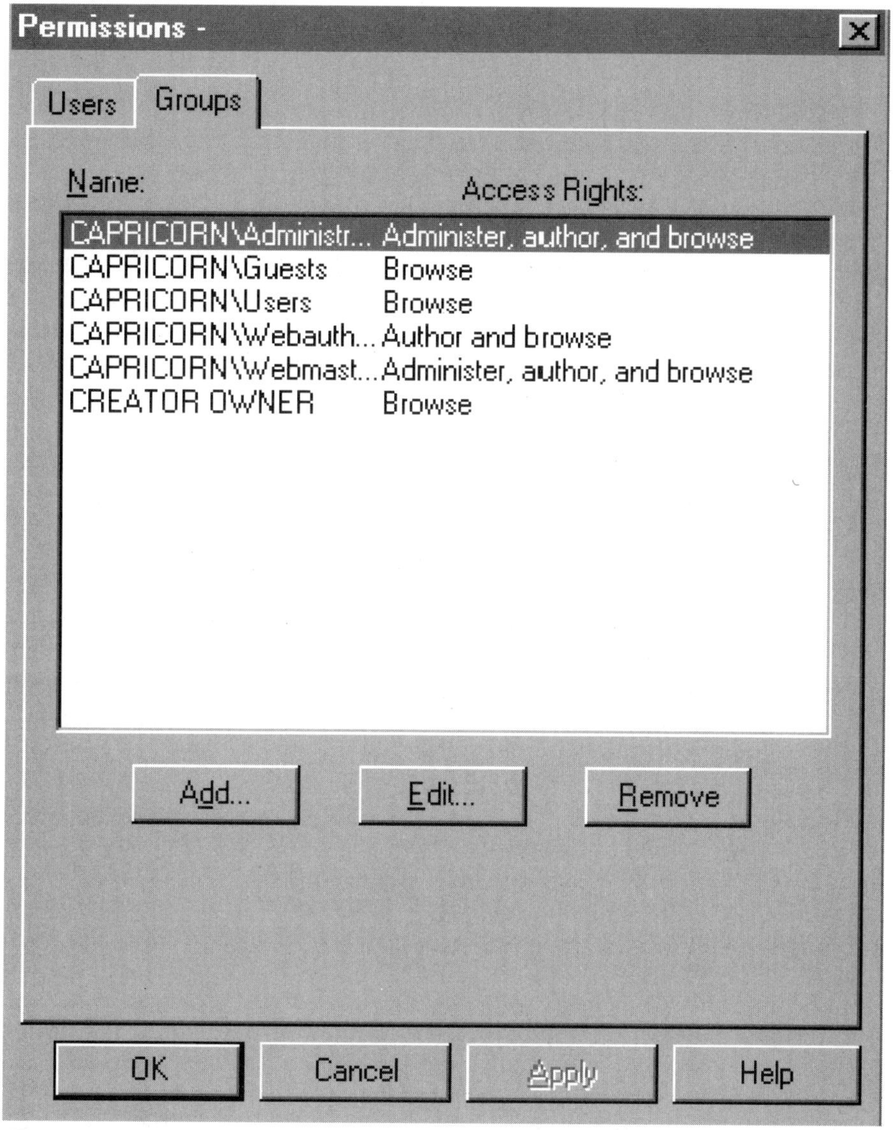

FIGURE 13.5 When Microsoft FrontPage talks to an IIS Web server, it uses NT groups to grant authoring and administration permissions.

the server itself maintains and that have no relationship with NT users and groups.

With such servers, FrontPage always runs with the identity and permissions of the server. You have no choice but to make the document not writable by the Web server user.

Other FrontPage Security Issues

We now turn our attention to other potential FrontPage security issues.

Password Sniffing

FrontPage usually uses the standard HTTP Basic authentication scheme to control who is allowed to use its authoring and administrative functions. This means that user names and passwords can be intercepted by network eavesdroppers. Once intercepted, a malicious user can use the password and his own copy of FrontPage to make unauthorized changes to the site. The documents are also passed back and forth in unencrypted format, allowing them to be intercepted and possibly modified in transit. This is an important consideration if FrontPage is used over the Internet.

The exception to this is when FrontPage extensions are running on Microsoft IIS. Under these circumstances, the client and server use Windows NT challenge/response authentication, which does not involve transmitting passwords in the clear (see Chapter 10). The documents themselves are still passed in unencrypted form, however.

To avoid these problems, FrontPage97 can be set up to use the SSL protocol to make a connection to the Web site. Provided that the server supports SSL, the user name, password, and the contents of all the documents transferred are encrypted. You can require that FrontPage use SSL for its authoring functions by specifying this as an option when you install FrontPage using the *FrontPage Administrator* program (NT) or *fpsrvadm.exe* (UNIX).

If your server does not support SSL, it's possible to use the Secure Shell program to set up an encrypted channel between the remote machine and the Web server. FrontPage thinks that it's talking to a server running on the user's personal computer, but in fact the transmissions are being encrypted and relayed to the real Web server somewhere else. This trick is explained in the Secure Login with SSH box earlier in this chapter.

As some protection against password guessing, FrontPage allows you the option of forcing authors to choose passwords that are complex. If the FrontPage configuration parameter *ComplexPasswords* is set to a non-zero value, FrontPage will insist that all passwords be at least eight characters and include one or more non-alphabetic character. Passwords that contain part of the user name will also be rejected.

On UNIX servers, you can add this parameter to FrontPage's global configuration file, *frontpage.cnf* (usually located in the */usr/local/frontpage/version2.0/* directory), or to the appropriate per-server configuration file. On NT systems, the configuration file is named *frontpg.ini*, and is located in the NT system directory. Note that setting this parameter will have no practical effect for IIS servers, since FrontPage doesn't currently allow users to change their passwords.

CGI Script Uploads

FrontPage97 gives authors the option to upload CGI scripts and make them executable. It's difficult to write secure, bullet-proof CGI scripts, and small bugs can have disastrous consequences. If the FrontPage parameter *NoExecutableCGIUploads* is set to a non-zero value, the FrontPage extensions will never set the executable bit on uploaded files. This gives you a chance to manually inspect the uploaded scripts and set the execute bit if everything seems safe. Remember to mark CGI scripts as read-only after you set the execute bit. Otherwise, the user may be able to overwrite the CGI script with a different executable. This feature is disabled by default.

Save Form Results to an Absolute Path or Pipe

FrontPage can be configured to allow authors to send the contents of fill-out forms to absolute path names or to pipe the results to arbitrary programs for further processing (UNIX servers only). Unless you trust your authors highly, either of these features can present a security risk. They are disabled by setting the parameters *NoSaveResultsToAbsoluteFile* and *NoSaveResultsPipeTo* to a non-zero value. This is the default.

You can allow fill-out forms to pipe their results to certain trusted programs by creating a parameter named *SaveResultsPipeToAllows*, whose value is a comma-separated list of programs you trust. *NoSaveResultsPipeTo* should be set to zero for this to work.

Authors Can Change Access Control Remotely

By default, FrontPage allows remote authors and administrators to change the access control restrictions on FrontPage-created directories. If you are worried that an author might inadvertently open up access to a confidential part of your Web site, you can disable the ability to change access control remotely by setting the parameter *AccessControl* to zero.

Logging

By default, FrontPage does not log authoring operations. The server records the access to a FrontPage executable, but it doesn't indicate what was done. You can enable extensive FrontPage logging by adding a parameter named *Logging* with a non-zero value to the FrontPage configuration. With this option enabled, a file named *_vti_log/author.log* located within each top-level directory records information about when each authoring operation was done, who did it, and what was changed.

If you turn on logging, you should also enable the parameter *NoSaveResultsToLogDir* by setting it to a non-zero value. This prevents authors from saving the results of fill-out forms to the log directory and overwriting the log file.

Server-Side Includes

Prior to version 2.0, the *DiscussionGroup* and *SaveResults* FrontPage WebBot's allowed remote users with no authoring privileges to upload HTML code that contained server-side include instructions. If the server-side include feature were enabled on the server, the remote user could then execute commands on the server host, using the Web server's permissions.

Although this hole has reportedly been patched in version 2.0 of the extensions, it is still possible for authorized Web authors to upload files containing server-side includes. It's recommended that, as a precaution, you disable (as described in Chapter 8) the server-side include "exec" feature in all directories managed by FrontPage. Similarly, servers that can process active server pages should have this facility limited or inactivated.

The HTTP PUT Protocol

FrontPage and similar Web publishing extensions use custom CGI scripts and the HTTP POST method to upload files to the server. Interestingly, Web publishing capabilities were built into the HTTP protocol using methods named PUT (to upload a new document) and DELETE (to delete an existing document). These methods have never been used for their intended purpose, perhaps because the first wave of Web servers emphasized browsing over authoring.

Recently, this situation has begun to change. Netscape Navigator Gold, versions 3.0 and higher, comes with a built-in HTML editor. Users can create new HTML documents in a WYSIWYG environment, then upload them to the server of their choice, using either the FTP protocol or with HTTP PUT. This development suggests that future servers from Netscape will have a built-in Web publishing system based on the HTTP protocol. In a related development, the draft HTTP/1.1 protocol puts renewed emphasis on Web server upload capabilities. Together, these things suggest that HTTP-based authoring will become more important in the future.

There are some advantages to using HTTP rather than FTP to upload files to the server. Administration is simpler. You don't have to worry about running an FTP server on top of the Web server, and you don't have to worry about setting up user accounts for each Web author—all access control is done through the Web server itself. In addition, HTTP PUT is potentially more secure than FTP. You can use SSL to transmit documents across the Internet in encrypted form, and if your HTML browser and editor support it, use HTTP/1.1 digest authentication to avoid transmitting access passwords in the clear. A major disadvantage is that, at the time this was written, at least, there was only one HTML editor and a scant handful of Web servers that supported HTTP PUT.

If you run the Apache Web server or one of its derivatives and wish to experiment with the cutting edge of Web publishing, you can use a Perl script called *nph-publish*, which allows the server to respond to the PUT method. Authors can upload files either to a special staging area or directly to the Web document root. If you prefer Web authors to be registered users of the host, the way MS IIS does things, you can configure *nph-publish* to assume the identity of the author before it makes any modifications to the file system. Otherwise, you can create accounts known only to the Web server and use normal HTTP per-directory access restrictions to control who has authoring privileges.

Full instructions for installing and using *nph-publish* comes with the package. You can find it at the URL listed at the end of this chapter.

An Upload Staging Area

Regardless of whether Web authors use HTTP, FTP, FrontPage, TELNET, or file sharing to get files from their personal computer to the server, there is always a risk that an unscrupulous author (or a cracker using a hijacked author account) will upload something that shouldn't be on the Web site. It could be a shell script or executable that will be used to gain further privileges on the system, a Trojan horse, a malicious applet, pirated software, or pornography. Many problems with executables can be avoided by configuring the server carefully to ignore CGI scripts that are outside the tightly controlled *cgi-bin* directory and by configuring the upload system to avoid creating files with execute permissions. Other types of unwanted content are harder to detect and avoid.

One way to improve this situation is to use a staging area. Authors don't have direct access to the Web document root. Instead, they upload files to a staging area that is kept in a separate location. At regular intervals, a script inspects the contents of the staging area. If the files satisfy certain sanity checks, the script transfers them to the document root directory, making them accessible to the public (Figure 13.6).

The staging area may be a directory somewhere on the server host machine, or it may be on a different machine altogether. If you are using a firewall system to protect the Web server from the Internet or, vice versa, your local area network from the Web server, a trust relationship can be set up between the staging machine and Web server so that authors can update the Web site without having to cross the firewall to do it.

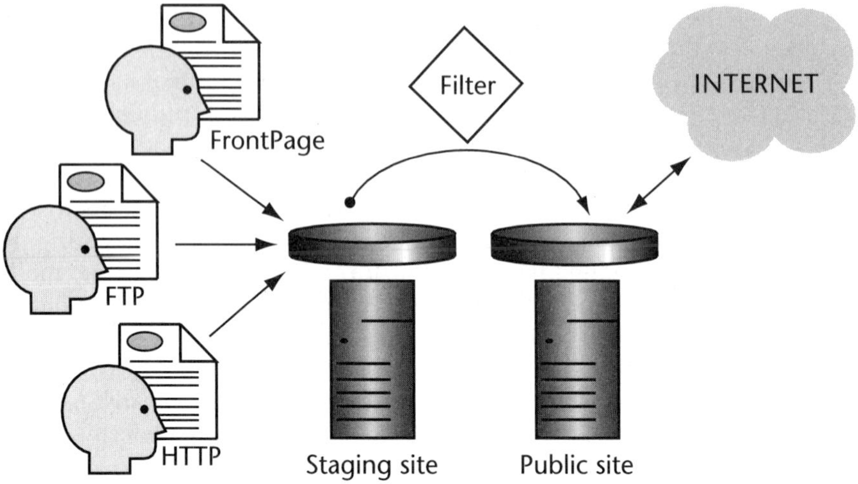

FIGURE 13.6 A staging area gives you an opportunity to monitor what's going on the Web site *before* it goes live.

Filtering Content

The script that transfers files from the staging area to the Web document root can be a simple wrapper around one of the file transfer programs described below, or it can be a sophisticated program that checks each file against a series of filter rules before performing the transfer. Things that you might want to filter against include

- **File Name** Check that the file name doesn't contain strange characters or is a "hidden" UNIX file (one that begins with a dot).
- **File Extension** Check that the file extension corresponds to one of the known MIME types (*.html*, *.htm*, *.jpg*, *.mov*, etc.). You can enforce content policy in this way. For example, if your site allows Java applets but forbids ActiveX controls, you can allow Java *.jar* and *.class* files but block ActiveX *.cab* archives.
- **File Mode** Uploaded files should not be world-writable and probably not executable. You can either block the transfer of files that don't have proper permissions or simply normalize the permissions to something safe.
- **File Ownership** Files in the staging area should be owned by one of the authorized Web authors. If the transfer script finds one that's not, it should flag this fact for investigation.
- **File Content** On many UNIX systems, the *file* command can correctly identify the content of a surprising number of file types. If this command is available, you can use it to make sure that the file's content

matches its extension. If it doesn't, someone may be pulling a fast one. For example, the following is the output of running *file* on three typical Web files.

```
lstein> file test.cgi wilogo.gif frametest.html
test.cgi:        Bourne shell script text
wilogo.gif:      GIF image data, version 87a, 94 x 68,
frametest.html: HTML document text
```

In this case, we discover that *test*.cgi, a CGI script, is written in a shell scripting language, something that should be avoided. A pointer to a version of *file* that recognizes many file types can be found at the end of this chapter.

The filter should assemble one list of files that have passed the tests and another list for the files that failed. The rejects should be logged and moved to an area where they won't be transferred with the rest of the files. The list of accepted files should be passed to the next phase of the script, where the files are actually transferred.

Transferring Files

Files that have passed the filtering tests can be transferred to the Web server's document root. If the staging area and the document root are on the same machine, you can just move or copy the files from within a script. If the staging area is on a different machine, you'll have to transfer the files physically or across the network.

There are a variety of ways to physically move files from the staging area to the Web server machine.

1. Copy the entire staging site to tape using the *tar* command or equivalent, then dump the tape to the Web document tree.
2. Burn the contents of the staging area onto a writable CD-ROM, carry it over to the Web server, and mount it. This has the virtue of practically guaranteeing that the site won't be vandalized. Previous CD-ROMs can be archived to keep a record of the site's contents at any time.
3. Copy the staging area onto a removable Zip, Jaz, or SyQuest drive. Throw the write-protect tab and mount it on the Web server. This also prevents vandals from making unauthorized "improvements."

If the site changes more than once a day, physical transfer methods are inconvenient. In many cases, you'll want to synchronize the staging area with the Web site automatically across the network by

1. *Pulling* files from the staging area to the server via FTP, HTTP, or remote-copy

2. *Pushing* files from the staging area to the server via FTP, *rdist*, *rsync*, or remote-copy.

Pulling Files from the Staging Area to the Web Server

There are several utilities that can be run on the Web server machine at regular intervals to pull the contents of the staging area across the network. Which one you choose depends on what you feel comfortable with, as well as with such practical factors as whether your firewall system can be configured to support this type of transfer. If possible, you should configure the staging area so that it will accept only transfer requests from the server machine.

One of the easiest methods to pull material from the staging area across the net is to use an FTP client that can do bulk transfers from the command line. One such client, *ncftp*, is a well-supported freeware program. You can use it to recursively fetch the entire contents of the staging area, updating only those files that are newer than the ones already present in the document root. Similar functionality can be found in the multiple "mirror" scripts available on the Internet, many of which are implemented as Perl programs. You'll find a variety of such scripts at the sites listed in Online Resources.

An alternative to FTP is to use the HTTP protocol to make the transfer. This involves running a Web server on the staging area. The Web server should be accessible only to Web authors and to authorized IP addresses. You can think of it as a "development server." A number of Perl scripts are available for automatically moving the contents of the staging area to the "live server" by making the appropriate series of URL requests. My favorite is the freeware product, *w3mir*.

Another pull method is to use the Berkeley *rcp* command to recursively copy the contents of the staging directory. Unlike the previous methods, which tend to abolish file ownership and permissions information, *rcp* preserves file and directory modes. If run as root, it will also preserve file ownership information. Unfortunately, it doesn't handle symbolic links well.

All pull methods are slightly awkward to automate. They also suffer from a more important defect: To some extent, they all require the machine used for the staging area to trust the Web server to pull just the files that are meant for it. However, the Web server is just the machine that you don't want to trust.

Pushing Files from the Staging Area to the Public Server

A more satisfactory method for transferring files across the network is to run a program on the staging machine that pushes files to the Web server. Not only does this improve the trust relationships, but there are several utilities designed to automate this process.

On UNIX systems, the most versatile utility is *rdist*, which was originally designed for upgrading multiple machines' system binaries from a single master copy maintained on a server. *rdist* will copy entire directory hierarchies while maintaining file ownerships, modes, modification dates, and symbolic links. Unlike any of the pull methods, *rdist* will also delete files from the Web server if they've been deleted from the staging area, ensuring that the two document trees are exact copies of each other. It can be compiled to transmit across a secure authenticated channel, such as the Secure Shell, and can be set up to log its activity to a file or to e-mail. Be sure to obtain a recent copy of *rdist* because the older version, which ran SUID to root, contains a security hole.

A similar utility, *rsync*, has somewhat fewer features than *rdist* but is easier to set up. It too can be configured to use Secure Shell to transfer files from the staging area to the Web server. Its main advantage over *rdist* is that it updates files by transferring only their differences, thus conserving bandwidth.

Finally, you can use any of the old UNIX standbys *tar*, *cpio*, or *afio* to push files across the net by brute force. As an example, here's how to use *cpio* to copy the entire staging area across an encrypted channel using *ssh*, the Secure Shell's equivalent of *rsh*. The names of the files to transfer are stored in a file called *ok_to_transfer*, which we assume has previously been assembled by the filter program.

```
lstein> cd /usr/staging_area
lstein> cat ok_to_transfer | cpio -o | \
                  ssh www cd /usr/local/etc/httpd\; cpio -i
```

The *tar*, *cpio*, and *ssh* programs are all available for Windows NT, as well as for UNIX. See the listing at the end of this chapter for information on obtaining them.

Using Source Code Control

If you have many Web authors and the site changes rapidly, you can combine the idea of a staging area with a source code control system, such as CVS or RCCS. The source code control system will help you keep track of what has changed on the Web site and who is responsible for changing it. If used properly, a major benefit of source code control is the ability to back track easily if a file is inadvertently deleted or modified.

Administering the Web Server Remotely

Web servers require regular administration. Log files need to be reviewed, new directory trees added, usage statistics compiled, CGI scripts installed, and communications parameters tweaked. Web servers offer a variety of remote administration schemes to accomplish these tasks, from simple UNIX servers that require you to TELNET in and edit configuration files from the command line to Windows NT servers that use RPC calls to administer the server via a graphical user interface. Many servers also provide a Web-based interface providing you with the ability to reconfigure the server from a Web browser anywhere in the world.

Administration by Remote Login

If you are using a UNIX-based Web server, such as Apache or NCSA *httpd*, that requires you to perform administrative tasks using text-based commands, you'll need to provide an incoming login service for the server host. The risk of running this type of service is that a network eavesdropper may intercept your communications and possibly intercept your password, enabling him to make unauthorized modifications to the site.

If possible, I recommend that you disable both the incoming TELNET and *rlogin* servers, and replace them with the encrypting Secure Shell. A public key certificate is not required to use Secure Shell's cryptography. Other encrypting login programs include SSL-TELNET and *stel*.

If an encrypting network login program is not an option, I recommend that you enable incoming TELNET rather than the Berkeley *rlogin* server. *rlogin* poses a significant security risk because of its easily subverted notion of "trusted hosts."

Two other precautions will reduce the risk of providing login services on the Web server. If you know that all logins will be coming from a defined set of Internet addresses (for example, from within your local area network, from the firewall machine, or from the IP address of your home machine), you can use Wietse Venema's freeware TCP wrapper, *tcpd*. This package allows you to restrict access to any *inetd*-based service by hostname or IP address. The wrapper is also designed to detect and prevent host name and IP address spoofing attacks. *tcpd* is easy to install and simple to use.

If you can't predict in advance what IP addresses you and other Web administrators will be connecting from, you can reduce the chance of a login password being stolen by using a one-time password system.

Administration via RPC

Some Windows NT Web servers, in particular IIS, have a graphical user interface called *Internet Service Manager* that uses NT remote procedure calls (RPC) to configure, start, and stop the server. It can be run on the same machine the server runs on or used across an NT domain to administer a server via remote control. Within an intranet protected by a firewall system, this program is safe from outside threats (though not safe from insider attacks).

On a system connected to the Internet, the *Internet Service Manager* program cannot be used remotely unless you leave NetBIOS services bound to TCP/IP, a configuration that is not recommended (see Chapter 9, Restrict Network Access to NetBIOS Services). One way to work around this problem is to run an alternate network protocol, such as Novell NetWare or NetBEUI, on both the Web server and the machine you wish to administer it from. Because neither protocol is routed across the Internet, they are not vulnerable to outside attack.

Administration via Dial-in

An effective way to establish a private connection between the server and a machine you wish to administer it from is to attach a modem to the server and dial in. In order to eavesdrop on a dial-in, an intruder would have to tap your phone line.

Many UNIX systems are already set up to accept incoming text-only logins. With a somewhat larger investment of time, you can add on a PPP server, allowing you to administer the server with TCP/IP-based tools. Both incoming text connections and PPP provide additional security checks and interoperate with one-time password systems. If you install PPP, be careful *not* to inadvertently provide IP forwarding services from the Web server to other machines in your local area network. If you do, you will have created a potential back door into your network.

On Windows NT systems, you can use Remote Access Server (RAS) to establish a dial-in connection. RAS offers a variety of nice features, including the ability to run TCP/IP and other network protocols across the connection. After establishing an RAS connection, you can use the *Internet Service Manager* to administer the IIS server. Again, be careful to configure RAS so that dial-in access is to the Web server machine only, not to the entire LAN.

Administration via the Web Browser

Many commercial Web servers allow you to administer the server from a Web browser, enabling you to perform routine administration from anywhere in the world. Some products, such as Netscape's Commerce server, use a separate server daemon to accomplish this. The administration server runs on its own separate TCP port. Others, such as IIS, use the same server to accomplish both administration and routine Web services.

When used within an intranet protected by a firewall system, browser-based administration is safe from external (but not internal) threats. Security issues arise when you try to use the browser to control a server that's accessible to the Internet. Because of the risk of network eavesdropping, I recommend that you establish an SSL connection between the browser and server before attempting any administration. Many servers offer the option of forcing SSL connections when accessing a particular directory. If this option is available, you should consider enabling if for the directory that holds administrative scripts.

You may encounter problems if you have to cross a firewall to contact the Web server and if the server is one that uses a separate network port for its administrative functions. If this happens, you have to coordinate with the firewall administrator to allow Web traffic to reach the administrative port.

Some UNIX-based remote administration servers are intended to be run with superuser privileges. The administrative server that comes with various Netscape servers falls into this category. You should treat with skepticism any vendor's instructions to run a server with superuser privileges. The consequences of a software bug in a program that runs as root are much more severe than the consequences of a bug in a program that runs with no special privileges. On closer inspection, it may turn out that by judiciously setting the SUID bit of a few of the key CGI scripts that the server uses to do its job you can run the administrative server as an unprivileged user.

If you don't use the server's Web-based administrative functions, you should disable them. If they are implemented as CGI scripts or DLLs, remove execute permission from the scripts or the directories they reside in. If the administrative functions are built into the server, see if your vendor provides a way to deactivate them.

IIS administrators should be aware that this server's Web-based administrative scripts are enabled by default. You must explicitly turn off this feature by removing execute permission from the directory */scripts/iisadmin*.

Access to the Server for Web Developers

Web developers need access to the server to install and test CGI scripts and modules. For most intents and purposes, developers can be treated as Web authors but be given the additional privilege of having write-access to the server's script and plug-in directories.

Developers should be discouraged from working directly on the live Web server. Unfinished and incompletely tested scripts pose a security risk if an outsider discovers them, and a lot of ongoing development work makes the task of monitoring the server for suspicious activity more difficult. If feasible, research and development should be performed on a separate development machine that's protected from the outside world by a firewall or strong access restrictions. When scripts are fully debugged, they should be moved to the live server. If this is unfeasible, it's best to run a second, completely separate, server on the machine. Protect this development server with strong access restrictions so that people outside your organization cannot gain access to it.

Checklist

1. Does your site have separate category(ies) for Web authors, developers, and administrators?

   ❍ No

   ☑ Yes

   It's generally a good idea to distinguish between users who have a right to work on the Web site from those who don't have that right. Even if everyone in your organization is currently a legitimate Web author, you may eventually need to add a user that doesn't have this privilege. It will be a lot easier to set this up later if you've already established the appropriate groups.

2. Does your site enforce Web authoring restrictions at the file system level?

   ❍ No

   ☑ Yes

   A policy that requires authors to log in under a specific account name and uses the operating system's file system access control lists and directory permissions to control access provides better fail safes than one that relies entirely on login restrictions. In some cases, such as the FrontPage extensions running on UNIX systems, you have no choice and must rely on the remote authoring server software to enforce access restrictions for you.

3. Does your site provide multiple mechanisms for authors to update the site, or a single one?

   ☑ Single mechanism

   ❍ Many mechanisms

   The more ways you provide for authors to update the site, the more things there are that can go wrong. Try to keep things simple so that you can keep track of what goes on.

4. Does your site provide a way for authors to authenticate themselves without sending passwords in the clear?

   ❍ No

   ☑ Yes

   Many possible ways for Web authors to access the server, including plain FTP, TELNET, NFS, and unencrypted HTTP, transmit user names and passwords in the clear. If this information passes through an untrusted network, such as the Internet, it could be compromised. Encrypting variants of these protocols provide greater security, as does Windows NT's challenge/response type of authentication, which does not send passwords in the clear.

5. Does your site provide a way for authors to update the site without sending the updated files in the clear?

   ❍ No

   ✓ Yes

   Even if the user name and password used to log in are secure, the content of updated pages isn't. If pages contain confidential information, they may be compromised if they pass across an untrusted network. Encrypting file transfer protocols protect against this eventuality.

6. Does your site use a staging area for file uploads?

   ❍ No

   ✓ Yes

   By having Web authors upload new and changed files to a staging area rather than directly modifying files on the Web server, you have a chance to catch errors, anomalies, and intentional vandalism before they go live. The script that moves files from the staging area to the live server can perform a variety of consistency checks, and more important, it can log the changes.

7. Does your site use a source code control system?

   ❍ No

   ✓ Yes

   If your site changes rapidly and/or has many authors, a source code control system can keep things from getting out of control. It can also get you out of some tight spots.

8. Do Web developers work on scripts and modules on the "live" server?

   ✓ No

   ❍ Yes

   For a variety of reasons, it's not a good idea to develop server-side scripts on the live server. It's much better to limit development work to a separate private server and move them to the live server only after they've been thoroughly debugged and tested.

Online Resources

Remote Control for Windows NT

pcANYWHERE

http://www.symantec.com/

WinFrame

http://www.citrix.com/

WinDD

http://www.tek.com/Network_Computers/Products/WinDD

NTrigue

http://www.ntrigue.com/

WinCenter

http://www.ncd.com/pwin/pwin.html

UNIX Network Access Control

Wietse Venema's TCP Wrapper Suite

ftp://ftp.win.tue.nl:/pub/security/

Secure Shell

http://www.cs.hut.fi/ssh/ (UNIX freeware version)
http://www.datafellows.com/f-secure/ (Windows & Macintosh versions)

SSL-Based TELNET

ftp://ftp.psy.uq.oz.au/pub/Crypto/

Stel

ftp://ftp.dsi.umin.it/

One-Time Password Systems

S/Key

ftp://thumper.bellcore.com/pub/nmh/skey/

SECURID

Security Dynamics, One Alewife Center, Cambridge, MA 02140;
Tel: 617-547-7820; Fax: 617-354-8836

SecureNet

Digital Pathways, 201 Ravendale Drive, Mountain View, CA 94043;
Tel: 415-964-0707; Fax: 415-961-7487

Server Publishing

FrontPage

http://www.microsoft.com/frontpage/

nph-publish

http://www.genome.wi.mit.edu/~lstein/server-publish/

wu-ftp

http://www.wustl.edu/ftp

file File Content Determination Program

ftp://ftp.ee.cornell.edu/pub/file/

Running a Staging Area

ncftp batch FTP client

ftp://ftp.probe.net/pub/ncftp/

mirror, gmirror, pmirror, etc.

ftp://ftp.sunsite.unc.edu/pub/Linux/system/file-transfer/

rdist

ftp://usc.edu/pub/rdist/rdist.tar.gz

rsync

ftp://samba.anu.edu.au/pub/rsync/

afio

ftp://sunsite.unc.edu/pub/Linux/system/Backup/

cpio

ftp://prep.ai.mit.edu/pub/gnu/

CVS Source Code Control System

ftp://prep.ai.mit.edu/pub/gnu/

Printed Resources

Hunt, Craig, *TCP/IP Network Administration* (O'Reilly & Associates, Inc., 1992).

Thorough introduction to fundamentals of TCP/IP networking, including instructions on setting up PPP and SLIP servers.

Liu, Cricket, Peek, Jerry, Jones, Russ, Buus, Bryan, and Nye, Adrian, *Managing Internet Information Services* (O'Reilly & Associates, 1995).

Detailed reference guide for managing many traditional UNIX-based information services, including FTP, gopher, mail, and net news.

Russel, Charlie, and Crawford, Sharon, *Running Microsoft Windows NT Server 4.0* (Microsoft Press, 1997).

A good source of practical information for setting up NT dial-ins and PPTP servers.

Chapter 14

Web Servers and Firewalls

out expanding people's access to network resources. all about limiting access to the network. Where these two 's meet is at the firewall, a system designed to make the in carefully controlled and monitored ways.

n enables you to accomplish two goals: You can provide 'rganization with access to the World Wide Web without world to peek in; and you can erect a barrier between an oftware, your organization's public Web server, and the n that resides on your private network.

irewall is simple. In a traditional open system, all hosts etwork (LAN) have direct access to the Internet and are le to attack from the outside. The security of the LAN is curity of the weakest host. A single insecure host will break in. Once in, it is easy, by stealing legitimate users' system software with doctored copies, and other such ier hosts at the site. Not only is it difficult to protect an ack, but it's difficult to detect. A network administrator g to monitor suspicious activity on tens or hundreds of rsonal computers.

Firewalls address this problem by interposing a specially configured gateway machine between the outside world and the site's inner network. Direct traffic between hosts on the inner network and the world at large is forbidden. Instead, all traffic must first go to the gateway, where software decides whether the traffic can be allowed through or rejected. This effectively divides the network into an "inner" trusted network (that is, the LAN), and an "outer" untrusted network (that is, the Internet). The border zone between the outer and inner networks is known as the "security perimeter." Now the job of protecting the LAN becomes a whole lot simpler. Instead of protecting a motley horde of individual hosts from compromise, you can focus your efforts on protecting the single gateway machine. If the gateway is secure, the LAN is secure.

There are two basic implementations for firewall systems. In the "dual-homed gateway" approach (Figure 14.1a), the firewall machine, called a "bastion" to give it that medieval castle feeling, has two network cards, one connected to the inner network and the other connected to the untrusted network. The machine is set up so that network packets reaching one card are not relayed to the other. By default, the two networks are completely isolated. However, because there's always a need for some communication between the inner and outer networks, specialized programs, called "proxies," are run on the firewall machine. The job of a proxy is to selectively forward information from one network to the other. Typically, a different proxy is responsible for each service: one for mail, one for FTP, and so on. Proxies can determine which network packets to forward by looking at the source and destination addresses, by examining the packet type, by examining the source and destination ports, or even by checking the data contained within the packet. Network packets are never transferred directly; their data is extracted and repackaged in new packets before ferrying the information across the gateway.

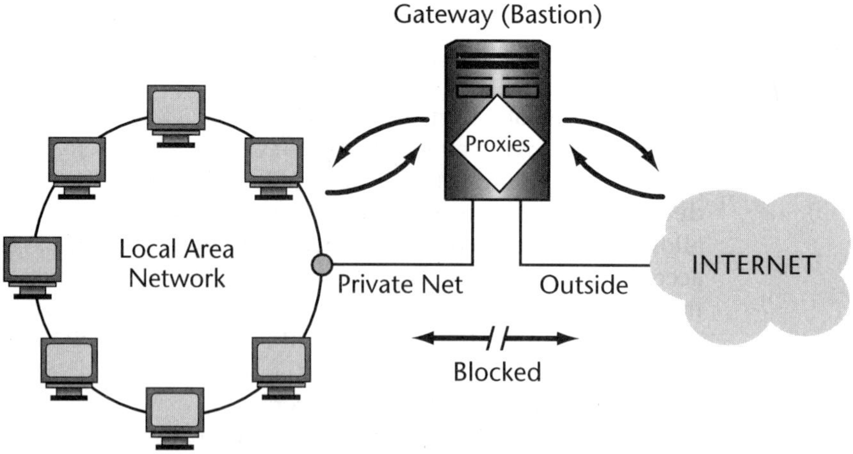

FIGURE 14.1a In the older dual-homed gateway firewall configurations, the gateway machine has two network interface cards; one is connected to the outer network, the other to the inner.

In the "screened-host gateway" approach (Figure 14.1b), a network router is used to control access to the inner network. The router restricts communication between the outer and inner networks by ensuring that network packets originating within the outer network can reach only the well-secured bastion machine where proxies retransmit the data to the inner network after examining it. In most cases, the machines on the inner network are completely invisible to the outer one. Outbound packets from the inner network are either restricted to the firewall machine, where they must again be chaperoned to the Internet through a proxy program, or are allowed to pass directly through the router after satisfying certain filtering rules to determine that they are safe.

A close cousin of this approach is the "screened subnet gateway," in which the router gives the outer network access to a small subnetwork, known as the "demilitarized zone." The bastion host sits in the demilitarized zone, as well as any other servers that you want to make available to the world, such as Web or FTP servers. Another router, situated between the demilitarized zone and the internal network, provides an extra dose of security against attack if either the bastion host or the external router is compromised. This topology is discussed further in a later section.

In a well-designed firewall system, there's no effective difference between the dual-homed and the screened-host systems. In each case, the internal network appears to the outside world to contain a single well-protected machine, the bastion host. All outgoing traffic from the internal network to the outside world appears to originate from the bastion, and all incoming traffic is directed to that machine. Software on the bastion checks each piece

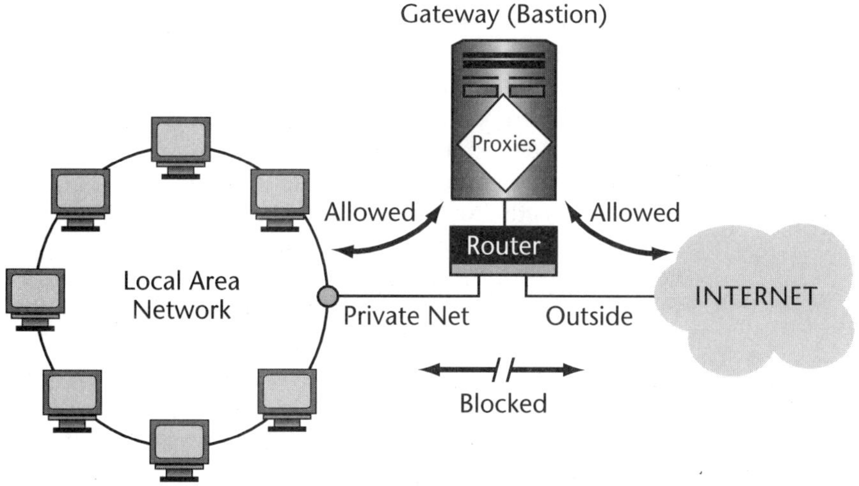

FIGURE 14.1b The screened-host gateway uses a router to forward all traffic from the outer and inner networks to the gateway machine.

of network data as it arrives, logs it, and allows it to pass through if it satisfies the rules and regulations set down by the firewall administrators.

Many organizations have installed firewall systems that are not strictly firewalls at all. They are network routers that have been configured to block "dangerous" net traffic while allowing "safe" traffic through. This type of system can be difficult to administer effectively because of the difficulty in creating effective filtering rules. Even a seemingly innocuous change in a routing table can have unintended effects. Because routers are not primarily designed for security purposes, they don't ordinarily log network activity, making it difficult to determine whether the system is working properly or even whether you are being attacked!

The essence of a firewall's security policy is embodied in the filters that allow or deny passage to network traffic. Proxy programs come in two flavors. There are "application-level" proxies, which are written for particular communications protocols. For example, one application-level proxy will be responsible for forwarding HTTP requests back and forth across the firewall, another responsible for FTP requests, and a third responsible for e-mail. Because application-level proxies understand the meaning of the information they're transferring back and forth, they can apply filtering rules based on the contents of the network packets. For example, if an organization decides to shield its employees against the potential dangers of ActiveX controls, it could set up an HTTP proxy to examine the contents of every HTML page crossing the bastion and quietly delete references to ActiveX. Application-level proxies can also filter network traffic by the IP addresses of the sending and receiving parties, the network ports at either end of the connection, and other features of the network packet headers.

In contrast to application-level proxies are "circuit-level" proxies—low-level, general-purpose programs that treat network packets as so many black boxes to be forwarded across the bastion or not. This type of proxy can filter only on the basis of header information in the network packets. Circuit-level proxies can disallow network packets that originate from prohibited sources, but they can't peek inside the packet to see if a legitimate-seeming packet is hiding some malicious activity. The main advantage of circuit-level proxies is their generality and speed. One proxy can handle many protocols and can often handle the latest whizzbang multimedia protocol long before a special-purpose, application-level proxy becomes available. Circuit-level proxies are often faster than their specialized brethren because their task is less computationally intensive.

SOCKS is a freeware circuit-level proxy that is widely used in older firewall systems (see the list of resources at the end of this chapter). Although it requires all software that uses it to be specially modified, most Web browsers and servers are already SOCKS-aware.

A newer form of circuit-level proxy is called a "stateful multilayer inspection gateway," or SMLI. An SMLI proxy has the ability to remember outgoing network packets and correlate them with subsequent incoming packets.

This gives the proxy much greater sophistication in filtering network connections than an ordinary packet filter or circuit-level proxy, and makes it possible to manage complex protocols that cannot be adequately monitored by watching a single packet at a time. Unlike SOCKS, no client software needs to be modified to support SMLI.

Systems that use the screened host or screened subnet architecture also have a third type of filtering available to them, called "packet filtering." Packet filtering uses the router's own routing tables to make decisions about which network packets to allow through and which to deny. Packets can be filtered by their source Internet address, their destination Internet address, the network interface they are received from, the service ports they are addressed to, and other information that they carry with them. Packet filters grant the firewall administrator a great deal of flexibility. If the bastion host doesn't happen to have a proxy that can deal with a certain type of network service, the packet filter can be reconfigured to let that service bypass the firewall entirely, effectively poking a hole in the firewall.

In all types of firewall systems, the security of the inner network depends on the security of the bastion host. Someone who gains access to the firewall or is able to reconfigure its security measures will most likely be able to break into other machines on the LAN. In screened-host systems, the router is also a potential weak link. To prevent either the bastion or the host from being compromised, firewalls are specially configured and stripped down. Typically, they run a "hardened" version of the UNIX or NT operating system, from which various vulnerabilities have been removed. Firewalls run no unnecessary services, contain no untrusted software, and keep a secure log of all activity.

Selecting a Firewall System

The subject of creating a firewall system from scratch is beyond the scope of this book. Good references on the subject can be found in the Printed Resources section at the end of this chapter. If you are an adventuresome and skillful UNIX system administrator, you can try your hand at building your own firewall system. The Trusted Information Systems Corporation offers a free firewall construction set called the Firewall Toolkit (FWTK). The FWTK comes complete with application-level proxies, authentication hooks, log filtering utilities, and administrative tools. The documentation, though terse, is comprehensive.

Under most circumstances, however, you will want to purchase a commercial firewall system. You'll get a system that has been extensively tested and that supports newer protocols, such as RealAudio; and such frills as graphical user interfaces for configuration and pager interfaces to alert you of possible break-in attempts. Most important, you'll have someone to call if something goes wrong. Many vendors offer turnkey systems that combine the appropriate hardware and software.

Because of the large number of competing firewall vendors, it can be difficult to choose among the conflicting claims and counterclaims for the system that's right for your organization. What follows is a list of the major features you should consider when firewall shopping, followed by a brief rundown of the seven major commercial firewall offerings.

- **Operating System** Firewall products are available that run on both UNIX and Windows NT systems. Neither operating system has an advantage over the other. In most cases, the firewall vendors have modified the operating system to harden it and make it more resistant against attack (some of these techniques were discussed in Chapters 8 and 9). Nor is it necessary for a network that is primarily Windows-based to have a Windows firewall, or vice versa. However, it is important to have a firewall system that you feel comfortable administering. If your expertise is in UNIX system administration, then a UNIX-based firewall will be the best choice.
- **Protocols Handled** Firewall systems inevitably lag behind the cutting edge of technology. All firewalls will handle FTP, e-mail, gopher, HTTP, NNTP, TELNET, and other common protocols, but they may not be able to handle new or unusual protocols, such as Pointcast, SNMP, or RealAudio. If you absolutely need to pass a new videoconferencing protocol across the firewall, make sure the system can handle it.
- **Filter Types** Network filters based on application-level proxies give you extensive control over what passes across the firewall; they are also able to analyze the contents of the data and modify it, if necessary. The downside is that this in-depth analysis carries a performance penalty, which may be noticeable in environments with heavy network traffic.

  Systems based on circuit-level proxies have better performance, and packet-filtering systems perform better still. However, both systems can regulate connections only on the basis of their source and destination addresses, their destination ports, and other components of the TCP/IP header. SMLI proxies provide a compromise between the two—better performance than an application-level proxy and better filtering capabilities than packet filtering systems.
- **Logging** A good firewall performs exhaustive logging. It also comes with tools to analyze and summarize the logs so that you can detect unusual activity.
- **Administration** Some firewalls are configured with graphical user interfaces. Others use text configuration files or a command-line program. Most firewalls provide a mechanism to administer the system remotely after carefully authenticating the administrator.

- **Simplicity** Good firewall systems are simple. The proxies are small, easy to understand, and can be verified by inspection. Some companies even make the source code to their system available for public inspection, a sign of their confidence in their software.
- **Tunneling** Some firewall systems provide the ability to set up an encrypting tunnel across the Internet in order to securely connect two networks in a single "virtual private network" (VPN). This can be a useful way to connect two branch offices or collaborators and may be cheaper than the alternative of leasing a dedicated telephone line for the purpose.

At press time, seven vendors accounted for most of the commercial firewall market.

1. **AltaVista (Digital Equipment Corporation)** This firewall system uses a combination of packet filters, application-level proxies, and circuit-level proxies. It runs on hardened versions of UNIX and Windows NT. Its major distinguishing features are extensive and customizable logging and log crunching and excellent performance under heavy load. Tunneling is provided as an add-on product.
2. **BorderWare (Secure Computing Corporation)** This UNIX-only system provides both application-level proxies and packet filtering. Administration is by graphical user interface only. Tunneling is available as an option.
3. **CyberGuard Firewall (CyberGuard Corporation)** This UNIX-only system covers all bases with a combination of packet filtering, application- and circuit-level proxies, and stateful inspection. Its many features are configured and managed using a well-designed graphical user interface. Performance under heavy load is good.
4. **Eagle (Raptor Systems)** Eagle uses application- and circuit-level proxies. It is available for NT and a variety of UNIX systems. Administration is primarily done via a graphical user interface. No tunneling is (currently) provided, nor is support for some of the more esoteric Web protocols such as S-HTTP or Quicktime. Like other application-level proxy systems, its performance degrades under heavy load.
5. **Firewall-1 (Checkpoint Software Technologies)** This system provides a combination of packet filtering and stateful inspection and is available for Windows NT and a variety of UNIX systems. Major selling points are an intuitive graphical user interface, and support for a large number of network protocols, including some of the more recent multimedia formats, and excellent performance. Tunneling is available as an add-on.
6. **Gauntlet (Trusted Information Systems)** This system, available either as a software-only package or as a turnkey combination of hardware and software, uses application-level proxies for filtering. A general circuit-

level, plugin proxy is available, as is packet filtering, but the latter is deprecated. Tunneling is supported as a separate product. Text-oriented and graphical administration interfaces are provided. Because of its reliance on application-level proxies, Gauntlet's performance is poor on a heavily loaded system. However, the product is unique in making its source code available for inspection.

7. **ON Guard (ON Technology Corporation)** This product is distinguished by using SMLI filters. It's also the only firewall in this group to run under a hardened version of Windows 95. Despite the Win95 interface, however, some people find its GUI confusing. Tunneling technology is not yet available.

Configuring a Firewall

The remainder of this chapter deals with the issues of configuring a firewall system to allow Web traffic to flow back and forth. In order to keep the discussion generic, I use a table-based format for describing routing tables that is not specific to any company's products. When describing application-level proxies, I show examples taken from the text-based configuration system used by the TIS Firewall Toolkit. It is easy to understand and fairly general.

Outgoing Web Access

With a firewall installed, there are two main issues: How to allow people within your organization to safely browse the Web, and how to make your organization's public Web site available to the rest of the world. We'll consider the problem of outgoing connections first.

Outgoing Connections Through a Packet Filter Firewall

If your firewall is of the older type that uses packet filtering for its access control, you need to provide filter exceptions for outgoing connections to the HTTP (port 80), FTP (port 21), SSL (port 443), and Gopher (port 70) services, as well as for the data sent back in response to those connections. A stylized representation of a firewall's filter table is shown in Table 14.1 (the format is borrowed from Cheswick and Bellovin, 1994).

The first column indicates the action to take—either to block the network packet or to allow it through. The next two columns indicate the source of the packet by TCP/IP address and by port. This is followed by the intended destination of the packet, again given as an address/port pair. The column

TABLE 14.1 Web Access Through a Packet Filter Firewall

Action	Src	Port	Dest	Port	Flags	Comment
block	*	*	*	*	*	Block all by default
allow	*{Internal net}*	*	*	80	*	Outgoing Web
allow	*	80	*	*	ACK	Incoming Web
allow	*{Internal net}*	*	*	21	*	Outgoing FTP control channel
allow	*	21	*	*	ACK	Incoming FTP control channel
allow	*{Internal net}*	*	*	≥1024	*	Outgoing FTP data
allow	*	≥1024	*	*	ACK	Incoming FTP data
allow	*{Internal net}*	*	*	443	*	Outgoing SSL
allow	*	443	*	*	ACK	Incoming SSL
allow	*{Internal net}*	*	*	70	*	Outgoing Gopher
allow	*	70	*	*	ACK	Incoming Gopher

labeled "Flags" contains other TCP header fields that can be used for filtering. For our purposes, the only important flag is ACK, which indicates that a network packet is a continuation of a conversation initiated earlier. In this example, *{Internal net}* is a shortcut for your organization's network address.

The first line blocks all access by default. Subsequent lines allow outgoing connections from any computer in your organization's internal network to any of the ports customarily used by the Web, FTP, SSL, and Gopher protocols. For each outgoing connection, a corresponding incoming connection is allowed, provided that it carries the ACK flag, indicating that it is an acknowledgement of a previously initiated connection. This prevents external hosts from initiating their own connections to your organization's machines.

Because FTP uses one network connection to transmit commands and another to transmit and receive data, and because the vanilla FTP protocol calls for the FTP server to *initiate* the data connection, it can be difficult to filter FTP connections correctly. The example shown here assumes that both the client and server FTP software understand the newer PASV (passive) command, which allows the client to initiate the data connection. The server will ordinarily use a high numbered port (greater or equal to 1024) for FTP data, so we allow this type of connection. All Web browsers use passive FTP connections, so you may need nothing more than this. See one of the printed firewall references for details if you need to support older FTP clients.

With these exceptions in place, browsers in your organization will be able to talk directly to Web servers outside. No modification of the browser software is necessary.

The filtering rules shown here are just the minimum needed to support Web browsers. You may also need rules that allow for outgoing e-mail (port 25), TELNET (port 23), and any other Internet services you require.

Outgoing Connections Through an Application-Level Proxy

If your firewall uses application-level proxies to provide Internet access, you'll need to enable separate proxies for each of the protocols commonly used on the Web, including HTTP, FTP, SSL, and optionally, Gopher. In some firewall systems, one proxy program will handle several or perhaps all of these protocols. In other systems, you'll need to configure a separate proxy for each one.

The TIS firewall toolkit comes with a single proxy, named *http-gw*, that handles both the HTTP and Gopher protocols. A separate proxy, named *ftp-gw*, is used for the FTP protocol. An SSL proxy is not available for the toolkit but is part of TIS's commercial system, as well as those of other vendors. (If you really want to use the FWTK for your firewall, there's a workaround for SSL that involves a generic proxy, called *plug-gw*, and a proxy Web server. See An SSL Proxy for the TIS Firewall Toolkit box for details.)

A proxy's job is to accept incoming connections from one side of the firewall, filter them, and forward them on to the other side. When a proxy is first installed, it is indifferent to whether it will service requests from the secure inner network or from the insecure Internet. You'll need to define who is permitted to use the proxy. In a basic configuration, any host on the inner network is allowed to use the proxies, and everyone else is refused access. Assuming that your LAN is the class C network at 193.49.189, here's a simple configuration that implements this basic idea.

```
# Rules for the FTP gateway
ftp-gw: denial-msg    /usr/local/etc/ftp-deny.txt
ftp-gw: welcome-msg   /usr/local/etc/ftp-welcome.txt
ftp-gw: help-msg      /usr/local/etc/ftp-help.txt
ftp-gw: timeout       3600
ftp-gw: deny-hosts    unknown
ftp-gw: permit-hosts  193.49.189.*
# Rules for the http/gopher gateway
http-gw: permit-hosts 193.49.189.*
```

The first six lines of this file set up defaults for the FTP proxy, including such things as the messages to deliver when a user is denied access or needs help. The line containing *deny-hosts* prohibits the use of the proxy by any machine that doesn't have a domain name system entry (almost always a good idea). The line containing *permit-hosts* allows any host in the internal network to use the proxy. Others are prohibited by default. A similar configuration line for the HTTP proxy applies the same access restrictions.

Most firewall products allow you to control which Web pages flow through the proxy. Some organizations, for example, are concerned about employees surfing the Web for recreational purposes during the work day. You can control the proxy so that access to certain sites or even certain URLs at those sites are out of bounds. Or you can restrict access to all but a few officially sanctioned sites. Because of the concern about the safety of Java applets and ActiveX controls (see Chapter 5), firewall products based on application-

An SSL Proxy for the TIS Firewall Toolkit

The TIS Firewall Toolkit provides an application-level proxy for HTTP but no support for encrypted Web connections using the SSL protocol. A workaround for this is to install an encrypting Web proxy on the outer network and use TIS's generic proxy *plug-gw* to forward the SSL proxy across the firewall to the Web proxy.

The Web proxy can be the same server you use to provide public Web service or a different one. The only requirement is that it support the SSL protocol.

1. Configure the Web proxy to accept proxy requests from the firewall machine but to reject them from elsewhere. The following lines in *httpd.conf* will do the trick with all Apache-derived servers.

```
ProxyRequests On
<Files http:*>
<Limit GET POST>
order deny,allow
deny from all
allow from gw
</Limit>
</Files>
```

   This example assumes that the firewall bastion is named *gw*.

2. Next, you'll configure *plug-gw* to forward SSL requests to the external server. Assuming that the external machine is named *www-external,* add the following line to the toolkit's configuration file.

```
plug-gw: port 443 193.49.189.* -plug-to www-external
```

   This tells the proxy that requests for port 443 (the standard SSL port) from hosts within the internal network are to be forwarded to the external server.

3. Arrange for *plug-gw* to be launched at system start by adding a line like the following to one of the *rc* boot scripts.

```
/usr/local/etc/plug-gw -daemon 443
```

   Start the proxy by entering the above command as the root user.

4. The last step is to configure each browser to use the firewall as its security proxy, by entering the firewall's name and port into the browsers' network configuration pages.

The system should now be configured correctly. Test it out by fetching a page from a secure server using an *https:* URL.

level proxies will optionally intercept HTML pages and filter out the <APPLET>, <SCRIPT>, and <OBJECT> tags. This mechanism can be defeated by a sufficiently determined employee and provides no protection against pages that are downloaded in encrypted form using SSL, but it does reduce the risk of active content brought in by casual surfing.

Once the HTTP and FTP proxies are installed and running, you need to configure every browser used on the internal network to direct its requests for URLs to the firewall. The mechanism varies somewhat from browser to browser. In Netscape Navigator, choose the menu commands *Options ->Network Preferences...->Proxies*, select *Manual proxy* from the list of radio buttons and press the *View* button to display a window showing the current proxy configuration (Figure 14.2). Type in the name or address of the gateway machine in the text fields labeled "HTTP," "Gopher," and "FTP." Unless you've configured the proxy to run on a nonstandard port, you should fill in the field labeled "Port" with the standard port numbers for HTTP, Gopher, and FTP, 80, 70, and 21, respectively. If you are running a private Web server on the internal network, you should also fill in the field labeled "No Proxy For" with the host name of the internal server. This will prevent the browser from trying to use the proxy to access a server that it can contact directly.

"SOCKS Host" should be left blank unless you are using a SOCKS-based circuit-level proxy. You may fill in the other fields if you have proxies that support them: the "Security proxy" field for SSL connections and "WAIS proxy" for the now little-used Wide Area Information Service protocol.

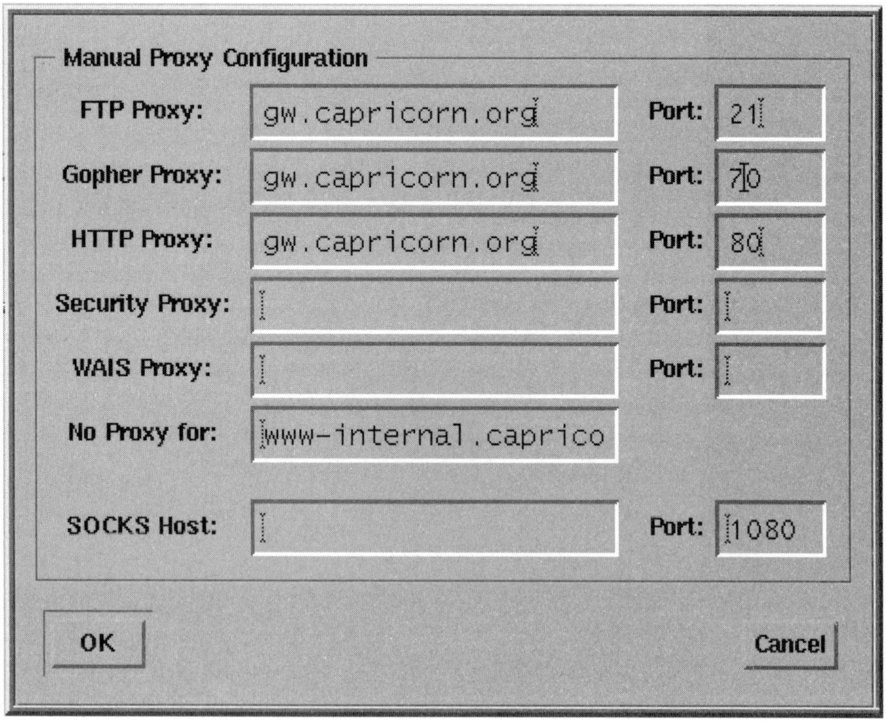

FIGURE 14.2 Configuring Netscape to use a firewall proxy involves entering the address and port number for each proxied service.

Proxy configuration in Internet Explorer uses a similar proxy configuration screen available under the *Edit->Options...->Connection* command. Unlike Netscape, which allows you to turn off proxying for one Web server host only, IE provides the flexibility of selectively disabling proxying for multiple hosts. If you have several internal servers that you don't want to go through the proxy to access, you can enter each one into the "Exceptions" field, separating each host name or IP address by semicolons. You can also enter addresses containing the * wild card to disable proxying for a range of hosts.

Netscape Navigator and Internet Explorer both have the feature of allowing you to set a site-wide proxy policy from a centralized configuration file. (See the Automatic Proxy Configuration section later in this chapter.)

Outgoing Connections Through a Circuit Proxy

If your firewall uses a circuit-level proxy such as SOCKS, the proxy will need to be configured to allow outgoing connections through the Web, FTP, SSL, and Gopher ports. In addition, the browser will need to be configured to direct its outgoing calls to the proxy. The SOCKS proxy is already supported by all commercial Web browsers. If you use a proprietary circuit-level proxy, you may need to make some code modifications to the browser (which may not always be feasible).

Here's the basic set of access control rules for a SOCKS proxy, configured to allow hosts inside the class C network 193.49.189 to get *out* but forbidding all use of the proxy from outside hosts.

```
#action #source       #netmask       #destination  #netmask
#deny the world access to the proxy
deny    0.0.0.0       0.0.0.0        193.49.189.0  255.255.255.0
#permit access to the proxy from anyone on the LAN
permit  193.49.189.0  255.255.255.0
```

Once the SOCKS proxy is active, you'll configure each browser in your organization to use it for access to the Internet. The process is identical to configuring the browser to use application-level proxies, except that you need only fill in the "SOCKS Host" and "Port" fields of the proxy configuration window. Other fields should be left blank.

Incoming Web Access

Once you solve the problem of providing outgoing Web services to your organization through the firewall, you need to worry about providing incoming Web services to the public. There are an endless number of ways to do this, but ultimately there are just a few possibilities to consider. This is because there are only three places where a Web server can be placed relative to a firewall system. It can go behind the firewall in the inner network, outside the firewall in the outer network, or run on the firewall machine itself.

The "Judas" Server

Although it might seem sensible, it's not a good idea to place the Web server on the firewall machine (Figure 14.3a). The problem is that Web server software cannot be trusted to be bug free, and any security holes in the server will compromise the integrity of the firewall. The only possible exception to this rule are Web servers that are certified by the firewall vendors themselves. The reason that these servers can be trusted is because they are minimal pieces of software that do little more than serve static HTML pages. They do not run CGI scripts, support server plug-ins, or handle active server pages. Therefore, they may not be adequate for many organizations' needs.

For similar reasons, although several vendors' Web servers have built-in proxy capabilities, it's almost never a good idea to install them on the firewall. However, proxy servers are useful in other situations, as we shall see later.

The "Sacrificial Lamb"

The safest place for a public Web server is outside the firewall, in the area between the firewall system and your organization's connection to the Internet service provider or regional access provider (Figure 14.3b).

In this "sacrificial lamb" configuration, the server is locked outside the castle gates, exposed directly to the predations of the waiting barbarians. You can now focus your efforts on making the Web server as secure as possible, making frequent and adequate backups, and monitoring the server logs for

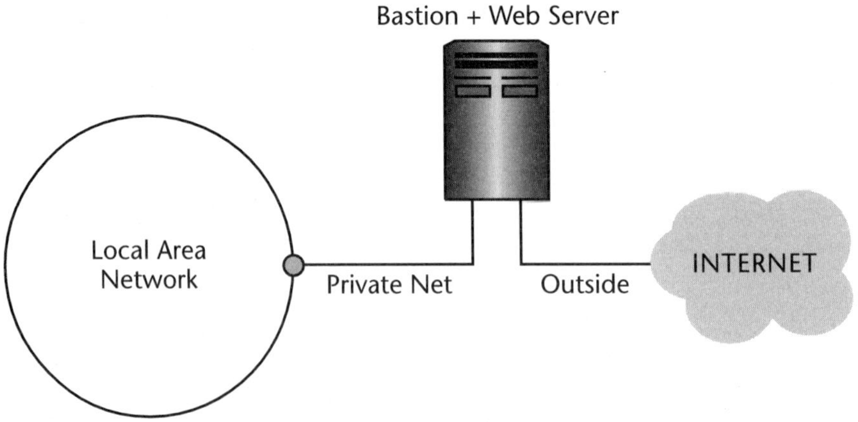

FIGURE 14.3a The "Judas" server (not recommended)

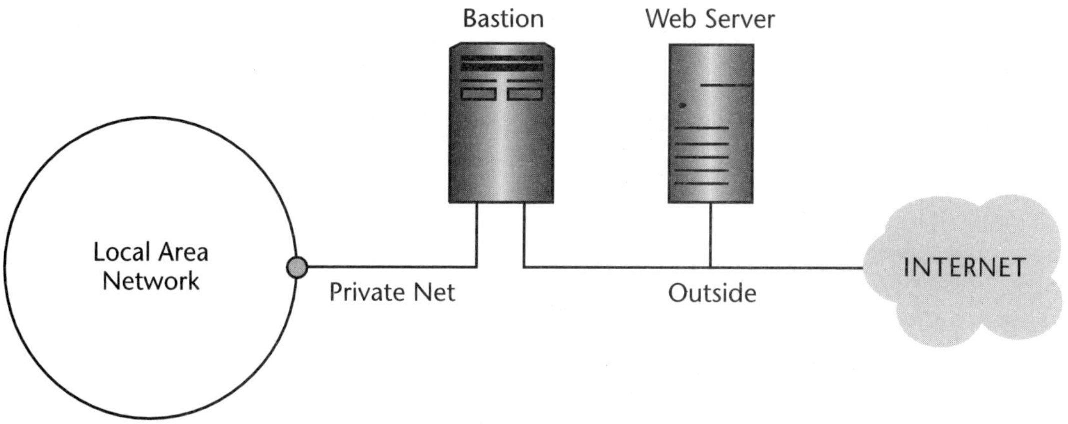

FIGURE 14.3b The "sacrificial lamb"

evidence of mischief. Even if worst comes to worst and the server is broken into, the integrity of the LAN has not been compromised.

Because communication between the LAN and the public Web server is deliberately restricted, it will not be simple for Web authors in your organization to use file sharing or remote login to update material on the Web site. In the most restrictive case, authors will have to physically transfer updated Web pages to the public server using floppy disk or tape, or even sit down at the server console and make changes directly. Chapter 13 discusses some strategies for remote administration.

Another problem with the sacrificial lamb configuration is that some firewall configurations do not provide an accessible area outside the security perimeter. The firewall may be plugged directly into a strand of fiber, an ISDN line, or a T1 line connecting the firewall machine to the Internet. In this case, you'll have to configure the firewall to allow limited access from the outside world into a Web server located on the inner network, either by modifying the firewall's packet filter, if it has one (see the section Poking Holes in the Firewall), or by using a reverse Web proxy (see Running a Reverse Web Proxy later in this chapter).

The "Private Affair" Server

If the Web server is not intended to be publicly available at all, the best location is behind the firewall in the inner protected network (Figure 14.3c). The server is freely accessible to your LAN but entirely invisible to the rest of the world. This is the configuration of choice for corporate intranets and for any application in which the server maintains confidential or sensitive information.

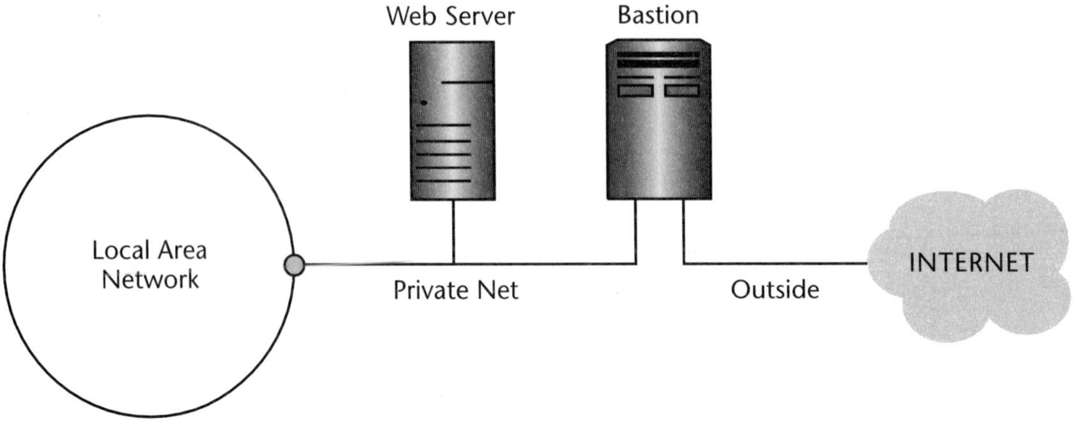

FIGURE 14.3c The "private affair" server

This configuration will not protect the server from insider threats, of course. You still need to put in the effort to make the Web server as secure as possible. You may even want to consider establishing internal firewalls between various departments within your organization, a strategy discussed in the next section.

Many organizations maintain a private Web site for the use of employees and a public site for material intended for public consumption. To avoid the inadvertent leakage of internal material into the public server, it's a good idea to keep them completely separate. If some material needs to be available on both machines, you can either push it from the private server to the public server on a regular basis (see Chapter 13), or you can let the public server pull the material from the private server when it needs to. One technique for accomplishing this is discussed in the Hybrid Server section later in this chapter.

The Doubly Fortified Server

If the Web server manages highly confidential information, you may be more concerned about insider threats than you are about the server being broken into via the Internet. In this case, you may want to set up an internal firewall system to protect the Web server from people who are connected to the LAN. Figure 14.3d shows this design. Obviously, there is no reason why this design can't be extended with more internal firewall systems.

A Demilitarized Zone Server

If your firewall system creates a demilitarized zone—a segment of network that is separated by routers on both the inner-network and outer-network

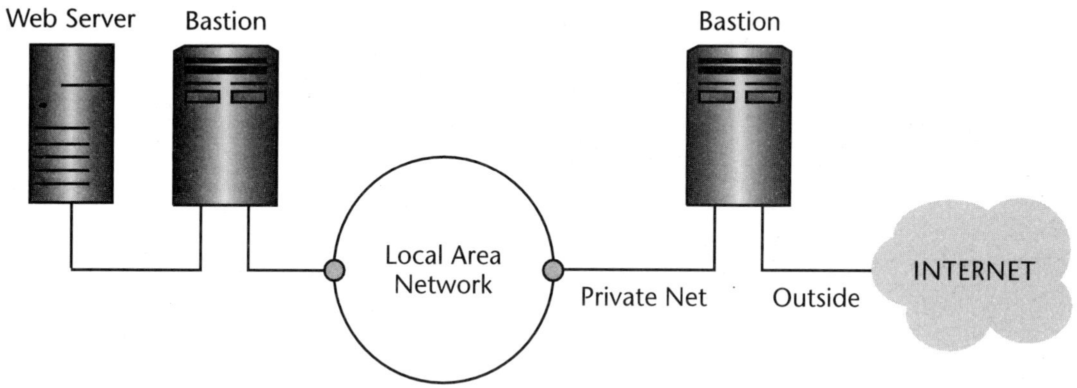

FIGURE 14.3d An internal firewall protects the Web server from insider threats.

sides—you can take advantage of this to create a Web site that is not as exposed as a sacrificial lamb configuration, but not as insular as a private affair server. Simply place the server inside the demilitarized zone (Figure 14.3e), then configure the routers and gateway so that hosts on both the inner and outer networks can establish HTTP connections with the server. Be sure to configure the firewall to block non-HTTP connections from the outside world, and to reject any attempt by the Web server to initiate a connection to the inner network.

You can take a similar approach with firewall systems that create a screened subnetwork. Place the Web server on the subnetwork alongside the bastion host and configure the router to allow HTTP traffic to flow from either side of the firewall to the Web server, but not to flow directly from the outer network to the inner one.

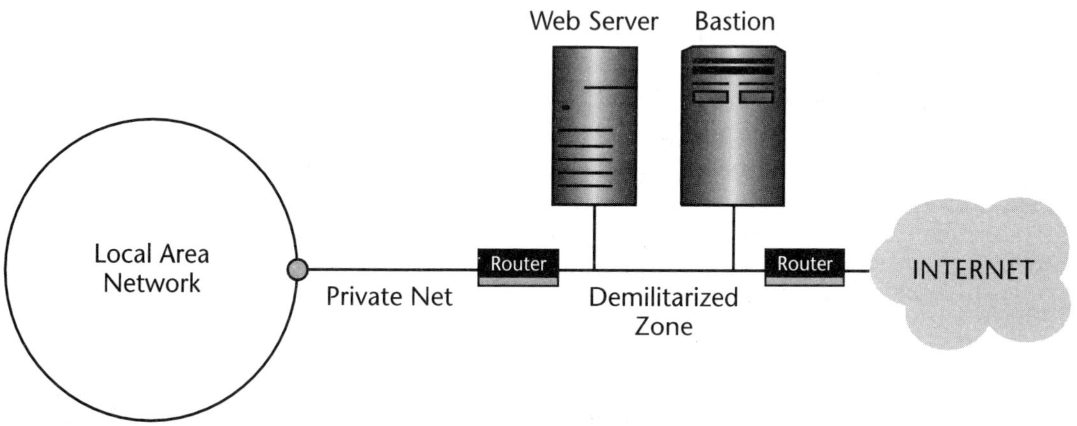

FIGURE 14.3e Placing the sacrificial lamb in the demilitarized zone.

Poking Holes in the Firewall

If you need to support a public Web server but your firewall configuration does not provide a convenient place to put the server outside the security perimeter or within a demilitarized zone, it may be possible to provide reasonably secure access to a server located within the internal network by selectively poking a hole in the firewall. This is not to be done lightly, as it may expose the internal network to a potential attack from a compromised Web server host. It is also only feasible if you are using a screened host or screened subnet type of firewall and have access to the router's filter tables. In some cases, the router that needs adjusting may be physically located at your Internet service provider, so this process will require some coordination.

In the example shown in Table 14.2, network packets sent from the protected internal network, *{Internal net}*, can travel to the bastion host, Gateway. Likewise, network packets from the outside world, *{World}*, are also allowed to travel to the bastion. Everything else is blocked. This is a basic screened-host firewall configuration.

To modify this configuration to allow for incoming calls to an internal Web server named *WebServer*, add rules something like what is shown in Table 14.3. The two new rules allow incoming requests from the Internet to be routed to the Web server, and for outgoing responses (with the ACK flag set) from the Web server to be transmitted to the Internet. Only packets directed to the Web server's HTTP port 80 will be honored.

Although this design restricts access from the outside world to the Web server, it doesn't restrict access from the Web server to other host machines on the LAN. Since the Web server is directly attached to the inner network, it has unrestricted access to the protected inner network. If the server is com-

TABLE 14.2 Simplified Screened-Host Firewall Filter Rules

Action	Src	Port	Dest	Port	Flags	Comment
block	*	*	*	*	*	Block all by default
allow	*{World}*	*	Gateway	*	*	World can talk to gateway
allow	*{Internal net}*	*	Gateway	*	*	Internal net can talk to gateway
allow	Gateway	*	*	*	*	Gateway can talk to everyone

TABLE 14.3 Filter Rule Exceptions for Incoming Web Services

Action	Src	Port	Dest	Port	Flags	Comment
allow	*	*	WebServer	80	*	Everyone can talk to server
allow	WebServer	80	*	*	ACK	The server can reply

promised, you're cooked. Although the fact that all restriction to the Web server from the outside world must be through port 80 might seem to offer the malicious hacker little foothold, this isn't true. There is plenty of mischief that a determined hacker can make on port 80 if he can find and exploit holes in the Web server, its modules, or CGI scripts. If you go this route, it is important to carefully configure and secure the server along the lines described in Chapters 8 and 9.

A Screened Network Segment for the Web Server

If you have an extra router available, an attractive alternative is to create a small screened subnetwork for the sole use of the Web server (Figure 14.4). The router separates the Web server from the rest of the internal network; its rules allow the Web server to talk to the firewall gateway using port 80 but blocks the server from talking to any other host in your organization or directly to the outside world.

The internal router's filter table looks like what is shown in Table 14.4. In effect, you've created a miniature packet filtering firewall for the sole use of the Web server. But here's a problem. If the public Web server can only talk

TABLE 14.4 Filter Rules for a Screened Public Web Server

Action	Src	Port	Dest	Port	Flags	Comment
block	*	*	*	*	*	Block all by default
allow	Gateway	*	WebServer	80	*	Gateway can talk to server
allow	WebServer	80	Gateway	*	ACK	Server can talk to gateway

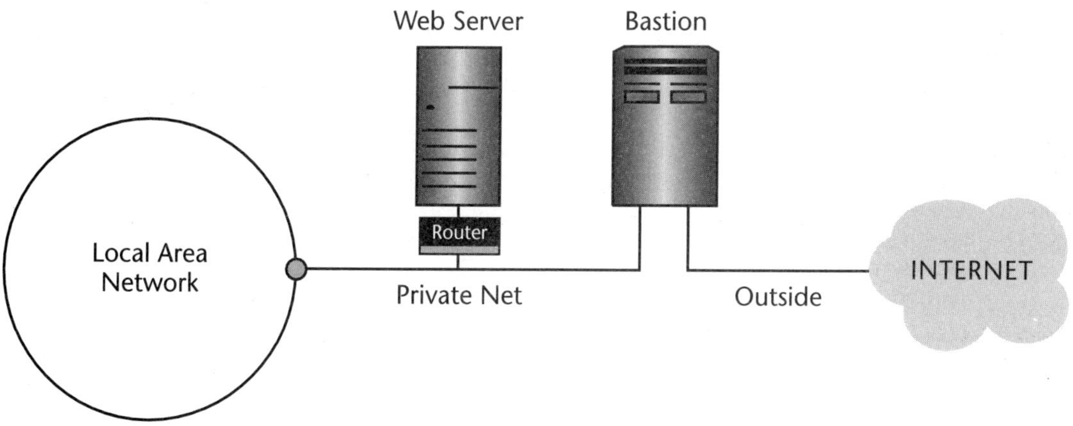

FIGURE 14.4 Placing the Web server on its own screened subnetwork insulates it from your organization while granting the outside world limited access to it.

to the firewall, how does the rest of the world get access to it? By running a reverse Web proxy. This is the topic of the next section.

Running a Reverse Web Proxy

The primary mission of firewall proxies is to allow people inside your organization to make outgoing connections to servers on the Internet. Their desktop software connects to a proxy on the firewall; it relays the request to the Internet server and forwards the servers' response back.

However, it's also possible to use application-level proxies in the reverse direction to grant people on the Internet controlled access to a Web server (Figure 14.5). As far as people on the Internet can tell, the firewall host is the Web server. However, it is only relaying requests to the real Web server, which is sitting behind the firewall in the protected internal network or, better still, on its own screened subnetwork. This lets you provide the outside world with controlled access to the server.

Details of setting this up depend on the particular proxy software you use. I will illustrate the concept with the HTTP proxy, *http-gw*, that is part of the freely available TIS firewall toolkit. When running in ordinary, forward proxy mode, *http-gw* listens to the HTTP port 80 for requests of this form:

```
GET http://www.animals.com/farm_frenzy/index.html HTTP/1.0
```

This is the type of request, complete with the protocol and host name, that is sent by Web browsers that have been configured to use a proxy. *http-gw* will check its configuration rules to determine the following:

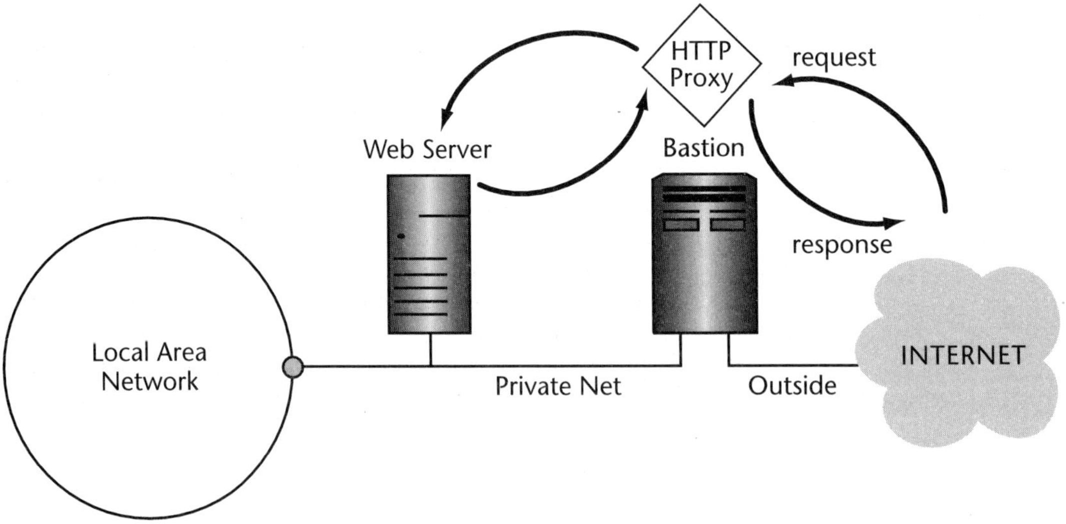

FIGURE 14.5 Reverse HTTP proxies forward URL requests from the outside world to a Web server located on the LAN.

1. Is the requesting host allowed to use the proxy?
2. If so, is the requesting host allowed to fetch files from the indicated remote host?

If the two rules are met, the proxy fetches the document pointed to by the URL and returns it, possibly after overwriting unsafe elements, such as ActiveX controls.

When running in reverse mode, the proxy receives requests like the following one from browsers that haven't been specially configured.

```
GET /farm_frenzy/index.html HTTP/1.0
```

Notice that there is no protocol or remote host in this URL. The remote browser thinks it is talking to a Web server that maintains the documents locally. The proxy server now asks its configuration the following questions.

1. Is the requesting host allowed to use the proxy?
2. If so, what server should the request be forwarded to?

If it can satisfactorily answer these questions, it forwards the request to the indicated Web server and retrieves the document. The following two lines in *http-gw*'s configuration file are all that is required to achieve both forward and reverse proxying.

```
http-gw: permit-hosts .193.49.189.*
http-gw: permit-hosts * -httpd www.capricorn.org -dest www.capricorn.org
```

The first *permit-hosts* directive allows all members of the internal network to use the forward proxy. There is no restriction on which remote Web servers they are allowed to contact. The second directive gives everyone else (*) access to the reverse proxy. The *-httpd* option makes the organization's public Web server, *www.capricorn.org,* the Web server to forward the request to. The *-dest* option restricts foreign sites' use of the proxy to fetching pages from the public server. This is to prevent others from taking advantage of the proxy to access remote sites.

This solution will allow the world nearly transparent access to an internal Web server through the firewall, without exposing the Web server host itself to the Internet. There are still some drawbacks to this approach. First, some of the advanced HTTP commands, such as the PUT command used to publish documents to the Web server, may not be available to the proxy. Ordinarily, this won't be missed. A more serious drawback is that certain holes in the Web server, such as those introduced by poorly written CGI scripts, can still be exploited remotely. The proxy merely forwards the attack.

A Hybrid Server

A hybrid approach that allows you to provide the world with access to the internal server without exposing it to the risks of running untrusted CGI programs and server plug-ins involves using two reverse proxies: one on an external sacrificial lamb Web server; one on the firewall. This scheme also overcomes one of the drawbacks of the sacrificial lamb configuration: keeping it up to date in an environment where there are many Web authors. If it's really secure, it won't allow remote logins or updates via file sharing, but this makes it difficult to update in a timely way.

The scheme is to set up the "kissing cousins" configuration shown in Figure 14.6. In this setup, an internal server is maintained behind the firewall and kept completely inaccessible from the outside world. The public server is a sacrificial lamb set up outside the firewall gateway. All insecure and untrusted Web services, including CGI scripts, FrontPage extensions, and server plug-ins, are run on the external server. In addition, anything that doesn't need to change very often, such as background information, logos, and icons, also live here. Pages that change frequently, however, are dynamically fetched through the firewall from a designated area on the internal server and forwarded to the outside world.

For the scheme to work, the sacrificial lamb must be a Web server that has built-in proxy capabilities. It will be configured in such a way that documents considered safe are proxied from the internal server via the gateway. Dangerous URLs, such as those that invoke CGI scripts and plug-ins, will be handled directly by the sacrificial lamb.

A variety of servers provide proxy capabilities. Examples include the freely available Apache and CERN servers, the Microsoft Proxy Server, and

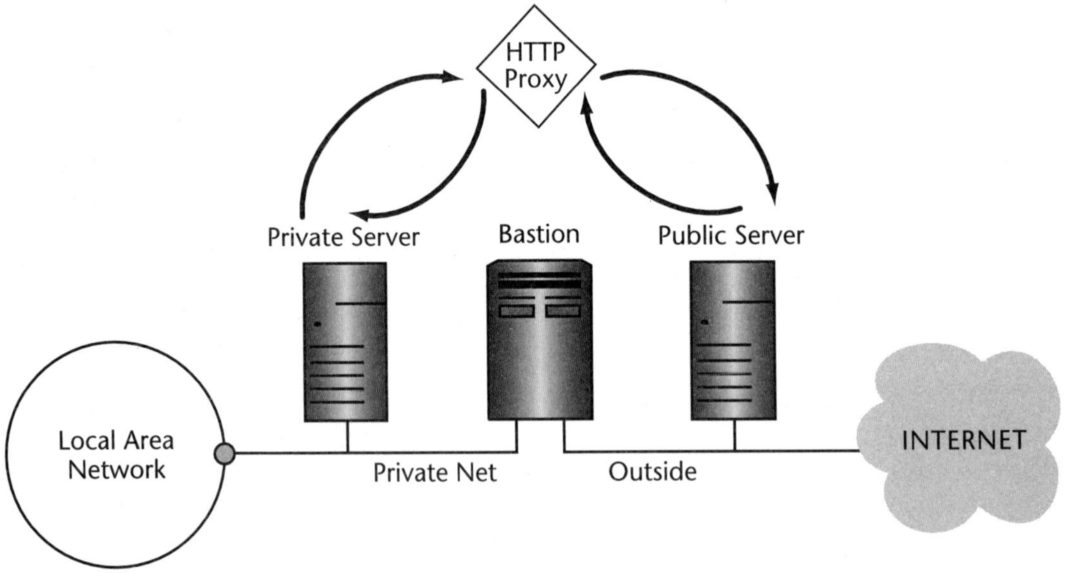

FIGURE 14.6 The "kissing cousins" configuration allows the public server to safely mirror static pages from the internal server.

the Netscape Proxy Server. I illustrate this example using the Apache server; modify as necessary for your software.

These host names are used in both Example 14.1 and in the next one on page 412:

Name	Description
www-internal	The internal server
www-external	The external sacrificial lamb server
gw	The firewall bastion host

EXAMPLE 14.1

1. **Prepare a "Public" Area on the Internal Server.** Within the internal server's document tree, create a directory named *pub.* All documents placed in this directory will be mirrored to the outside world.

   To be absolutely certain that Internet users cannot access documents outside this public directory tree, you should configure the internal server's access control to restrict access to all other directories to IP addresses within your organization, including the gateway. Modify the access restrictions for the */pub* directory so that the gateway has access. (See Chapter 10 for details.)

2. **Configure the Firewall to Allow the Internal and External Servers to Chat.** Edit the firewall configuration to allow the external server to access the internal server. This will be in addition to any outgoing Web access that you already provide. With the TIS firewall toolkit, the necessary entry will look like

   ```
   http-gw: permit-hosts www-external -httpd www-internal -dest www-internal
   ```

   In other words, the external server is allowed to use the firewall proxy to access the internal server only. All other use of the proxy from outside hosts is forbidden.

   Sites with a firewall that controls Web access via packet filtering rather than an application proxy should set up the routing filtering to look like what is shown below. The external server is allowed to send requests to the internal server, and the internal server can return data in response.

Action	Src	Port	Dest	Port	Flags	Comment
allow	*www-external*	*	*www-internal*	80	*	External server can talk to internal
allow	*www-internal*	80	*www-external*	*	ACK	Internal server can answer back

EXAMPLE 14.1 *(continued)*

3. **Configure the External Server to Mirror Some of its Documents from the Internal Server.** Make sure that the server is configured to act as a proxy. In the case of the Apache server, this requires the server to be configured and compiled with the proxy_module installed. For a firewall that uses an application proxy, add the following line to *httpd.conf.*

```
ProxyPass /pub/ http://gw/pub/
Redirect  /pub  http://www-external/pub/
```

The *ProxyPass* directive tells the server to forward all requests for URLs beginning with the */pub/* path name to the firewall gateway proxy by fetching a URL starting with *http://gw/pub/*. The firewall, in turn, forwards the request to the internal server. The returned document then is passed back through the firewall to the external server, and finally returned to the requester. The *Redirect* line is there so that the URLs *http://www-external/pub* and *http://www-external/pub/* behave in the same way.

For a packet-filter-based firewall, change the directive to point directly at the internal server.

```
ProxyPass /pub http://www-internal/pub
Redirect  /pub  http://www-external/pub/
```

For Web proxies that support it, you can turn on proxy cacheing in order to return frequently requested documents from a local cache maintained on the external server without passing the information through the firewall every time.

Creating a Cacheing Proxy Server for Internal Use

The Web consumes a lot of network resources. Whenever someone accesses a popular Web site, such as the AltaVista search service, its home page and all its graphics are retrieved across the network. For this reason, most browsers now cache frequently fetched pages and images on a local disk and retrieve the local copy rather than the network version if the cached version is not too old. Although this does reduce network use, consider what happens when multiple people from your organization access the same popular sites during the course of a day. Each browser fetches and caches the remote pages independently. The same pages may be fetched dozens or hundreds of times every day. Together, these redundant accesses may impose a significant load on the firewall system.

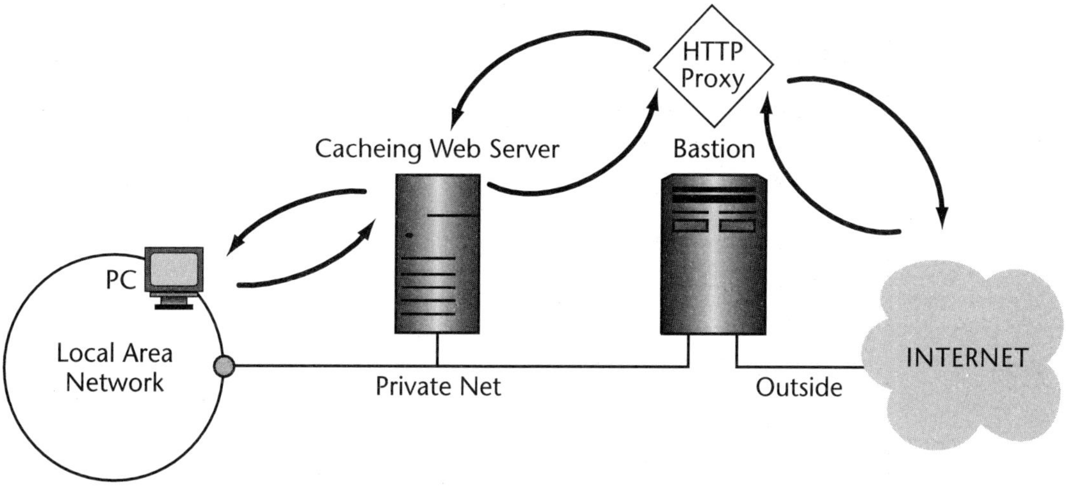

FIGURE 14.7 Using the internal Web server as a cacheing proxy allows you to reduce the load on the firewall.

Large Internet service providers, such as America Online, conserve network resources by providing its customers with a proxy Web server that caches the documents it fetches. A single popular document will be fetched only once a day rather than hundreds of times. This type of cacheing proxy is distinct from the simple HTTP proxy that forwards Web requests across the firewall machine. For medium to large organizations, a cacheing proxy is strongly recommended.

The most convenient place for a cacheing proxy is your organization's internal server. Start by configuring the internal server to act as a cacheing proxy server and to use the firewall as its proxy to the outside world. The internal server will forward all requests for Internet documents to the firewall system. Next reconfigure your organization's browsers to use the internal server as their proxy rather than the firewall (Figure 14.7). URL requests will go first to the internal server, then to the firewall, and finally to the outside.

Frequently requested documents will remain cached on the internal server. The sort of chaining proxy in Example 14.2 is essentially the reverse of what was described in the previous example.

Automatic Proxy Configuration for Browsers

Both Netscape Navigator (v2.0 and higher) and Internet Explorer (v3.02 and higher) allow you to administer their proxy configurations in a centralized way. This can greatly simplify the task of installing a browser on a new host

EXAMPLE 14.2

1. **Configure the Internal Server to Act as a Cacheing Proxy.** The details vary from server to server. The directives for the Apache UNIX server are as follows.

```
ProxyRequests On                    # turn the proxy on
ProxyRemote * http://gw             # forward all requests to the gateway

# Basic parameters for a 50 meg cache.
CacheRoot /usr/local/etc/httpd/proxy
CacheSize 50000
CacheGcInterval 4
CacheMaxExpire 24
CacheLastModifiedFactor 0.1
CacheDefaultExpire 1
NoCache www-internal localhost      # don't cache our own documents
```

2. **Limit Access to the Internal Server.** You want the internal proxy server to be used only by your own organization's hosts. Because the internal server runs behind a firewall, this happens automatically. However, it never hurts to have the Web server perform its own access control. If you are using the Apache server, add the following lines to *access.conf* (as before, assuming that your internal network uses the class C network at 193.49.189).

```
<File proxy:*>
<Limit GET POST>
order deny,allow
deny from all
allow from 193.49.189
</Limit>
</File>
```

3. **Configure the Firewall Proxy to Allow Outgoing Access from the Internal Server.** Because the internal server will be acting as the funnel for all outgoing requests, the gateway should be configured so that only the internal server can make web requests. Again, configuration details depend on the firewall in use. For the TIS firewall toolkit, the directive to add would be

```
http-gw: permit-hosts www-internal
```

Firewalls that use packet filtering will have to be configured to allow outgoing Web connections from the internal Web server. It is important that incoming connections still be forbidden, or you will have inadvertently opened up your internal Web server to the world!

4. **Configure Browsers on Your Site to Use the Cacheing Proxy.** Each browser at your site now needs to be configured to use the internal Web server as its proxy. Do this exactly as before, entering the internal Web server host name in the fields for the HTTP and FTP proxies.

machine or of simultaneously changing the proxy configuration of hundreds of previously installed browsers. To take advantage of this, you need an internal Web server; any brand will do.

1. Using a text editor, create a file that describes the desired proxy configuration. This file will contain a short JavaScript program that defines a single function, named *FindProxyForURL*. The most basic example follows. It directs all requests for URLs on external Web servers to the firewall and tells the browser to make direct contact with any hosts on the internal network.

```
function FindProxyForURL(url, host) {
   if ( isPlainHostName(host) || dnsDomainIs(host, ".capricorn.org") )
       return "DIRECT";
   else
       return "PROXY gw.capricorn.org:80; DIRECT";
}
```

   This function will be called by the user's browser every time she tries to load a URL. The input to this function is two values: the full requested URL and its host-name part only.

   The return value from the function is one of three strings.

   - DIRECT—Contact the server directly.
   - PROXY *proxy name:port*—Fetch the URL via the indicated application-level proxy host.
   - SOCKS *proxy name:port*—Fetch the URL via the indicated SOCKS proxy host.

   The return value can be a semicolon-delimited list of proxies, in which case the browser will try each one in turn until it gets a response.

   The preceding example uses the built-in *isPlainHostName()* and *dnsDomainIs()* functions to determine whether the desired URL is on the protected inner network or outside. The first function returns true if the URL's host-name part is a local host name (without dots). The second returns true if the host lives inside the indicated domain. If either of these functions returns a true value, the script returns the string DIRECT, telling the browser to contact the host directly. Otherwise, it returns an instruction to attempt to make a proxy connection through the firewall machine. If this attempt fails, the browser will try to make a direct connection. More examples of configuration scripts are given below.

2. Save the configuration file with a name like *proxyconfig.pac*, and place it somewhere in the internal Web server's document tree. The name is not important, but the *.pac* extension is.

3. Configure the Web server to recognize the *.pac* file type. Netscape and Microsoft browsers use a special MIME type, *application/x-ns-proxy-autoconfig*, for proxy configuration files. Some servers may already recognize *.pac* files as belonging to this type. Others will need to be configured.

In Apache and other NCSA *httpd*-derived servers, you should add this line to *httpd.conf* or *srm.conf*.

```
AddType application/x-ns-proxy-autoconfig .pac
```

4. Configure all browsers at your site to use this configuration file for their proxy configuration. Open the browser's proxy configuration window, select the radio button labeled "Automatic Proxy Configuration" and enter the URL of the proxy configuration file. For example, if the internal server is named *www-internal.capricorn.org* and the configuration file was placed in a subdirectory of the document tree named *admin*, the URL to enter is

```
http://www-internal.capricorn.org/admin/proxyconfig.pac
```

From now on, each time a browser launches, it will fetch the configuration file and use it to choose its proxies.

In addition to *isPlainHostName()* and *dnsDomainIs()* functions, the proxy configuration script has many other built-in functions available, allowing you to choose proxies based on the host name, patterns appearing in the URL requested, and even on the day of the week. Details are available among Netscape's release notes for Navigator 2.0 (see the end of the chapter).

A few common examples follow.

Set Proxy for a Numeric Subnet

Instruct the browser to make a direct connection to machines within the local network but to use the proxy for all other hosts. The *isInNet()* function expects parameters consisting of the host name, a network address, and a subnet mask.

```
function FindProxyForURL(url, host) {
   if ( isInNet(host,"193.49.189.0","255.255.255.0") )
       return "DIRECT";
   else
       return "PROXY gw.capricorn.org:80; DIRECT";
}
```

Internally, *isInNet()* performs a DNS lookup in order to go from host name to IP address. This can cause performance problems if your DNS server is slow.

Choose Different Proxies Based on the Protocol Type

Occasionally, proxies are spread across several firewall machines in order to minimize load. You can use the *shExpMatch()* function to pattern-match against the protocol part of the URL and select the proxy server to use.

```
function FindProxyForURL(url, host) {
   if ( isPlainHostName(host) || dnsDomainIs(host, ".capricorn.org") )
       return "DIRECT";
   else if ( shExpMatch(url,"http:*") )
       return "PROXY http-gw.capricorn.org:80";
   else if ( shExpMatch(url,"ftp:*") )
       return "PROXY ftp-gw.capricorn.org:21";
   else if ( shExpMatch(url,"gopher:*) )
       return "PROXY gopher-gw.capricorn.org:70";
   else
       return "DIRECT";

}
```

Fall Back to a Different Proxy If One Fails

This is just like the basic example, but it accommodates a network configuration in which there are backup firewalls to be used when one goes down.

```
function FindProxyForURL(url, host) {
   if ( isPlainHostName(host) || dnsDomainIs(host, ".capricorn.org") )
       return "DIRECT";
   else
       return "PROXY gw1.capricorn.org:80; PROXY gw2.capricorn.org:80;
               DIRECT";
}
```

Use the Proxy for External Servers, as Well as for the Public Web Server

This configuration is typical for organizations that have a public Web server located outside the firewall. Requests for URLs on machines within the local domain can all be direct, except for those on the public server, which must go through the firewall proxy.

```
function FindProxyForURL(url, host) {
   if ( (isPlainHostName(host)
          ||
         dnsDomainIs(host, ".capricorn.org")) &&
         !localHostOrDomainIs(host,"www.capricorn.org") )
       return "DIRECT";
   else
       return "PROXY gw.capricorn.org:80; DIRECT";
}
```

This function uses the awkwardly named *localHostOrDomainIs()*, which compares two host names in a way that allows for the possibility that the domain-name part might be missing from the first one.

Examining Firewall Logs for Signs of Server Compromise

One day your organization's public Web server is compromised by a teenager bent on wanton destruction. How will you know that the server has been broken into and the hacker is now attempting to penetrate your LAN? One way is by carefully tracking activity on the server machine itself, as described in the previous chapters. However, firewall logs give you another weapon with which to detect break-ins.

Ordinarily, the public Web server should be quiet regarding network traffic coming into your LAN through the firewall. Connections between the LAN and the server should be limited to outgoing connections initiated by your organization's employees. If the Web server suddenly starts initiating its own connections to the firewall, you've got a problem.

For example, an early component of an attack is the door-rattling approach of scanning all the ports on the firewall to see which ones are active. Many firewall products log attempts to access unused ports. All log failed attempts to access a proxy service. An example of such a port scanning attempt might show up in the logs like this.

```
May 22 8:13:10 gw kernel: tcp from www/193.49.189.62:1320 to gw/193.49.189.63 on unserved port 19
May 22 8:13:12 gw kernel: tcp from www/193.49.189.62:1321 to gw/193.49.189.63 on unserved port 20
May 22 8:13:14 gw kernel: tcp from www/193.49.189.62:1326 to gw/193.49.189.63 on unserved port 21
May 22 8:13:15 gw kernel: tcp from www/193.49.189.62:1327 to gw/193.49.189.63 on unserved port 22
May 22 8:13:17 gw telnet-proxy: [1414]: deny host=www/193.49.189.62 use of gateway
May 22 8:13:19 gw kernel: tcp from www/193.49.189.62:1331 to gw/193.49.189.63 on unserved port 24
```

Similarly, attempts to probe for weaknesses using the Sun RPC system show up in the logs as multiple attempts to connect to udp port 111.

As another example, here's what might appear in the logs if a compromised Web server makes repeated attempts to access the gateway's FTP server using guessed passwords.

```
May 22 09:04:24 gw ftpd [2940]: failed login from www/193.49.189.26, guest
May 22 09:04:40 gw ftpd [2949]: failed login from www/193.49.189.26, system
May 22 09:05:10 gw ftpd [2957]: failed login from www/193.49.189.26, root
```

Most firewall systems provide you with customizable log-crunching utilities that allow you to scan for suspicious behavior. Set these up to immediately report on *any* unexpected network activity that originates at the Web server. With any luck, you'll be able to stop the attack before any lasting harm is done to the server, the LAN, or your organization's reputation.

Checklist

1. Does your organization have a firewall?

   - ☑ Yes
   - ❍ No

   It is difficult to secure a local area network if every machine has direct access to the Internet. A firewall is recommended for any security-conscious organization.

2. Where is the public Web server (if any) in relation to the firewall?

   - ☑ Outside the firewall
   - ❍ On the firewall host
   - ☑ Inside the firewall on a screened subnet
   - ❍ Inside the firewall

   Web servers are untrusted software and should never be placed on the firewall machine. The public server should be located outside the firewall gateway. If it must be located inside for practical reasons, it's better to place it on its own protected subnetwork than on the main LAN backbone.

3. Where is the internal Web server (if any) in relation to the firewall?

   - ❍ Outside the firewall
   - ☑ Inside the firewall
   - ❍ On the firewall host

   The internal Web server belongs on the LAN, protected by the firewall—nowhere else.

4. How do employees browse the Web through the firewall?

   - ☑ They can't. Our security policy doesn't allow it.
   - ☑ We use a firewall proxy that was certified by the firewall vendor.
   - ❍ We installed on the firewall a full-featured cacheing Web proxy from a third-party vendor.
   - ❍ They log in to the firewall machine and use Lynx to get out.
   - ❍ No problem. The router allows port 80 traffic to flow back and forth freely.

   Use only the Web proxy that is provided with your firewall system or one that has been explicitly certified by the firewall vendor. The firewall software is a tightly integrated package. Installing other software may have unintended consequences.

5. How do you update the public Web server?

   - ☑ We TELNET to it from the LAN via the firewall.
   - ☑ We FTP to it from the LAN via the firewall.
   - ☑ We manually update it from CD-ROM/tape.
   - ❍ We use file sharing to mount its file systems across the firewall.
   - ❍ We TELNET/FTP to it from the Internet.
   - ☑ We TELNET/FTP to it from the Internet using an encrypted connection.
   - ☑ We TELNET/FTP to it from the Internet using a one-time password.
   - ❍ We use Web server extensions (for instance, FrontPage) to publish
     - ☑ From internal LAN to Web server
     - ☐ From Internet to Web server
     - ☑ From Internet to Web server, encrypted connections only
   - ❍ We mirror part of our internal site to the public server
     - ☑ Static documents only
     - ☐ CGI scripts, server extensions
   - ❍ We don't need to update it. It's the kind of Web server that generates all its pages from a database, and we have it connected directly up to our corporate relational database.

   Updating the public server from the Internet is a sensitive issue because of the ease with which passwords can be sniffed and documents intercepted.

   Any updates performed across the Internet (for instance, from employees' or clients' homes) should be performed over an encrypted connection or use a one-time password system (see previous chapters). Connections to the server from within your organization's LAN are safe from sniffers, but keep the number of authorized users on the server to a minimum. Any direct connection from the server to the LAN, whether it is a shared file system, a shared database, or the privilege to execute CGI scripts on an internal server, should ring alarm bells. (See the previous chapter for safe updating strategies.)

6. How do you monitor the Web server for compromise?

   - ❍ We don't. It's a secure Web server.
   - ❍ We've hired five people to read through the reams of server and firewall logs every day.
   - ☑ We have scripts that crunch the logs to filter out all expected activity. We examine what's left.

   Most "secure" Web servers transmit their documents in encrypted form but are not otherwise secured against break-in. Treat the server as any other untrusted host on the Internet and watch it carefully for suspicious activity. If logging is adequate, it will generate far more information than a mere mortal can wade through. It's essential to have an automated system of scripts and filters to sift the wheat from the chaff. Usually, it's better to design filters that remove the expected entries and send you the unexpected ones rather than look specifically for suspicious activity—who's to know all the suspicious activity in advance?

Online Resources

Firewall Products

Trusted Information Systems Firewall Toolkit

ftp://ftp.tis.com/pub/firewalls/toolkit/

SOCKS Proxy

ftp://ftp.nec.com/pub/socks/

AltaVista Firewall

http://www.software.digital.com/

BorderWare Firewall

http://www.sctc.com/

CyberGuard Firewall

http://www.cyberguardcorp.com/

Eagle Firewall

http://www.raptor.com/

Firewall-1

http://www.checkpoint.com/

Gauntlet Firewall

http://www.tis.com/

ON Guard Firewall

http://www.on.com/

Miscellaneous Documentation

Automatic proxy configuration for Netscape and Microsoft browsers

http://search.netscape.com/eng/mozilla/2.0/relnotes/demo/proxy-live.html

The Firewalls Mailing List

Subscribe by sending e-mail to *majordomo@greatcircle.com*. In the body of the e-mail message put `subscribe firewalls`.

An online archive of the list, along with a number of papers and other firewall resources, can be found at *http://www.greatcircle.com/firewalls/*

Printed Resources

Chapman, Brent, and Zwicky, Elizabeth, *Building Internet Firewalls* (O'Reilly & Associates, 1995).

A more practically oriented book that describes in detail how to build a firewall system.

Cheswick, William, and Bellovin, Steven, *Firewalls and Internet Security* (Addison-Wesley, 1994).

A detailed look at the principles of firewall design, with many amusing anecdotes from real-life experiences.

Bibliography

Amoroso, Edward, *Fundamentals of Computer Security Technology* (Prentice-Hall, 1994).

Chapman, Brent, and Zwicky, Elizabeth, *Building Internet Firewalls* (O'Reilly & Associates, 1995).

Cheswick, William, and Bellovin, Steven, *Firewalls and Internet Security* (Addison-Wesley Longman, 1994).

Christiansen, Tom, Schwartz, Randal, and Wall, Larry, *Programming Perl5* (O'Reilly & Associates, 1995).

Curry, David, *UNIX System Security: A Guide for Users and System Administrators* (Addison-Wesley, 1994).

Garfinkel, Simson, *Pretty Good Privacy* (O'Reilly & Associates, 1995).

Garfinkel, Simson, with Gene Spafford, *Web Security and Commerce* (O'Reilly & Associates, 1997).

Garfinkel, Simson, and Spafford, Gene. *Practical UNIX & Internet Security* (O'Reilly & Associates, 1996).

Howes, Tim, and Smith, Mark, *LDAP, Programming Directory-Enabled Applications with Lightweight Directory Access Protocol* (Macmillan Technical Publishing, 1997).

Hunt, Craig, *TCP/IP Network Administration* (O'Reilly & Associates, 1992).

Liu, Cricket, Peek, Jerry, Jones, Russ, Buus, Bryan, and Nye, Adrian, *Managing Internet Information Services* (O'Reilly & Associates, 1995).

Pfleeger, Charles, *Security in Computing* (Prentice Hall, 1996).

Rubin, Aviel, Geer, Daniel, and Ranum, Marcus, *Web Security Sourcebook* (John Wiley and Sons, 1997).

Russel, Charlie, and Crawford, Sharon, *Running Microsoft Windows NT Server 4.0* (Microsoft Press, 1997).

Schneier, Bruce, *Practical Cryptography,* 2nd Edition (John Wiley & Sons, 1995).

Smith, Richard E., *Internet Cryptography* (Addison Wesley Longman, 1997).

Sutton, Stephan, *Windows NT Security Guide* (Addison Wesley/Developers Press, 1997).

Index

D

F

G

H

I